Derek Sellen

Grammar
GOALS

UPDATED EDITION

Reference and practice for pre-intermediate to intermediate students

✓ B1-B2

✓ FCE-style activities updated for the 2008 specifications

✓ Audio CD/CD-ROM with exam practice for Paper 3, Use of English

Editor: Rebecca Raynes
Design and art direction: Nadia Maestri
Computer graphics realisation: Irene Mazza
Cover illustration: Anna and Elena Balbusso

First edition: March 2008

5   4   3   2   1

The CD contains an audio section (the recording of dialogues and stories in the volume) and a CD-ROM section
(13 complete tests for the FCE Paper 3, Use of English).
• To listen to the recording, insert the CD into your CD player and it will play as normal.
  You can also listen to the recording on your computer, by opening your usual CD player programme.
• If you put the CD directly into the CD-ROM drive, the software will open automatically.

Minimum system requirements:	
PC: – Pentium III processor – Windows 98, Me, 2000, XP – 64 Mb RAM (128Mb recommended) – 800x600 screen resolution 16 bit – 12X CD-ROM drive – Audio card with speakers or headphones	**MAC:** – Power PC G3 – OS X 10.1.5 – 128 Mb RAM free for the application

Our e-mail and web-site addresses are:
editorial@blackcat-cideb.com
www.blackcat-cideb.com

CISQ **CISQ**CERT
**TEXTBOOKS AND
TEACHING MATERIALS**
The quality of the publisher's
design, production and sales processes has
been certified to the standard of
UNI EN ISO 9001

ISBN 978-88-530-0824-4 Book + CD-Rom
ISBN 978-88-530-0825-1 Book

Printed in Italy by Stamperia Artistica Nazionale, Trofarello, Turin

INTRODUCTION

Aim and level

Grammar Goals *updated edition* is aimed at pre-intermediate to intermediate students who need to revise, consolidate and improve their grammar skills. It covers the complete grammar syllabus for the Cambridge ESOL First Certificate in English exam and has been revised for the new specifications starting December 2008.

Book organisation and approach

Grammar Goals approaches grammar in a clear simple way. It carefully avoids complicated jargon, relying more on easy to understand language. There are 110 units, each focusing on one area of grammar. The one-page explanations are clear and well balanced, and special attention has been paid to those points which are the most common source of errors. Each point on the theory page is lettered to enable easy reference when working on the exercises.

Using the book

It is not necessary to work through all the units in **Grammar Goals**. You can select those units which are appropriate to your needs. The clear contents, index and useful links on theory pages enable you to turn to relevant grammar areas to supplement a coursebook or revise points arising out of written work or classwork.

Exercises

The vast range of exercises enables students to practise thoroughly what they learn. Exercise types include: multiple-choice, gap filling, sentence transformation, identifying structures and word types, matching, word transformation, sentence correction, identifying formal/informal contexts, using grammatical structures within a text, and free writing.

Many of the exercises use narrative to create student-friendly, well-contextualised tasks which are fun to do. Many, in particular the dialogues and stories, are also recorded on the accompanying CD for students to check their answers and listen to the pronunciation of native speakers.

The wide variety of exercises include:

- Narratives with a range of recurring characters, such as Harry and Michelle the robbers, Nadia the teenage genius and Professor Makepeace the absent-minded inventor.
- Factual texts in the form of articles, ads, letters etc.
- Open exercises to give students the opportunity to practise the grammar points in a less guided way and apply grammatical knowledge to individual self-expression. These can be used in the classroom to occupy and challenge the most able students.

  Each unit begins with a contextualised task related to the main theory points, followed by a range of exercises to cover all the points in that unit, which can be attempted in the order the student chooses.

Review sections

Students preparing for the FCE exam can practise for it by doing the 12 Grammar Review Sections. The first 3 exercises of these sections follow the FCE format.

Appendices

The 17 appendices provide quick reference tables.

Audio CD/CD-ROM

The CD-ROM offers 13 complete tests for the FCE Paper 3, Use of English, which can be done online or printed off and carried out on paper.

Online material

A grammar check, which can be used as an entry or exit test, and extra tests are downloadable from our site: www.blackcat-cideb.com.

Also available online, downloadable as Mp3 files are the recordings of all the introductory paragraphs to the theory pages. These are indicated with the symbol: @

CONTENTS

UNIT 1 >> Present Simple

 Harry and Michelle **live** in London but they **travel** all over the world. Why **do** they **travel** so much? Because they **rob** banks. Harry **plans** the robberies while Michelle **prepares** the getaway routes. They **have** a lot of money but they **don't keep** it in the bank! So, **does** crime **pay**?

For information about form, see Appendix 1. For spelling rules about adding **-s**, see Appendix 13.

A USE

We use the Present Simple:

1 to talk about things which are **always/generally** true: *Water **boils** at 100 °C.*

2 to express **facts**: *60% of robberies **occur** in big cities.*

3 to talk about regular **actions** or **habits**, with **adverbs of frequency** (see Unit 64) or with expressions like **every day**, **every week**, **once a month**:
   *They **wash** the car **once a week**.*   *Harry **usually carries** a gun.*

4 to talk about **timetabled events** in the future (see Unit 15):
   *The plane for Lisbon **leaves** at 11.30 tomorrow.*

5 to **ask for factual information** about the present. For example:
   *Where **do** you **come** from?*   *What **do** you **do**?* (= What is your job?)

B INFORMAL/FORMAL

We generally use **don't/doesn't** in informal, spoken English and **do not/does not** in formal, written English.

Informal: e.g. A letter to a friend, in conversation.   *I **don't** like big cities.*
Formal: e.g. A letter for a job application.   *I **do not** smoke.*

C AVOIDING REPETITION AFTER *AND*, *OR* AND *BUT*

It is usual to omit the repeated subject after **and, or, but** in sentences like this:
*Nick often phones Jill **and** then **meets** her for dinner.*   (Not ~~and then he meets~~...)
*They go to a city restaurant **or look** for a country inn.*   (Not ~~or they look~~...)

Sometimes we can use **do** or **does**, **don't** or **doesn't**, to avoid repeating a phrase with a Present Simple verb, especially after **but**:
*I like football **but** my sister **doesn't**.*   *They don't want to help **but** I **do**.*

D *WHY DON'T YOU... ?*

We use **Why don't you...?** to make **suggestions** or **give advice**:
*'I'm lonely.' '**Why don't you phone** a friend?'*

E EMPHATIC USE OF *DO/DOES*

We can use **do** or **does** in an affirmative sentence to **make the verb more emphatic**:

1 **to deny an accusation**: *It's not true! I **do** study hard!*

2 or to **accuse somebody of something which they have denied**: *You **do** talk in your sleep!*

3 or to **add emphasis to a factual statement**: *I was right! The train **does** leave at 9.30!*

In writing, we may underline or italicise **do** or **does**:
*'I **do** love you,' he said.*   *She <u>does</u> understand.*

1 **A** Fill the gaps in the story with verbs in the Present Simple. Choose verbs from the list. Then listen and check your answers.

| ask | ask | *not earn* | *enjoy* | *find* | *give* | *knock* | *sleep* | *wash* | ~~not work~~ |

Slim Skinty and Ellie Tramper are very poor. They **(0)** *don't work* , so they **(1)** ....
any money. However, they **(2)** .... their lives. Slim Skinty often
(3) .... under a bridge or in the park. He **(4)** .... food in rubbish bins
and **(5)** .... his clothes in the river. He never **(6)** .... anyone for
money. In contrast, Ellie often **(7)** .... on the doors of big houses and
(8) .... for somewhere to stay. Sometimes the people **(9)** .... her
food and old clothes.

2 **A** Write Present Simple questions with the same meaning as items 1-6. Use the verb in brackets.

0	What is your weight? (*weigh*)	How much *do you weigh*?	
1	What is the meaning of 'smart'? (*mean*)	What ....?	
2	What is the price of these jeans? (*cost*)	How much ....?	
3	What time is the next train? (*leave*)	When ....?	
4	What is your job? (*do*)	....?	
5	What is her address? (*live*)	....?	
6	What would you like to do tomorrow? (*want*)	What ....?	

3 **B** Choose the best alternative in these contexts.

0 (a letter to a bank) I **don't**/(do not) have enough capital to start a small business next year...

1 (a conversation in a pub) Those guys **don't/do not** look very happy.

2 (a report to a professor) Most students **don't/do not** perform well in examinations.

3 (an article in a popular magazine for teenagers) Jez-E-bel, a new rock singer, **doesn't/does not** take drugs, says her agent.

4 (an article in the *Times*) The government **doesn't/does not** want to raise taxes.

4 **C** Complete sentences 1-4.

0 Slim Skinty sleeps in the open air but Ellie Tramper *doesn't.*

1 Slim .... travel in cars or lorries but Ellie .... **2** Slim .... ask people for things but Ellie .... **3** Harry always carries a gun but Michelle .... **4** I don't want to meet Harry but the police ....

5 **E** Use emphatic *do* or *does* to complete parallel sentences to the ones given.

0 Of course your brother likes you. Your brother *does* like you.

1 It's not true that I don't help my parents. I .... **2** You're wrong. Not everyone hates the school food. Some people .... like .... **3** You can't deny that you snore. You .... **4** Yes, he's more handsome with his new haircut. His new haircut .... make him .... **5** You're wrong. I always tell you that I love you. I .... **6** Don't tell me that London doesn't have rainy weather. London ....

OPEN EXERCISE

6 **D** Make suggestions for these situations. Use *Why don't you...?*

0 I feel ill. *Why don't you go to the doctor?* or *Why don't you take some medicine?*

1 I'm lonely.   **2** I'm bored.   **3** I've got no money.   **4** I've got toothache.   **5** I'm in love with Susie.   **6** I can't find this street.   **7** I can't find my wallet.   **8** I don't understand this exercise.

UNIT 2 >> Present Continuous

 Jill and Nick **are sunbathing** on the beach in Hawaii. I**'m watching** them from the hotel window. White seagulls **are flying** overhead and the waves **are** gently **lapping** against the sand. They**'re enjoying** the peace but Beth, their secretary in the UK, has a problem, so she**'s dialling** their mobile number now.

For information about form, see Appendix 1.
For spelling rules about adding **-ing**, see Appendix 4.

Ⓐ USE

We use the Present Continuous:

1 for things we are doing or for things which are happening **now, at this exact moment, at the moment of speaking**:
*The teacher**'s helping** me.*

2 for things we are doing or things which are happening **during this period of our lives** (but not permanently):
*My football team **is losing** a lot of matches.*

at the moment of speaking	during this period of his/her life
*My sister **is phoning** me from Bangkok.*	*My sister**'s travelling** all over the world.*
*Jill**'s talking** to Nick.*	*Jill**'s staying** at the seaside for two weeks.*
*Nick **is lying** on the beach.*	*Nick **is learning** chess.*

3 to talk about **changes** which are happening over a period of time, with verbs like **improve/increase/get worse/rise/fall**.
*The average temperature **is increasing**.*   *Prices **are rising** rapidly.*

4 to talk about a **planned action** in the future (see Unit 15).
*I **am flying** to Mallorca tomorrow.*   *We**'re meeting** at the airport.*

Ⓑ AVOIDING REPETITION AFTER *AND*, *OR* AND *BUT*

Sometimes we can use **am, is, are** or **am not, isn't** or **aren't**, to avoid repeating a phrase with a Present Continuous verb, especially after **but**:
*Nick is reading **but** Jill **isn't**.*
*They're sunbathing **but** I'm **not**.*

It is usual to omit the repeated subject and the auxiliary verb (**am/is/are**) after **and, or, but** in sentences like this:
*Beth is looking at the accounts **and adding** the figures.* (**Not** ~~and she's adding~~...)
*Brigitte is sitting at her desk **but** not **paying** attention to the clients.*

1 **Ⓐ** Read this story about a robbery at Buckingham Palace. Fill the gaps with verbs from the list in the Present Continuous. Use the short forms where possible. Then listen and check your answers.

> arrest   attack   communicate   cut   do   drink   fly   fly   get
> go   happen   hide   land   shoot   ~~steal~~   strike   take   turn

Harold Baker is inside the palace. He (0) *is stealing* a painting of the Queen. Michelle Harris
(1) .... a helicopter overhead. They (2) .... by radio.

Michelle: What (3) .... you ....?

Harry: I (4) .... in the wine cellar and (5) .... the Queen's champagne.
What (6) .... outside?

Michelle: Big Ben (7) .... midnight. I think that everyone (8) .... to bed.

Harry: Good! I (9) .... the wires of the alarm system. Now, I (10) .... the painting off the wall. (11) .... you .... the helicopter on the palace roof?

Michelle: Yes. But wait! One of the Queen's soldiers (12) .... at me. Bullets
(13) .... all around me. It's dangerous.

Harry: Wait! The dogs (14) .... me. Help! The guards (15) .... me.

Michelle: Good luck, Harry. I (16) .... off the radio and (17) .... out of here. Goodbye.

2 **Ⓐ** Put all the verbs in the Present Continuous form. Then write the number of each verb in the correct column of the table.

a. Shelley and Babs (0 *study*) *are studying* business at university. Now, they (1 *exercise*)
.... and (2 *chat*) .... at the gym. Shelley (3 *lift*) ....
weights and Babs (4 *ride*) .... an exercise bicycle.

b. Neil and Eddie (5 *eat*) .... dinner in a restaurant. Neil (6 *finish*) .... his last course but Eddie (7 *eat*) .... his soup. Eddie (8 *play*) .... in a rock group. They (9 *record*) .... a new CD in London. He (10 *tell*) .... Neil about it.

c. Sue (11 *work*) .... very hard at school this term. So, now, she (12 *not dance*)
.... She's too tired. She (13 *watch*) .... the other dancers in the disco.

now at the moment of speaking	during this period of her/his life
	0

3 **Ⓐ** Write Present Continuous sentences about the changes in the table. Use each verb only once.

> change   disappear   fall   get better   get worse   ~~improve~~   increase

	before	this year	your sentence
His English mark	55%	75%	0 His English is improving.
The price of sugar	£1.00	£0.85	1
The population	364,000	398,000	2
Her maths mark	86%	98%	3
Fashion for men	Black suits	All colours	4
His French mark	75%	65%	5
Tigers in India	200,000	25	6

UNIT 3 >> Present Simple or Present Continuous?

> Kevin Scoremore **plays** football for Crunchester United. He **scores** lots of goals. But he **is not playing** very well this afternoon. The other team **is winning** 3-0 and the referee **is sending** Kevin off the pitch. His team-mates **are protesting**: 'Kevin never **fouls** other players. He always **obeys** the rules.'

Ⓐ PRESENT SIMPLE AND PRESENT CONTINUOUS

Present Simple	Present Continuous
• is used for things which happen **always, often, generally, usually, normally, every week** etc. *Sheila **plays** the piano.*	• is used for things which are happening at **this moment, now**: *Sheila **is cooking** dinner.*
• is used for things which are unchanging for a long time. They are **permanent**: *I **live** in Britain.*	• is used for things which may change. They are **temporary**: *Luigi **is living** in Britain for a few months.*

Compare: *What **do** you **do**?* = What is your job?
*What **are** you **doing**?* = What are you doing at this moment/these days?

Ⓑ STATE VERBS

There are some verbs which we **do not use** in the continuous form:
We say: *I **want** an ice-cream.* (Not *I am wanting...*) (see Unit 84)

These verbs describe **emotional** and **mental states** (e.g. *like, hate, know*), use of the **senses** (e.g. *hear, smell*) or **possession** (e.g. *own, belong*). See Appendix 5 for a full list.

With **see, smell, hear, feel, taste,** we often use **can** when we perceive something through our senses:
*I **can smell** the perfume.* (Not *I am smelling the perfume.*) (see Unit 85)

Ⓒ *BEING* + ADJECTIVE

We say: *I **am** ill.* (Not *I am being ill*)   *He **is** rich.* (Not *he is being rich*.)

But it is possible to use **am/is/are being** + **adjective** to **describe how someone is behaving.**
*He **is being** lazy.*   *He is lazy.*
*They're **being** silly.* (= now)   *They are silly.* (= always)

Ⓓ *ALWAYS DOING*

If we use **always**, it is usually with a Simple verb: *I **always go** to school.* (See Unit 1)
But we can use **always** + **Present Continuous** to place emphasis on a repeated action, often when we are **complaining** or **praising somebody**.
*Jenny **is always gossiping** about her friends.* (complaint)
*Bob **is always saying** nice things about people.* (praise)

1 Ⓐ In each item 1-6, fill one gap with a Present Continuous verb and the other with the same verb in the Present Simple form. Use any suitable verb.

0   Joe Sutton is a boxer. He runs six miles every day but today he is ill, so he is running only one mile this morning.

1   Harry and Michelle .... banks. But tonight, they .... Buckingham Palace.

2   The Metalheads .... in Glasgow tonight. They usually .... their number one hit, Metal Heart.

3   Randy, the American astronaut, ... several million miles through space every year. But today he is on holiday. He .... to Brighton by train.

4   Ben is a gourmet. He often .... Italian food but tonight he .... paella.

5   Francesca is an artist. She .... a portrait of the Prime Minister. She often .... pictures of famous people.

6   Roger Scoop .... a photograph of Myra. He .... photographs of all the stars.

2 Ⓐ Ⓑ Circle the correct form of the verb in these sentences.

0 He knows/is knowing a lot of famous people.

1 Do you understand/Are you understanding his ideas?   2 She's Chinese but she speaks/is speaking Japanese now.   3 Look out! He drives/'s driving very fast towards us.   4 'Where's Joe?' 'He reads/is reading a magazine in the sitting room.'   5 This island belongs/is belonging to a millionaire.   6 What do you want/are you wanting to do?   7 They own/are owning a flat in New York.   8 Do you like/Are you liking the new CD?   9 How much does this coat cost/is this coat costing?   10 Turn up the volume. Nobody can hear/is hearing the music.

3 Ⓐ-Ⓒ Choose the correct alternatives for 1-15 in this passage. Circle your answers. Then listen and check your answers.

Tonight, Brett Starkey, the radio commentator, (0) is broadcasting/broadcasts live from the Adelphi Theatre in Liverpool.

Brett: It's nine o'clock and the audience (1) are waiting/wait for the Metalheads to begin their concert. Ah! Now the group (2) is coming/come onto the stage. As you (3) are knowing/know, Kelvin usually (4) is playing/plays keyboards but tonight he (5) is performing/performs solo in New York, so Ben, a local musician, (6) is playing/plays with the group. The audience (7) aren't clapping/don't clap. I (8) am thinking/think that perhaps the Metalheads (9) are losing/lose popularity these days. Now, they (10) are singing/sing their first number, 'How (11) Are You Knowing/Do You Know It's Love?' I (12) am hearing/hear/can hear the fans singing too. Their enthusiasm (13) is increasing/increases. Everything (14) is being/is OK now. Their fans (15) are still loving/still love the Metalheads.

4 Ⓓ Read the following passage about Danny. Then, write seven sentences about Danny and his teachers. In each sentence, use *always* with one of the verbs from the passage in the Present Continuous.

Danny is the worst pupil in his class. Every day he falls asleep in the lessons. He forgets to bring his book to school. He fights with the other boys and he teases the girls. He plays tricks all the time. One day, he brought his pet mouse to school and put it in the teacher's pocket. His teachers complain about him every day. But when he goes home, he is a different person. He helps his mother all the time and loves playing with his baby sister as often as he can.

0   Danny is always falling asleep in the lesson.

UNIT 4 >> Past Simple

 Roger Scoop **became** a reporter in 1985. He **worked** for different national newspapers and **interviewed** a lot of famous people. He **travelled** all over the world and **wrote** front-page news stories. However, in 1995, while he **was** in Asia, some terrorists **kidnapped** him and **held** him prisoner for a year.

For information about form, see Appendix 1.

Ⓐ USE

We use the Past Simple to talk about something in the past:

1 to **tell a story**: *The terrorists* **kidnapped** *Roger. They* **took** *him into the jungle.*

2 for something which was **true in the past**: *The Romans* **built** *good roads.*

3 with **time expressions** referring to finished times:
One hour ago/Two years ago/Last night/Yesterday/Last month/In 1992, we **took** *the exam.*

4 with **questions** to ask about somebody's past: *Where* **were** *you born?*

Ⓑ *BE, HAVE GOT* AND *LIE*

The verbs in this section sometimes cause problems for learners when they are used in the past:

Be

Remember that the Past Simple is the same in all persons except in the past tense of **be**.

I/she/he/it	**was**	*I* **was** *home last night.*
we/you/they	**were**	**Were** *they at the party?**

* We never use **did** or **didn't** to form past questions or negative sentences with **be**.

Have got

We used **had** in the Past Simple where we use **have got** in the present:

I've got a Mercedes. I **had** *a Ferrari but I sold it.*   (Not ~~I had got a Ferrari~~...)
Didn't *you* **have** *a pet when you were a child?*   (Not ~~Hadn't you got a pet~~...?)

Lie and lay

to lie	(= to be in a horizontal position)	*Yesterday, I* **lay** *in bed until 12.*
to lie	(= not to tell the truth)	*I* **lied** *about the accident.*
to lay	(= to put something down	*I* **laid** *the baby on its bed.*
	= to produce an egg)	*The hen* **laid** *an egg.*

Ⓒ NOT REPEATING THE VERB

We can avoid repeating a Past Simple verb by using **did** or **didn't**, especially after **but**:
I enjoyed the film but my sister **didn't**.
I asked her to help and she **did**. (See Unit 1C)

Ⓓ USE OF EMPHATIC *DID*

We can use **did** in Past Simple affirmative sentences to add emphasis in the same way as we use **do** or **does** in the Present Simple (see Unit 1E). For example:
You're wrong about the result of the match. Manchester **did** *beat Liverpool.*

1 **A** **B** Fill the gaps in the continuation of Roger's story with verbs in the Past Simple. Choose them from this list.

| agree | be | become | begin | demand | discover | enjoy | fly | follow | forget |
| have got | hide | lose | release | sell | step | surround | think | try | not work |

The terrorists (0) *demanded* a million pounds. The army (1) .... to rescue Roger but the terrorists (2) .... in the jungle and the army's plans (3) .... Finally, Roger's newspaper (4) .... to pay the ransom and his captors (5) .... him. Roger (6) .... that he (7) .... free at last! He (8) .... back to Britain but as soon as he (9) .... off the plane, photographers (10) .... him. At first, he (11) .... the attention and he (12) .... his story for a lot of money. However, the Press (13) .... him everywhere. They (14) .... that he (15) .... three different girlfriends and, as a result, he (16) .... them all! Roger (17) .... to hate the Press. Luckily, the media soon (18) .... his story and Roger (19) .... a normal reporter again.

2 **A** **B** Complete these sentences about Roger Scoop, using suitable verbs.

0 When *did he become* a reporter? In 1985.
1 Where .... in 1995? He .... to Asia. (use: *go/travel*)
2 Why .... the terrorists .... him? Because they .... money.
3 Why .... the terrorists .... him? Because the newspaper .... the ransom.
4 How .... he .... to Britain? He ....
5 .... he .... his story to the Press for a lot of money? Yes, he ....
6 How many girlfriends .... he ....? Three.
7 .... he .... being famous? No, he ....

3 **B** Choose the correct Past Simple form of *to lie, to lie* or *to lay* for these sentences.

0 They lay on the beach from 9 a.m. until noon.
1 Harry .... about the robbery.   2 The hens .... three eggs yesterday.
3 I .... my wallet on the table and forgot to pick it up.   4 Jessica .... in the bath for hours until the water got cold.   5 As soon as I .... my head on the pillow, I fell asleep.   6 Nobody collected the letters; they just .... on the mat.

4 **C** Substitute *did* or *didn't* for one of the verbs in each sentence.

0 Bob passed the exam but Julie failed. *Bob passed the exam but Julie didn't.*
1 Tom gave me a present but Sam forgot. ....
2 Rocky didn't climb the mountain but I climbed it. ....
3 I didn't see the film but Martin watched it. ....
4 Prices rose in France but they remained the same here. ....

5 **D** Complete the parallel sentences to the ones given by using emphatic *did*.

0 It's not true that I forgot to post the letters. *I did post the letters.*
1 I'm right. It was Columbus who discovered America. .... America.
2 I'm positive that I locked the safe before I left. I ....
3 My sister isn't lying about going to Oxford University. .... to Oxford University.
4 No, you're wrong, I didn't fail my English exam. I ....

UNIT 5 >> Past Continuous

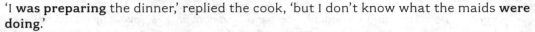

> @ 'What **were** you **doing** at 5.35?' asked Inspector Davis.
> 'I **was preparing** the dinner,' replied the cook, 'but I don't know what the maids **were doing**.'
> 'I **was hoovering** the carpets,' said Lucy, 'and Ella **was cleaning** the bathroom.'
> 'Did you see the murder?'
> 'No, we **were** all **working**.'

For information about form, see Appendix 1. For spelling rules about adding **-ing**, see Appendix 4.

Ⓐ USE

We use the Past Continuous to talk about a **particular moment** in the past:
*Lucy **was hoovering** at 5.35.* (= She was in the middle of hoovering at 5.35)

We often use the Past Continuous and the Past Simple in the same sentence:
*They **were cooking** dinner when somebody **knocked** at the door.*
(= They were in the middle of cooking dinner at that moment)

We use the Past Continuous for the action which was **in the middle of happening** (they were cooking).

We use the Past Simple for the **sudden completed action** (somebody knocked).

We do **not** use the Past Continuous to talk about two actions which follow each other:
*He **shot** the bank manager and **ran** away.* (**Not** ~~was shooting/was running~~)

Notice the difference between these questions:
'What **were** you **doing** when the murder took place?' 'I **was cooking**.'
'What **did** you **do** when the murder took place?'   'I **called** the police.'

Ⓑ WHEN AND WHILE

Sometimes we use **when** with the Past Simple and we use a Past Continuous verb in the other part of the sentence:
***When** I **saw** him, he **was carrying** a gun.*
*We **were cleaning** the windows **when** it **started** to rain.*

Sometimes we use **when** or **while** with the Past Continuous:
*I **had** an accident **when/while** I **was going** to town.*
***When/While** they **were arguing**, the baby **started** crying.*

Sometimes we use **while** with two Past Continuous actions happening at the same time:
***While** I **was cooking** dinner, my brother **was watching** a video.*
*She **was flying** to Paris **while** we **were doing** the exam.*

1 **A** **B** Fill the two gaps in each sentence with one verb in the Past Simple and the other verb in the Past Continuous form.

I (**0** *cook/ring*) was cooking dinner when the phone rang. While I (**1** *talk/knock*) ....
on the phone, my neighbour .... at the door. She (**2** *cry/be*) ....
because there .... a mess in her house.
She said, 'I (**3** *have/call*) .... a bath when my husband .... me to
watch TV. (**4** *watch/reach*) While I .... the news on TV, the water
.... the top of the bath. The ceiling (**5** *collapse/end*) .... just as the
programme ....'
While I (**6** *listen/arrive*) .... to her story, the police .... They
(**7** *want/come*) .... to warn me that smoke .... from my kitchen
window. When I (**8** *return/burn*) .... to the kitchen, I saw that the dinner
.... While I (**9** *put/arrive*) .... out the flames, my guests
.... While I (**10** *apologise/explode*) ...., the cooker
....

2 **A** **B** There are three verbs in each item 0-7. Circle the one verb which it is most natural to change to the Past Continuous form. Write the verb in the Past Continuous in the space at the end of the sentence.

0 Two teenagers robbed a bank. But the police caught them while they
(hid) the money.   were hiding

1 Charles played the violin but in the middle of his performance a woman
stood up in the audience and shot him.   ....

2 Mike met a beautiful girl while he travelled to Barcelona and fell in love
with her.   ....

3 When Tracy climbed the mountain, she found an eagle's nest and
stole its eggs.   ....

4 When I arrived in the middle of the party, everybody danced and nobody
greeted me.   ....

5 While the guards took the gold to the bank, two robbers stopped their
van and threatened them.   ....

6 We sailed across the ocean when we thought that we saw a mermaid.   ....

7 Jason broke into the castle and rescued the Princess while the guards slept. ....

3 **A** **B** Rewrite these sentences. Use *while* with the correct form of the verb. Use verbs from this list.

act   climb   dream   eat   sing   talk   teach   telephone   travel

0 In the middle of Mr Smith's class, I sneezed.   While Mr Smith was teaching,
                                                             I sneezed.

1 During her speech, the students fell asleep.   ....

2 He became ill on his journey through Africa.   ....

3 The alarm clock rang in the middle of her dream.   ....

4 In the middle of the play, the actor forgot his words. ....

5 The dog began to howl during their song.   ....

6 During our dinner, the table collapsed.   ....

7 In the middle of my call, someone knocked at the door. ....

8 During our journey up the mountain, it began to snow.   ....

UNIT 6 >> Present Perfect (1)

 Nick is talking on the phone to Beth, his secretary in England. 'What'**s happened**?' 'Everything'**s gone** wrong. I'**ve lost** the key to the office. The computer'**s stopped** working. Our customers **haven't received** their orders. The tax inspector **has decided** to investigate the company. And my boyfriend'**s left** me for another girl...'

For information about form, see Appendix 1.

Ⓐ USE

We use the Present Perfect:

1 for things which have happened **from the past until now** (See Unit 8):
*Nick **has managed** the company for six years.*
(= He started to manage the company six years ago and he manages it now.)

2 for things which we have done in our lives when **we don't give an exact date**:
*Jill'**s travelled** all around the world.*
*Beth'**s passed** seven exams.*

3 if we are speaking in an **unfinished time period**. At 11 a.m. Beth says:
'I'**ve posted** the letters.' (unfinished time period — it is still morning)

But in the afternoon or evening, she says:
'*I posted them this morning.*' (finished time period — the morning has finished)

4 if what happened **then** is **still important now**:
*I'm unhappy. My boyfriend'**s left** me.*
*I can't get in the office. I'**ve lost** the key.*

Ⓑ IT'S THE FIRST TIME...

When we talk about the first, second time etc. that we have done something, we use the Present Perfect:
*It's the **first time** (that) Beth'**s looked** after the office.* (Not ... ~~the first time she looks~~...)
*It's the **second time** he'**s asked** that.* (Not ... ~~the second time he asks that~~.)

Ⓒ DIFFERENCES IN MEANING

The Present Perfect and the Present Continuous have different meanings:
*Now I **have finished** my work.* = I finished a few moments ago.
*Now I **am finishing** my work.* = I am in the process of finishing at this moment.

We sometimes use the Present Perfect with a Present Simple or Present Continuous verb in the same sentence. This shows that the Present Perfect action has happened **first**.
*After I **have had** breakfast, I **go** to work.*
*He **is waiting** outside because he **has lost** his key.*

1 Ⓐ Here are descriptions of a fashion show, a football match and a murder investigation. In each case, the writer is describing what has happened until now. Put the verbs in the correct places in the correct form. Then listen and check your answers.

A. The Fashion Show: ~~arrive~~ change fall send take wear

The fashion show is ready to begin. The audience **(0)** have arrived and **(1)** .... their seats. All the top magazines **(2)** .... journalists to report on the show. The models **(3)** .... into the new range of clothes. Let's begin. Oh! Claudette, the first model, **(4)** .... over. This is the first time she **(5)** .... such high heels.

B. The Football Match: *blow defend miss score send win*

It is nearly full time. Nobody **(6)** .... Liverpool **(7)** .... two penalties and Manchester United **(8)** .... well. The referee **(9)** .... off two players for serious fouls. Now, he **(10)** .... the whistle. It's the end of the match. Neither team **(11)** ....

C. The Murder: *arrest be examine find inform question take*

Inspector Dixon is now at the murder scene. Sergeant Trent **(12)** .... there for an hour. The Inspector is asking him a lot of questions. '**(13)** .... you .... any evidence? **(14)** .... you .... the witnesses? **(15)** .... you .... the victim's family? **(16)** .... the police photographer .... photos of the crime scene? **(17)** .... the police doctor .... the body? **(18)** .... we .... the murderer?'

2 Ⓐ Fill the gaps with verbs from the list. Use the Present Perfect in positive, negative or question forms. Use a short answer if suitable.

> *cover dance disappear dream drink drive eat end fall flirt*
> *forget go ~~hear~~ hold invite put see shake throw tip wear*

0 Have you heard the news? Bob McGive has invited Slim Skinty to his party!
1 Slim doesn't feel comfortable. He .... a suit and tie before.   **2** '................... Slim .... hands with a millionaire before?' 'No, he ....'   **3** Slim is very hungry. He .... for a week. He .... the whole plate of caviar into his mouth!   **4** Look at Slim and Bob's daughter, Celia. I think they .... in love.   **5** They .... together five times tonight. And each time, Slim .... Celia very closely.   **6** Slim and Celia .... into the garden. It is very dark. The clouds .... the moon.   **7** '................... you .... my daughter?' Bob is asking. 'She ....!'   **8** Bob .... Slim out of the house. He's angry because Slim .... with Celia.   **9** Slim .... too much of Bob's whisky. He can't walk straight.   **10** Celia .... soon .... Slim. She's dancing with another man.   **11** The party .... All the guests .... away in their expensive cars. Bob .... out the lights.   **12** Next morning, Slim is waking up. '................... I .... everything? Did I really go to a millionaire's party last night and dance with his daughter?'

3 Ⓐ Put the verb in each item 1-10 in the Present Perfect form. Then show why we use the Present Perfect by writing A1, A2, A3 or A4.

A1 = action from past until now   **A2** = an action/actions in our lives at no exact date
A3 = unfinished time period   **A4** = past action is still important now

0 I've lived in Glasgow for ten years.		A1
00 Can you help me? I've lost my way.		A4
1 My brother (*meet*) .... the President.		....
2 At 10 p.m. he said, 'I (*enjoy*) .... this evening very much.'		....

3 I feel sick. I (*eat*) .... some out-of-date food. ....
4 Steve (*win*) .... gold medals at five Olympic Games. ....
5 He (*teach*) .... French for six years. ....
6 Sheila (*get*) .... divorced twice. ....
7 I (*travel*) .... through the Sahara Desert seven times. ....
8 Jill and Nick (*manage*) .... their company for twelve years. ....
9 The boss asked at 10 a.m.: ' (*see*) .... you .... Sam this morning?' ....
10 Sam is very unhappy. His boss (*dismiss*) .... him. ....

4 **Ⓐ** **Look at these three parts of a story about Bob and his brother. In two cases, the actions take place in an unfinished time period. Use Present Perfect verbs. In the other case, the actions take place in a finished time period. Use Past Simple verbs. Use verbs from the list. Then listen and check your answers.**

arrive   be   be   break   ~~do~~   find   find   fire   have   lose
read   start   take   tell   visit   walk   watch   work

A It is 3 p.m. Bob has come home. He is talking to his brother, Ricky.
  Bob: What (0) *have* you *done* today?
  Ricky: I (1) .... some films on TV. I (2) .... *HI* magazine. My friends
      (3) .... me. I (4) ....a great time. (5) .... your day ....
      good?
  Bob: No, I (6) .... my job.
  Ricky: Never mind. Let's watch TV.

B It is 3 p.m. next day. Bob has come home.
  Ricky: (7) .... you .... your new job this morning?
  Bob: No. I (8) .... a taxi but the taxi (9) .... down. Then, I (10) .... to
      the office but I (11) .... late. And my new boss (12) .... me.
  Ricky: Never mind. Let's watch TV.

C They continue talking.
  Bob: But this afternoon I (13) .... successful.
  Ricky: Good! (14) .... you .... a new job?
  Bob: No. But I (15) .... a job for you. I (16) .... the factory that you'll start
      tomorrow.
  Ricky: But I (17) .... never .... in a factory before.
  Bob: Never mind. Let's watch TV.

5 **Ⓐ Ⓑ** **Rewrite the second sentence using a Present Perfect verb so that it gives the same information as the first sentence.**

0 Damien began to write novels five years ago and he still writes novels.
  Damien *has written novels for five years.*

1 Sam began playing the piano six years ago and he still plays the piano.
  Sam ....

2 Tina is visiting America for the first time.
  It's the first time ....

3 I did one grammar exercise at 10 a.m. and another exercise at 11 a.m.
  .... two grammar exercises this morning.

4 He's very happy because he is the winner of the chess competition.
  He's very happy because ....

5 Do you know the Principal of the school?

....? (use: *meet*)

6 Does she have a driving licence?

.... her driving test? (use: *pass*)

7 Kim stopped writing to me twenty years ago and she still doesn't write to me.

.... for twenty years.

8 Myra is getting married for the fifth time.

This is the ....

9 Can the twins speak Spanish?

.... Spanish? (use: *learn*)

10 The manager began working here ten years ago.

The manager ....

11 She cannot remember anything because of the accident.

She .... her memory because of the accident. (use: *lose*)

12 The last time Joe drank alcohol was ten years ago.

Joe .... for ten years.

6 **C** **Read this description. In each item, put one of the verbs in the Present Perfect form and the other verb in the Present Continuous form.**

THE BILLIONAIRE'S BIRTHDAY PARTY

0 The musicians have arrived and are playing 'Happy Birthday'. (*arrive/play*)

1 The dancers .... on their costumes and .... on the stage. (*put/perform*)

2 The guests .... the food which the chef .... (*eat/prepare*)

3 The alarms .... because a gatecrasher .... the grounds. (*ring/enter*)

4 The guards .... him and .... him away. (*arrest/take*)

5 The billionaire .... out the candles and .... the cake. (*blow/eat*)

6 Now he .... the presents which his friends .... him. (*open/give*)

7 Now the guests .... at the fireworks which the servants .... (*look/light*)

8 The actress's helicopter .... in the garden and she .... the billionaire. (*land/congratulate*).

9 The billionaire .... the actress because she .... to marry him. (*kiss/agree*)

10 Now the party .... and the guests .... in their big cars. (*finish/leave*)

OPEN EXERCISE

7 **A** **B** **Complete these sentences in any suitable way using Present Perfect verbs.**

1 It's the first time ....

2 It's the seventh time ....

3 It's the ninth time ....

4 It's the hundredth time ....

5 I .... never .... before.

6 She .... never .... before.

UNIT 7 >> Present Perfect (2)

 Inspector Davis is investigating a murder in a hotel. He **has already questioned** the cook and he **has just finished** interrogating the maids. He **hasn't interviewed** the manager **yet**. He **still hasn't discovered** the motive for the murder. He**'s never encountered** such a puzzling crime.

A ALREADY, JUST, YET, EVER, NEVER, STILL

We often use the Present Perfect with **already, just, yet, ever, never, still.**

These words refer to a **time period between the past and now.**

He's **already** questioned the chef.	(at some time before now)
Have you **ever** seen a murder?	(in your life until now)
He's **just** finished interrogating the maids.	(a very short time before now)
There has **never** been a murder in this hotel.	(in all the past time until now)

We use **yet** to say that **something hasn't happened**:
*The murder happened an hour ago. Inspector Davis hasn't found any clues **yet**.* (not until now)

We use **still** to emphasise that **we've waited a long time**:
*The murder happened two months ago. He **still** hasn't found any clues.* (not until now)

B POSITION

Notice the position of these words:

1 We usually put **already, ever, just, never** directly **before the past participle**:
   *He's **already questioned** the maids.*   *Have you **ever helped** the police?*

2 We usually put **yet** at the **end of the sentence**: *He hasn't found any evidence **yet**.*

3 We usually put **still** directly in front of **hasn't, haven't**:
   *He **still hasn't** written his report.*   *They **still haven't** found the murderer.*

C STILL

We can use **still** with different tenses:

He **still hasn't paid** his bill.	(from past until now)
He **still works** in the garage.	(there is no change in the present from the past)
After he left school, he **still visited** the teachers.	(there was no change in the past)
He **will still study** when he's 90 years old.	(no change in the future)

Still goes after **am, is** or **are**:
*They **are still** ill.*   *I **am still** tired.*

D BEEN/GONE

We use **have/has been to** when we have visited a place and **have come back again**:
we have finished the trip.   *Sarah's **been to** China. She came home yesterday.*

We use **have/has gone to** when we have departed but **haven't come back yet**:
we haven't finished the trip.   *Paul **has gone to** Glasgow. He's there now.*

1 **A** **B** Nick and Jill have a new secretary, Brigitte, in the office. Write sentences with *already, just, still* or *yet* for situations 1-10. Use the verbs in bold in the correct tense and:

already (x 3)   *just (x 2)*   *still (x 3)*   *yet (x 3)*

0 Brigitte must **photocopy** some important documents. Nick asked her to do it a week ago.
  Brigitte still hasn't photocopied the documents.

1 Her boyfriend gave her a 1kg box of chocolates yesterday. She **ate** all of them this morning.
  ....

2 Nick asked her to **bring** his coffee three hours ago. But Brigitte is too busy eating chocolates.
  ....

3 Five minutes ago, she **e-mailed** her boyfriend.
  ....

4 There are some faxes to **send**. She will send them soon.
  ....

5 Jill asked her to **telephone** Mr Branson. 'I did it two hours ago,' she says.
  ....

6 Two minutes ago, she **finished** painting her nails.
  ....

7 Six hours ago, Mr Branson asked Brigitte to **give** Nick an urgent message. The message is on
  her desk. ....

8 She got her monthly salary at noon. She **spent** it in her lunch hour. Now she has no money.
  ....

9 She wants to **ask** for a pay-rise. She is waiting until tomorrow to ask.
  ....

10 Nick wants to **dismiss** Brigitte. He is waiting until the end of the day.
  ....

2 **A** **B** Rewrite these sentences inserting *already* or *yet* or *still*.

0 Don't look for your key. I've unlocked the office.
  I've already unlocked the office.

1 He started working in Spain in 2000 but he hasn't learnt Spanish.
  ....

2 She wants to work in India but she hasn't got a visa. She'll go to the embassy tomorrow.
  ....

3 He's only sixteen but he's made two hit CDs.
  ....

4 I bought his last CD ages ago but I haven't listened to it.
  ....

5 I promised to buy her a meal a long time ago but I haven't done it.
  ....

6 I hope you've studied the book – the exam's tomorrow.
  ....

7 I didn't go the cinema with them because I've seen the film.
  ....

3 **A** **B** Complete these questions using the verbs from the list.

choose   dye   ~~fall~~   feel   meet   ride   rise   see   swim   take   travel   write

0   Have you ever fallen off a ladder?

1   .... your parents ever .... you to Disneyland?

2   .... you ever .... a Sumo wrestling match?

3   .... your friend ever .... her hair?

4   .... the teachers ever .... you to be football captain?

5   .... you ever .... a famous TV star?

6   .... you ever .... happy during an exam?

7   .... prices ever .... by 100% in a year?

8   .... your uncle ever .... a novel?

9   .... your friend ever .... in the Atlantic?

10   .... that cowboy ever .... a wild horse?

11   .... Nick and Jill ever .... to China?

4 **C** Use *still* with a verb in a suitable tense.

0   He was crying last night and he is crying now. He is still unhappy. (*be*)

1   When he moved to London, he .... his friends in the village. (*visit*)

2   You are lazy. You began three hours ago but you .... the work. (*not finish*)

3   In 2050, ... we .... cars? (*drive*)

4   Bob's company closed but he .... rich now. (*be*)

5   I'm thirsty. They .... my drink. (*not bring*)

6   I asked for a drink three times but they .... it. I got very angry. (*not bring*)

7   He borrowed my mobile three weeks ago but he .... it back. (*not give*)

5 **A** - **C** Read about Richard. Then rewrite sentences 1-2 and 3-5 inserting *already, yet and still* in the correct places.

> Richard wants to be a doctor. He has passed his school examinations in Biology and Chemistry. Next year, he wants to study at medical school. He failed his exam in Physics, so he has special classes at school.

0   Richard has passed his examinations in Biology and Chemistry.
    Richard has already passed his examinations in Biology and Chemistry.

1   He hasn't started medical school.

    ....

2   He is studying Physics.

    ....

> Bob McGive owns two islands. He wants to buy Tahiti. He began negotiations with the Tahitian government seven years ago.

3   Bob has bought two islands.

    ....

4   He hasn't bought Tahiti.

    ....

5   He is negotiating with the Tahitian government.

    ....

6 Ⓓ Read the passage in the box and then put either *has/have been* or *has/have gone* in the gaps in the sentences. Use short forms or short answers where possible.

> Lisa, Sally, Hugh, Tom and Pete all live in Leeds but they are travelling in Europe. At the moment, Lisa's in Amsterdam. Pete was in Holland last week but now he's in Germany. Sally is in Zurich. Last week, she was in Vienna. Hugh's in his flat in Leeds, looking at photos from his trip to Brussels. His friend, Tom, has photos from Paris, Milan and Venice.

0 'Where's Lisa?' 'She's *gone* to Amsterdam.'
1 '...................................... Pete .... to Holland?' 'Yes, he ....'
2 'Is Pete in Holland?' 'No, he .... to Germany.'
3 Hugh .... to Brussels for a holiday.
4 Hugh .... to fewer places than Tom.
5 But Tom .... n't .... to Brussels.
6 'Is Sally in Vienna?' 'No, she .... to Switzerland.'
7 Lucky Sally! She .... to Vienna.
8 How many places .... Tom .... to?
9 'What about you? .... you .... to Leeds?'
  'No, but I .... to Leicester.'
10 '...................................... already .... to Holland,' said Pete.
11 'I'd like to see Sally.' 'You can't. She .... to Zurich.'

OPEN EXERCISES

7 Ⓐ-Ⓒ Now write three sentences for each situation. Write one sentence with *already*, one with *yet* and one with *still*.

> Nick wants to sell products in Russia. He wants to visit St Petersburg next year. Last year, he made a business trip to Moscow. His company is continuing to sell products to the USA.

1 ....
2 ....
3 ....

> Myron wants to win another Oscar. He won two Oscars in 1956 and 1967. He is over 70 years old but he continues to act. After his next film, he wants to retire.

4 ....
5 ....
6 ....

> Slim Skinty needs money. He sold his coat last week. He wants to sell his trousers but nobody wants to buy them. I want to buy his socks but I'm waiting until I get my wages.

7 ....
8 ....
9 ....

8 Ⓐ Make 3 questions with *Have you ever...?* for each person in your class or group of friends. Invent some embarrassing questions.

For example: Have you ever asked anyone to marry you?
Some serious questions: Have you ever studied ancient Greek?
Some ridiculous questions: Have you ever travelled to Mars?

UNIT **8** >> Present Perfect (3)

> Myron **has known** Myra Marvellosa **for** nearly thirty years. He was her second husband but they **haven't been** friends **since** their marriage ended in divorce.
> Myron says: 'She **has replaced** every part of her body with cosmetic surgery **since** she was twenty.'
> Myra replies: 'He**'s told** lies about me ever **since** I left him for a younger man.'

Ⓐ *FOR* AND *SINCE*

We often use the Present Perfect tense with **for** and **since**:

*Myra **has worked** in Hollywood **for** twenty-five years.*
*Myron **has hated** Myra **since** 1981.*

We use **for** when we mention the **length of a period of time**:

... **for** *five minutes*   ... **for** *six weeks*   ... **for** *nine months*

We use **since** when we mention the **beginning of a period in the past**:

since + date/special event	since + action in the past
... *since 1990/... since my last birthday*	... *since I telephoned you/... since they got married*
... *since Christmas/... since June 8th*	... *since we came on holiday/... since I had breakfast*
... *since the wedding/... since breakfast*	... *since I was sixteen years old/... since I was born*

We often use negative Present Perfect verbs with **for** and **since**:

*I **haven't seen** a Myra Marvellosa film **since** I was a child.*

<u>Remember</u>: we cannot use the Present Simple in these sentences:

          *I **have studied** English **for** five years.*   Not ~~I study English for five years~~.
          *I **have lived** in London **since** 2003.*   Not ~~I live in London since 2003.~~

Ⓑ *HOW LONG... ?*

Questions with **How long...?** and the Present Perfect often have an answer with **for** or **since**:

*'**How long has** she **known** Myron?'*   *'**For** thirty years.'* or *'**Since** 1978.'*

We can ask:

*How long **is it** since I saw you?* or *How long **has it been** since I saw you?*

Ⓒ *IT'S AGES/IT'S BEEN AGES SINCE...*

We can use **It** + **is** + **time period** with **since** + **past verb**:

*It**'s** ages/ten years/a week since I saw you.*
or *It**'s been** ages/ten years/a week since I saw you.*

1 Ⓐ Write sentences with: *for* + number of years OR *since* + date OR *since* + event. Use negative verbs if necessary.

0 2004: Last number one hit for the Metalheads. (*have a number one hit*)
The Metalheads haven't had a number one hit since 1999.

1 November 2007: last victory for Crunchester United Football Team. (*win a match*)
....

2 Harry went to prison: seven bank robberies by Michelle. (*rob seven banks*)
....

3 10 years ago: Nick and Jill establish their agency. (*manage an agency*)
....

4 Last December: Billy Buttons disappeared. (*see*)
Nobody ....

5 Summer 2002: my last holiday. (*have a holiday*)
I ....

6 5 years ago: Myron's last film. (*make a film*)
....

2 Ⓐ-Ⓒ Read about Claudette's modelling career and then complete items 1-12. Use the words in brackets, putting the verbs in the correct tense. In one case, use a negative verb.

Claudette came to France from England in 1997. Her name was Sandra Wiggins but she changed it to Claudette. She began her modelling career eight years ago. A year later, she joined the fashion house of Jean Grotesque. Claudette and Jean have a close relationship and a year ago, they bought a villa together near Paris. All the famous stars come to Jean's fashion shows now. Claudette also has her own American TV show. She got the contract for the show in 2005. At first only 200,000 people watched but now her show has twenty million viewers every week. Jean Grotesque began to broadcast her show in Europe after he bought FABTV Satellite Station. Now she is famous all over the world. But she never goes back to England.

0 How long has Claudette lived in France? Since 1997. (*live in France*)

1 ....? Since 1997. (*call herself Claudette*)

2 Claudette .... a model .... eight years. (*be*)

3 .... Jean Grotesque's Fashion House?
.... seven years. (*model for*)

4 Claudette and Jean .... for .... (*live together*)

5 Jean's fashion shows .... Claudette began modelling for him. (*be successful*)

6 ....?
.... 2005. (*have her own TV show*)

7 The viewing figures .... from .... to .... 2005. (*rise*)

8 FABTV .... Jean bought the station. (*broadcast her show*)

9 Claudette .... she started her career. (*become famous*)

10 Claudette .... she became a model. (*return to England*)

11 It .... over ten years since she came to France.
(*be*/two possible answers)

12 How long .... since she moved into the villa?
(*be*/two possible answers)

UNIT 9 >> Present Perfect Continuous

 Myron is appearing on a television chat show. He**'s been telling** stories about Myra. 'She**'s been drinking** heavily since the failure of her last film. She**'s been taking** drugs.' But Myron doesn't know that Myra **has been listening** from another room in the studio. The television company **have been planning** this for a long time. Their viewing figures **have been falling** but tonight's show is special!

For information about form, see Appendix 1.

A USE

We use the Present Perfect Continuous:

1 to talk about a continuous action which **started in the past and is still continuing**:
He**'s been telling** *stories for a long time.* (he is still talking)
She**'s been having** *a violin lesson.* (she is still in the lesson)
My tooth **has been aching.** *I must go to the dentist.* (it is still aching)

2 to give information about a **long continuous action that has just stopped**:
*It***'s been snowing.** (it's just stopped)
The viewing figures **have been falling.** (but now they've just stopped falling)

3 for a **regular activity from the past until now**.
We often use a time expression with **for** or **since**:
I **have** *been making films* **for** *one year.*
He **has been acting since** *he was four.*
*They***'ve been studying** *this unit* **for** *twenty minutes.*
*I***'ve been studying** *English* **since** *I was seven.*

B *HOW LONG* + PRESENT PERFECT CONTINUOUS

We often make questions which begin **How long...?** with a Present Perfect Continuous verb.

We often use **for** (+ the period of time) and **since** (+ the point of time when the action began) with this tense (see Unit 8).

'***How long have*** *you* ***been planning*** *this programme?'*   '***For*** *two months.'*
'***How long has*** *she* ***been watching*** *TV?'*   '***Since*** *the programme began.'*

1 **Ⓐ Ⓑ** Use verbs from the list in the Present Perfect Continuous form to complete this conversation between Inspector Davis and Police Officer Clark. Then listen and check your answers.

communicate   do   fly   send   sit   surround   take   talk   ~~wait~~   waste   watch

Davis: How long (0) *has* Harry *been waiting* outside the Bank of England?

Clark: He (1) .... in his car for three hours.

Davis: What (2) .... Michelle ....?

Clark: She (3) .... the bank through binoculars from a window. Also, a helicopter (4) .... overhead. And someone (5) .... signals from a boat on the Thames.

Davis: (6) .... Harry .... with Michelle?

Clark: No, and she (7) .... to him.

Davis: Well, everything's under control. Extra police (8) .... up positions on the rooftops for the last hour. Soldiers (9) .... the area. Harry and Michelle (10) .... their time. They cannot rob the bank.

2 **Ⓐ Ⓑ** Complete these sentences using the items in brackets. Use the Present Perfect Continuous form of the verbs. Use capital letters where necessary.

0 Why are your clothes dirty? *Have you been playing* football? (*you/play*)

1 I've looked for you everywhere. Where .... ? (*you/hide*)

2 Why is Jim at the door? .... to our conversation? (*he/listen*)

3 The boss is going to dismiss them. .... late for work. (*they/arrive*)

4 Diane will win the competition. .... every day. (*she/practise*)

5 Mum's tired because .... up early. (*she/get*)

6 Get up, lazy bones! How long .... in bed? (*you/lie*)

3 **Ⓑ** Study these situations. Then make sentences using Present Perfect Continuous verbs. Use *for* or *since* in each example.

0 He began to play football a short time ago.
He *hasn't been playing for* a long time. He's *been playing for* a short time.

1 The policeman began watching Harry at 8 o'clock.
He .... 8 o'clock. He .... seven hours.

2 Myra began to drink when her film failed five years ago.
Myra .... her film failed. Myra .... five years.

3 Mina began her career as a jazz singer twelve years ago. She still makes CDs.
Mina .... with a jazz band .... twelve years.
She .... CDs .... a long time.

OPEN EXERCISE

4 **Ⓐ** For each situation, write a Present Perfect Continuous question, as in the example.

0 You look very tired.   *Have you been working hard?*

1 You've got a black eye.   ....?

2 Your clothes are wet.   ....?

3 You're coughing and sneezing.   ....?

4 The room looks nice.   ....?

5 You've got lipstick on your cheek.   ....?

Present Perfect Continuous

UNIT 10 >> Present Perfect Simple or Continuous?

> **@**
>
> Interviewer: How long **have** you **been going** out together?
> Couple: We**'ve been dating** each other for thirty years. We**'ve written** thousands of love letters and **telephoned** each other every night.
> Interviewer: Why **haven't** you **got married** before?
> Couple: We**'ve been saving** up to buy a ring!

Ⓐ PERMANENT OR TEMPORARY SITUATIONS

We prefer to use the **Present Perfect Simple** for permanent situations or for **longer time periods**:
I've lived in England for six years. (this is my permanent home)
We've written thousands of love letters. (over a period of thirty years)

We prefer the **Present Perfect Continuous** for **temporary situations** or for **shorter time periods**:
We've been staying in a honeymoon hotel. (a temporary situation)
We've been looking for a house for a year. (a comparatively short time)

But it is often possible to use either the Present Perfect Continuous (to put emphasis on the length of time) or the Present Perfect Simple.
I've been dating her for thirty years. or *I've dated her for thirty years.*

Ⓑ *HOW LONG* AND *HOW MANY*

We ask:
How long have you been writing to her? (we are interested in the **continuous** length of time)
But *How many letters have you written?* (we are interested in the **number** or **amount**)

Ⓒ EMPHASIS ON ACTIVITY OR COMPLETED ACTION

We often use the Present Perfect Continuous if we are interested in the **activity**. Perhaps it is completed or not: *They've been saving up for a long time.*

We use the Present Perfect Simple if we want to **emphasise** that the action is **complete, finished**:
They've saved up enough money. Now they can get married.
(they're not saving now — the process of saving money is complete)

Here are more examples:
I've been reading this book. I'm on chapter five. It's very exciting.
I've read this book. Now I can take it back to the library. (finished)
She's been cooking dinner. That's why the house smells of fish.
She's cooked dinner. Now we can sit down and eat. (finished)

Ⓓ OTHER USES WITH THE PRESENT PERFECT SIMPLE

We use the Present Perfect Simple (not the Continuous):

1 with **already, ever, never, yet**: *I haven't saved enough money yet.*

2 with verbs like **know, forget, notice**: *I've known her for a year.*

3 to talk about **short sudden actions**: *I've broken the window.*   *She's had an accident.*

4 to talk about the last time we did something: *I haven't eaten meat since 1998.*

1 Ⓐ Ⓒ Ⓓ Fill the gaps with verbs from the list in either the Present Perfect Simple or the Present Perfect Continuous form. Then listen and check your answers.

come   do   enter   hide   land   rob   never steal
steal   succeed   switch   wait   watch   not watch

Harry and Michelle are sitting in a car near the Bank of England.

Harry: The police (0) *have been watching* us for three hours.

Michelle: Good! So they (1) .... the Tower of London.

Harry: Exactly. We (2) .... a lot of famous places but we

(3) .... the Crown Jewels before!

Michelle: Our partner, Bart, is radioing me. Hello, Bart! What (4) .... you

.....................................?

Bart: I (5) .... the helicopter inside the Tower. I (6) ....

off the alarm system and I (7) .... the main building.

Harry: (8) .... you .... the jewels yet?

Bart: No. I'm in the cellar. I (9) .... here for an hour.

I (10) .... for the guards to go away.

Michelle: It's OK. All the soldiers (11) .... here to the Bank.

Nobody is at the Tower. Our plan (12) ....!!! We're ready to act!

2 Ⓐ Ⓒ Ⓓ Put the verb either in the Present Perfect Continuous or the Present Perfect Simple tense.

0 I (*paint*) *'ve been painting* a picture. That's why I've got red paint on my nose.

1 I (*dance*) .... the tango many times. But I (*never dance*)

.... the waltz.   2 I (*wash*) .... my hair. That's why

I didn't answer the phone when you called.   3 They (*repair*) ....

the cooker. But it's still not working.   4 Sorry I'm late. I (*look*) .... for a

present for my sister.   5 I (*choose*) .... a present and I (*send*)

.... it to my sister.   6 I (*not write*) .... the report yet.

I (*wait*) .... for the information.   7 The match (*finish*)

.... The referee (*blow*) .... the final whistle.

8 She (*choose*) .... a new car. But she (*not pay*) .... for

it yet.   9 I'm angry because someone (*talk*) .... about me behind my back.

3 Ⓐ - Ⓓ Nick and Jill are back from holiday. Complete their questions to Beth. Use the Present Perfect Continuous except where only the Present Perfect Simple is possible.

0 *Have* you *answered* all the letters? (*answer*)

1 How long .... you .... about the computer problems? (*know*)

2 .... the other secretaries .... hard? (*work*)

3 .... Brigitte .... late for work? (*arrive*)

4 .... you .... the letters in the files every day? (*put*)

5 Is that your new Mercedes in the car park? How long .... you

.... it? (*own*)

6 How can you afford an expensive car? .... you .... the

company? (*rob*)

7 .... Brigitte .... the office phone to speak to her boyfriend? (*use*)

UNIT 11 >> Continuous or Simple?

 Slim Skinty **has slept** in many strange places. Last week, he **slept** in a garage. Recently he**'s been sleeping** in a cow shed. But wherever he sleeps, he always **dreams** about being a millionaire.

Ⓐ PRESENT PERFECT, PRESENT SIMPLE, PAST SIMPLE

- We use the **Present Perfect** tenses if we are talking about the **period of time from then until now**:
  *Slim **has slept** in many strange places.*   *He**'s been sleeping** in a cow shed.*
- We use the **Present** tenses if we are talking about the **present time period**.
  *He always **dreams** about being a millionaire.*   *He**'s snoring** now!*
- We use the **Past Simple** tense if we are talking about something that happened **then**:
  *He **slept** in a cow shed two weeks ago.*   *He **met** Ellie Tramper last year.*

Ⓑ PRESENT PERFECT VS PAST SIMPLE

We use the **Present Perfect** tenses when we **don't give an exact time** in the past:
Something has happened at some time between the past and now.
*I**'ve** never **slept** in a cow shed.*   *He**'s been sleeping** under bridges.*

But we use the **Past Simple** if we give or ask for a **specific time reference** in the past:
*I **got** my first job **when I was sixteen.***   ***When did** you **leave** school?*

We often refer to a past period of time without using an actual time phrase:
*He **left** school and **started** his first job.* (we understand that this was in the past)

Ⓒ PRESENT PERFECT FOR A RECENT EVENT/ACTION

We use the Present Perfect for an action which has a **strong connection with the present**.

Present Perfect	→ connection with present	Past Simple	→ finished action
*I**'ve lost** my key.*	I can't open the door.	*I **lost** my key.*	I told the police.
*He**'s found** a penny.*	He can buy a chip.	*He **found** £500*	He spent it all.
*They**'ve been** ill.*	They still look pale.	*They **were** ill.*	But they're OK now.
*The war**'s finished.***	We can go home.	*The war **finished.***	The soldier returned.

You can see that the choice of Present Perfect or Past Simple affects the meaning:

*Slim **has saved** enough to buy a coat.* The tense choice suggests that Slim has not yet bought the coat.	*Slim **saved** enough to buy a coat.* The tense choice tells us that he bought the coat.

Ⓓ *FOR, SINCE AND AGO*

We use the **Present Perfect** tenses with **for** and **since** (see Unit 8).
*He**'s lived**/**'s been living** on the road **for** the last ten years/**since** 1998.*

But we can use the **Past Simple** with **for** if the action finished in the past:
*He **lived** in the mountains **for** a year from 2000-2001.*
*He **didn't go** to the dentist's **for** twenty years. Then he had ten teeth out.*

We use the **Past Simple** with **ago**:
*I **began** to work here six months **ago**.*   *Where **were** you five hours **ago**?*

1 Ⓐ-Ⓒ Read this story and put the verbs in a suitable tense. Choose from the Present Perfect, the Present Simple or the Past Simple. Use short forms where possible. Then listen and check your answers.

Last week, Slim Skinty (**0** *go*) went for a job interview. Bob McGive (**1** *ask*) .... him some questions. 'Why (**2** *want*) .... you .... to be managing director of my sausage factory?'

'I (**3** *eat*) .... a lot of sausages in my life,' Slim (**4** *reply*) .... , 'so I (**5** *know*) .... a lot about sausages.'

'(**6** *manage*) .... you ever .... a large company?'

'No, but in 1983, I (**7** *organise*) .... a party for all the tramps in the town. We (**8** *find*) .... some out-of-date sausages in your factory dump and we (**9** *have*) .... a barbecue.'

'I see. And how much (**10** *earn*) .... you .... now, Mr Skinty?'

'I (**11** *not earn*) .... anything at the moment. You see, I (**12** *have*) .... never .... a job in my life.'

'Well, Mr Skinty, you (**13** *give*) .... some very interesting and original answers to my questions.' Bob (**14** *pause*) ....

'So, (**15** *decide*) .... you .... to give me the job?'

'No, I (**16** *negative short answer*) .... But, tell me, why (**17** *decide*) .... you .... to apply for this job?'

'Because it (**18** *be*) .... warm in this interview room. And I (**19** *sell*) .... just .... my winter coat to buy some sausages for my supper!'

2 Ⓐ-Ⓓ Rewrite these sentences, using the verbs in brackets.

0 Helen moved to Scotland in 1999.
  Helen has lived in Scotland since 1999. (*live*)

1 Slim sold his only coat last week.
  .... a week. (*not wear*)

2 Bob has owned this factory for fifteen years.
  .... (*buy*)

3 Slim never sleeps in a bed.
  .... since he became a tramp. (*not sleep*)

4 Bob has eaten caviar and venison only since he became a millionaire.
  .... when he was not so rich. (*not eat*)

5 Slim knows everyone in the village.
  .... since he came there. (*meet*)

6 Bob opened a new factory in Russia a few days ago.
  .... (*just open*)

7 Nobody has seen Slim's cat since last Christmas.
  .... at Christmas. (*disappear*)

8 When did Bob and his wife get married?
  .... married for long? (*be*)

9 Bob's son was short last year but now he's tall.
  .... a lot since last year. (*grow*)

10 I've visited California. It was in 2005.
  In 2005, I .... (*visit*)

3 **A** - **D** Rewrite these sentences as in the examples, using the words in brackets. Change the verb tense from Past Simple to Present Perfect or vice versa.

  0 Paul bought a new car a few days ago.
  Paul has just bought a new car. (*just*)

  00 Kelly has taught English for ten years.
  Kelly began to teach English ten years ago. (*ago*)

  1 I chose a present for my friend.
  .... (*already*)

  2 Kevin began to play for Crunchester United in 2000.
  .... (*since*)

  3 Tim wants to pass his driving test next month.
  .... (*yet*)

  4 The journalists interviewed Myra half an hour ago.
  .... (*just*)

  5 Phil and Julia have been married since May.
  .... (*in May*)

  6 Boris has played the violin for sixteen years.
  .... (*ago*)

  7 When Meg came to Wales, she began to speak Welsh.
  .... (*since*)

  8 The police did not arrest Harry but they are planning to.
  .... (*yet*)

  9 Barry began to collect stamps when he was twelve years old.
  .... (*since the age of*)

  10 Colin failed the exam three times last year.
  .... (*still*)

4 **C** **D** Which is better? A (Past Simple) or B (Present Perfect) Why?

  0 Sally **A. passed** / **B. has passed** the exam. Now she can go to university.
  Because there is a strong connection to the present.

  1 Sally **A. passed** / **B. has passed** her exam and went to university.
  ....

  2 Uncle Joe **A. lost** / **B. has lost** his false teeth. He is very upset.
  ....

  3 Leonardo da Vinci **A. painted** / **B. has painted** the 'Mona Lisa' in the sixteenth century.
  ....

  4 I **A. finished** / **B. have finished** painting a picture. Bob McGive wants to buy it.
  ....

  5 Our house **A. burnt** / **B. has burnt** down. We are homeless!
  ....

  6 Uncle Joe **A. lost** / **B. has lost** his false teeth. But he found them and ate his pie.
  ....

  7 Jimmy **A. was** / **B. has been** absent from school a lot recently. The teacher is angry.
  ....

8 Henry VIII **A. was / B. has been** the King of England for many years.

....

9 Kylie **A. got / B. has got** engaged to Robbie. Everybody is very surprised.

....

10 Lisa **A. was / B. has been** engaged to Terry. But now she has given him back the ring.

....

5 Ⓐ - Ⓓ Are these sentences correct? Either put a tick (✓) at the end or put a cross (✗) and rewrite the sentence, changing the tense of the verb.

0 She lives in Scotland since May.   ✗ *She has lived/has been living in Scotland since May.*

1 They bought a new car last year. ....

2 Did you see the new Tom Craze film yet? ....

3 Ben already beat Phil at tennis three

   times this year. ....

4 English is becoming important since it

   became a world language. ....

5 She's been looking for a new boyfriend

   since Tom left her. ....

6 Sally is learning French for a long time. ....

7 I've broken my leg when I was a child. ....

8 They're sleeping downstairs since the

   bedroom ceiling collapsed. ....

9 In June, I've passed my driving test

   but then I crashed my car. ....

10 It's raining since 2 a.m. ....

OPEN EXERCISES

6 Ⓐ - Ⓓ Put any suitable verb in the gaps. Use either the Past Simple or the Present Perfect form.

A Nick and Jill (1) .... their company in 1998. At first, they (2) .... a lot of money but recently they (3) .... a big profit. As a result, they (4) .... new offices – they are expanding!

B Kevin Scoremore (5) .... football in many countries during his career. In 1998, he (6) .... in Italy and in 1999, a German club (7) .... him for 5 million pounds. Recently, he (8) .... for Crunchester United. He is a very popular player here.

7 Ⓐ - Ⓒ Use a suitable verb either in the Present Perfect or in the Past Simple.

1 Somebody .... my wallet. I must call the police!

2 Somebody .... my wallet. But the police caught the thief.

3 My team .... another game. Now they're bottom of the league.

4 My team .... again last month so I stopped supporting them.

5 He .... a lot of alcohol at the party. I'm glad he didn't drive home.

6 She .... a lot of alcohol. Don't let her drive home.

7 .... you .... this window? Help me clear away the glass.

8 .... you .... the window during the disco last month?

UNIT 12 >> Past Perfect

 Sebastian Ace finally defeated Max Blastov last year. In 1990, Blastov **had tried** to blow up the embassy. In 1995, he **had threatened** to boil the world's oceans. In 2000, he **had invented** a laser that would drill a hole in the moon. Ace **had** always **stopped** Blastov's plans. But Blastov **had** always **escaped**. Finally, last year, Ace captured Max.

For information about form, see Appendix 1.

Ⓐ USE

We use the Past Perfect to talk about an **action** or state in the past **that happened at a time before another action** in the past:

past (then)	farther in the past (before then)
Ace stopped Blastov's plans. Blastov tried to destroy the world.	But he **had** always **escaped.** Ace **had known** about Blastov's plans.

We normally use the Past Perfect if we tell the story like this:
*Ace destroyed Blastov's secret island. He **had arrived** by mini-submarine.*
(the story goes back)

But we normally use the Past Simple if we tell the story like this:
*Ace **arrived** on the island by mini-submarine. He **destroyed** Blastov's HQ.*
(the story goes forward)

We can use the Past Perfect in the past in a parallel situation to the Present Perfect in the present.

time period: past to present	time period: far past to near past
She**'s** just shot the ambassador. They**'ve** never **found** his secret HQ.	She**'d** just **shot** the President when Ace arrived. They **had** never **found** his secret HQ until Ace helped them.

Ⓑ PAST PERFECT WITH CERTAIN WORDS

We often use the Past Perfect with:

1 **after, although, because, before, until, when.** We use it for the earlier action:
*She arrived late **because** her car **had broken** down.*

2 **already** and **never**: *I arrived at 6 p.m. but Tom **had already gone**.*

3 **for** and **since**: *John met his old girlfriend in 2007.*
*He **had** not **seen** her **for** five years.* (from 2002 (far past) to 2007 (main past))
or *He **had** not **seen** her **since** 2002.*

4 with a time expression with **by...**:
***By** 2006, Ben **had won** the championship ten times.* (= in the period up to 2006)
But we say: *In 2005, Ben **won** his tenth championship.* (In 2005 + Past Simple)

Ⓒ FUNCTION: EXPRESSING REGRET

We often use the Past Perfect **to express regret for failed plans/hopes** etc.
*Max **had hoped/had planned** to become the ruler of the world.* (= but he didn't)

1 Ⓐ Ⓑ **In 1-10, put one verb in the Past Simple and one in the Past Perfect form.**

0 Chris (*visit*) *had visited* many countries in Europe, so he (*want*) *wanted* to travel to Asia.

1 First, he (*visit*) .... India. He (*never be*) .... there before.

2 After he (*see*) .... many cities, he (*decide*) .... to visit the mountains.

3 He (*meet*) .... a holy man who (*live*) .... in a cave for 60 years.

4 The holy man (*dream*) .... about Chris even before he (*arrive*) .... at the cave.

5 After he (*talk*) .... to the holy man, Chris (*change*) .... his mind about life.

6 His friends in Britain (*be*) .... worried. Chris (*not write*) .... to them for a long time.

7 His girlfriend (*look*) .... for him in India. Nobody (*see*) .... him.

8 When she (*find*) .... him, he (*already give*) .... all his money to the poor.

9 She (*return*) .... to Britain without Chris. He (*decide*) .... to live in the cave forever.

10 She (*hope*) .... to marry him but, after this, she never (*fall*) .... in love again.

2 Ⓐ Ⓑ **Use eleven Past Perfect verbs and three Past Simple verbs to complete this story. Choose the verbs from the list.**

attach	become	~~destroy~~	die	explode	fall	give
hate	help	meet	meet	place	steal	track	try

In 1999, Ace (**0**) *destroyed* Blastov's secret headquarters on Surf Island. Blastov's girlfriend, Tigra, (**1**) .... Ace because she (**2**) .... in love with him. They (**3**) .... for the first time in Istanbul ten years before but, at that time, Tigra (**4**) .... Ace. She (**5**) .... to poison him. They (**6**) .... again in 1997. Ace (**7**) .... nearly .... after Tigra (**8**) .... a cobra in his bed. In 1998, after Ace (**9**) .... Tigra to South America, she (**10**) .... a mini-bomb to his suitcase but luckily it (**11**) .... not .... Finally, however, the two enemies (**12**) .... lovers and Tigra (**13**) .... Ace the plans which she (**14**) .... from Blastov.

3 Ⓐ Ⓑ **Rewrite each item as one sentence, using at least one Past Perfect verb in each case. Use the words in brackets.**

0 He was a reporter. Then, he became a novelist.
Before he became a novelist he had been a reporter. (*before*)

1 Dickens sympathised with poor children. He had to work in a factory as a child.
.... (*because*)

2 In 1853, Dickens wrote his tenth novel.
.... (*by the end of 1853*)

3 In the 1850s, Dickens was the most popular writer in the world.
.... (*by/become*)

4 Dickens visited America. Then he wrote *Martin Chuzzlewit*.
.... (*after*)

5 Dickens visited America for the first time in 1841.
.... (*before 1841/never*)

6 His health began to deteriorate but he travelled all over the country to read from his books.
.... (*although/already*)

OPEN EXERCISE

4 Ⓐ - Ⓒ **Write a story about Tigra, Max and Ace. Use Past Simple and Past Perfect verbs.**

UNIT **13** >> Past Perfect Continuous

 When I visited Istanbul in 1998, I met several famous people. Sebastian Ace **had been spying** for nearly thirty years. Gloria Gluttony **had been writing** books about Turkish food for over twenty years. And Serena Dervish **had been performing** as a belly-dancer for fifty years!

For information about form, see Appendix 1.

Ⓐ USE

We use the Past Perfect Continuous to talk about a **continuous action** that had been happening up to the time that something else happened.

from far past to 'then'	'then'
He **had been living** in London,	but then he moved to York.
It **had been raining** for three hours.	Then, the sun began to shine.
She **had been waiting** for an hour.	Finally, the bus came.

We also use the Past Perfect Continuous for a **regular activity** from the **far past** until 'then'. We often use a time-expression with **for** or **since**:

I **had been studying** Spanish **for** one year before I moved to Spain.
He was a famous musician. He **had been playing** the piano **since** the age of four.

Ⓑ PAST PERFECT SIMPLE VS PAST PERFECT CONTINUOUS

We use the **Past Perfect Simple**:

1 for short, quick actions: *He **had scored** a goal.*

2 to emphasise that an action had been **completed**:
*She **had cooked** dinner.* (= it was ready to eat)

We use the **Past Perfect Continuous**:

1 for longer, continuous actions:
*She **had been writing** a letter.*   *He **had been playing** for an hour.*

2 to emphasise that someone had been **doing something continuously** up to a time in the past: *She **had been cooking** dinner.* (we don't know if she had finished)

Remember: we cannot use certain verbs in continuous tenses. (See Appendix 5)

Ⓒ PAST PERFECT CONTINUOUS OR PAST CONTINUOUS?

We use the **Past Continuous** when we want to show that someone was **in the middle of doing something** at a time in the past: *When I saw him, he **was talking** to his friends.*

We use the **Past Perfect Continuous** when we want to show that someone **had just been doing something** at a time in the past:

*When I saw him, he **had been talking** to his friends.* (but he had just stopped)

Ⓓ QUESTIONS WITH *HOW LONG...?*

We often make questions which begin **How long...?** with a Past Perfect Continuous verb. We often use **for** and **since** with this tense:
'**How long had** you **been waiting** before the police arrived?'
'**For** ten minutes.'   or   '**Since** 10 o'clock.'

1 **A** Read this information and then complete 1-8 with Past Perfect Continuous verbs.

> Sebastian Ace, the international spy, moved to Istanbul in 1970. He began working for the Russians in 1972. However, in 1975, he began selling secrets to the Americans. In 1980, he began to smuggle guns. In 1988, he began to help the Iranian secret service. In 1983, the Swedish Intelligence Service began to investigate him and in 1990, the Turkish police started following him. In 1993, he gave information to the Japanese government for the first time and in 1995, he began sending micro-film to the Chinese. In 2000, he was still working for all these countries.

0 I met Ace in 1998. He *had been living in Istanbul* for 28 years.
1 Tigra met Ace in 1996. He .... for one year.
2 A spy attacked Ace in 1999. He .... for 11 years.
3 The customs service arrested him in 1987. He .... for 7 years.
4 He visited Tokyo in 2001. He .... for 8 years.
5 The Turkish police closed the case in 2000. They .... for 10 years.
6 The Russians gave him a medal in 2001. He .... for 29 years.
7 The Swedes arrested him in 2000. They .... for 17 years.
8 The CIA helped him to escape in 2001. He .... for 26 years.

2 **B** **D** Fill the gaps with suitable verbs in either the Past Perfect Continuous or the Past Perfect Simple.

0 She *had been listening* to a CD by the Young Metalheads but then I interrupted her.
1 After they .... chess, they played poker.
2 Everyone was shocked. Someone .... Lady Alice. (use: *kill*)
3 Lord Robert was innocent. He .... golf when the murder .... (use: *play/happen*)
4 Someone .... Lady Alice while she .... (use: *shoot/sleep*)
5 The mechanic .... the car, so they were able to drive home. (use: *repair*)
6 The mechanic .... the car but he went home without finishing the job.
7 They played Vivaldi in New York but before that, in L.A., they .... Mozart.
8 At 3 a.m. Joe complained because I .... the guitar loudly since midnight.
9 How long .... films before you won your first Oscar?
10 How long .... Phil before you got engaged? (use: *know*)
11 The police asked Harry how long he .... banks with Michelle.
12 Before he went to prison, Harry .... to 2000 robberies. (use: *confess*)

3 **C** Fill the gaps with verbs in either the Past Perfect Continuous or the Past Continuous.

0 Nobody was on the beach; everyone *was swimming* in the sea. (*swim*)
1 When Gillian .... for an hour, her mother told her to stop. (*swim*)
2 Bob .... all morning, so he was very tired. (*exercise*)
3 When I came to the gym, Bob .... He was in the weights room. (*exercise*)
4 After he .... for an hour, Hugh had a snack. (*study*)
5 'Where was Hugh yesterday?' 'He .... in the library.' (*study*)
6 She .... at the bus stop when it began to rain. (*wait*)
7 She .... at the bus stop but, when it began to rain, she went home. (*wait*)

UNIT **14** >> *Used to*

@ Here is part of a history book from 3050 AD:
People **used to** eat food but now we take nutro-injections. They **used to** travel by car and plane but now we go from place to place by matter-transfer chambers. They **didn't use to** have thought communication systems; instead they **used to** use mobile phones. People **used to** be very primitive. But now we are civilised!

For information about form, see Appendix 1.

Ⓐ USE

We use **used to** to talk about **habits in the past**, for things which we **always/usually/often did** in the past. We don't do these things now.

*People **used to travel** on horseback or on foot.*
*She **used to be** a teacher but now she's a bookseller.*
***Did** you **use to be** a teacher before you became a writer?*
***Did** your grandfather **use to travel** by steam train?*
*Films **didn't use to be** so violent.*
*She **never used to want** to get married but now she does.*

Note: We can also use **would** to talk about habits in the past. See Unit 26E.

Ⓑ *USED TO* AND PAST SIMPLE

We use **either used to** or the Past Simple for **habits in the past**:
*I **used to live** in London.   or   I **lived** in London.*

If we choose **used to**, it is clear that we do **not** live in London **now**.

We use the Past Simple, **not used to**, for a past action which was not a habit.
*I **bought** a new car in March. (Not ~~I used to buy a new car~~.)*
*But I **used to buy** a new car every year. (= it was a regular habit)*

Ⓒ HABITS IN THE PRESENT

We use **used to** only about the past. For a habit in the present, we use a normal Present Simple verb.
*We **used to live** in caves. (past habit)*
*She **sleeps** in a cave when she **goes** to the mountains. (present habit)*
*She **used to go** dancing every night. (past habit)*
*Her sister **goes** dancing every night. (present habit)*

Note: Do not confuse **used to do** with **be used to doing** (see Unit 80).
We can use **be used to doing** in all tenses.

1 Ⓐ Fill the gaps with *used to* + verb. Then listen and check your answers.

Hugh Carter is interviewing Dave Innocence, a pop star from the 80s.

Hugh: (**0** *be*) Did you use to be famous?

Dave: Yes, everybody (**1** *know*) .... my name. I (**2** *live*) .... a life of luxury. I (**3** *drive*) .... a pink limousine. I (**4** *buy*) .... new clothes every day. I (**5** *wear*) .... very expensive after-shave. The band (**6** *eat*) .... in the best restaurants. Girls (**7** *scream*) .... when they saw us in the street.

Hugh: Marvellous! (**8** *write*) .... you .... your own songs?

Dave: No, I (**9**) .... n't. I (**10** *not play*) .... the electric guitar. I (**11** *not sing*) .... on my CDs. My manager (**12** *hire*) .... people to sing and play. All I (**13** *do*) .... was stand on the stage and mime! But everyone (**14** *buy*) .... our CDs. So I was rich.

2a Ⓐ Ⓑ Read about Dave. Then write 9 short sentences with *used to* + verbs from the story.

From 1984 to 1988, Dave lived in the USA. He ate hamburgers every day but he never drank cola. He wore cowboy clothes and carried a gun. He bought a pink Cadillac and drove from New York to Los Angeles every summer. He met a Texan girl and sent her roses every day. Finally, he asked her to marry him but she refused. He recorded a sad song about her and the Texas radio played it for many years. On hearing the song, Dave cried. Dave didn't believe in love previously but now he does.

0 Dave used to live in the USA.
1 ....
2 ....
3 ....
4 ....
5 ....
6 ....
7 ....
8 ....
9 ....

2b List the five Past Simple verbs in the story which could not be also expressed by *used to*. One has been done for you.

bought, ..., ..., ..., ...

3 Ⓐ - Ⓒ In these sentences, use verbs either with *used to* or in the Present Simple tense.

0 I used to go to school by bicycle but now I go by bus. (*go/go*)
1 Maggie loves riding. Every weekend, she .... her pony. (*ride*)
2 Fiona also loves riding. She .... her pony every weekend but now she is too busy. (*ride*)
3 When Jill was a child, her grandmother .... her stories. (*tell*)
4 Now Jill .... the same stories to her own children. (*tell*)
5 London .... the biggest city in the world. (*be*)
6 In the Stone Age, people .... stone tools. (*use*)
7 English people .... more coffee than tea nowadays. (*drink*)

OPEN EXERCISE

4 Ⓐ Ⓑ Look at exercise 1. Write a similar interview between Hugh Carter and a film star/sports star/politician from the 80s.

REVISION 1 >> First Certificate Practice

1 For questions 1-12, read the text below and decide which answer, A, B, C or D, best fits each gap. There is an example at the beginning (0).

DOLPHINS

Like whales, dolphins are mammals, not fish, and most species (0) A in the sea. Since ancient times, people (1) ..... many stories about dolphins. For example, there is a Roman tale about a dolphin which rescued a boy after he (2) ..... into the sea. The Ancient Greeks and Romans often (3) ..... images of dolphins in their works of art, showing that they (4) ..... them as an important part of their environment. Nowadays, dolphins still (5) ..... a fascination for us. There (6) ..... many popular films and TV series about them and, in the 60s, the custom of swimming with dolphins (7) ..... . People wanted, and still (8) ....., to get as close to dolphins as possible. However, recent evidence has contradicted the idea that dolphins only (9) ..... non-aggressive behaviour. Doctor Mary Fisher, a marine biologist, (10) ..... this but by the end of the century, after a series of observations, she had changed her opinion. Human beings can be aggressive towards dolphins: many nations (11) ..... them but now only Sri Lanka and Japan (12) ..... to hunt them on a large scale for meat and oil.

0 (A) live	B are living	C living	D lives
1 A tell	B told	C have told	D were telling
2 A had fallen	B had fall	C felt	D was falling
3 A include	B had included	C were including	D included
4 A regarded	B have regarded	C use to regard	D had been regarding
5 A are holding	B hold	C held	D use to hold
6 A have been	B had been	C are being	D use to be
7 A beginned	B has been beginning	C began	D begun
8 A were wanting	B wanted	C had wanted	D want
9 A are exhibiting	B exhibit	C have exhibited	D use to exhibit
10 A used to believe	B is believing	C believes	D had been believing
11 A hunt	B had hunt	C use to hunt	D used to hunt
12 A continues	B are continue	C continuing	D continue

2 For these questions, read the text below and think of the word which best fits the gap. Use only *one* word in each gap. There is an example at the beginning (0).

ON DOLPHIN BEACH

'You (0) *are* all welcome to this beach. I have already (1) .... you a lot about dolphins. What more (2) .... you want to know? Perhaps you didn't (3) .... that the killer whale is not really a whale but a large species of dolphin. I expect all of you (4) .... seen dolphins in aquariums. They perform tricks for the public but they (5) .... do anything which is not part of their natural behaviour. In the past, some of these creatures (6) .... to live in very poor conditions. People didn't (7) .... to care about preventing cruelty to animals in zoos or aquariums. But now there are strict regulations. And from this beach, you can see wild dolphins. Look! Some are (8) .... out of the water now. Have you (9) .... seen such a beautiful sight? I have (10) .... observing these wonderful creatures since I (11) .... a child but I (12) .... grown tired of them yet!'

3 For these questions, complete the second sentence so that it has a similar meaning to the first sentence, using the word given. Do not change the word given. You must use between two and five words including the word given. There is an example (0).

0 John wore a uniform when he was in the army.
John *used to wear a uniform* when he was in the army. *USED*

1 Dinner is ready! Come and eat!
I .... dinner! Come and eat! *COOKED*

2 I started repairing the car at 9 a.m. and I'm still doing it.
I .... since 9 a.m. *HAVE*

3 Ben did his homework and then he went out with his friends.
After ...., Ben went out with his friends. *HAD*

4 I last played tennis in June.
I .... June. *SINCE*

5 I'm drying my hair but it's still wet.
I .... yet. *DRIED*

6 I've never seen a ballet before.
This is .... a ballet. *FIRST TIME*

7 Is your brother an early riser?
Does .... early in the morning? *GET*

8 I was not a good basketball player but now I play in the league.
I .... well but now I play in the league. *TO*

OTHER PRACTICE

4 Complete these sentences using the verb given in the most suitable tense (or with *used to* + verb).

0 This is the first time she *has won* the championship. (*win*)
1 It was the second time that she .... the President. (*meet*)
2 Why .... the police .... you last night? (*telephone*)
3 They .... along the motorway when the accident occurred. (*drive*)
4 My uncle .... but he stopped after his heart attack. (*smoke*)
5 I tried to contact him but he .... already .... out. (*go*)
6 We .... the medicine for three days but we don't feel better. (*take*)
7 Helena still .... her room – it's disgusting. (*not clean*)
8 This wallet .... to me. It's mine! (*belong*)
9 The car .... to you. You must ask Tim if he'll lend it to you. (*not belong*)
10 The puppy ....! Nobody can find her. (*disappear*)

OPEN EXERCISE

5 Write suitable questions for these answers. Use present or past verbs.

0 *What do you do on Saturdays?* or   I play tennis.
 How do you relax after an exam? etc.

1 ....   Because I was ill.
2 ....   At Platform 5.
3 ....   On the Internet.
4 ....   Since 2003.
5 ....   I was having a bath.
6 ....   No, I didn't.

UNIT **15** >> Present Continuous and Present Simple for the future

 THE WEDDING: The veteran Rolls Royce **picks** up Julie and her father at 1.45 p.m. They **arrive** at the church at 2.00 p.m. Julie **is wearing** a satin dress with a lace veil. Phil and the best man, Frank, **go** to the church earlier. Frank **is bringing** the ring. And it**'s** all **happening** next Saturday!

Ⓐ PRESENT CONTINUOUS FOR FIXED PLANS

We use the **Present Continuous** to talk about the **future** when there is a **fixed agreed plan**.

*Julie **is wearing** a satin dress.* (decided plan for next Saturday)
*Phil **is bringing** the ring.* (definite arrangement)

But we **cannot** use the Present Continuous when there is no fixed programme and when we talk about things which we cannot control.

~~*It's raining at the wedding.*~~
~~*Frank is falling in love with a bridesmaid.*~~

Ⓑ PRESENT SIMPLE FOR TIMETABLES

We use the Present Simple to talk about the **future** when there is a **fixed timetable**.
We often use it to talk about **travel times, film times, school times** etc.

*The car **picks** up Julie and her father at 1.45.* (timetabled event)
*The wedding service **starts** at 2.00.* (timetabled event)
*Shall we go and see the new George Clooney film? It **starts** at 9 pm.* (film time)
*The English lesson **starts** at 10.15.* (school time)

We **don't** use the Present Simple if we have made a personal arrangement.

*Phil **is meeting** all his old girlfriends tomorrow.* (**Not** ~~*Phil meets*~~...)
*They**'re having** a final dinner together.* (**Not** ~~*They have*~~...)

It is possible to use **either** the Present Continuous **or** Simple to talk about timetabled events. The Present Simple generally sounds less personal and more official:

*Bob**'s arriving** at 6.00.* *His plane **arrives** at 6.00.*
*They**'re flying** to Barbados after the wedding.* *They **fly** to Barbados after the wedding*

1 **A B** Complete these sentences with the verbs in brackets. Use the Present Simple for travel times/ceremony times/fixed timetabled arrangements. Use the Present Continuous for personal arrangements.

0 Julie *is going* to a club with her friends on Thursday night. (*go*)

1 Phil .... with his friends at The Bachelor's Arms on Friday. (*drink*)

2 The wedding car .... Julie and her father at 1.45. (*collect*)

3 The marriage service .... for an hour. (*last*)

4 Phil's father .... the ceremony with a video camera. (*film*)

5 The wedding reception .... at 4 p.m. (*begin*)

6 The best man .... a speech at some time during the meal. (*make*)

7 Julie .... presents to the bridesmaids and the page boys. (*give*)

8 The taxi .... the bride and groom to the airport at 9 p.m. (*take*)

9 The plane .... for the Bahamas at 11.05. (*depart*)

2 **A B** Rewrite the information in these sentences, using the Present Simple if possible; otherwise use the Present Continuous. Use suitable verbs, negative if necessary.

0 There is a plane leaving London for Barcelona at 9.25 tomorrow.
The plane for Barcelona *leaves at 9.25 tomorrow*.

1 The lecture is from 5 o'clock to 6 o'clock next Friday.
The lecture .... at 5 o'clock and ....at 6 o'clock next Friday.

2 I have an appointment to meet Anne in the hotel bar at 6.15.
I ....

3 We have cancelled our meeting with the lawyer on May 12th.
We .... the lawyer on May 12th.

4 Can you tell me the leaving time of the next coach to Belfast, please?
What time ...., please?

5 We've got tickets to go to the football match next Saturday.
We ....

6 There is a train to Bristol every day except Sunday.
The Bristol train .... on Sundays. (use: *run*)

3 **A B** Use the Present Simple for the more official context in each pair of sentences. Use the Present Continuous for the less formal context.

0 The night train *leaves* at 3 a.m. tomorrow. Jim *is leaving* by coach tomorrow. (*leave*)

1 I .... my girlfriend at 6 tonight. The board of directors .... at 9 a.m. tomorrow. (*meet*)

2 Jez-E-bel .... her new song on Pop TV tomorrow night at 8.10. The children .... a play for their friends tomorrow. (*perform*)

3 Next Friday, Brian .... his new job. Mum .... to cook at about 6. (*begin*)

4 My friend .... a new nightclub next month. The President .... the new hospital next weekend. (*open*)

5 We .... Tina's birthday tomorrow. The government .... the anniversary of the revolution next May. (*celebrate*)

UNIT 16 >> *Be going to*

 Fred Giles is talking to Molly the cow: 'They**'re going to make** a film in Mockham. The actors **are going to spend** lots of money here. We**'re** all **going to be** rich and famous.' Molly is thinking: '**Am I going to be** a star?'

Ⓐ USE

We use **be going to** (I**'m**/he**'s**/she**'s**/it**'s**/we**'re**/you**'re**/they**'re going to** + verb):

1   when we have **already decided** or we **intend** to do something in the future:
   *They**'re going to make** a film in the village.* (definite intention)
   *I**'m going to invite** all my friends to act in the film.*

2   when there are **sure signs** that something is going to happen in the future:
   *The critics don't like the film. It**'s going to be** a failure.*
   *Hollywood actors are rich. They**'re going to spend** lots of money here.*

3   or when something is **on the point of happening**:
   *The engine's on fire. The plane**'s going to crash**.*
   *Phoebe Cute is always drunk. The director**'s going to sack** her.*

Ⓑ PRONUNCIATION

In American slang, people say or write: *I**'m gonna do** it.* instead of *I'm going to do it.*
The British often pronounce **going to** as 'gənə' in conversation.

Ⓒ PRESENT CONTINUOUS AND *BE GOING TO*

The difference between **be going to** and the Present Continuous for the future is very small and they are often interchangeable in sentences like those in A1 but **not** in A2 or A3.
*They**'re making** a film. = They**'re going to make** a film.*

We also use **be to** and **be about to** for future events:
*They **are about to** arrive in the village.* (action on the point of happening)
*They **are to** film here for twenty-eight days.* (planned action)

See Unit 94 for more information and practice on these infinitive constructions.

Ⓓ *WAS/WERE/HAD BEEN GOING TO*

We use **was/were going to** when someone wanted to do something in the past but didn't succeed in doing it:
*Myra **was going to star** in the film but the director sacked her.*
*They **were going to film** in the USA but it was too expensive.*

We sometimes use **had been going to** in the same way, especially when the situation is more distant:
*I **had been going to go** to university in 2006 but I failed my exams.*

We also use these forms when we report speech (see Unit 102):
'I'm going to the disco.'   →   *She said that she **was going** to the disco.*
'I was going to read the paper.' →   *He said that he **had been going** to read the paper.*

1 **Ⓐ** Complete this conversation between two villagers with verbs from the list, using *going to*. Use short forms where possible. Use a negative form if necessary. Then listen and check your answers.

be (x 4)   benefit   ~~make~~   play   put   remember   star   stay   tell   want

A: They (0) 're going to make a film in the village next year.

B: Really? What (1) .... it .... about?

A: That's a secret. They (2) .... anyone until next year.

B: (3) .... any famous actors .... in it?

A: Tom Craze and Phoebe Cute (4) .... the lead roles.

B: (5) .... Myra Marvellosa .... in it?

A: No, she's too old. She (6) .... 65 next birthday.

B: (7) .... the actors .... in the village? I bet all the hotels

(8) .... up their prices. And after the film's release, lots of tourists

(9) .... to come here.

A: Perhaps. Or perhaps the film (10) .... a flop (= a failure). Then

nobody (11) .... it and the village (12) .... at all.

2 **Ⓐ** Rewrite 1-8 using *be going to* and including the word in brackets.

0 Do you plan to go to the USA next year?
   Are you going to go to the USA next year? (go)

1 Our parents have cancelled their plans to go on holiday to Greece.
   .... (aren't)

2 I forecast heavy rain in the south-east tomorrow.
   It .... (heavily)

3 He is driving carefully. There's no danger.
   He .... (crash)

4 Crunchester are a better team than Liverpool. They are playing tomorrow.
   .... Liverpool tomorrow. (beat)

5 Why do you want to give Jeremy the sack?
   .... you .... Jeremy? (dismiss)

6 The engine is dangerous. Do you expect an explosion?
   The engine is dangerous. ....? (it)

7 There's a very high wind. Is it dangerous for the tree?
   There's a very high wind. .... down? (fall)

8 The grape harvest is very good. I'm looking forward to next year's wine.
   The grape harvest is very good. Next year's wine .... (excellent)

3 **Ⓑ** Rewrite the sentences which are inappropriate. Tick those which do not necessarily need changing.

0 In a disco: 'I'm gonna steal your girlfriend. What you gonna do about it?' ✔

1 In a teenage magazine: 'Jez-E-bel's gonna be the greatest rock star since Elvis Presley.'
   ....

2 Letter to Cambridge University: 'My son's gonna study Politics at Trinity College next year.'
   ....

3 In a Hollywood film: 'Help! The alien's gonna kill me.'

....

4 In a club: 'And now we're gonna play our latest hit for you.'

....

5 The judge in a law court: 'Harold Baker, you're gonna go to prison for ninety-nine years.'

....

6 In *The Times*: 'What is the government gonna do about unemployment?'

....

4 ⓓ For each situation 1-10, write a sentence with *was/were going to*.

0 The decision to build a new motorway did not get the government's approval.
They were going to build a new motorway.

1 The snowstorm wrecked Chris's plans to climb Everest.
Chris ....

2 Max had planned an attack on the United Nations but Ace prevented him.
Max ....

3 There was a change of plan, so that Derek started his new job in July, not April.

....

4 Ben decided not to go ahead with the sale of his car.

....

5 Phoebe wore the blue dress, not the special red dress, to the Oscar ceremony.

....

6 Tim decided not to send in his application for the new job.

....

7 The government cancelled the construction of the new hospital.
They ....

8 Roger's trip to the United States did not go ahead.

....

9 The Metalheads broke up before the recording of a Christmas CD.
The Metalheads ....

10 Lisa jilted her fiancé, Bill, and married Ted instead.

....

5 ⓐⓓ Rewrite 1-7 using *am/is/are/was/were going to*.

0 What did you intend to study at university?
What were you going to study at university?

1 Do you plan to continue your career as an actress?

....

2 They wanted to study at Oxford but they failed their examinations.

....

3 We had decided to visit our aunt in Australia but she died.

....

4 I have decided not to accept the job at the Tax Office.

....

5 Has Emma agreed to pay for the broken furniture?

....

6 Why did your brother plan to steal the money?

....

7 The weather forecaster had predicted rain.

The weather forecaster had said that ....

6 Ⓓ Read the text and the example. Then write five sentences with *had been going to* and a suitable verb.

> At 16, Phoebe Cute agreed to marry her childhood sweetheart, Tim, but her mother stopped her. Phoebe was training to be a ballet dancer in England but her mother sent her to drama school in the USA. A director offered her a starring role in *Titanic 2* but the US government refused her a work visa. Phoebe wanted to buy a house in Hollywood but she had to come back to Britain; she planned to make a British film but the production company went bankrupt. She had decided to give up acting but Tom Craze asked her to star in his new movie. She plays his childhood sweetheart.

0 *Phoebe had been going to marry her childhood sweetheart.*

1 ....

2 ....

3 ....

4 ....

5 ....

OPEN EXERCISE

7 Ⓐ Write sentences with *be going to* for each situation.

0 It's cold and there are heavy clouds.
   It's going to snow. // There's going to be a blizzard. etc.

1 There is a fire in the roof of the old wooden town hall.

....

2 The police have identified Harry's fingerprints on the gun.

....

3 Tom Craze called the director 'a stupid idiot'.

....

4 The armed terrorist is in the crowd near the President.

....

5 Kevin is with the ball in front of an open goal.

....

6 The government needs more money.

....

7 Phoebe Cute is in the fashion store with her credit card.

....

8 Phil has brought roses and champagne for Julie.

....

9 Mick is driving on the wrong side of the road.

....

10 The lifeguard is swimming out towards Tina.

....

UNIT **17** >> *Will* and *shall*

> 'Madame Magistar **will look** into your future. My predictions **will change** your life. Your boss **will promote** you. You'**ll meet** the girl of your dreams. You'**ll travel** all over the world. You **won't** ever **be** poor.'
> 'But **will** I **pass** my next grammar test?'

For information about form, see Appendix 1.

Ⓐ USE

We use **will**:

1 for things that we **decide to do now**, at the moment of speaking:
*I'**ll ask** Madame Magistar to read my palm.*
She predicted good luck.
*I'**ll buy** a lottery ticket.*

2 when we **think** or **believe** something about the **future**:
*Her predictions **will** probably **come** true.*
*In 2099, the world **will be** peaceful.*

3 when we talk about **possibility** and **probability**, and after: **I think, I expect, I promise, I hope, I'm sure** and similar verbs:
*I **expect** I'**ll be** rich.*
*I **promise** she'**ll help** you.*
*She'**ll probably charge** a lot of money.*

4 to make an **offer**, **promise** or **threat**:
*I'**ll help** you. (offer)   I **won't leave** you. (promise)   You'**ll pay** for this! (threat)*
*You'**ll see**! (= You'll see that I am right)*

We also use **Shall I...?** to **offer** to do something:
*It's hot in here. **Shall I** open the window?*

5 to make an **invitation**, using **will** or **won't** (for 'strong' or persuasive invitations):
*Will you **come** to the party?   Won't you **have** some tea?*

6 to **refuse** something strongly, using **won't**:
*I **won't lend** you the money.*

7 to make a **request**:
*It's cold. Please **will** you **switch** on the heating?*

We also use **will/shall** in *if*-clauses: see Unit 106.

Ⓑ AFTER *AND, OR* AND *BUT*

It is not necessary to repeat **will/shall** after **and** if the subject does not change:
*I'**ll look** into your future **and change** your life. (Not ... ~~and I'll change~~...)*

Ⓒ SUGGESTIONS

We use **Shall we... ?** to make a suggestion:
*Shall we **ask** the fortune-teller? = Let's ask the fortune-teller.*

1 **A**-**C** Read about a new baby and her three uncles. Fill the gaps with verbs with *will, shall or won't*. Use verbs from the list. Use short forms where possible. Then listen and check your answers.

> appear   ask   be   change   not do   do   not drink
> have   hurt   kill   laugh   not look   pass   say   not stop

Uncle Sam: (0) *won't* you *look* at the new baby? She's very pretty.

Uncle Joe: Perhaps she (1) .... an entertainer when she's an adult. She
(2) .... ten number one hits and she (3) .... on television a lot.
But she (4) .... crying. What's the matter?

Uncle Sam: (5) .... you .... me the bottle? She's hungry.

Uncle Bill: She (6) .... from it. She's not hungry, so she must need changing.
(7) .... you .... her nappy, Joe?

Joe: No, I (8) .... that! I don't know how. (9) .... we ....
Aunt Betty to help us?

Sam: No, she (10) .... at us and (11) .... that men are useless.
I (12) .... it.

Bill: Be careful! You (13) .... her.

Sam: There, she's quiet at last. I (14) .... anyone who wakes her up!

Now, classify the ways that the uncles use *will/shall* by referring to 17A 1-7 and 17C.

1 = to decide suddenly   2/3 = to predict   4 = to make an offer, promise or threat
5 = to invite   6 = to refuse   7 = to request   C = to suggest

0 *A5*   1 ....   2 ....   3 ....   4 ....   5 ....   6 ....   7 ....
8 ....   9 ....   10 ....   11 ....   12 ....   13 ....   14 ....

2 **A** **C** Rewrite these sentences, using *will* and the words in brackets. Use the negative form if necessary. Use *shall* for suggestions (see 17C).

0 Do you agree to be a member of the quiz team next year?
   Will you take part in the quiz team next year? (*take part in*)

1 The government promises not to raise taxes next year.
   The government promises that they .... (*increase*)

2 Everyone is sure that the end of the war is near.
   Everyone is sure that .... much longer. (*last*)

3 Jenny thinks that Bob is sure to fail his driving test.
   Jenny is sure that Bob .... (*pass*)

4 It's all right. I have decided not to tell the teachers about the fight.
   It's all right. I .... (*tell*)

5 It's very hot. Is it possible for you to switch on the air conditioning?
   It's very hot. Please ....? (*switch*)

6 Let's decorate the bedroom. ....? (*decorate*)

7 Crunchester are sure to win the league. I am right!
   Crunchester .... league champions. ....! (*be/see*)

8 It's hot. I've got an idea – the beach!!!
   It's hot. I've got an idea – I .... at the beach. (*go swimming*)

9 Mary isn't here yet. I'm expecting her to arrive later.
   Mary isn't here yet. She .... (*probably*)

10 Let's go to the cinema. ....? (*go*)

UNIT 18 >> *Will, going to,*
Present Continuous, Present Simple

> 'Look!' said Pete. 'It's snowing. I**'ll get** my toboggan.' Later, he met Steve. 'I**'m going to go** tobogganing on the hill. Are you coming?'
> 'I**'m meeting** the manager at the bank. It **closes** in half an hour. But I**'ll join** you later.'

A WAYS OF TALKING ABOUT FUTURE ACTIONS

There are four ways to talk about future actions. For example, Pete says:

1 *Look! It's snowing. I**'ll get** my toboggan.*
   (a sudden idea, use **will**) but later, when he meets Steve, he says:

2 *I**'m going to go** tobogganing.*
   (this is what I want/have already decided/intend to do, use **be going to**) or:

3 *I**'m meeting** the manager.*
   (this is a fixed personal plan (perhaps I've already made an appointment), use the **Present Continuous**)

4 *It **closes** in half an hour.*
   (there is a fixed timetable, use the **Present Simple**)

B DIFFERENCE IN USE OF *BE GOING TO* AND PRESENT CONTINUOUS

In many cases, we can use the Present Continuous and **be going to** interchangeably:
*I**'m going to meet** the manager tomorrow.* = *I**'m meeting** the manager tomorrow.*

But in some cases, we do not have this choice:
We can say: *I think it **will snow** again tomorrow.*
or: *It **is going to snow** tomorrow.*
But not *It is snowing tomorrow.* (There is no fixed plan/it is beyond our control)

We can say: *The dog's angry. It**'s going to bite** her.* (on the point of happening)
or: *The dog's angry. It**'ll probably bite** her soon.* (prediction)
But not *The dog's angry. It's biting her soon.* (not a fixed arrangement)

We use **be going to** when the present evidence strongly suggests a future event:
*He's driving very fast. He**'s going to crash**.* (**Not** *he is crashing*.)

13 **1** **A B** Choose the best alternative in each case. Then listen and check your answers.

Pete reached the top of the hill. Rosie and Rachel were already waiting there.
'(0) We're going to ride/We're riding down the hill on our Super-Sled,' said the girls. '(1) I'll go/I'm going faster than you,' said Pete. 'No, (2) you won't/you aren't,' laughed Rosie. 'Listen!
(3) I'm giving/I'll give you a kiss if you beat us.' 'And. (4) I give/I'll give you a pound every time you beat me,' said Pete. They went down the hill several times but the girls always won.
'I've got a plan,' Pete told Steve the next day. '(5) I'm going to practise/I practise every day until next weekend.' 'I've got an idea too,' said Steve. ' (6) I'm going to improve/I'm improving the shape of your toboggan. Then (7) it goes/it'll go faster.' They prepared for a week. On Friday, they phoned the girls. '(8) We are/We're going to be on the hill tomorrow.
(9) We're going to beat/We're beating you. (10) You'll see/You're seeing.' The girls laughed.
'Have you heard the weather forecast for tomorrow? The temperature (11) is rising/is going to rise. The snow (12) is going to melt/is melting. Goodbye Pete. And thank you for the money.'

14 **2** **A B** Which is better: *will or be going to*? Choose the most suitable way to complete the sentences. Use *'ll, 'm, 's, was, were going to*. Then listen and check your answers.

Pete felt lonely. He found the photo of an old girlfriend. 'I know!' he thought. 'I (0) 'll phone her.'
He asked her to meet him. 'I'm busy,' she said. 'I (1) .... meet my husband.'
Pete decided to go to the disco. 'I (2) .... look for a new girlfriend,' he told Steve.
'I (3) .... come too,' said Steve. 'I (4) .... meet Dave in the pub, so
I (5) .... phone him to let him know my change of plan.'
Pete saw a beautiful girl at the disco. 'I (6) .... ask her to dance,' he thought.
They danced all night. Pete (7) .... to ask her for another date but she said,
'I (8) .... emigrate to Brazil tomorrow. I (9) .... send you a postcard.'
Pete had a new plan. 'I (10) .... join a dating agency,' he explained to Steve. A girl
at the agency interviewed him. 'I (11) .... tell you the truth,' she said. 'I like you very
much. I (12) .... have a holiday in the Bahamas next week. Please come with me.
Pete told Steve about the girl. 'I (13) .... to accept. Then I remembered. My team
(14) .... play Liverpool next week. I can't go with her.

3 **A B** In each story A and B, use: a verb with *going to*, a verb with *will* (a sudden idea), a Present Simple verb, a Present Continuous verb.

A 'Give me your money or I (1 *kill*) .... you,' said the robber.
Pete gave him his wallet and he escaped. Pete went home and told Steve. '(2 *report*)
.... you .... it?' asked Steve. 'No, I (3 *visit*)
.... a new girlfriend this weekend. I haven't got time to tell the
police. My train (4 *leave*) .... in fifteen minutes.'

B Diane (1 *live*) .... in a flat with her friends. At the moment, she lives with
her parents. When she told her brother, Pete, he said at once, 'I (2 *help*) ....
you.' He (3 *bring*) .... his van next Saturday to help her move her furniture.
He (4 *finish*) .... work at 5.30, so she can't move until the evening.

C Pete told Steve: 'I (0 *go*) 'm going to the library in a few minutes.' 'OK, I (1 *come*)
.... with you.' 'But the library (2 *close*) .... at midday
on Tuesdays,' said Dave. 'They (3 *not extend*) .... the opening hours until
next year.'

UNIT 19 >> Future Continuous and Future Perfect

Fabian: Can I call you at midnight?
Maria: No, **I'll be sleeping**. (thinks: I **won't have come** back from the disco)
Fabian: OK, can I call you at 9 tomorrow morning?
Maria: No, I**'ll be working**. (thinks: I **won't have got** up)

For information about form, see Appendix 1.

Ⓐ FUTURE CONTINUOUS: USE

We use the Future Continuous to say **we'll be in the middle of doing something at a particular moment in the future**:
I **will be watching** TV at 9.35. (= I will be in the middle of the action)

Thus, we use the Future Continuous in a similar way to the other continuous tenses:

Past Continuous:	Present Continuous:	Future Continuous:
I *was eating* at 8 yesterday.	It's 8. I'*m eating*.	I'*ll be eating* at 8 tomorrow.

We also use it for a continuous action which will continue throughout a particular time period:
I **will be watching** TV from 6 to 9 p.m. (= I will be continuously busy during this period.)

We also use it:

1 for a planned or timetabled event in the future:
   I **will be going** to London next Saturday.   The film **will be starting** at 11.15.

2 the question form to ask about someone's plans, especially if we want to make a request or an offer afterwards:
   Will you **be visiting** Grandma tomorrow? Can you give her this note?

3 to imagine/predict what somebody is doing now:
   Don't ring Jenny now. She'**ll be revising** for her exams. (= I believe that she's revising)

Ⓑ FUTURE PERFECT: USE

We use the Future Perfect for an action which will occur at some time **between now and a future time**. We do not give an exact time for the action.
I am planning to change my job at some time between now and next year. I say:
I'**ll have changed** my job by the end of next year.

Bill wants to go out at 7 p.m. You can't cook and eat before 7.30. You say:
Let's go later. I **won't have finished** dinner by then.

Ⓒ FUTURE PERFECT WITH *BY* AND *ALREADY*

We often use the Future Perfect with a time expression with **by**. Compare:
In 2018, I will finish university. (In 2018 = exact date)
By 2018, I **will have finished** university. (By 2018 = at some time between now and 2018)

We often use the Future Perfect with **already** (as with the Present and Past Perfect):
By noon, I **will already have discussed** it with him.

* It is possible to use **shall** (more formal) instead of **will** in these tenses after I and we.
We **shall be staying** in Rome tomorrow.
We **shall have left** Rome by Friday.

1 Ⓐ **Choose a verb from the list and use it in the Future Continuous in the gaps in this conversation.**

<u>cook</u>   dance   get   have   paint   study   wash   watch

0 'Can I phone you at 6 o'clock?'   'No, I'll *be cooking* my dinner.'
1 'Can I call you at 6.30?'   'No, I .... a soap opera.'
2 'Can I call you at 7?'   'No, I .... *Grammar Goals*.'
3 'Can I see you at 7.30?'   'No, I .... my fingernails.'
4 'Can I meet you at 8.00?'   'No, I .... my hair.'
5 'Can I come round at 8.30?'   'No, I .... a shower.'
6 'Can I pick you up at 9?'   'No, I .... ready to go out.'
7 'Can I see you at the disco?'   'No, I .... with my boyfriend.'

2 Ⓑ Ⓒ **Look at this environmental forecast for the next century. Write sentences using *By 2100* and a Future Perfect verb.**

Between now and 2100

item	event	item	event
0	change in the weather patterns	4	using up of all earth's resources
1	rise in global temperatures	5	development of new fuels
2	destruction of the rainforest	6	disappearance of many species
3	building of a colony on the moon	7	first landing on Mars by China

0 By 2100, the weather patterns *will have changed*.
1 By 2100, global temperatures ....
2 By 2100, human beings ....
3 By 2100, we ....
4 By 2100, we ....
5 By 2100, scientists ....
6 By 2100, many species ....
7 By 2100, Chinese astronauts ....

3 Ⓐ - Ⓒ **Read the text and then complete the sentences with verbs in either the Future Continuous or the Future Perfect.**

Next year, Phoebe Cute is going to make two films. From January to May, she will star in *Fear Circles*. Then, from August to December, she will go to Israel to star in *Woman in Green*. In June she is going to get married to the director Stefan Grex. In the following month, they are planning to have a honeymoon, first of all in Italy and then, from the middle of July, in Iceland. Stefan is joining her in Israel at Christmas.

0 In April, Phoebe *will be filming* *Fear Circles*. (*film*)   1 By June, she .... making that film. (*finish*)   2 She .... married in June. (*get*)   3 They .... Italy by late July. (*already leave*)   4 Her enemies think she .... a divorce before the end of the year. (*get*)   5 In the autumn, she .... in Israel. (*work*)   6 By the end of the year, she .... two films. (*complete*)   7 They .... Christmas in Israel. (*spend*)   8 By the end of the year, she .... at least three countries. (*visit*)
9 When they meet in Israel, Stefan .... her for several months. (*not see*)

UNIT 20 >> When, before, after, as soon as, until, while

> **When** you **arrive** at our twelve-star hotel in Alpville, our friendly staff **will welcome** you. **After** you **have rested** in your suite, our Swedish team **will give** you a free relaxing massage. Then, at your first meal, our orchestra **will play** a symphony **while** you **eat**.

A PATTERNS TO TALK ABOUT THE FUTURE WITH *WHEN, BEFORE, AFTER, AS SOON AS, UNTIL,* AND *WHILE*

After time expressions such as **when, before** etc. a present tense form is used although this refers to future time.

time-clause with present verb	future verb
When you *arrive,*	the staff *will welcome* you.
Before you *have* dinner,	you *will have* a massage.
After you *leave* the massage centre,	we *will escort* you to the dining room.
As soon as you *enter* the dining room,	the orchestra *will begin* to play.
While you *eat/are eating,*	they *will perform* a symphony.
Until you *finish* your meal,	the orchestra *will play.*

The time-clause can come second. Note that no comma is necessary in this case:
The orchestra will play until you finish your meal.

We use a similar grammar pattern with **if** (See Unit 106):
If I go to that hotel, I won't have the massage. (**Not** *If I will go*)

B WHILE/AS WITH PRESENT CONTINUOUS

We often use **while** or **as** with the Present Continuous. The action in the **while/as** part of the sentence is a long continuous action:
As you are approaching the hotel, you will see a lake. (**Not** *will approach*)
While you are eating, the orchestra will play. (**Not** *will eat*)

C + IMPERATIVE

We often use an imperative verb in this kind of sentence:
When the fire alarm rings, go to the emergency exit.
As soon as you've finished packing, call a taxi.

D WHEN, BEFORE ETC. + PRESENT PERFECT

We use **when** + Present Perfect when we want to show clearly that the **first action** will/must finish before the second action takes place:
When I have paid the bill, I'll go to the disco.

But *When I pay the bill, I'll give the waiter a tip.* (The two actions happen at more or less the same time.)

Here are some more examples with the Present Perfect:

time-clause with Present Perfect verb	future verb
After I *have paid* the bill,	I'll go to the disco.
As soon as I *'ve got* back to my room,	I'll phone you.
Until they *have prepared* our room,	we will wait in the hotel foyer.

1 **A** **C** **D** Fill the gaps with verbs from the list in the correct tense – Present Simple, Imperative, Present Perfect or Future with *will*.

be   cruise   fly   give   provide   recommend
relax   return   serve   spend   take   visit

Following your massage, our Italian chef (0) will provide a twelve-course meal. After you
(1) .... a peaceful first night on our king-size water-filled beds, our French
waitresses (2) .... a splendid breakfast. As soon as you (3) ....
ready, a helicopter (4) .... you to a ski-station where Swiss instructors
(5) .... you individual lessons. That night, you (6) .... on the lake
before you (7) .... to the hotel. Next day, you (8) .... in our leisure
centre until a chauffeur-driven limousine (9) .... you to the airport. Please, when you
(10) .... your friends, (11) .... our hotel to them.

2 **A** **D** For each pair of sentences, complete one sentence with a Present Simple verb and the other with a Present Perfect verb. Put the other verbs in a suitable form.

0 When I phone Sally, I'll give her your best wishes. (*phone/give*)
   When I have phoned Sally, I'll ring you to tell you her news. (*phone/ring*)

1 When they .... married, they .... on their honeymoon. (*get/go*)
   When they .... married, they .... to be faithful. (*get/promise*)

2 When the election .... place, we .... who is the new President.
   (*take/know*)
   When the election .... place, ... you .... for the
   Socialists? (*take/vote*)

3 When you .... Jay Horn's new novel, ... you .... it
   to me? (*read/lend*)
   When you .... Jay Horn's new novel, ... special attention to page 54.
   (*read/pay*)

4 When they .... the new dam, they .... the best construction
   materials. (*build/use*)
   When they .... the new dam, it .... cheap electricity. (*build/supply*)

3 **A** **B** **D** Combine each pair of sentences into one sentence.

0 First, we'll arrive at Heathrow Airport. Then, we'll transfer to another plane.
   As soon as we arrive at Heathrow, we'll transfer to another plane.

1 The committee will vote. Then, they'll announce the winner.
   After ....

2 I won't make a decision yet. I need to see the latest sales figures.
   ....

3 She'll get married. First, she'll go out with all her friends.
   .... before ....

4 Sue will send me a cheque. Then, I'll deliver the computer.
   .... until ....

5 The firework display will begin. First, there'll be a carnival procession.
   .... before ....

6 The sun will rise. Dracula will vanish.
   .... as soon as ....

REVISION 2 >> First Certificate Practice

PAPER 3 PART 1

1 For questions 1-12, read the text below and decide which answer, A, B, C or D, best fits each gap. There is an example at the beginning (0).

HYPERSONIC FLIGHT

Scientists in America are developing a hypersonic plane, the X-43A. It **(0)** A speeds of 11,585 kph, ten times the speed of sound. In the future, it **(1)** ..... from New York to London in 40 minutes. There **(2)** ..... be an extensive series of tests before the plane **(3)** ..... even a human pilot. The first unpiloted test flight **(4)** ..... place next month. In order to achieve hypersonic speed, the plane **(5)** ..... off under its own power. Instead, a B52 bomber **(6)** ..... it on its back to an altitude of 7,300 metres. At this height, a special rocket **(7)** ....., taking the X-43A to its test speed of Mach 7. Three test flights **(8)** ..... place by the end of this year. However, unless there is a technological breakthrough, it **(9)** ..... several decades before commercial passengers use hypersonic aircraft. As soon as they **(10)** ..... the tests successfully, scientists are going to begin planning piloted flights. Perhaps, in the middle of the 21st century, you **(11)** ..... from Europe to the USA in under an hour. Who knows what developments **(12)** ..... by then?

0	A will reach	B	will reaching	C	will reached	D	will reaches
1	A won't fly	B	will fly	C	will be fly	D	is flying
2	A will have	B	is going to	C	will go to	D	will be going to
3	A will be carry	B	will be carries	C	carries	D	carrying
4	A will be take	B	will have taken	C	is going take	D	takes
5	A will take not	B	will take	C	will not take	D	not will take
6	A will carry	B	will be carry	C	carry	D	is carry
7	A will be igniting	B	will be ignite	C	will ignite	D	ignite
8	A are going to take	B	will have taken	C	will be taking	D	will take
9	A will be	B	was	C	was going to be	D	is
10	A have completed	B	completed	C	are complete	D	will have completed
11	A will be travel	B	travel	C	travelled	D	will be travelling
12	A will be occurring	B	will have occurred	C	will occur	D	are occurring

PAPER 3 PART 2

2 For these questions, read the text below and think of the word which best fits the gap. Use only one word in each gap. There is an example at the beginning (0).

MORE ABOUT THE X-43A

Why **(0)** will the development of the X-43A be important in the future? When its development **(1)** .... complete, it will improve access to space. Scientists estimate that the project will cost 185 million dollars but it **(2)** .... make space flight cheaper after it **(3)** .... come into operation. **(4)** .... the same technology **(5)** .... to be useful for commercial flights? Some believe the X-43A **(6)** .... never carry passengers because of its high acceleration. However, major airlines are interested in faster craft, so maybe in the future we will all **(7)** .... travelling at hypersonic speeds. Going to New York from Europe **(8)** .... be like going to the local shops! But **(9)** .... such planes going **(10)** .... mean higher levels of pollution? By the end of the century, technology will **(11)** .... reduced our journey times but will it also **(12)** .... destroyed the planet?

PAPER 3 PART 4

3 For these questions, complete the second sentence so that it has a similar meaning to the first sentence(s), using the word given. Do not change the word given. Use from two to five words including the word given. There is an example (0).

0 Peter is going to meet his cousin at 4.30 p.m.
Peter is meeting his cousin at 4.30 p.m. *MEETING*

1 Colin is going to write the marriage proposal. Then, he's going to post it.
After .... the marriage proposal, he's going to post it. *WRITTEN*

2 Jill has a meeting about the company accounts from 2 to 3 p.m.
At 2.30 p.m., Jill .... the company accounts. *WILL*

3 We will extinguish the fire. Then we'll immediately start to rebuild the house.
As .... extinguished the fire, we'll start to rebuild the house. *SOON*

4 The temperature is dropping; there's a definite forecast of snow.
The temperature is dropping; .... snow. *GOING*

5 Maggie will go home after she has visited her sick aunt.
Maggie will visit her sick aunt .... home. *GOES*

6 The government will build twenty hospitals before December 31st.
The government .... by the end of the year. *HAVE*

7 The departure time of the Moscow train is 6.45 tomorrow morning.
The .... 6.45 tomorrow morning. *AT*

8 Robin is driving non-stop across Europe at 100 kph. It is 6 p.m.
By midnight, Robin .... 600 kilometres across Europe. *WILL*

OTHER PRACTICE

4 All these sentences are about the future. Put a verb from the list in the most suitable form in each gap.

not admit   arrive   contact   cook   enter   finish   get   not depart
phone   receive   return   snatch   take   wait   watch   write

0 By 2025, all the refugees will have returned to their homes.

1 Don't call me at the usual time tomorrow evening. I .... dinner.

2 'I'm going to buy some fish and chips.' 'Good idea. I .... some too.'

3 According to the timetable, the next train .... until tomorrow morning.

4 Sheila will be occupied at 6.35 – she .... her favourite soap.

5 I believe that by the end of this century we .... life in other galaxies.

6 Look at Harry! He .... Sue's handbag. Stop him before he can do it.

7 The doctors .... him to hospital until the nurses' strike ....

8 Come and see us after midday. Nick .... all his business letters by then.

9 As soon as Phoebe .... the room, ... a photo of her with her new boyfriend.

10 Don't phone me at 10.30 – Pete .... at that time.

11 Look at this schedule – the plane .... in London at 1 a.m.

12 By the time we arrive, Stella .... our e-mail, so she .... for us at the airport when we get there.

UNIT **21** >> *Can, could, be able to*

You **can read** about the ghost of Mockham Castle in many guidebooks. I saw it myself in 1998. **I couldn't believe** my eyes! It **could hover** above the floor. It **was** even **able to pass** through walls. Even now, **I cannot think** of it without trembling. **Can** you **understand** how I feel?

For information about form, see Appendix 2.

Ⓐ USE

We use **can** to talk about present or future time:
*I **can cook** very well.*   *I **can cook** dinner tomorrow.*

We use **can** or **can't** to talk about:

1 general ability: *Ghosts **can appear** and **disappear**.*   ***Can** ghosts **swim**?*
2 something **we can do** at a **particular time** (often with verbs like **see, hear, feel, smell** etc.):
*I **can hear** the ghost but I **can't see** it.*   ***Can** you **feel** anything?*
3 permission: *Tourists **can visit** the East Tower but they **can't visit** the dungeons.*

We use **could** or **couldn't** in the same way as **can/can't** but to talk about the past:
*When I saw it, it **could hover** above the floor.*   *I **couldn't see** it clearly.*

Ⓑ *CAN* AND *COULD* REFERRING TO PRESENT TIME

We also use **can** or **could** (more formal) about present situations:

1 to ask for **permission**:   ***Can** I **unlock** this door?*   ***Could** I **use this pen**?*
2 to **offer to help** somebody: ***Can** I **help** you find the way?*   ***Could** I **help** you?*
3 to **request** something: ***Can** you **help** me?*   ***Could** you **tell** me about the ghost?*

Ⓒ TALKING ABOUT POSSIBILITY WITH *CAN* AND *COULD*

We also use **could** to talk about **possibility** in the present or future:
*It **could rain** later.*   *I **could win** the competition.*   *He **could be** ill.*

We use **could have** to talk about a **possibility** in the **past which didn't happen**:
*I **could have won** the race but I broke my leg.*   *It **could have rained** but luckily it didn't.*

We use **can't** to talk about **impossibility** in the **present** or **future**:
*You **can't be** serious! (= You must be joking.)*   *It **can't** possibly **snow** before January.*

Ⓓ ALTERNATIVES TO *CAN/COULD*

We use **be able to** with the same meaning as **can** (ability) in various tenses and always with a modal, a perfect tense and *to*-infinitive:
*She's **unable to/isn't able to** understand me.*   *(= She can't understand me.)*
*He **must be able to** pay the bill.*   (**Not** ~~He must can pay the bill.~~)
*I'd like **to be able** to speak English perfectly.*   *They **have been able to** help us.*

We usually use **was/were able to** (**not could**) in the past to talk about something which was difficult to do at a particular time:
*I **was able to win** the race. (**Not** ~~I could win the race.~~)*   *She **was able to find** her passport.*

But in the negative, we can use **either couldn't** or **wasn't/weren't able to**:
*He **wasn't able to find** his keys.*   or   *He **couldn't find** his keys.*

Managed to and **succeeded in** are sometimes used in the affirmative instead of **could** to emphasise that **something was difficult or challenging**:
*I **managed to** open the door.*   *We **succeeded in** solving the problem.*

1 **A B** Complete the second items with phrases with *can* or *could*. Use the negative if necessary.

0 He is a very skilful football player. He *can play* very skilfully.

1 She asked very politely: 'Is it possible to borrow your dictionary?'
She asked: '.. ?'

2 I didn't know how to read until I was seven. I .... until I was seven.

3 I've never learnt how to ride a bicycle. I ....

4 Was your brother able to swim when he was a child?
.... when he was a child?

5 'Please pass me the water,' he said directly. '...?' he asked.

6 He is an excellent violinist but he has never learnt the guitar. He ....
very well but he ....

7 She is a very fast runner. She .... very fast.

8 They weren't able to find the treasure. They ....

9 Did the soldiers have permission to go home at the weekends?
.... at the weekends?

10 They are unable to travel abroad because they've lost their passports.
.... because they've lost their passports.

11 Pete was a better swimmer than Jane when they were children.
Pete .... better than Jane when they were children.

2 **A B** Fill the gaps with verbs from the list. Use *can, cannot, could, couldn't* with the verbs.

> appear   be   explain   ~~feel~~   guarantee   look   remember
> see   sleep   solve (x 2)   spend   tell   vanish   visit   win

0 When the ghost passed near me, I *could feel* a cold wind.

1 It .... from one room and .... in another.

2 I was scared. For several nights, I ....

3 Even now, I .... every detail of the experience.

4 Nowadays, tourists .... the castle for a small fee.

5 The owners .... that they will see the ghost but they
promise that they .... at the places where it has appeared.

6 Nobody .... why the ghost haunts the castle.

7 .... the ghost .... the spirit of a murder victim? (= is it possible?)

8 When I saw the ghost I .... if it was male or female.

9 I .... only .... a white shape with two eyes.

10 It is a mystery. Nobody .... it in the past and nobody
.... it now.

11 This is Lord Mockham's challenge. You .... £2,000 if you
.... the night alone in the castle.

3 **A D** Complete the questions and answers 1-8 using *can, be able to* etc.

0 Dave had studied entomology, so he identified the butterfly easily.
Was Dave able to identify the butterfly? **Yes, he was.**

1 Ben was a good swimmer when he was six years old.
....? Yes, he could.

2 Martina had studied hard and passed her exams.

....? Yes, she was.

3 The climbers found it impossible to climb Mount Everest.

....? No, they weren't.

4 Inspector Davis found the solution to the mystery.

.... to solve .... Yes, ...

5 Brigitte learnt how to fly an aeroplane when she was a girl.

....? Yes, she could.

6 But she didn't learn how to fly a helicopter.

....? ....

7 The circus elephants rode bicycles!

....? Yes, they were.

8 Sarah knew the answers to all the questions in the quiz.

....? Yes, she was.

4 Ⓐ - Ⓒ **Identify these sentences with *could* and *can't* by writing a number 1-7 after each.**

1 = past of can, ability in the past   **5** = possibility present or future
2 = polite way of asking for permission   **6** = possibility in the past
3 = polite way of offering help   **7** = impossibility in the present or future
4 = polite way of requesting something

0 It could rain tomorrow. 5

1 I couldn't swim until I was 25. .....
2 Could you lend me £5? .....
3 Her husband could be the murderer. .....
4 Could she be in love with me? .....
5 Could you help me? .....
6 It can't be true! .....
7 Could I help you? .....
8 The price of coffee could rise soon. .....

9 They could dance very well when they were young. .....
10 Could I taste this cheese? .....
11 Could I pass you anything? .....
12 Could you give me the money soon? .....
13 He could be ill – I'm not sure. .....
14 Your cake is delicious. It couldn't be better! .....
15 I could have won! .....

5 Ⓐ **There are places in this story where you could replace an existing phrase with *could*, *couldn't* + verb. Underline the phrases and mark them with a number, then write the substitutes below, as in the example.**

Victor Frankenstein grew up in Switzerland but, when he was seventeen, his father said he had permission to go *(0)* to university in Germany. He found it impossible to make friends but he was a brilliant student of science. Soon he had the ability to create a monster. However, it was impossible for him to control the monster. It was difficult for Victor to ask for advice because nobody would believe him. The monster ran away and lived in the forest. It lived near a family of refugees and listened to their conversation. After a few months, it had gained the ability to speak German. But the monster was unable to find companions because everyone was afraid of it. Frankenstein wanted to forget the monster but it was impossible for him to escape his destiny.

0 *he could go*   **4** ....
1 ....   **5** ....
2 ....   **6** ....
3 ....   **7** ....

6 **ⓓ** Complete the sentences with a suitable tense of *be able to* plus a verb from the list. Use a negative if necessary.

arrest   buy   exorcise   find   forgive   look
pass   pay   raise   sell   spend   solve   take

0   No one *has* ever *been able to spend* the night alone in the castle dungeons.
1   Last year, a bishop visited Mockham Castle but he .... the ghost.
2   Ghosts can easily escape because they .... through walls.
3   Lord Mockham would like to .... the entrance fee for tourists.
4   Lord Mockham .... his taxes next year as life at the castle is expensive.
5   Lady Mockham lost her jewels a few days ago and she .... them yet.
6   'The ghost stole them!' 'Madam, we .... a ghost,' said the police.
7   '......... anybody ever .... a photo of the ghost?' 'No, they haven't.'
8   Lord Mockham has the jewels; he .... them for a million pounds one day.
9   'When the insurance company pay me, I should .... another castle,' he thought.
10 Unluckily for Lord Mockham, the police .... the mystery. ....(use: Present Perfect)
11 Lord Mockham ....after the castle next year because he'll be in prison.
12 Lady Mockham wants a divorce. ' I .... my husband for stealing ....my jewels!'

7 **ⓓ** Rewrite these sentences using the correct tense of the word in brackets.

0   Ben was able to climb the wall. *Ben managed to climb the wall.* (*manage*)
1   Nadia managed to beat the chess computer. .... (*succeed*)
2   Nick was able to get a bank loan. .... (*manage*)
3   She achieved her ambition; she married Bob. .... (*succeed*)
4   It was difficult but Lois passed the exam. .... (*succeed*)

OPEN EXERCISE

8 **ⓒ** Complete these sentences in any suitable way using *could have* + past participle.

0   *He could have stolen the money/robbed the bank etc.* but the police were guarding it.
1   .... but the fire brigade arrived.
2   .... but his parents stopped him.
3   .... but there was a snowstorm.
4   .... but they forgot to bring their wallets.
5   .... but he fell ill.
6   .... but she lost the recipe.
7   .... but we had run out of money.
8   .... but they didn't want to.

UNIT 22 >> *Must*

 Film producer: '*Star Trip VIII* was a success — we **must make** *Star Trip IX*. Brendan Boone **must play** Captain Kork. But **we mustn't give** Myra a part. She's too old to play the alien princess — she **must be** over 70! She **must be getting** an old-age pension!'

For information about form, see Appendix 2.

A USE

We can use **must** to talk about the present or the future time:
*We **must start** filming now.*
*We **must finish** the film next year.*

If we want to talk about the past, we use **had to** (see Unit 23).

We use **must**:

1	to say that something is **necessary**:	*We **must start** filming.* *The actors **must start** rehearsing their lines.*
2	to talk about **laws** and **regulations**:	*We **mustn't film** violent scenes.* *The actors **must have** a break every three hours.*
3	to give an **order**:	*The extras **must be** here at 6 a.m.* *Brendan Boone **must stop** forgetting his lines!*
4	to **recommend** something:	*Star Trip V is great. You **must see** it!* *The director **must give** Lola Louche an audition — she's very good!*
5	to express a strong **personal wish**:	*I **must see** Brendan Boone's new film.* *I **must get** the part!*

B DEDUCTION

We use **must** to make a **deduction from evidence**. We are sure that something is true. We can also use the continuous* form (**must be getting**) when we are sure that something is happening at this moment.

evidence	deduction
She isn't in the film studio. *She has a lot of wrinkles.* *They aren't in the studio.* *She's over 70*	*She **must be** ill.* (= I'm sure that she's ill) *She **must be** 70.* (= I'm sure that she's 70) *They **must be filming** in the town.* (now, at this moment) *She **must be getting** a pension.* (continuously during the present period)

* Remember there are some verbs we cannot use in continuous tenses (see Appendix 5).

1 **Ⓐ** Fill the gaps with *must, mustn't* and suitable verbs.

0 When you join the army, you *must wear* a uniform. **1** To save electricity, you
.... off the lights. **2** You .... TV all day. It's bad for your sight.
3 After he/she/it, we .... -s to a Present Simple verb. **4** I ....
smoking. It's bad for me. **5** I'm very thirsty. I .... a cup of tea. **6** That hotel is
very good. You .... there. **7** In many parks, you .... on the
grass. **8** Children .... to cross the road safely. **9** We .... a
verb with *to* after *can* or *must*.

2 **Ⓐ Ⓑ** Captain Kork has landed on a new planet. Make sentences with *must* or *mustn't*. Also,
match the sentences with Theory points in A and B by writing A1-5 or B after each one.

0 It is necessary to take our breathing apparatus with us.
We must take our breathing apparatus with us. (A1)

1 It is forbidden to break the Galactic Laws.
We .... ( )

2 Obey orders. Make sure that you don't lose contact with the mother ship.
Obey orders. You .... ( )

3 It is forbidden by Galactic Law to use our weapons against the aliens.
According to the Law, we .... ( )

4 Look at those buildings. They prove the existence of an intelligent life form.
Look at those buildings. An intelligent life form .... here. ( )

5 It is important to find a way to communicate with them.
We .... ( )

6 There are voices in my head. The aliens seem to have telepathic abilities.
I can hear voices. The aliens .... ( )

7 'Captain Kork,' said the alien princess, 'I have a strong desire to marry you.'
'Captain Kork,' said the alien princess, 'I .... ( )

8 Our planet has beautiful underground caves. Go there on your honeymoon.
Our planet has beautiful underground caves. You .... ( )

9 That was very good. I really want to see *Star Trip X*.
That was very good. I .... ( )

3 **Ⓑ** Use either *must* + verb or *must be* + verb-ing to complete these sentences.

0 The dog is sleeping. His legs are moving. He *must be dreaming*. (*dream*)
1 Doctor, this is a very common illness. There .... a medicine for it. (*be*)
2 Your dad has got a Ph.D. He .... the answer. (*know*)
3 Joanne and Luigi are shouting. They .... (*quarrel*)
4 Sara is upstairs in her bedroom. It's very quiet. She .... (*sleep*)
5 I can smell tobacco. Someone in the house .... (*smoke*)
6 There is smoke and fire at the top of the volcano. It .... (*erupt*)
7 I can't see the children. They .... (*hide*)
8 The bank manager is angry with Joe. He .... him some money. (*owe*)
9 Bob McGive is very rich. He .... a lot of cars. (*own*)

OPEN EXERCISE

4 **Ⓐ** Write a set of rules for: students/astronauts/library users/train passengers/soldiers/one
other group.

UNIT 23 >> *Have to, don't have to* and *mustn't*

Uncle Joe **has to be** careful with his health. Last week he **had to come** into hospital because of heart problems. He **mustn't smoke**, **mustn't eat** sweet things and he **mustn't drink** alcohol. But he **doesn't have to give** up flirting with the nurses. The doctors think that romance is good for him!

Ⓐ USE

Have to is used to express **necessity** or **obligation**:

*Do you **have to take** any special medicine?*   (= is it necessary for you to take it?)
*The nurses **have to look** after the patients.*   (= they are obliged to look after them)

Ⓑ SIMPLE TENSES OF *HAVE TO*

We can use **have to** in other simple tenses. For example:

*Joe **will have to return** to hospital next year.**   *Joe **had to come** into hospital last week.*
*Joe **has had to change** his eating habits.*   *Joe **had** never **had to follow** a special diet before.*

* But we can also use the present form to talk about the future:
*Joe **has to see** the doctor next week.*

We can use **have to** in the continuous form for a temporary continuing obligation:
*Joe **is having to** rest a lot at the moment.*

Ⓒ *HAVE GOT TO*

We can also use **have got to** in the present (less formal) with the same meaning as **have to**:

*Joe's **got to be** sensible about smoking.*   *I've **got to visit** him.*

Ⓓ CASES WHERE WE USE *HAVE TO*, NOT *MUST*

We use **must** only to **talk** about the **present** and the **future**.

We use **have to**, not **must**:

1   to talk about the **past** (see Unit 22A): *Did you **have to have** an aspirin last night?*
2   after another modal: *It's Sunday! You **can't have to go** to work!* (Not ~~can't must~~)
3   as a **to-infinitive**: *I wouldn't like **to have to get** up early.* (Not ~~to must~~)
4   in **perfect tenses**: *I've **had to work** since sunrise.* (Not ~~I have must~~…)

Ⓔ *HAVE* TO VS *MUST*

Often, we can use either **must** or **have to**, but we prefer **have to**:

1   when **other people** or the **situation** make it necessary for us to do things:
    *I **have to remember** her birthday or she will get angry.* (= the situation makes it necessary)

2   for questions: *Do you **have to go**?*   *Does/Will she **have to do** the exam tomorrow?*

But we often use **must** to give **personal feelings**:
*I **must remember** her birthday.* (= I think it is important)

Ⓕ *DON'T HAVE TO* VS *MUSTN'T*

There is an **important difference** between **don't/doesn't have to*** and **mustn't**.
*I'm rich. I **don't have to work**.* (= it is not necessary for me to work)
*I'm suffering from stress. I **mustn't work**.* (= it is forbidden for me to work)

* We can also use **needn't** to give the same meaning. See Unit 28.

1 Ⓐ Ⓑ Ⓓ Ⓔ **Read the text and then complete the sentences. In each sentence, use a suitable tense of *have to*.**

> Joe has had an eventful life. His family was poor so he got a full-time job when he was fourteen. In 1939, the government called him up to join the army. As a soldier, he fought in North Africa and Singapore. In 1960, he got married but in 1961 his wife, Molly, threw him out of the house. She divorced him and he paid her a lot of money. Now he is over 80 years old. His last tooth fell out two years ago, so now he wears false teeth. He has a weak heart, so next year he's going to have an operation. But he is still happy.

0 When he was fourteen, he *had to go to work*.
1 He .... in 1939.
2 He .... to North Africa and Singapore.
3 In 1961, he .... the house.
4 .... Joe .... his wife .... ? Yes, he ....
5 He .... false teeth for two years.
6 Next year, ...
7 He .... to survive all his life. (use: *struggle*)

2 Ⓐ Ⓔ Ⓕ **Rewrite these sentences. Use *have to, don't have to* or *mustn't*.**

0 It isn't necessary for Joe to take the medicine any more.
Joe *doesn't have to take the medicine any more*.
1 The doctors have forbidden Joe to eat fatty food like fish and chips.
Joe ....
2 The doctor insists that Joe does special exercises every morning.
Joe ....
3 The doctors insist that Joe doesn't lift any heavy weights.
Joe ....
4 Visits to the doctor are only necessary once a month.
Joe .... more than once a month.
5 The insurance company pays for Joe's hospital treatment.
Joe .... his treatment himself.
6 Is it necessary for Doctor Spencer to give Joe an X-ray?
.... ?
7 It isn't necessary for the nurses to check Joe's temperature.
....
8 The doctors insist that Joe stops going to discos!
Joe ....
9 Doctor, is it important that Joe changes his diet?
Doctor, ... ?

3 Ⓒ **Joe's friend, Dan, and his doctor are asking him questions. Use *have got to* (informal) for the friend and *have to* (formal) for the doctor + the verbs in brackets.**

0 Dan asks: '*Have* you *got to go* back to hospital soon?' (*go*)
1 Dan asks: '.................. your daughters .... you?' (*look after*)
2 Dr Spencer asks: '.................. you .... your own shopping?' (*do*)
3 Dr Spencer asks: '.................. the nurse .... you when you bathe?' (*help*)
4 Dan asks: '.................. the doctor .... you a regular check-up?' (*give*)

UNIT 24 >> *May* and *might*

Nick and Jill saw Madame Magistar, the fortune teller. 'This time next year, you **may be** lying on a beach in the Bahamas. The US president **might ask** you to help him solve his financial problems. You **might** even **become** the richest people in the world. So, you **may as well** pay me a lot of money now. It's nothing to billionaires like you.'

Ⓐ *MAY/MIGHT* FOR POSSIBILITY

We use **may** or **might** to talk about **possibility** in the **present** or **future**:

*Beth **may be** ill.* (now)   *The President **may ask** you for help.* (future)
*She **might be** in London.* (now)   *You **might go** to the Bahamas.* (future)

Often we use **may** for something which is possible and likely. We tend to use **might** for something which is possible but not so likely. We are less certain.

*It **may rain**.* (e.g. 70% possible)   *It **might** even **snow**.* (e.g. 40% possible)

Ⓑ OTHER USES

We also use **may***:

1 to talk about and ask for permission:
  *You **may smoke**.*   *You **may** not **park** here.*
  ***May** I **smoke**?*   ***May** she **come** to your party?*

2 to offer help: ***May** I **help** you?*

If we want to ask especially politely, for example with a stranger, we use **might***:

***Might** I **leave** now, sir?*   ***Might** we **use** this table?*   ***Might** I **help** you?*

* **May** is more formal than **can**, and **might** is a lot more formal than **could** in these cases.

Ⓒ CONTINUOUS FORMS

We can use a continuous* form (**may/might be doing**) to refer to a particular moment in the present or future or to a long continuous action.

*This time next year, you **may be swimming** in the Bahamas.*
'Where's Madame Magistar?'   *'She **might be resting**.'*

Sometimes we can use either form:

*I **may meet** Hugh at 6 p.m.*   or *I **may be meeting** Hugh at 6 p.m.*

* Remember there are some verbs which we do not use in a continuous form (see Appendix 5).

Ⓓ *MAY/MIGHT AS WELL...*

We use **may/might as well** + **basic verb**. It means that this action is the **best available choice**.

*You **may as well** pay me.* (= it's a sensible course of action)
*I'm bored. **I might as well** come to the shops with you.* (= it's a less boring thing to do)

Ⓔ *MAY BE/MAYBE*

Be careful when you use **... may be...** (a verb form written as two words) and **maybe** (written as one word: = *possibly, perhaps*). The sentences in A and B have the same meaning but are different in grammar:

A: *John **may be** ill.*   *The children **may be** lost.*   *We **may be** late.*
B: ***Maybe** John is ill.*   ***Maybe** the children are lost.*   ***Maybe** we'll be late.*

1 🅐🅑 Write sentences with *may*, basing them on sentences 1-8 below.

0 Perhaps Madam Magistar possesses magic powers.
  = *Madam Magistar may possess magic powers.*
1 But it's possible that she's a fraud.
  = But ....
2 Some scientists asked to inspect her equipment.
  = They asked: '...?'
3 The police are considering whether to ban her show.
  = The police ....
4 She offered to read the Prime Minister's palm.
  = She said to the PM, '..?'
5 She forecast the possible end of the world in 2000.
  = She said, '.. in 2000.'
6 Some people ask to see her in private.
  = Some people say, '..?'
7 She tells people that it's impossible to change destiny.
  = She says, 'You ....,'
8 Tru-Ads plc offered to advertise her show.
  = Tru-Ads plc asked, '...?'

2 🅐🅒 Use *may/might be* + verb-ing or *may/might* + verb to rewrite these sentences. Use the verbs in brackets in the correct form.

0 Perhaps John is in the middle of telephoning his girlfriend.
  John *may be phoning his girlfriend.* (*phone*)
1 Perhaps Madeleine knows the answers to these questions.
  .... (*know*)
2 I think Ben's in the middle of a chess game with his professor.
  .... (*play*)
3 Myra is possibly meeting the President from 6 to 8 tomorrow evening. At 7.30, Myra
  .... (*meet*)
4 Perhaps Carmen will understand the exam question.
  .... (*understand*)
5 'Where's Sally?' 'Sally is watering the flowers in the garden, I think.' 'Where's Sally?'
  '.. .' (*water*)
6 Kevin has recovered from his broken leg but perhaps he will break it again. Kevin has recovered
  from his broken leg but .... (*break*)
7 It is possible that the new laptop will cost more than £1,000.
  .... (*cost*)
8 I think that Tom is in the process of falling in love with Maria.
  .... (*fall*)
9 Ali's playing his guitar at the disco but perhaps he'll rest from 10.30 to 11.00. At 10.45, Ali
  .... (*not play*)

3 🅐🅓🅔 Fill the gaps either with *may, maybe* or *may be*.

0 There may be rain tomorrow.   1 .... it'll rain tomorrow.   2 She says that she
.... as well marry Tom.   3 I haven't seen Tom. He .... still sleeping.
4 I can see an important-looking person – .... he's the boss.   5 I think the teacher
.... angry.   6 The Loch Ness Monster .... not exist.   7 The workers
.... getting ready for a strike.   8 The stray dog .... belong to the
butcher.

UNIT 25 >> *Should, ought to, had better*

Myron and Myra **shouldn't be** quarrelling but they are!
'Myra, you're crazy. You **should see** a psychiatrist.'
'You **should be sitting** in a cage at the zoo. Someone **ought to kill** you.'
'You'**d better not threaten** me again. You're crazy...'

For information about form, see Appendix 2.

Ⓐ *SHOULD/OUGHT TO*

We use **should** or **ought to** to give advice, to say that it is good or right to do something:
*Are you lonely? You **should find** some new friends.   We **ought to look** after the environment.*

We use **shouldn't** or **oughtn't to** to say that it is inadvisable or wrong to do something:
*Are you tired? You **shouldn't work** so hard.   We **oughtn't to destroy** the rainforests.*

We often prefer to use **ought to/oughtn't to** when it is morally right or wrong to do
something: *She **oughtn't to tell** lies.* (but we can also use **should** in these cases)

* Remember: **Ought to** is more formal than **should** and is used less frequently.

Ⓑ *HAD BETTER*

We can use **had better** to give advice when we want to say that a course of action is more
sensible/more practical/wiser in a specific situation.
*I'**d better not tell** a lie.*   (= it isn't practical, someone might find out I am lying)
*I **oughtn't to tell** a lie.*   (= it is wrong)

We can use **had better** to make implied threats: *You'**d better be** quiet!*

We **do not** use **had better** for general advice/statements:
*We **should/ought to** obey the law at all times.* (**Not** ~~We had better obey~~...)

Ⓒ CONTINUOUS FORM

We can use a continuous* form (**should/ought to/had better be doing**) to refer to a
particular moment in the present or future or to a long continuous action.
*They **shouldn't/oughtn't to be quarrelling**.*   *I'**d better be going** now.*

* Remember there are some verbs which we do not use in a continuous form (see Appendix 5).

Ⓓ *SHOULD/OUGHT TO AND MUST*

There is normally a clear difference between **should/ought to** and **must**.

should/ought to	must
*You **should/ought to revise** for the exam.* (= it's a good idea to revise)	*You **must revise** for the exam.* (= I order you/it's absolutely necessary to revise)
*You **shouldn't/oughtn't to park** there.* (= I advise you not to park there)	*You **mustn't park** there.* (= I forbid you to/it is forbidden to park there)

But sometimes we use **should/ought to** instead of **must** to make orders or instructions
sound more polite: *You **should/ought to concentrate** more in class.* (this is really an order)

Ⓔ *SHOULD* FOR PROBABILITY

We use **should** to say that something will probably happen (predictions):
*The train **should arrive** on time.* (= it is probable that the train will arrive on time)
*Don't worry. It **shouldn't rain** tomorrow.* (= it's unlikely to rain tomorrow)

We also use **should** to draw a probable logical conclusion from the evidence:
*The phone rings. I say: 'That **should be** Jenny.'* (= I'm expecting Jenny to ring)

70   **27** *Should have done, ought to have done*   **105** *Suggest, insist, request etc.*
110 More about conditionals   **Appendix 5**

1 **Ⓐ** Marvin Mindset, the fashionable psychiatrist, is advising Myra. Fill the gaps with *should/shouldn't* + verbs from the list. Then listen and check your answers.

attack ~~be~~ be control meditate pay spend

0 Myra, you shouldn't be jealous of other actresses. **1** You .... every morning to calm your nerves. **2** You......................... more than you earn. **3** You......................... me $40,000 before you go. **4** You......................... angry with me for telling you the truth. **5** You .... your violent temper. **6** You .... me with that stiletto. Help!!!!

2 **Ⓐ** Look at these ideas. Use *ought* if it is a moral idea. Use *should* in the other cases. Use the negative form where necessary.

clean give go go help obey ~~tell~~

0 People oughtn't to tell lies. **1** You .... other people at all times. **2** He .... his car – it's very dirty. **3** She .... near the dog – it's dangerous. **4** We .... more money to charity. **5** She .... out with that boy – he's a liar and a cheat. **6** Everyone .... the law.

3 **Ⓐ Ⓑ** Complete the second sentence in each item using the words in brackets. Supply any other necessary words.

0 Myron thinks it's a good idea for Myra to stop making films. (*had better/make*)
Myron says: 'She'd better not make any more films.'

1 The gunman wants his victims to give him their money. (*had better*)
He says: ' .... '

2 I believe in equal pay for women and men. (*ought/earn*)
Women .... the same as men.

3 The gunman doesn't want his victims to tell the police. (*had better*)
He says: ' .... '

4 Bob has long dirty hair and he has a job interview tomorrow. (*had better*)
His friends say: '....................................... and .... your hair before tomorrow.'

4 **Ⓒ** Make sentences with *should/shouldn't be* + verb-ing. Use the verbs in brackets.

0 Jack is at the disco, but he has an exam tomorrow.
He shouldn't be dancing. (*dance*)   He should be revising. (*revise*)

1 Colin is driving his car. At the same time, he's talking on his mobile phone.
He .... carefully. (*drive*)   He .... (*use*)

2 Maria is watching TV. It's her grandmother's birthday.
She .... (*watch*)   She .... (*phone*)

3 Stella is buying an expensive dress but she has no money in the bank.
She .... (*save*)   She .... (*buy*)

4 Petra is sleeping. It's 8.50. Her job starts at 9.00.
She .... to work. (*go*)   She .... in bed. (*lie*)

5 **Ⓐ-Ⓔ** Choose the best answer.

0 That liquid is highly poisonous: You **mustn't**/shouldn't/had better not drink it.

1 The bible says that we **had better not/oughtn't to/shouldn't to** laugh about religion.

2 There are a lot of dark clouds. You **ought/had better/must** take an umbrella with you.

3 The weather forecaster said that it **had better not/shouldn't/mustn't** rain tomorrow.

Should, ought to, had better

UNIT 26 >> *Would, would like, would rather*

> Hugh invited Claudette for a meal.
> '**Would** you **like** fish and chips?' he asked. 'Or **would** you **rather have** bacon and eggs?'
> 'I**'d like** caviar and champagne,' she replied. 'When I was a child in a poor family, I **would dream** about luxuries like that.'
> 'OK,' said Hugh, 'but **would** you **pay** the bill, please?'

For information about form, see Appendix 2.

Ⓐ USE

We use **would** when we are **imagining a situation or an action** that might occur:
'**Would** you **marry** John?' 'No, I **wouldn't**.'
I **would** *never* **tell** *a lie.*

Ⓑ WOULD LIKE...

We use **would like** to talk about our **wishes**/to **invite someone**/to **offer something**:
*I***'d like to** *go to Brazil.*   **Would** *you* **like** *to come to the party?*   **Would** *she* **like** *tea?*

Compare:
Would *you* **like** *water or champagne?*   (= What do you prefer to drink now?)
Do *you* **like** *champagne?*   (= Do you like it generally?)

We often answer the question: **Would you like...?** by saying **Yes, please.** or **No, thank you.**

Ⓒ WOULD RATHER DO/WOULD RATHER HAVE DONE

We use **would rather** + **basic verb** to say what we **prefer**. We often use it with **than**.
*I***'d rather have** *champagne.* **Would** *you* **rather eat** *at the Ritz* **than** *at the Hilton?*

If we are talking about a **past situation** where we preferred something but failed to achieve it, we use **would rather** + **have** + **past participle**:
*We went to London but I***'d rather have gone** *to Paris.*

Ⓓ ASKING AND REFUSING

We can use **would** to **ask someone to do something** for us. It is polite to add **please**:
Would *you* **open** *the window,* **please**?

We can use **wouldn't** when someone **refuses to do something**:
I asked her to help me but she **wouldn't**.   *They* **wouldn't let** *me talk.*

Ⓔ HABITS IN THE PAST

We can also use **would** to talk about **habits in the past**.
When Claudette was a child, she **would dream** *about...* (= she often dreamed...)

We can **only use** it to refer to **habits**, **but not** to permanent states:
We can say: *When I was a student, I* **used to live** *in York* (see Unit 14).
But not ~~I would live in York~~.

1 **A**-**E** Read the interview with Claudette and write sentences with similar meanings to items 1-7. Use *would* or *wouldn't* in each sentence. Then listen and check your answers.

0 Is it better for you to have a rich, ugly husband or a poor, handsome husband?
Would you rather have a rich, ugly husband or a poor, handsome husband?

1 When I was a child, I often imagined living in a palace – so I prefer a rich husband.
.... (*would* x 2)

2 Can you imagine yourself ever agreeing to pose in the nude for a magazine?
....

3 No, I always refuse to do that kind of thing. I prefer not to become a sex object.
.... (*would* x 2)

4 Before you were a model, did you use to read fashion magazines?
....

5 No. Even now, I like going to the cinema more than watching a fashion show.
....

6 Do you want to return to England to live? Or is it better for you to live in France?
....

7 I prefer not to live in England. But now I want a drink, so stop asking me questions!
.... (*would* x 2)

2 **B** Put *do* or *would* + *like* in the gaps.

0 Would you like to have a coffee?

1 .... you .... British television?   4 .... you .... visiting old churches?

2 .... you .... to look at these photos?   5 I .... to give you this present.

3 .... you .... to visit my home?   6 .... your son .... English food?

3 **C** Write a sentence using either *'d/would rather (... than)* or *'d/would rather have...*

0 I don't want to go to a restaurant. I prefer to eat at home tonight.
I'd rather eat at home tonight.

1 Frozen vegetables are not as good to eat as fresh ones.
I ....

2 The girls didn't like the football match; they wanted to watch the fashion show.
....

3 Where would you like to live, in an apartment block or a house with a garden?
....

4 He married Shirley but he was in love with Penny.
....

5 I want to marry a kind person, not a beautiful one.
....

4 **D** Write four sentences with *wouldn't* about Tom.

> Tom refused to do his homework. Not only that, but he disobeyed his father when he asked him to clean his room. He also ignored a note from his sister asking him to cook dinner. 'I'm not going to wash up,' he shouted. 'I might take the dog for a walk but I won't give it a bath.'

0 *Tom wouldn't do his homework.*

1 ....   3 ....

2 ....   4 ....

UNIT 27 >> *Must have done, can't have done, wouldn't have done etc.*

There's blood on this knife. The murderer **must have used it**. This door is still locked. He **can't have come** through it. So, **could** he **have entered** the room through the window?

It's fairly small but he **might have squeezed** through it.

For information about form, see Appendix 2.

Ⓐ DEDUCTION AND PROBABILITY

If we are certain that something happened in the past, we use **must have + past participle** of the verb:

*There's blood on the knife. The murderer **must have used** it.*

We can use **can't have + past participle** when we think that something in the past was **not possible** or was **very surprising**:

*The door's still locked. He **can't have come** through it.*
*Lord Brian loves Lady Alice! He **can't have murdered** her!*
*There were guard dogs in the garden. He **couldn't have got** past them.*

We can use **may have/might have/could have + past participle** to show that something perhaps happened in the past:

*Perhaps Lady Alice knew the murderer. She **may have unlocked** the door.*
*The window's very small but he **might have climbed** through it.*
*Someone dropped a glove. It **could have been** the murderer.*

Ⓑ DUTY IN THE PAST

If we **did not do something necessary** in the past, we use **should have/ought to have + past participle**:

*The guards **ought to have checked** the cellars but they didn't.*
*I **should have revised** for the exam.*

We use the negative to show that we **did something wrong**:

*They **shouldn't have touched** the evidence until the police came.*

Ⓒ INTENTION IN THE PAST

If we **intended to do something** in the past or were ready to do something but **did not actually do it**, we use **would have + past participle**:

*The police **would have arrived** more quickly but the road was blocked.*
*I **would have said** goodbye but I didn't know you were leaving.*

1 Ⓐ Use *must have, can't have, may have* + past participle of verbs from the list.

do   fall   have   ~~help~~   hire   kill   love   poison   scream   wear

0 There are two sets of footprints in the garden.
Someone must have helped the murderer.

1 There are a lot of fingerprints.
The murderer .... gloves.

2 Nobody heard anything.
Lady Alice ....

3 Her personal guard dog is dead.
Someone .... it.

4 Lord Brian was in Scotland playing golf.
He .... it.

5 Lady Alice was very beautiful.
She .... a lover.

6 Lady Alice treated her servants badly.
One of them .... her.

7 Lord Brian is very rich.
He .... an assassin.

8 The guards are very lazy.
They .... asleep.

9 Lord Brian seems very relaxed.
He .... his wife very much.

2 ⒶⒷ Use continuous forms of items from the list to fill the gaps.

could/do   can't/drive   must/listen   can't/read   might/read   ~~must/sleep~~
shouldn't/sleep   can't/watch   must/watch   should/watch   can't/wear   must/wear

0 The murder happened at 3 a.m. Most people in the house must have been sleeping.

1 The footprints are very wide and large.
The murderer .... boots.

2 What .... Lady Alice .... before she fell asleep?

3 The TV is out of order – so she .... a film.

4 There is no book on her bedside table.
She ....

5 There are headphones next to the bed.
She .... to music.

6 There are no tyre tracks in the lane.
The murderer .... a car.

7 I've punished the security guard.
He ....

8 The guard .... the house.

9 I've just found a magazine under the bed.
She .... that.

10 The murderer has planned this very carefully.
He .... the house.

11 She always locks her diamond ring in the safe at night.
She .... it.

3 **A** **B** Present or past? Use either *must/can't* etc. *have done* or *must/can't* etc. *do* to fill the gaps.

0 There is a new car in Mick's garage. He must have sold the old one. (*must/sell*)

1 There are a lot of ski-shops in this area.
It .... a lot. (*must/snow*)

2 Joanne isn't wearing her ring.
She .... the engagement. (*must/break off*)

3 Hugo had grey hair yesterday but today it's black.
He .... it. (*must/dye*)

4 Colin's name is not on the list.
He .... the exam. (*can't/pass*)

5 Diana is in love with my brother.
She .... mad! (*must/be*)

6 Sally isn't at school today.
She .... an accident. (*may/have*)

7 Gina isn't at school today.
She .... the flu. (*may/have*)

8 Helen's been away for a week but she's back today.
She .... the flu. (*must/have*)

9 Tom used to be in love with my sister.
He .... mad. (*must/be*)

10 Ben's car has stopped.
He .... up with petrol. (*should/fill*)

11 Ben's car has stopped.
He .... the garage quickly to get help. (*should/phone*)

4 **A**-**C** Circle the correct answer.

0 Martin loved Stella. He **should have/can't have/must have/(would have)** married her but she rejected him.

1 They **can't have/might have/can have/mustn't have** met Phil in Glasgow. He was here with me in Brighton.

2 Hugo looked good last night but he **might be/might have been/can't have been/can't have** wearing a wig.

3 Sam was the office manager; he **should/ought/must/would** to have checked the accounts.

4 Ali was the team captain; the players **shouldn't have/should have/must have/wouldn't have** supported his decision.

5 Dan **would have/shouldn't have/can't have/can have** come to the party but he was ill.

6 James **might be/might have been/must have been/must be** a spy when he lived in Asia but I'm not sure.

7 The President told a lie; therefore, he **ought to have/must have/can have/mightn't have** resigned instead of continuing in office.

8 Ben **would have/can't have/must have/might have been** bought a new car but he didn't have enough money.

9 Tina **must have/couldn't have/might have/would have** stolen the money. She is extremely honest.

5 **A-C** Complete the second sentences. Choose ONE of the modal verbs in the brackets to include in your answer.

0 John didn't go to the disco because he had broken his leg.
John *would have gone to the disco* but he broke his leg. (*can't/would*)

1 The teacher wanted Sara to finish her homework before Monday but she didn't.
Sara .... before Monday. (*must/should*)

2 Ben planned to take part in the chess competition but he lost the entry form.
Ben .... but he lost the entry form. (*can/would*)

3 Marisa had to take the medicine before dinner but she forgot.
Marisa .... but she forgot. (*must/should*)

4 The Socialists were going to win the election but it was cancelled.
The Socialists .... but it was cancelled. (*must/would*)

5 They predicted snow yesterday but the wind direction changed.
It .... yesterday but the wind direction changed. (*might/can*)

6 I was wrong to be angry with Anna.
I .... with Anna. (*should/shouldn't*)

7 Look at those floods! I'm sure there was a lot of rain last night.
Look at those floods. It .... a lot last night. (*might/must*)

8 There was nearly an accident but luckily I stopped the car in time.
There .... an accident but luckily I stopped the car in time. (*could/must*)

9 I'm very surprised that you knew about my engagement!
You .... about my engagement! (*can't/shouldn't*)

OPEN EXERCISE

6 **B** Make sentences with *should have/shouldn't have* about the members of the Collins family.

Yesterday the Collins family had a bad day. Pauline needs to practise the violin every day but she spent the whole day watching TV. Jack's car was very dirty but he played golf all afternoon. It's still dirty! Trevor didn't have a shower – his girlfriend said that he stank! Betty burnt the dinner because she was reading a magazine while she was cooking. Mandy tore her best dress because she wore it on a walk through the forest. The police arrested Simon because he rode his bicycle at night without a light. He'd forgotten to repair it. Sheila didn't mend a hole in her pocket and so she lost her wallet. She had a thousand pounds in it.

0 Pauline *should have practised the violin* .   *She shouldn't have watched TV.*
1 Jack ....   He ....
2 Trevor ....   His girlfriend ....
3 Betty ....   She ....
4 Mandy ....   She ....
5 Simon ....   He ....
6 Sheila ....   She ....

Must have done, can't have done, wouldn't have done etc.

UNIT 28 >> *Need, needn't, needn't have*

The Collins family **needed** a holiday — they'd been working hard. They chose a small hotel in Spain. But it rained all the time, so they **needn't have brought** the suncream or the swimsuits. They **didn't need** their walking boots either as the rain flooded the footpaths. They **needn't have come** abroad — there's plenty of rain in England!

For information about form, see Appendix 1.

Ⓐ USE

We use **need** to talk about something which is or isn't urgent or necessary:

*They **need** a holiday.*
*He **doesn't need** a new car.*

Note that the negative form of **need to** in the present can also be **needn't** + **verb**.

*Bob **doesn't need** to borrow* ⎫
*Bob **needn't** borrow* ⎭ *any money.* (= it isn't necessary for him)

don't need to/needn't + **verb** have a very similar meaning to **don't have to** (see Unit 23):

*We **needn't reserve** a room. = We **don't have to reserve** a room.*

Ⓑ *NEED* + VERB-ING = A PASSIVE MEANING

We can also use **need** + **verb-ing** to say that it is necessary to wash, clean, repair, mend etc. something:

*The room **needs cleaning**.*
*This hotel **needs modernising**.*

Alternatively, we can use a passive form (see Unit 100E):

*The room **needs to be cleaned**.*
*This hotel **needs to be modernised**.*

Ⓒ *NEEDN'T HAVE DONE* VS *DIDN'T NEED TO DO*

We use **needn't have** + **past participle** when we did something which wasn't necessary:

I studied hard. But they cancelled the exam, so it wasn't necessary.
*= I **needn't have studied** hard.*

She made 50 sandwiches for the picnic. It rained, so there was no picnic.
*= She **needn't have made** the sandwiches.*

There is a difference in use between **needn't have...** and **didn't need to...**:

*I studied hard but then they cancelled the exam. = I **needn't have studied**.*
*I didn't study; but I passed the exam easily. = I **didn't need to study**.*

1 Ⓐ Ⓒ Use the correct form of *need* (present, past or future, positive, negative or question form) to complete these sentences. Use the verbs in brackets.

0 He isn't able to find a wife. He *needs to join* a dating agency. (*join*)

1 His work was very difficult. He .... all about nuclear physics. (*know*)

2 I had a terrible headache yesterday. I .... an aspirin. (*take*)

3 They'll start a new company next year. They .... an accountant. (*employ*)

4 He'll probably fail the driving test. I think he .... it again. (*take*)

5 I .... at least eight hours a day or else I get bad-tempered. (*sleep*)

6 Bob's been arrested! .... he .... a lawyer? (*hire*)

2 Ⓑ Write sentences with *need* + verb-ing. Also use a passive to express the same meaning.

0 His hair is untidy. = *It needs combing/brushing.   It needs to be combed/brushed.*

1 The computer's out of order. ....

2 The car's covered in mud. ....

3 The hospital is really old-fashioned. ....

4 The garden is very dry. ....

5 The room is very smelly. ....

6 There's a hole in my jacket. ....

3 Ⓒ Make sentences with *needn't have* about these situations.

> Last week, Pauline practised the violin every day. Her mother bought a new dress to wear at Pauline's concert. Trevor booked a hotel room to go on holiday with his girlfriend. Mandy filled in an application form for a job at the local factory. Simon lent Trevor £1,000 so he could go on holiday. Sheila bought a new dog basket for her puppy.

0 They've cancelled the concert. Pauline *needn't have practised every day.*

1 Her mother ....

2 The local factory has closed. ....

3 Trevor's girlfriend has left him. ....

4 Trevor doesn't want to go on holiday now. Simon ....

5 Sheila's dog has disappeared. ....

4 Ⓒ Ⓔ Make sentences with EITHER *needn't have* OR *didn't need to* for these situations.

> Last month, Pauline went to London to see an art exhibition. Betty lent Trevor her cookery books but he didn't read them. Mandy bought a new computer. But she didn't buy a DVD player. Simon watched videos instead of revising for his exam. Sheila painted her flat herself instead of hiring a professional painter.

0 The same art exhibition is now on at Pauline's local museum.
   Pauline needn't have gone to London.

1 The exhibition in London was free. She .... for the entrance ticket.

2 Trevor has just cooked a perfect dinner. ....

3 Mandy has won a computer in a competition. ....

4 She has also won a DVD player. ....

5 Simon has got an A grade in his exam. ....

6 We all admired the newly painted flat. She .... a professional decorator.

7 But now a fire has destroyed her flat. ....

REVISION 3 >> First Certificate Practice

1 For questions 1-12, read the text below and decide which answer, A, B, C or D, best fits each gap. There is an example at the beginning (0).

LOST TRAVELLERS

You (0) A heard about the mystery of the ship called the *Marie Celeste*. When it was found, drifting at sea, it was completely empty. Nobody (1) ..... explain the disappearance of the crew. Pirates might have attacked the ship and removed them. Or they (2) ..... victims of bad weather. Could a freak wave have swept them overboard? This is not the only mystery of a lost crew. In August 1978, a plane (3) ..... at a Sydney air-strip. When it failed to arrive, search parties went out and (4) ..... locate the small plane in the middle of semi-desert. The plane was in good order but the pilot and crew had vanished. No one (5) ..... to explain this mystery either. A more famous event was the disappearance of Amelia Earhart, a pioneering female aviator, in 1937. Her plane (6) ..... somewhere over the Pacific Ocean. But some people believe she (7) ..... on a remote island although there is no proof of this.

Other lost travellers have survived. The survivors often (8) ..... accusations of cannibalism. In fact, we can find many cases where travellers (9) ..... succeeded in reaching safety without eating parts of their dead companions. (10) ..... society to punish such transgressors? Or (11) ..... accept that in extreme situations we (12) ..... suspend normal laws of human behaviour?

0 (A) must have	B can have	C couldn't have	D need have
1 A couldn't	B can't	C can	D is able
2 A may have	B maybe	C may be	D may have been
3 A should have landed	B shouldn't have landed	C must have landed	D had to land
4 A could have	B were able to	C must	D had to
5 A could	B has been able	C ought	D has had
6 A was able to crash	B must crash	C must have crashed	D must have crash
7 A was able to survive	B could survive	C can't have survived	D had to survive
8 A must to face	B maybe	C have to face	D would face
9 A would have	B shouldn't have	C had to have	D wouldn't have
10 A Should	B Ought	C Can	D Is able
11 A should we	B ought we	C could we have	D do we need
12 A shouldn't	B ought	C need to	D must to

2 For these questions, read the text below and think of the word which best fits the gap. Use only *one* word in each gap. There is an example at the beginning (0).

SURVIVORS

There (0) must be millions of stories about survivors, from ship wrecks, plane crashes and other misadventures. I myself and my companions (1) .... have lost our lives when our light aircraft crashed on a remote mountainside. We (2) .... to survive on the small amount of tinned food we were (3) .... to rescue from the wreck. We (4) .... to have remained by the plane and waited for rescue but some of us decided to try to reach the nearest village. We (5) .... have been crazy! We set off with a map, down the mountain slope and into thick jungle. How (6) .... we have known that the map contained errors and that we (7) .... have headed more to the west? We (8) .... have died in the jungle but, on the sixth day, a local Indian hunter spotted us. He (9) .... have been very surprised to see a group of men and women in ragged clothes in the rain forest! We soon found out that we (10) .... have panicked. A rescue team had arrived at the site of the crash and airlifted the other survivors to hospital. We ourselves (11) .... have been enjoying modern medical care instead of existing in the jungle.

After our experience, we know the value of the first rule of survival. You (12) .... leave the site of the crash.

PAPER 3 PART 4

3 For these questions, complete the second sentence so that it has a similar meaning to the first sentence(s), using the word given. Do not change the word given. Use from two to five words including the word given. There is an example (0).

0 It was wrong for Tim to tell everyone about my secret love affair.
   Tim *shouldn't have told everyone* about my secret love affair. *SHOULDN'T*

1 I prefer to wait in the garden: this hall is very dark.
   I .... garden than in this dark hall. *RATHER*

2 She was a very good skater when she was a child.
   She .... when she was a child. *COULD*

3 My grandfather used to go for long walks in the forest until the day he died.
   My grandfather .... in the forest until the day he died. *WOULD*

4 Rain is coming through the hole in the roof; it's a good idea to mend it.
   Rain is coming through the hole in the roof; we .... it. *BETTER*

5 It's not necessary for us to go shopping; there's plenty of food in the fridge.
   We .... shopping; there's plenty of food in the fridge. *DON'T*

6 Nobody's going to read these old magazines; why don't I burn them?
   Nobody's going to read these old magazines; I .... then. *WELL*

7 I'm warning you. Don't phone my girlfriend again!
   I'm warning you. .... my girlfriend again! *YOU'D*

OTHER PRACTICE

4 If you can substitute *would* for *used to* in these sentences, put a tick (✓) in the box and rewrite the part of that sentence. If you cannot replace *used to* by *would*, put a cross (✗) in the box and write nothing.

0 When I lived in Spain, I used to go to the beach every night. ✓ *would go*

1 When I was child, I used to live in the country. ☐ ....

2 When I was in the army, I used to visit my girlfriend secretly. ☐ ....

3 When she was a teenager, she didn't use to talk to her parents. ☐ ....

4 When I lived in London, I used to work in a bank. ☐ ....

5 When I lived in London, I used to row on the Thames. ☐ ....

6 During the 90s, they used to stay in the same hotel each summer. ☐ ....

7 When I was a child, I used to own a red bicycle. ☐ ....

8 Did you use to visit the night clubs when you lived in Paris? ☐ ....

UNIT 29 >> The indefinite article

Clara and Billy grew up in **an** industrial town. There were factories and tall blocks of flats. There were **some** large houses with gardens for managers and factory owners. Clara lived in **a** house like this in **an** exclusive part of town. Her father was **a** barrister and her mother was **a** university lecturer.

Ⓐ *A* VS *AN*

We use **a** if the next word begins with a consonant or 'w' or 'y' sound:
a grammar book (consonant)   *a one way street*   *a university lecturer* (sound 'w'/'y')

We use **an** if the next word begins with a vowel sound (**a, e, i, o, u**) or silent 'h':
an industrial town   *an honest person*   *an hour-long journey*

Ⓑ USE

A/an are indefinite articles.

1 We use them with **singular* countable nouns the first time we refer** to a person, animal or object:
*They grew up in **an** industrial town.* (first time we refer to this town)
*She lived in **a** house.* (first time we refer to this house)

2 We use **be + a/an + noun** to talk about **people's jobs** etc.:
*Her father is **a** barrister.*   *He was **an** actor.*   *Carlos is **a** Mexican.*

We can also use the indefinite article to **talk in general** about **members of a profession, species** etc.:
A dentist earns a lot of money.   *A horse is a herbivorous animal.*

But notice the alternative structure with a plural noun in D below for general statements: *Dentists earn a lot of money.*

3 We also use **a/an** to talk about **cost, frequency** and **speed**:
*It costs £5.00 **a** litre.* (cost)   *Clara goes to school six days **a** week.* (frequency)
*He drove at 100 miles **an** hour.* (speed)

Per is used in the same way: *£5.00 **per** litre/100 miles **per** hour/six days **per** week*

Ⓒ *ONE*

We use **one** instead of **a/an** when **the number is important**.
*There is only **one** car factory in the town.*   But *Yesterday I visited **a** factory.*
*There were three people, **one** man and two women.* But ***A** man was standing outside the bank.*

Ⓓ SOME/NO ARTICLE

When we refer to a plural noun for the first time we often use **some**:
There is a large house in the suburbs. → *There are **some** large houses in the suburbs.*

But we use **no article**:

1 when we are referring to all houses/all cars etc. **in general**:
Large families need to live in large houses.
Cars are useful but bicycles are more environmentally friendly.

2 with a plural noun if we are not interested in indicating the quantity:
There were factories and tall blocks of flats.

3 in expressions like this with **of**:   *a block **of flats***   *a box **of chocolates***

1 **A B** Put *a* or *an* in Chapter 1 of Clara and Billy. There are 16 more places where the indefinite article is missing. Then listen and check your answers.

> **CLARA AND BILLY: Chapter 1 continued**
>
> But Billy came from _{0. a} ∨ very different background. His mother was dancer in nightclub and his father was unemployed builder. Clara was tall, clumsy girl with big hands and feet. She came from elegant neighbourhood but she wasn't elegant person. Billy was giant. He wanted to be boxer or basketball player. He didn't have intelligent or handsome face but he had deep brown sensitive eyes. They met in youth club. Clara had rich boyfriend but when she saw Billy she felt shiver along her spine. She knew he was special person for her. Billy had similar sensation; love affair was beginning.

2 **B** Complete the second sentence using *a/an*.

0 I paid £6 for one litre of petrol. The petrol cost *£6 a litre*.
1 I drove 65 kms in one hour. I drove at ....
2 I serve customers in a shop. I'm ....
3 I attend church on Sundays and Tuesdays. I go to church twice ....
4 Clara comes from the north of England. .... northerner.
5 Luigi comes from Italy. Luigi is ....

3 **A - C** Put *a/an* or *one* in the gaps.

0 There is *one* table and eight chairs.
1 He has only .... pair of glasses.
2 They drove at 150 kms .... hour.
3 It takes .... hour, not two, to reach York.
4 You mustn't take more than .... capsule.
5 He is .... very good disc jockey.
6 There is room for .... more person in the bus.
7 She lives in .... village near Dover.
8 These apples cost £1.00 for .... kilo or £ 3.00 for five kilos.
9 The grapes cost £2.00 .... kilo.

4 **D** In each pair of items, use *some* in one and *X* (no article) in the other.

0 A Charles has bought *some* new books.
  B He loves reading *X* modern novels.
1 A Don't disturb the nests of .... rare birds.
  B Dave saw .... rare birds in his garden.
2 A I bought .... new shoes in London.
  B I always choose .... leather shoes.
3 A Bill and Rita are .... teachers.
  B There are .... teachers in the pub.
4 A I like .... English apples very much.
  B She baked .... apples in the oven.

UNIT 30 >> The definite article

This is **the** second part of **the** story of Clara and Billy. They got married and lived in a small flat — **the** rooms were damp and **the** heating didn't work in the winter. Sometimes, Clara sat all day in **the** town library just to keep warm. Her parents hated **the** idea of **the** marriage and didn't want to see her.

Ⓐ USE

We use the definite article — **the** — when we refer to:

1 a **singular** or **plural noun** already mentioned:
*I ate an apple and some pears — **the** apple was sweet but **the** pears weren't ripe.*

2 anything which we **identify definitely**:
*Clara went back to **the** flat where they lived.*
*She wore **the** jewels which her other boyfriend had given her.*

3 a **part of a known thing**:
***the** top of the mountain   **the** middle of the room*
***the** end of the relationship   **the** start of the lesson etc.*

4 **musical instruments**:
*to play **the** piano/**the** violin/**the** drums/**the** guitar etc.*

5 words like this:
In the town: ***the** post office/**the** library/**the** supermarket/**the** shops/**the** museum etc.*
*I'm going to **the** cinema.*   *She's sitting in **the** library.*
In the house: ***the** bathroom/**the** front door/**the** garden/**the** dining table etc.*
*I put my clothes in **the** wardrobe.*   *He opened **the** front door.*

Ⓑ SHARED KNOWLEDGE

We use **the** with a singular or plural noun when it is clear which person or thing we are talking about:
*This is **the** second part of the story. (we already know that the story exists/we know that after the first part, there will be a second part)*
***The** rooms were damp and **the** heating didn't work.*
(we already know about the flat — so we know that the rooms and the heating exist even though this is the first time the writer mentions them)

Ⓒ GENERALISATIONS

If we are talking about a general idea, we **do not use the**. Many languages use **the** in sentences like this, so it is an easy mistake to make:

general idea (without *the*)	specific (+ *the*)
Men and women often don't understand each other.	***The** men and women at the club often argue.*
Love affairs sometimes end in tears.	***The** love affair between Clara and Billy went wrong.*
Parents and children sometimes quarrel.	***The** parents took their children to school by car.*

Ⓓ NO ARTICLE

Remember it is often not necessary to use an article when we refer to a plural noun for the first time (see 29D).
*She bought apples and pears from the shop. (also possible: She bought **some** apples and pears)*

18 **1** **A**-**C** There are 20 more missing articles (*a, an, the*). Insert them as in the example. Then listen and check your answers.

> **CLARA AND BILLY: Chapter 2 continued**
>
> *0 the*
> But Billy was reacting badly to ^ situation. He hated restrictions of his new life. He went out to pub and drank with his friends from past. Clara sometimes wore rings which her first boyfriend had given her. One day they had huge quarrel. Billy hit Clara and she called police. They took him to police station and he spent two nights in cells. After that, Billy disappeared. He went to Scotland and worked on farm. He still drank too much and farmer soon dismissed him. Over next years, he spent money which he earned on drink and lost jobs which he found. One day, twelve years later, Clara got letter: 'I'm always thinking of you. I'm sorry. Please see me.' Clara was successful journalist now working for newspaper in London but she replied to letter and agreed to meet him at station in Nottingham on anniversary of their wedding. It would be first time they had met since they split up.

2 **C** Insert *the* in these sentences if necessary. Write G (= general) or Sp (= specific) in the space at the end of each item.

0 Elephants are mysterious, powerful animals and have always fascinated me. *G*

1 In this zoo, zoo-keepers feed animals three times a day; tourists often watch. ....

2 I like meeting foreign students because we can have interesting conversations. ....

3 I like foreign students at this school because their courses are interesting. ....

4 She introduced me to friends who were visiting her. ....

5 Friends are an important part of all our lives. ....

6 In early decades of the last century women started campaigning for the right to vote. ....

7 Many people believe that aliens are trying to communicate with us. ....

8 In film which I saw, American army had to fight aliens which had landed. ....

9 Do you agree that computers have changed our way of life dramatically? ....

3 **A**-**D** Fill the gaps with *the* or **✗** (= no article).

0 Can you tell me where *the* toilet is?

1 Joan is cooking in .... kitchen.

2 I live on .... top floor of an apartment block near Hyde Park.

3 Please pass .... salt and pepper.

4 Cheryl went to the chemists and bought .... sticking plasters.

5 She is going to visit .... friends in Liverpool.

6 There were three routes but .... main one led along .... bottom of .... valley which we had seen from .... train.

7 My aunt loves .... flowers, so .... roses which you sent her were a welcome gift.

8 I'll meet you in .... park near .... bus station.

9 She played .... violin for her family and friends.

10 In this town, many craftsmen used to make .... violins by hand.

11 She's playing with .... dog in .... garden.

UNIT 31 >> More about articles

 Clara travelled from **the** south to Nottingham by train. Billy travelled from **the** north. They planned to meet at Nottingham Station. **The** sun was shining in **the** sky and Clara was thinking about Billy. What had he been doing for **the** last twelve years? Had he been in prison? Had he been in hospital? The train crossed **the** River Trent. It was stopping at Platform 1.

Ⓐ USES OF *THE* WITH NAMES ETC.

We also use **the**:

1 with words like **sky, sun, moon** (there is only one): *Look at* **the** *moon above* **the** *sea.*
2 with **names of hotels, cinemas, theatres, restaurants**: *the Ritz/the ABC Cinema*
   but not with: hotels, restaurants which end in **'s**: *We ate at Macdonald's*
3 with **names of mountain ranges, rivers, seas, oceans, deserts**, and **some lakes**:
   The Alps/The River Thames/The Pacific Ocean/The Kalahari Desert/The Great Lakes
4 with **radio**. We say: *to listen to* **the** *radio* but *to watch TV*
5 with **cardinal points**: *the north   the south-east   the west*
6 with **parts of the body** in prepositional phrases, especially with **in** (see also Unit 33B):
   He went red in **the** *face.   They hit him in* **the** *stomach.*

We also use **the** when we are talking generally: *He is a specialist in treating* **the** *heart.*

Ⓑ NO ARTICLE

We use **no article** with:

1 **people** (including family members such as 'Granddad'), **books** or **plays** etc.:
   I saw David today. (**Not** ~~the David~~)   *I've read Hamlet.   We saw Granny.*
   Except if it is part of the name: *I saw The Marriage of Figaro.*
2 **places**:
   • **towns, cities, countries** etc.: *She went to France.* (**Not** ~~the France~~)
     Except when there is a word like *Kingdom/States/Republic* as part of the name, or
     the name refers to a group of islands: *the Republic of China   the West Indies*
   • names of **planets, stars** etc.: *They landed on Mercury.*
     But *the sun, the moon, the Milky Way*
   • **streets, addresses** etc.: *She lives in Park Lane.   It's in Trafalgar Square.*
     But *the High Street, the M20 (motorway)*
   • **stations, airports** etc.: *I arrived at Waterloo Station/Platform 1/Heathrow Airport.*
3 **lakes, single islands, continents, mountains**: *Lake Superior, Easter Island, Everest, Asia*
4 **sports** or **games**: *to play chess/tennis/football/baseball* etc.
5 **meals**: *to eat/have/cook breakfast, lunch, dinner, supper*
   He had breakfast. But *He ate* **the** *breakfast which Sally cooked.* (a particular breakfast)
6 **names of colours**: *My favourite colour is red.   Blue is a beautiful colour.*
7 **names of illnesses**: *He's got bronchitis.   She died from cancer.*
   Except *the Plague   We also sometimes say:* **the** *'flu: I've caught* **(the)** *'flu.*
8 **certain expressions with go and be**: *to go to work/to school/to university/to church/*
   to prison/to hospital/to bed/to be in hospital/to be at home/to go home:
   She goes to work every day.   They went home.   She is at home.
   Compare: *He went to* **the** *hospital to visit his sick friend.* (a particular visit)
           He went to hospital because he had a weak heart. (for treatment)
9 **expressions with by**:
   They travelled **by air/by train/by road/by taxi** etc.   *It is made* **by hand/by machine.**
10 some **special days** and **festivals**: *Christmas (Day)/Easter (Day)/Thanksgiving*
11 **abbreviated writing**: in newspaper headlines, academic notes, instructions, notices, etc.
    POPE VISITS USA (headline)   *DON'T PARK IN FRONT OF GATE* (notice)
    REMOVE SCREWS FROM TOP SHELF (instructions)

1 🅐🅑 Insert *a, an, the* where necessary. There are 15 more missing articles. Then listen and check your answers.

> **CLARA AND BILLY: Chapter 3 continued**
>
> *O. the*
> But when ∨train stopped at Nottingham Station, she didn't get out of carriage. She saw Billy on platform – as train started moving again, he saw her through glass of window. But it was too late. She travelled as far as York Station, stayed overnight in Baker's Hotel, and then returned to London by coach. They never tried to meet again. Billy bought farm in Republic of Ireland near River Shannon and married Irish girl. Clara worked for *Times* in several countries – Russia, United States, Netherlands. Twenty years later, when Clara died in hospital, they found photo of Billy in her handbag. Billy died on same day. Last word he spoke was her name: 'Clara!'

2 🅐🅑 Write *the* or *✗* (= no article) in each gap. You may need to consult an encyclopaedia or atlas for some of these or ask an English friend.

0   ✗ Manchester

1 .... Milky Way	8 .... Buckingham Palace	15 .... United Arab Emirates
2 .... Mercury	9 .... Statue of Liberty	16 .... Sicily
3 .... Oxford Street	10 .... Trafalgar Square	17 .... Houses of Parliament
4 .... London Airport	11 .... Slattery's Hotel	18 .... Everest
5 .... M1 motorway	12 .... Red Lion pub	19 .... Andes
6 .... capital of France	13 .... Olympic Stadium	20 .... Thames
7 .... National Theatre	14 .... Victoria Station	21 .... Lake Michigan

3 🅐🅑 Put *a, an, the* or *✗* (= no article) in the gaps.

0   She went to *the* hospital to apply for a job as *a* nurse.

1   John was late this morning so he went to .... school by .... taxi.

2   I ate .... breakfast in .... burger restaurant in .... High Street.

3   I enjoyed .... dinner which your mum cooked on .... Christmas Day.

4   Bernie played .... chess in .... National Championship.

5   They went to .... bed early last night soon after having .... dinner.

6   He was punched in .... eye.

7   .... Grandad is visiting us tomorrow.

8   Is .... red the best colour for this picture?

9   I......... plague is a very rare disease nowadays.

4 🅑 Abbreviate these instructions, notices and headlines. Omit articles and the items in italics.

0   Don't walk on the lawns or the flower beds. *Don't walk on lawns or flower beds.*

1   Enter the castle by the bridge over the moat. ....

2   The warring nations *have* accepted an offer of peace. ....

3   The Prince *is* to marry a supermarket assistant. ....

4   A single woman *is* looking for a flat in Canterbury. ....

5   Add the sugar to the mixture using the spoon. ....

UNIT 32 >> Countable and uncountable nouns

 'In many languages, the word for furniture is plural. But in English, furniture is an uncountable noun. It isn't singular, so we can't use *a* and we can't make it plural by adding *-s*.' (from Professor Grammar's English Language ~~Advices~~ — sorry! Advice Website)

Ⓐ COUNTABLE NOUNS

Countable nouns have a **singular** and a **plural form**. Most countable nouns add **-s** to form the plural (*door → door***s**/*hill → hill***s**). But remember the spelling changes which occur in some cases. See Appendix 13 for more information about spelling, irregular plural forms etc.

Ⓑ UNCOUNTABLE NOUNS

Uncountable nouns have only **one form**. They are not singular or plural, so don't use **a/an** or add **-s**. But we often use **some**: *I need **some** money, **some** water* etc.

Many uncountable nouns:

1 **refer to substances** like:
   bread chocolate water coffee cheese meat plastic butter wood glass milk petrol soap sugar toothpaste

2 **refer to abstract ideas, emotions** etc. like:
   education grammar health knowledge love wealth

3 are uncountable in English although they are countable in some other languages. e.g.:
   accommodation advice baggage behaviour equipment furniture homework information luggage news nonsense progress spaghetti travel weather

4 have a countable noun which refers to the same area of meaning. For example:

uncountable	accommodation	publicity	work	travel
countable	flat, house etc.	advertisement	job, post etc.	journey

See Appendix 8 for a list of uncountable nouns.

Ⓒ *CHEESE* OR *CHEESES*?

Many nouns can be used as countable nouns or as uncountable nouns. For example:

uncountable	countable
I like **chocolate**. (= substance)	I bought a box of **chocolates**. (= individual sweets)
He has white **hair**.	He has five **hairs** on his head. (= individual hairs)
It's made from Indian **cloth**. (= substance)	He cleaned the car with **a cloth**. (= a countable item)
Give me a kilo of **cheese**.	Swiss **cheeses** are delicious. (= types of cheese)
I like drinking **tea**.	I've tried many **teas**. (= types of tea)
She found some **work**.	This is **a work** by Picasso. (= a work of art) Drive slowly past the **roadworks**. (special use)
Travel is exciting. (in general)	He described his **travels**. (special use)
I bought some writing **paper**.	The Times is **a** famous British **paper**. (= newspaper)
Life is difficult. (abstract, general meaning)	I read about the lives of British kings. (particular)
This book's about **education**.	He had **a** good **education** at a private school.

Ⓓ *A PIECE, A BIT*

We often use words like **piece** or **bit** (informal) with uncountable nouns. For example:
*He gave me **a piece of advice**.   Can you give me **a bit of paper**?*

29 The indefinite article   35 *Some, any, no*   37 *A lot, lots of, much, many*
39 *A few, few, a little, little*   Appendices 8, 13

1 **Ⓐ** **Complete these sentences. Take the correct form of the verbs from the list.**

belong/belongs   don't/doesn't   has been/have been   is/are (x 5)   make/makes
meet/meets   play/plays   suit/suits   taste/tastes   want/wants   was/were

0 The police sometimes *make* mistakes.
1 Plastic scissors .... safer for children than metal ones.
2 Economics .... a popular subject at university.
3 The jar of olives in the fridge .... to me.
4 Tight jeans .... you because you've got a good figure.
5 The news .... on Channel 4 at 5 p.m. but I missed it.
6 All the sheep .... in the field.
7 The manager of the three companies usually .... the workers on Friday.
8 There .... some strange phenomena in the city lately, including UFOs.
9 When they visit our town, the orchestra .... classical and pop music.
10 What .... the criteria for choosing members of the committee?
11 The journalists from the newspaper .... to ask you some questions, sir.
12 The spaghetti .... very good.
13 The new pieces of equipment .... work.
14 Literature .... my favourite subject.

2 **Ⓑ Ⓒ Ⓓ** **Write *a, an, some* in the gaps. Put a cross (X) if none of these are possible.**

0 I need *some* equipment.   00 I don't like *X* soup when the weather is hot.
1 I've got .... good news about the football match.   2 He brought .... heavy luggage
with him.   3 He's done .... good work.   4 Can you lend me .... suitcase – mine is
broken.   5 Did you buy .... shampoo?   6 I like .... travel very much.   7 She
gave me .... piece of useful information.   8 It will be .... fine weather tomorrow.
9 Would you like .... food or drink?   10 This is .... very comfortable
accommodation.   11 The windows are made of .... glass.   12 Waiter! There is ....
long black hair in my soup!   13 This soup needs .... extra salt.   14 Please give me
.... advice.   15 Would you like .... glass of cola?   16 We listened to ....
music last night; .... Spanish orchestra was playing.   17 Add .... milk and ....
litre of water to the mixture.

3 **Ⓒ** **The italicised words are most frequently uncountable. Explain their use as countable nouns in these sentences by writing one of the letters A–C.**

A the word refers to different types/a particular type
B the word refers to objects made from the material or pieces/portions of the material
C this is an unusual technical/professional use of the word

0 This shop sells *cheeses*. A
1 I used three *cloths* to clean the floor. ....
2 I'd like two *sugars* in my tea. ....
3 Please give me three *coffees*. ....
4 This is a special bullet-proof *glass*. ....
5 French and Italian *wines* are the best, I think. ....
6 You should pay the *moneys* to the clerk of the court. ....
7 South American *coffees* are different from African *coffees*. ....

4 **B** **D** Rewrite the sentences using the words in brackets.

0 I'm looking for a place to live in this area.
I'm looking for some accommodation in this area. (*accommodation*)

1 He was carrying a heavy suitcase and a heavy rucksack when I saw him.
.... (*some*)

2 These scissors don't cut very well.
.... (*pair*)

3 She told me three interesting things about the history of Brighton.
.... (*pieces*)

4 My grandmother gave me a helpful suggestion about choosing a wife.
.... (*advice*)

5 Shall we buy a new table and chairs for the living room?
.... (*furniture*)

6 People have gone on journeys since the beginning of civilisation.
.... a part of life since the beginning of civilisation. (*has*)

7 I ate a very good meal at Joseph's house.
.... (*food*)

5 **D** Can you complete these phrases with suitable items from the list? Use a dictionary if necessary. If there is more than one possibility, write both/all. You can use words more than once.

bread   cake   chocolate   cloth   fish   garlic
gold   grass   hair   honey   inspiration   milk   ~~paper~~   ~~plastic~~
sand   shampoo   soap   sugar   toothpaste   veal

0 a sheet of *paper/plastic*   **6** a loaf of ....   **12** a jar of ....
1 a bar of ....   **7** a grain of ....   **13** a stroke of ....
2 a blade of ....   **8** a lump of ....   **14** a carton of ....
3 a tube of ....   **9** a lock of ....   **15** a roll of ....
4 a sachet of ....   **10** a fillet of ....   **16** an ingot of ....
5 a slice of ....   **11** a clove of ....

6 **A**-**D** Here is an exercise from Professor Grammar's English Language Advice Website. Refer back to the theory and Appendix 12 and circle all the correct items. In each case, 0 to 4 items may be correct.

0 A some furnitures	B a furniture	ⓒsome furniture	Ⓓa piece of furniture
1 A some advice	B some advices	C some pieces of advice	D an advice
2 A countries	B countrys	C peoples	D monkeys
3 A some equipment	B an equipment	C equipments	D a equipment
4 A informations	B some informations	C information	D an information
5 A tomatoes	B potatoes	C heros	D volcanoes
6 A feet	B teeth	C geese	D tooths
7 A knives	B wives	C leaves	D thieves
8 A a children	B some children	C the childs	D a child
9 A passers-by	B passer-bys	C parents-in-law	D boyfriends
10 A a sheep	B 100 sheep	C 100 sheeps	D a flock of sheeps
11 A stimuli	B crises	C a crisis	D a stimulus
12 A some news	B the news are	C the news is	D a piece of news

13 **A** to do research **B** to do researches **C** to do a research **D** to do researchs
14 **A** destinations **B** a destination **C** some destination **D** a piece of destination
15 **A** knowledges **B** ideologies **C** ideas **D** theorys

7a Ⓐ-Ⓒ Read this passage about Brighton. Underline all the nouns. Then answer the questions which follow.

Brighton is one of the liveliest towns in the country; in fact, in 2001, it officially became a city, a sign of its <u>vitality</u> and importance. For a long time it has been a popular holiday resort for townspeople, mainly because of its long stretches of beach and its location near the capital. It offers the chance for relaxation and excitement. Its most distinctive building is the Royal Pavilion, built in the style of Indian and Chinese architecture by a prince in the eighteenth century. Inside, the rooms are decorated with expensive materials such as marble and silk. With the evolution of the railways in the nineteenth century, the journey from London became much quicker, increasing Brighton's popularity as a holiday destination. It also has a dolphinarium for the amusement and education of children and adults as well, several streets of small shops known as The Lanes, and hotels which combine elegance with comfort. For more information about Brighton or advice about accommodation and entertainment, ask at one of the local tourist bureaux.

7b List the nouns which are uncountable in this text.

0 vitality
1 ....
2 ....
3 ....
4 ....
5 ....
6 ....
7 ....
8 ....
9 ....
10 ....
11 ....
12 ....
13 ....
14 ....
15 ....
16 ....
17 ....

7c Some of these uncountable nouns can be countable in other contexts. Use them in their plural form to fill the gaps in 1-3.

0 There are many beautiful beaches along the south-west coast of England.
1 Children often play games using ...., small hard round balls of glass.
2 He gave his children good .... at schools and colleges in Switzerland.
3 Blackpool is another famous holiday resort with lots of .... for visitors.

7d Find two examples of plural nouns which don't have the form singular noun + -s.

1 .... 2 ....

OPEN EXERCISE

8 Ⓒ Use these words as both countable and uncountable nouns.

0 exercise I get a lot of exercise at the gym. I did three grammar exercises today.
1 cheese ....
2 education ....
3 glass ....
4 hair ....

UNIT 33 >> Possessive adjectives and pronouns

Sly Sally, the Pickpocket Queen, even stole from **friends of hers** at a party. 'Hey, give me that Rolex, it's **mine**!' 'That wallet isn't **yours**!' 'Stop. Bring back that car. It's **ours**!' Back at **her** flat, Sly Sally looked at the things. 'They were **yours**. But now they're **mine**.'

Ⓐ FORM

Here are examples of the **possessive adjectives** and **possessive pronouns**:

my/mine	It's **my** Rolex!	That Rolex is **mine**!
your/yours	It isn't **your** house.	Is it **yours**? (for **you** singular or plural)
his/his	Is that **his** car?	Yes, it's **his**. (adj. and pronoun have the same form)
her/hers	It's **her** flat.	Everything in it is **hers**.
its*	She stole Myra's dog — this is **its** platinum collar.	
our/ours	She's driving **our** car.	Hey, that's **ours**!
their/theirs	Her friends lost **their** possessions.	These things are **theirs**!
one's*	It's easy to lose **one's** way.	

* There are no equivalent possessive pronouns for **its** and **one**.

Ⓑ POSSESSIVE ADJECTIVES: USE

We often use possessive adjectives:

1 with **parts of the body**: *She cleaned **her** teeth.*   (**Not** ~~She cleaned the teeth~~.)
with our **personal clothes**: *She put on **her** clothes.*   (**Not** ~~She put on the clothes~~.)
But, after a preposition, we prefer to use **the** for the recipient of the action:
*The bullet wounded him **in the** shoulder.* (See Unit 31A)

2 + **own**, to **emphasise ownership**:
*This is **my own** car.* (= I haven't borrowed or hired it; it's mine!)
*They don't live with me; they have a flat of **their own**.*

Remember: we do not generally use **she/her/hers** to refer to countries:
*France has changed **its** foreign policy.* (rarely used: **her** foreign policy)

Ⓒ POSSESSIVE PRONOUNS: USE

We use possessive pronouns to replace **my/your/his/her/our/their + noun**:
*It's **mine**!* (= it's my car/my Rolex/my house etc.)

We often use them with **of**:
*I recognise that diamond. It's **one of mine**.* (= one of my several diamonds)
*She stole from **friends of hers**.* (= from some of her several friends)
*He used to be a **teacher of ours**.* (= one of our several teachers)

We often use them in comparative sentences: *My jewels are **more valuable than yours**.*

Ⓓ ITS/IT'S

Notice the difference between **its** and **it's**:
its = possessive adjective: *The dog ate **its** dinner.*   *I like London, especially **its** shops.*
it's = short form for **it is** or **it has**: *It's hot today.*   *It's been cold since Tuesday.*

Their, **there** and **there** are also different:
Their = of them/**there** = opposite of here/**they're** = they are

1 Ⓐ Ⓑ Put one word in each gap. Use possessive adjectives, *own*, *the*.

0 She's washing *her* hair.

1 I'm not wearing a wig! It's .... hair!

2 The dog recognises members of .... household but attacks strangers.

3 The police shot him in .... leg.

4 Raise .... hand if you want to answer a question.

5 He gave him an injection in .... thigh.

6 I took off .... jacket and prepared to fight.

7 Use .... pens! Stop borrowing mine!

8 Does the hostel provide bedding or do we bring .... sheets?

9 No, I won't lend him a razor. He should buy one of ....

2 Ⓐ - Ⓒ Fill the gaps with *my, mine, your, yours, his, her, hers* etc. Then listen and check your answers.

Slim Skinty hasn't got a house of (0) *his* own. Sometimes (1) .... sister lets him stay in (2) .... house or in a shed of (3) .... in (4) .... garden. Often he sleeps in farmers' fields. When they tell him that the land is (5) ...., he replies: 'The land isn't (6) .... It belongs to us all. It's (7) ....! I may be poor, but I love this life of (8) .... You have (9) .... cars, houses and foreign holidays. But I don't want to change (10) .... life for a middle-class life like (11) ....'

3 Ⓒ Rewrite the second part of each item. Use a pattern with *of* from 33C.

0 You can tell Bob everything. He's one of our friends. *He's a friend of ours.*

1 Do you know them? Are they some of your teachers? ....?

2 I'm always biting my nails. It's one of my habits. ....

3 She can't resist buying new shoes. It's one of her weaknesses. ....

4 I can introduce you to the Prince. He's one of my cousins. ....

5 Do you see those people? They used to be my neighbours. ....

6 Phil doesn't want to meet Pat. She's one of his ex-girlfriends. ....

7 I like doing DIY. It's one of my hobbies. ....

8 We know your parents. We used to be their close friends. ....

9 I hope you like this soup. It's one of my special recipes. ....

10 Of course Molly helped Don. He's one of her old friends. ....

4 Ⓓ Put *it's, its, their, there* or *they're* in the gaps.

0 Look. *It's* snowing.

1 .... are 300 sheep in this field.

2 My friends aren't here – .... out driving in .... car.

3 The farmers said that .... land has decreased in value since 1995.

4 The crocodile opened .... jaws and showed all .... teeth.

5 .... been a long time since I saw my first girlfriend.

6 What I like about Italian food is .... variety.

7 I think this dog is ill. .... lost .... appetite.

8 France and Germany redrew .... frontiers after the war.

9 France is famous for .... wine and cheese.

UNIT 34 >> Possessive 's/s'

 Silvio Copiman is a great painter. Last week an American collector bought one of Silvio's paintings for $10,000,000. But it had Picasso's signature on it. Even the experts' examination didn't show that it was a fake!

Ⓐ ADDING 'S/S' TO SHOW POSSESSION

We use **'s** to show that something belongs to somebody:

singular noun not ending in -s	's	*Silvio's studio my brother's bike*
plural noun ending in -s	'	*The two brothers' house.*
plural noun not ending in -s	's	*The children's toys. The men's changing rooms.*
singular noun ending in -s 1 most names etc. 2 classical Greek and Roman names	's '	*St James's Park/Boris's house* *Sophocles' plays*

'**Whose** car is this?' 'It's Jane's.'   '**Whose** ring did you find?' 'The Princess's.'

Ⓑ OTHER USES OF 'S/S'

We use **'s** to indicate other kinds of relationship, not only possession. For example:

function:	*the women's changing room* (the room for the women)
time:	*three days' holiday a week's rest*
creation:	*Silvio's paintings Shakespeare's plays Einstein's theories*
places:	*Italy's biggest cathedral Britain's finest film*

We can use a **name** + **'s** to refer to someone's **home** or **restaurant** etc.
I stayed at Colin's last night.   We ate at Pepe's.

We also use **'s** in the **names** of **kinds of shop** etc. — *the grocer's, the dentist's* — but in modern usage, we often omit these: *I'm going to the dentist.*

There are other cases where, if the meaning is clear, we can use only the word with **'s**:
It isn't my jacket. It's my wife's. (= my wife's jacket)

Sometimes apostrophes are ambiguous: *My sisters' photo* can mean:
1) a photo which shows my sisters or 2) a photo which belongs to my sisters.

Ⓒ EXPRESSING RELATIONSHIPS BETWEEN NOUNS WITHOUT 'S/S'

1 We don't normally use **'s/s'** when we talk about a relationship between things, and between people and places:
the wing of the aeroplane **Not** ~~the aeroplane's wing~~
the Queen of England   the President of the Republic

2 We often use **noun + noun** for a relationship between things:
*the **city gate*** **Not** ~~the city's gate~~

3 We prefer to use the preposition **of** when there is a long phrase:
*What's the name **of** the teacher at the college with red hair?*

4 We do not use **'s** with **the + adjective** (see Unit 62D):
*the condition **of the poor*** **Not** ~~the poor's condition~~

Ⓓ DOUBLE P5OSSESSIVES AND TWO OR MORE OWNERS

We sometimes use a double possessive: *This is Silvio's wife's cousin.*
For two owners of one thing, we add **'s** to the final name: *Bob and Janet's car.*
But if each own a car, we say: *Bob's and Janet's cars.*

1 Ⓐ Ⓑ Ⓓ **Find 10 more places in the text where you can replace a phrase with an expression using 's or s'. Underline the complete phrase which your expression replaces. Then listen and check your answers.**

> The main enemy of Silvio is Sam Woodison, who edits *Artbreak*. This magazine is the bible for the art collectors. The article by Sam in the issue of last month showed that the paintings in the collections of several famous millionaires are the work of Silvio. All these paintings have the names of famous artists on them. But Sam says that they are worthless. The collectors are the victims of the wife of Silvio. She sells the paintings of her husband in her gallery in the Street of Saint Mark in Boston. Silvio is lucky; the beauty of his wife makes the collectors careless.

0 *Silvio's main enemy*

1	6 ....
2	7 ....
3	8 ....
4	9 ....
5	10 ....

2 Ⓑ Ⓒ **Some of the expressions 1-9 are not usual. Replace them with a compound noun (noun + noun). Put a tick next to the expressions that need not be replaced.**

0 the church's tower *the church tower*
1 the computer's keyboard ....
2 the class's register ....
3 the artist's talent ....
4 the millionaire's mistake ....
5 the plant's pot ....
6 the car's seat ....
7 the garden's pond ....
8 a shop's assistant ....
9 the books' shelf ....

3 Ⓐ Ⓑ Ⓓ **write these sentences using 's or s'.**

0 I visited the birthplace of Charles Darwin. *I visited Charles Darwin's birthplace.*
1 She wore the dress of her sister to the dance. ....
2 He stole the girlfriend of his best friend. ....
3 The room of the children is quite large. ....
4 I've lost the e-mail address of Mr Jones. ....
5 The birthday of Elaine is April 20th. ....
6 What's the name of the wife of the friend of Bill? ....?
7 The new CD by the Metalheads is great! ....
8 I borrowed the car of George and Martha. ....
9 The sister of Ben went inside the cage of the gorillas. ....
10 The problems of the company of Nick and Jill are serious. ....
11 The dog of my brothers is black and white. ....

UNIT 35 >> *Some, any, no*

 Guy is asking Will **some** questions about his holiday.
'Did you meet **any** beautiful girls? Did you drive **any** fast cars?'
'No, but I read **some** good books. **Some** people don't waste their time like you.'
'Well, I bet you had **no** fun.'

Ⓐ SOME, ANY, NO

We use **some** (positive) or **any** (with **negative** verbs and **questions**) or **no** (= not) with:

1 **plural nouns**: *He went out with **some** local **girls**.   Have you seen **any** handsome **boys**?*
*Will has **no girlfriends**. = Will hasn't got **any girlfriends**.*

2 or **uncountable nouns**: *He drank **some** fruit **juice**.   Has he found **any treasure**?*
*Will didn't drink **any alcohol**. = Will drank **no alcohol**.*

We also use **any** in sentences with negative words such as **never, hardly, without**:
*He's got **hardly any** friends.*   *She did it **without any** help.*

Ⓑ ANY IN OPEN QUESTIONS

We frequently use **any** in open questions:
*Did you meet **any** famous people?*   *Have you got **any** photos?*

But we usually use **some** in questions if:

1 we are **offering something**: *Would you like **some** biscuits?*
2 we are **asking for something**: *Can you give me **some** tickets, please.*
3 we **expect** the answer 'yes': *Did you buy **some** tickets?* (I expect that you bought some)

Ⓒ SOME, ANY AND NONE WITHOUT A NOUN

We can use **some** and **any** without a noun if the meaning is clear:
*He didn't give any sweets to Jenny but he gave me **some**. He didn't give Billy **any**.*

We use **none** (a pronoun) to replace **no + noun** if the meaning is clear:
*He gave **none** to Billy. (= no sweets)*

Ⓓ ANY FOR UNRESTRICTED CHOICE

We can use **any** in positive sentences when **any** means that it doesn't matter which:
*Visit me at **any** time.*   (= the time is not important)
*Choose **any** number* between 1 and 5.*   (= Choose 1 or 2 or 3 or 4 or 5.)
*Notice: in this meaning we can use **any + singular noun**.

Ⓔ COMMON USES OF SOME, ANY, NO, NONE

1 If we want to talk about the remaining quantity of something, we use **some left**, **any left, none left, no + noun + left**: *There's **some** soup **left**. Do you want **some more**?*
*Is there **any** coffee **left**? Sorry, there's **none left**. = There isn't **any left**.*

2 We use the expressions *It's **no good**./It isn't **any good*** to mean that the situation is hopeless. ***It's no good.** I can't do this exam.*

3 We often use **any longer/no longer**: *I can't stay awake **any longer**. = I can **no longer** stay awake.*
Notice: that **any longer** usually goes at the end of the clause.
No longer usually goes before the main verb (or after forms of **be**).

4 We often use **just any** with a derogatory meaning: *She doesn't want to see **just any** film.*

Ⓕ STRESSED SOME AND ANY

If we <u>stress</u> **some** or **any** when we are speaking, we suggest some kind of limitation:
*He has <u>**some**</u> friends.* (but not enough)   *I don't kiss just <u>**any**</u> boy!* (= I choose carefully)

1 **A**-**D** Fill the gaps with *some, any* or *no* as appropriate. Then listen and check your answers.

Will: I had (0) *some* good conversations with local islanders.

Guy: Did you find (1) .... good beaches? And I'm sure you visited (2) .... exciting nightclubs.

Will: No, I didn't go to (3) .... But I had (4) .... long games of chess with (5) .... old men in the village square. I didn't win (6) .... They were better than (7) .... player I've ever met.

Guy: Did you buy (8) .... designer clothes?

Will: No, there weren't (9) .... Western stores. There were only (10) .... local shops where you could buy (11) .... kind of tropical fruit that you wanted. I bought (12) .... every day.

Guy: So there were (13) .... girls, (14) .... parties and (15) .... fun. How boring! Poor Will!

Will: But I found (16) .... treasure on the island and now I'm a millionaire. So I don't need (17) .... sympathy from you.

2 **A**-**E** Fill the gaps in 1-10 with *some, any, no* or *none*.

0 'Please, give me *some* water – I'm dying of thirst.'

1 'I've got hardly .... money. Could you lend me ....?' 'Yes, of course I'll lend you .... But there's .... in my wallet. I'll get .... from upstairs.'

2 I'm free all next week. I can meet you on .... day.

3 I can't make .... sandwiches. There's .... bread left.

4 I don't like all Mozart operas but I like ....

5 'Would you like .... vodka?' 'No. I'm a teetotaller – that means I drink .... alcohol.'

6 I passed a whole week without doing .... work.

7 There's .... time left – we can't finish the work now.

8 'Could you give me .... leaflets about the festival?' 'No, I'm sorry, there are .... left. But they're printing .... new ones. I'll have .... next week.' 'That's .... good. I need them today.'

3 **E** Write sentences using *just any*.

0 She only buys designer handbags. *She doesn't buy just any handbag.*

1 He only goes to the best parties. ....

2 She only buys top quality meat. ....

3 I'm very careful about the TV programmes I watch. ....

4 He published his stories in the most exclusive magazines. ....

5 The lawyer only chooses certain cases. ....

4 **E** Use patterns with *some, any* or *no* to write sentences based on 1-10.

0 John has no special preference in books. *John reads any books.* (*reads*)

1 They've eaten all the ice cream. .... (*There/no*)

2 Tim likes the 7th and the 9th but no other Beethoven symphonies. .... (*some*)

3 I don't care which city I visit tomorrow .... (*ready to visit*)

4 It's hopeless. Marianne will never phone me. .... (*good*)

5 She chooses her clothes very carefully. .... (*doesn't buy*)

6 He is not a student at this university now. .... (*longer*)

UNIT 36 >> *Something, anything, nothing* etc.

 Ken sent this message to his girlfriend:
'Darling, I love you so much! I'll do **anything** for you. I'll go **anywhere** just to be with you. There's **nothing** that can keep us apart!'
But she replied: 'Sorry, I'm not in love with you any longer. Goodbye!'

Ⓐ WORDS BEGINNING *SOME-*, *ANY-* AND *NO-*

for things:	something	anything	nothing
for people:	somebody or someone*	anybody or anyone*	nobody or no one*
for places:	somewhere	anywhere	nowhere

* These words with **-body** and **-one** have the same meaning.
These words follow the same rules as **some**, **any**, **no**.

Remember: we say ***go anywhere*** not ~~go to anywhere~~.

*I can hear **something**.*
*The robbers are hiding **somewhere**.*

***Somebody** has robbed the bank.*
*Would you like **something** to eat?*

*I can't see **anything**. Turn on the light!*
*I didn't meet **anyone** at the disco.*

*Did you go **anywhere** last weekend?*

***Nobody** is wrong.*
*We went **nowhere** last weekend.*

***Nobody** visited her in hospital.*

Ⓑ *ANY* FOR UNRESTRICTED CHOICE

We use **anyone/anything/anywhere**: to say it doesn't matter who, where etc.

*I'll do **anything** you want.*	(= it doesn't matter which thing)
*It's easy! **Anyone** can do it.*	(= it doesn't matter which person)
*I will go **anywhere**.*	(= I'll go to London or New York or Paris etc.)

In a negative sentence we often use, ***just anyone*** etc., often with a derogatory meaning:
*I don't want to stay **just** anywhere.* = Where I stay is important.

Ⓒ COMMON STRUCTURES WITH *SOME-*, *ANY-* AND *NO-* WORDS

1 We can use **else** after **someone**, **anything** etc.

   *John was in the park but I saw **no one else**.* (= I saw only John)
   *Would you like **anything else**?*

2 We can use **something**, **nobody**, **anywhere** etc. with an **adjective**:

   *I gave her **something nice**.*
   *She did **nothing wrong**.*
   *Have you been **anywhere interesting**?*

3 We can use **something**, **nobody**, **anywhere** etc. + **to** + **verb**:

   *I want **something to drink**.*
   *He's got **nothing to do**.*

1 **A**-**C** Here are some of the problems which TROUBLE-BUSTERS have to deal with. Fill the gaps with *some-*, *any-* or *no-* words. Then listen and check your answers.

> **TROUBLE-BUSTERS Incorporated**
>
> Is somebody making you unhappy? Is there nowhere for you to escape your problems? Is something else on your mind? Stop worrying. We can help anyone! Anytime! Anywhere! Call us for free advice.

A (0) *Someone* is following me. I don't know why. I haven't done (1) .... wrong. But a man in dark glasses in a long black coat is always behind me (2) .... that I go. The police say that they can't do (3) .... Help me, please.

B I haven't got (4) .... to talk to. (5) .... has phoned me all week. I'm really lonely. I don't go (6) .... in the evenings because I'm too shy. Is there (7) .... which you can do to help me?

C I wanted to go (8) .... exciting, so I booked a holiday in Egypt with a travel company. But at the airport, the airline told me that (9) .... had reserved a ticket for me. So I went (10) .... I don't know (11) .... who can help me.

D My life is completely boring. There isn't (12) .... good in my life. There's (13) .... in this town to go in the evenings. I do (14) ...., go (15) ...., meet (16) .... Please give me some ideas.

2 **A**-**C** Fill the gaps with a *some-*, *any-* or *no-* word plus *to* + verb.

0 Is there *anywhere to go* in your town in the evenings? (*go*)
1 I'm very tired. I've got .... me look after the house. (*help*)
2 I need to buy .... her for her birthday. (*give*)
3 I can't find .... me how to operate this machine. (*show*)
4 The market has closed down. There's .... fresh food in the town. (*buy*)
5 I need to go .... during the next few weeks. (*relax*)
6 I haven't found .... the tap. Can you recommend a plumber? (*fix*)
7 There isn't .... in the shops – they've sold everything! (*buy*)

3 **A**-**C** There are 10 more places in this text where you can replace a phrase with a *some-*, *any-* or *no-* word. In one case use *else* with the word. Underline the exact phrases and write the words in order below.

> Matt has been <u>to a place</u> every night for the last week. He always finds a person to dance with or to have dinner with. But tonight he is going out with a person who is very special. Her name is Fiona. He thinks no other person is as beautiful and kind. She says that she will go to all kinds of places and that she will eat all kinds of food. But Matt thinks that there is no place in his town which is good enough for a person like her. Can any of the people here give him some advice? Do you know a place he can take her? He will go to any place in the world just to please her.

0 *somewhere*	3	6	9 ....
1	4	7	10 ....
2	5	8	

UNIT 37 >> *A lot of, lots of, much, many* (1)

 It's Bob McGive's 50th birthday and there are **lots of** reporters at his house in Scotland. 'How **many** mansions have you got? How **much** money do you spend each year? Do you have **a lot of** beautiful girlfriends? Is there **much** gold in your private vaults?'

Ⓐ USES WITH NOUNS

a lot of/lots of (with plural or uncountable in all sentences)	many (with plural nouns in negative sentences and questions)	much (with uncountable in negative sentences and questions)
*I have **a lot of** friends.* *I haven't got **a lot of** food.* *Have you got **a lot of** money?*	*I haven't got **many** friends.* *Have you got **many** books?*	*I haven't got **much** food* *Has she got **much** money?*

Ⓑ FORMAL AND INFORMAL CONTEXTS

We can use **many** in positive sentences but in informal spoken English we prefer to use **a lot of/lots of**.

*I know **a lot of/lots of** people.* (spoken English)
*I have visited **many** countries in Europe.* (more formal English)

We use **lots of** only in very informal situations:

*Did you get **lots of** things in the sales, Kate?* *There are **lots of** night clubs around here.*

In very formal situations, we find **much** in positive sentences:
*There was **much** confusion about the new plan.* (very formal)

Ⓒ *HOW MUCH/HOW MANY* IN QUESTIONS

We use **How much...?** and **How many...?** to ask **questions about quantity**:

***How much** cheese did you buy?* (uncountable) ***How many** biscuits have you eaten?* (plural)

We can use **How much...?** or **How many...?** without a noun if the meaning is clear:
***How much** do you earn?* *Did you like the plums? **How many** have you eaten?*

Ⓓ ALTERNATIVE PHRASES

There are other phrases which we use in a similar way to **a lot of**:

a (great/large/small) number of + plural noun: *I've got **a number of paintings**.*
a (great/large/small) amount of + uncountable noun: *She ate **a huge amount of food**.*
plenty of* + plural *or* uncountable noun: *I had **plenty of friends/plenty of food**.*
a great deal of + uncountable noun: *It caused me **a great deal of worry**.*

* we often use **plenty of** to mean a **sufficient number/amount**:
  *Don't worry — we've got **plenty of** fuel for the winter.*

Ⓔ *A LOT, LOTS, MUCH, MANY* WITHOUT A NOUN

We can use **a lot/lots/much/many** without a noun if the meaning is clear:
*'Did he spend a lot of money?' 'No, not **much**.' or 'Yes, **a lot**.'* (**Not** ~~Yes, much.~~)
*'Were there many people there?' 'No, not **many**.' or 'Yes, **lots**.'* (**Not** usually Yes, many.)
*'I met a lot of tourists at the party.' 'Did you meet **many**?'* (= ... meet many tourists?)

1 **A C** The journalists are questioning Sebastian Ace. Fill the gaps. Choose *much* or *many* for questions and negatives. In other cases use *a lot (of)*. Then listen and check your answers.

How (0) much information can you give us about your life as a spy? How (1) .... secret missions have you carried out? Have you killed (2) .... enemy spies? Is there (3) .... danger that your enemies still want to kill you? Did you receive (4) .... help from the CIA? How (5) .... time did it take to train to be a spy? How (6) .... times have you fallen in love with an enemy spy? There are (7) .... stories about you. How (8) .... of the legend is true? All I can tell you is that I've listened to (9) .... questions and now I want to sleep.

2 **A C D** Rewrite the sentences using the word in brackets.

0 Can you tell me the number of tourists who visit your country each year?
   How many tourists visit your county each year? (*how*)

1 Modern cities produce tons and tons of rubbish every day.
   .... (*amount*)

2 What is the salary for teachers in your country?
   .... in your country? (*much*)

3 A great number of people visit the Glastonbury Festival every year.
   .... (*many*)

4 There were a lot of swimmers who wanted to take part in the gala.
   .... (*plenty*)

5 Do you need a lot of equipment for the concert or a little?
   .... (*how*)

3 **B D** Which is more likely? Choose the suitable alternative.

0 From an e-mail to your friend: I hope we have much/(lots of) good weather this summer.

1 From a conversation with a bishop: Is there still **lots of/a great deal of** opposition to women priests?

2 From a report in the *Times*: **Many/Lots of** teachers disapprove of the government's education policy.

3 From a chat with your friend: I've got **many/lots of/a great number of** new CDs.

4 From a speech in Parliament: This could lead to the solution of **many/lots of** economic problems.

5 From a speech in Parliament: There has been **much/many/lots of** controversy about the legalisation of drugs.

4 **E** Shorten these items by crossing out any words which can be omitted.

0 'Did you get a lot of e-mails from your friends over the summer?' 'No, I didn't get many e-mails.'

1 I have some problems with learning new computer skills but my friends don't have a lot of problems.

2 The homework was easy. There wasn't much work to do.

3 Were you hungry? You've eaten a lot of food.

4 'Have you visited many Web-sites today?' 'No, not many Web-sites.'

5 There hasn't been much bad weather this month but there'll be a lot of bad weather in the winter.

6 He doesn't know much information about his own home-town.

A lot of, lots of, much, many (1)

101

UNIT 38 >> *A lot of, lots of, much, many (2)*

@ Mrs Bagmouth likes gossip **very much**. She likes watching soap operas on TV **very much** but it's **a great deal** more interesting to spy on her neighbours.

Ⓐ *A LOT, LOTS, MUCH, VERY MUCH* AS ADVERBS

- We can use **a lot/lots of/very much/many** as **adverbs** in questions, affirmative and negative sentences. They are often placed at the **end of the clause**:
  *I like England **very much/a lot**.*   *Have you played cricket **a lot/very much**?*
  *I don't go to the cinema **very much/a lot/a great deal** as I prefer the theatre.*
  Notice: that **very much** often occurs with verbs such as **like, love, want**:
  *They **want** to go to the circus **very much** but they can't.*
  Notice: We use **much** in questions and negatives but **not** in affirmative sentences:
  *You haven't spoken **much** today.*   *Have you travelled **much**?* Not ~~I like Italy much~~.
  We can use **lots** in affirmatives and questions but only in very informal situations:
  *I've travelled **lots**.* (very informal)   *Have you worked **lots** today?*
- We use them in **short answers**: *'Did you enjoy the film?' 'Yes, **a lot/lots/very much**.'*
  *'Do you like her?' 'No, **not a lot/not much/not very much**.'*
- In formal English, **(very) much** can come before some verbs expressing enjoyment, such as **prefer/enjoy/appreciate**: *I **much prefer** Picasso's art to Matisse's.*
  With **like/dislike**, this is only possible in **negative sentences** or after **very**:
  *They **very much disliked** the exhibition.*   *I **didn't much like** her wedding dress.*

Ⓑ MODIFYING COMPARATIVES

We can use **much, very much, a lot** and **a great deal** with comparatives (see Unit 67):
*I spent **a lot more** money this week.*   *He's **much shorter** than his sister.*
But we use **very** in front of adjectives and adverbs:
*He is **very intelligent**. (**Not** ... ~~much intelligent~~.)*   *She drove **very fast**.*

Ⓒ MODIFYING *MUCH, MANY, A LOT*

We can use **too, so, as, very** in front of **much** or **many**:
*He's eaten **too much** chocolate.*   *There's **so much** noise that I can't study.*
*I want **as many** sweets as she's got.*   *There aren't **very many** people here.*
We also use:

a great many + plural noun:	*I've got **a great many friends** in London.*
quite or **rather** + **a lot** :	*He earns **rather a lot/quite a lot** of money.*
much or **far** or **rather** + too much/too many:	*She's eating **much too much** ice cream.*
	*There are **rather too many** people.*
much + **too** + adjective:	*That bed is **much too small**.*

Ⓓ *MUCH/MANY + OF*

We use **much of** or **many of** before determiners (e.g. **a/the/this/his**) and before pronouns:
***Many of the** students have gone home.*   *How **much of the** castle did you visit?*
*I saw the film but I didn't enjoy **much of it**.*

Ⓔ *OTHER USES*

There are certain idioms which use **a lot** or **much**. For example:
- **not to be much of**: *He **isn't much of** a dancer.* (= He isn't a good dancer.)
- **to see a lot of/not to see much of**: *I haven't **seen much of** her recently.* (= I haven't met her...)
- **to think a lot of/not to think much of**: *The boss **thinks a lot of** her.* (= He values her.)
We also use **much + else** in negative sentences or questions: *I didn't like **much else**.*

1 Ⓐ Read the text and find 9 more places where you can use *a lot (of), many, much* instead of existing phrases. Underline the exact phrase that you are replacing and write the necessary words in the order in which you would use them.

'I give <u>hundreds of thousands of pounds</u> to charity each year. I don't spend a big amount on myself. I have hundreds of friends but no girlfriends; I've been happily married for a great number of years. Yes, I have a large amount of wealth but I think about other people a great deal and try to help them. A number of rich people believe that the rest of society has a great number of problems and that money can't do a great deal to help. But, in my view, that's not right. So, is there a larger amount of information you want or is that enough?'

0	*a lot of money*	5	....
1	....	6	....
2	....	7	....
3	....	8	....
4	....	9	....

2 Ⓑ Write sentences whichs use the word(s) in brackets and a comparative adjective or adverb.

0 My suitcase weighs 60 kilos but yours weighs 250. (*a great deal*)
My suitcase is a lighter deal heavier than yours.

1 Sam is 1 metre 55 centimetres tall but his sister is 1 metre 75. (*much*)
Sam ....

2 Her handbag cost £45 but mine cost £250. (*very much*)
My handbag ....

3 My brother has an intelligence quota of 120 but I have one of 180. (*much*)
I ....

4 12 accidents occurred on the valley road and 56 on the mountain road last year. (*a great deal*)
The mountain road ....

5 Tom is sometimes rude but Graham behaves extremely politely. (*a lot*)
Graham ....

3 Ⓐ Ⓒ Ⓓ Ⓔ Fill each gap with one word. Then listen and check your answers.

0 Nobody likes Mrs Bagmouth very much.

1 Mrs Bagmouth doesn't think .... of her neighbours.

2 She has made a great .... enemies because she gossips far .... much.

3 .... of her neighbours refuse to speak to her .... of the time.

4 They would .... appreciate it if she stopped gossiping.

5 'Mr Black isn't .... of a gardener,' she told me. 'His garden is .... too untidy!'

6 'Mrs Smith can't cook. She puts .... too .... salt in her food.'

7 'I like Miss Brown a great .... What a shame that she is .... too ugly to find a boyfriend.'

8 'Mrs Brown can cook but she can't do much .... She has no other skills.'

9 'I don't .... like Miss Green's fashion sense. .... of her clothes are so .... out of date that a dinosaur wouldn't wear them!'

10 'Miss White eats .... too .... sweets. She's .... too fat.'

UNIT 39 >> A few, few, a little, little

 In 1995, **a few** people came to the Metalheads's first concert and they earned **a little** money. They were very happy. It was a good beginning. Last Saturday, **few** people came to see the Metalheads' final concert and they earned **little** money. They were very miserable. It was a sad ending.

Ⓐ SUMMARY OF USES OF *A LITTLE, LITTLE, A FEW, FEW*

A few/a little have a **positive** idea. **Few/little** have a **negative** idea:

He has **a few friends**.	(some – plural noun/positive idea)	He often visits them.
He has **few friends**.	(not many – plural noun/negative idea)	He is lonely and unhappy.
He has **a little money**.	(some – uncountable/positive idea)	He can buy a magazine.
He has **little money**.	(not much – uncountable/negative idea)	He can't buy enough food.

The use of **few/little** is rather formal; in everyday English, we tend to use **not many** or **not much**: *I have **few** friends.* (formal)   *I have**n't** got **many** friends.* (more common)

Ⓑ NEGATIVE AND POSITIVE SENSES

We also use **only a few/only a little** in everyday English. This gives a **negative sense**:
*I have **only a little** money. Help me.*   *She's got **only a few** books. Lend her some.*

When we use **quite a few**, this emphasises the **positive sense**:
*I have **quite a few** friends.* (= many)

Ⓒ USING *A FEW, A LITTLE* WITHOUT A NOUN

We can use **a few** and **a little** without a noun if the meaning is clear, for example in short answers: *Have you seen many plays by Shakespeare?*   *Yes, **a few**.*
Did you buy any cheese?   *Yes, **a little**.*

We can use **a little** as an adverb at the end of a clause with words such as **like, enjoy**:
*I liked the film **a little**.*

Ⓓ *A LITTLE, A FEW* WITH ADJECTIVES AND COMPARATIVES

We can use **a little** with a negative adjective or a comparative word:
*He is **a little** sad today.*   (**Not** *a little happy*)
*She is **a little** stupid.*   (**Not** *a little intelligent*)
*He ran **a little faster** than before.*   *There is **a little more** ice cream.*

We can use **a few** with **more**: ***A few more** people came to the party than I expected.*

There are some adjectives using **little** and a **past participle**, for example:
*It is a **little known** fact that male sea horses give birth.*
*The word 'lugubrious' is **little used** nowadays.*

Ⓔ *A FEW/FEW/A LITTLE/LITTLE + OF*

We use **a few of/few of…** and, less commonly, **a little of/little of…**, followed by **the, my, this** etc:
***A few of the** protesters caused trouble.*   (= a small number of them all)
*We gave **a little of the** cake to our friends.*   (= a small amount of the whole)
*I understood **little of what** she was saying.*   (= I didn't understand much)

1 **A** **B** **E** Fill the gaps with *a few, few, a little* or *little*. In some cases you also need to add *of*.

0 Joe Sutton has won *few* big fights in his boxing career. The media have paid little attention to him. He is rather sad about this.

1 Myra has won .... Oscars and has had .... success in the theatre as well as starring in many films. She thinks she has had a great career.

2 However, ... film directors want to work with Myra. She has walked out on a film quite .... times. She is a difficult person to work with.

3 .... criminals have escaped from Inspector Baxter. He has received quite .... medals for his efficiency. Well done, Inspector!

4 Only .... models earn more than Claudette. She has put on .... weight but she is still very slim.

5 Kevin Scoremore has scored .... goals this season. There is .... doubt that this is one of his most unsuccessful seasons.

6 Nick and Jill own .... companies. Most of them make .... profit, so they are not rich. But with .... luck, they may be rich soon!

7 Harry has robbed quite .... banks. But he needs to be .... more careful – the police have arrested him many times.

8 Sly Sally has stolen quite .... things from houses in her street with the result that .... her neighbours have asked the police to make her move. Sally has offered to return .... what she has stolen but it is not enough.

9 .... what Mrs Bagmouth gossips about is based on fact but .... her stories are completely accurate, I regret to say.

2 **C** Write answers to these questions, using *a few* or *a little*.

0 Have you visited all the countries in Europe? No, but I've visited a few.

1 Did she drink all the cola? No, but ....

2 Did he need a lot of equipment? No, but ....

3 Will you do all the exercises? No, but ....

4 Have you done all the washing up? No, but ....

5 Have you written all the Christmas cards? No, but ....

3 **A** **B** **D** There are 10 more phrases in the text which can be replaced by *few/a few/little* or *a little*. Underline the exact phrases and write the words in the order in which they occur below the text.

Not enough people came to the Metalheads' last concert. But a small number of fans waited for them after the show and wanted their autographs. It made them slightly happier. After all, there are not a lot of bands who stay together for more than a small number of years. They have had a small number of number one songs and there are not many people who don't possess a Metalheads CD. It's slightly sad that the band are breaking up. All they needed was a small amount of luck but, instead, there were a small number of unfortunate incidents – their record company went bankrupt and their manager died! Not many bands have had such bad luck!

0 Few   **2** ....   **4** ....   **6** ....   **8** ....   **10** ....

1 ....   **3** ....   **5** ....   **7** ....   **9** ....

UNIT 40 >> Reflexive and reciprocal pronouns

 I've got a great idea for a play. I thought of it **myself.** First, there are the members of two families who hate **one another.** Second, a girl and a boy from opposing families fall in love with **each other.** Then, they're separated from **each other.** Finally, they kill **themselves.** Isn't it an original idea?

Ⓐ USE

We use reflexive pronouns (**myself, yourself, himself/herself/itself/oneself,* ourselves, yourselves, themselves**) when the **subject** and **object** are the **same person**:
*I cut **myself.***   *He looked at **himself.***   *You (plural) should please **yourselves.***

* We only use **one/one's/oneself** in quite formal English.

But we also use reflexive pronouns in sentences like these:
His book** is about **himself.   ***Mirrors** show us **ourselves** as others see us.*

Ⓑ EMPHASISING INDEPENDENT ACTION BY USING REFLEXIVES

We use **verb + myself, yourself, himself** etc. **+ object** when **we do something for ourselves:** *She washed **herself** an apple.* (= *She washed an apple **for herself.***)

We use **verb + object + myself, yourself, himself etc.** when we want to make it clear that **another person didn't do it:**
*I cooked dinner **myself.*** (= My mother/friend etc. didn't cook dinner)

We use **by + myself, yourself, himself** etc. when we do something **without help:**
                 *I cooked dinner **by myself.*** (= without help)
or when **we are alone:** *She was sitting **by herself.*** (= alone, with nobody)

Ⓒ DIFFERENCES IN THE USE OF REFLEXIVE PRONOUNS IN ENGLISH

Often verbs which are reflexive in many other languages are not reflexive in English.
They met each other in the town.   **Not** ~~They met themselves.~~
They married each other.   **Not** ~~They married themselves.~~

Other examples include: **shave, shower, dress, feel, hurry, meet, open, relax, stop.**

You can often use expressions with **get** to translate reflexive verbs in these languages, e.g. **get... bored, dressed, lost, married, ready, rich, used to** (see Unit 81), **upset, wet.**

Ⓓ COMMON EXPRESSIONS WITH REFLEXIVES

behave yourself = behave well
help yourself = serve yourself
enjoy yourself = have fun
make yourself at home = feel comfortable when you are a guest
do it yourself = doing your own household repairs etc. *Many British people enjoy* **DIY.**
Other expressions use **self-**, e.g.: **a self-**taught student = (s)he has taught him/herself

Ⓔ RECIPROCAL PRONOUNS — *EACH OTHER, ONE ANOTHER*

We use the reciprocal pronoun **each other** when the action is **between two people/things**, not reflexive: *They kissed **each other.***   *He connected the computers to **each other.***
For more than two people/things, we use **one another:**
*The team shook hands with **one another.***   *A corridor joins all the rooms to **one another.***
Notice the difference between **reciprocal** and **reflexive pronouns.**
*Romeo and Juliet killed **themselves.***   (= They each committed suicide)
*Romeo and Juliet killed **each other.***   (= Romeo killed Juliet and she killed him)

1 Ⓐ Ⓔ Here are two more ideas for plays. Do you recognise the stories? Fill the gaps with *-self/-selves, each other* or *one another.*

A Three witches meet **(0)** *one another* in the mist and make a prophecy. As a result, a man and his wife encourage **(1)** .... to kill the King. The wife goes mad because she hates **(2)** .... The man's friends abandon him because they want to save **(3)** .... The man and the King's friend fight **(4)** .... The man dies.

B A prince and his uncle hate **(5)** .... Then the ghost of the prince's father shows **(6)** .... to the prince. 'Your uncle killed me!' The prince blames **(7)** .... for not taking revenge. Finally, the whole family dies because they've all poisoned or stabbed **(8)** ....

2 Ⓐ Ⓑ Ⓓ Rewrite these sentences using verb + *myself, yourself, himself* etc.

0 She cut her finger with the bread knife. *She cut herself with the bread knife.*

1 He had a good time at the party. .... at the party.

2 The sick man couldn't put his clothes on without help.
....

3 They looked at their reflections in the mirror.
....

4 He pulled the trigger and the bullet went in his own foot.
.... in the foot. (use a form of *shoot*)

5 Did you all have a good time at the beach?
....?

6 It's not good to feel guilty.
One shouldn't .... (*blame*)

7 Relax – you're my guests.
.... at home.

8 Young children often behave badly when there are no adults to control them.
.... (*don't*)

3 Ⓐ-Ⓔ Choose the correct alternative.

0 After the match, they showered **themselves/their selves/–/theirselves.**

1 The five friends congratulated **one another/each other/them/–.**

2 The dog cut **it's self/it'self/itselves/itself** on some broken glass.

3 Nobody helped us. We did it **our self/weselves/ourselves/by our self.**

4 She really enjoyed **–/herself/her self/with me** at the match.

5 The twins agreed to meet **themselves/each other/one another/with themselves** after they'd finished classes.

6 Uncle Joe is so ill that he can't feed **himself/him self/his self/by himself.**

7 We were afraid to be **by ourselves/ourselves/our self/by ourself** in the darkness.

8 I cooked **myself/myself dinner/each other dinner/themselves dinner.**

9 The class was so long that I **got bored/bored myself/bored self/bored.**

10 He's a **self-taught/self-made/self/self-done** man. He **riched/enriched himself/got rich/riched himself** without any help.

UNIT **41** >> *Each, every, none, all, most, some, both*

Buy our second-hand cars. **Every** kind of car is in our showrooms, from family saloons to jeeps. **Each** one is a bargain. **All** of our cars have new engines and fresh paintwork. **None** of our cars has a hidden problem. **All** our customers are happy. We're open **every** weekday and **most** Sundays.

Ⓐ SUMMARY OF THE USES OF *EACH*, *EVERY* ETC.

quantifier	+ singular noun	+ plural noun	+ uncountable noun	+ of the/ of my etc.	+ the
each	✓			✓	
every	✓				
none				✓	
all		✓	✓	✓	✓
most/some		✓	✓	✓	
both		✓		✓	✓

Each car is perfect. We tested **each of the** cars.*
Every kind of car is* in our showrooms.   ⎫
None of the cars has* a problem.   ⎬ * **each**, **every** and **none** with singular verb
                                              ⎭

All drivers must pass a test.   *All advertising is dishonest.*
All of the cars/All the cars are safe.
Most/Some cars are dangerous.   *Most/Some petrol is unleaded.*
Most/Some of our cars have airbags.
Both twins/Both of the twins/Both the twins bought a car. (same meaning)

Ⓑ EVERY

1 We use **every** when we are thinking of **all the people/items together**. We use **every** for **3 or more things**.
   We use **each** when we are thinking of **each person/item individually**. We are more likely to use **each** with small groups: *He has three brothers and I met **each** one.*

2 There are four pronouns which begin **every-**: **everything**, **everybody** and **everyone**, **everywhere**. In subject position, they go with singular verbs.
   Everything is all right.   *Everyone likes her.*   *Everywhere is closed.*

3 In most cases, we cannot use **all** instead of **every-** pronouns:
   Everything's OK. **Not** ~~All is OK.~~   *I like everybody in school.* **Not** ~~I like all...~~

4 No preposition is necessary with **everywhere**: *I've been everywhere.* **Not** ~~to everywhere.~~

5 We often use expressions like: **every day/every week/every year** etc.
   Compare: *I worked all day.* (from 9 till 5)   *I worked every day.* (Monday to Friday)
   Everyday (as one word) is used as an adjective: *She has everyday problems.*

6 We can combine **every** and **few**: *They go on holiday every few weeks.*

Ⓒ POSITION OF *EACH*

We can use **each** in mid-position in a sentence with a plural verb:
They have each received a present. (**or** *Each of them has...*)

We can place **each** after the object of a verb:
She gave them each a kiss. (**or** *... gave each of them...*)

1 Ⓐ **Rewrite these sentences, using the word(s) in brackets.**

0 Every washing machine in our shop has a year's guarantee.
All of the washing machines in our shop have a year's guarantee. (*all of*)

1 There are no machines in the shop which have out-of-date parts.
.... (*has*)

2 There are no modern washing powders which damage your clothes.
.... safe for your clothes. (*every*)

3 Our second-hand books are almost all in good condition.
.... (*most*)

4 All of our books have special plastic covers.
.... (*each of*)

5 In each of our two shops you can buy specially signed copies by the author.
.... specially signed copies by the author. (*of/sell*)

6 The Krazy Kat night club gives free drinks to all its clients.
.... free drinks at the Krazy Kat. (*client*)

7 The dancing girls do not perform in any other club.
.... (*none*)

8 There is a 100% customer satisfaction rate.
.... are satisfied. (*of*)

2 Ⓐ - Ⓒ **Find the correct answers. More than one may be possible.**

0 All things/Every things/Everything/All in the shop is second-hand.

1 Most people/Most the people/Most of people/Mostly person like me.

2 They looked at everywhere/everywhere/in everywhere/all the places for her.

3 Both his/Both of/Both this/Both of his parents are teachers.

4 The robbers stole all/everything/every things/each thing in the room.

5 He loves all of animals/every animal/each animal/most the animals in the zoo.

6 Does everybody/Do everybody/Does everyone/Do all want a drink?

7 At the office yesterday, all computers/every computers/none computers/all the computers broke down.

8 They each/Every student/Each student/All the students receives a report.

9 In formal English, we say: 'none of the books is/are/was/were interesting.'

10 They each chooses/They each choose/Each of them choose/Each of them chooses a CD.

11 I'm so tired – I've been working every days/all day/all days/everyday.

3 Ⓐ - Ⓒ **Reformulate the sentences, using the words in brackets.**

0 All of the models at the fashion show are famous. (*Every*)
Every model at the fashion show is famous.

1 Every designer has a new style. (*Each of*) ....

2 All the fashion magazines have sent a journalist to the show. (*Every*) ....

3 All the people in the audience are celebrities. (*Each*) ....

4 The designers work hard from Monday to Sunday. (*day*) ....

5 All the people want to wear designer clothes. (*Everyone*) ....

6 The fashion models are all beautiful. (*None/ugly*) ....

UNIT 42 >> *Both, either, neither*

> **Both** Bob McGive and Slim Skinty went to the village school. **Neither** of them did well in their exams. They had to choose **either** to work hard and try to become rich **or** to be lazy and enjoy a simple life. Now Bob's a billionaire and Slim's a tramp. But **neither** Bob **nor** Slim is miserable.

Ⓐ *BOTH, EITHER, NEITHER* TO LINK TWO THINGS, PEOPLE, GROUPS

	+ singular noun	+ plural noun	+ of the/my/these etc. + plural noun	often paired with:
both	✓	✓	✓	... and...
either	✓	✓	✓	... or...
neither	✓	✓	✓	... nor...

Both the millionaire and the tramp went to that school.
Both men went to that school. = *Both of the men/Both of them went to that school.*

I haven't met either man. *We didn't meet either the teachers or the students.*
I haven't met either of the men/either of them.

Neither man is unhappy. *Neither the teachers nor the students are happy.*
Neither of the men/Neither of them is* unhappy. (See D)

Ⓑ POSITION OF *BOTH* WITH VERBS AND PRONOUNS

We can use **both** in mid-position in a sentence with a verb:
*They **both went** to the disco.* (before main verb) *They **were both** happy.* (after **be**)
*They **will both** go home soon.* (after auxiliary)

But for special emphasis we can place **both** directly after the subject:
*We **both** will go home soon.* *They **both** were happy.*

We can also use **both** directly after (not before) the plural personal object pronouns **us**, **you**, **them**: *She kissed **us both**.* *I'll take **you both** to the disco.*

Ⓒ POSITIVE AND NEGATIVE

We usually use **either** in a negative sentence, but also in positive sentences:
*I don't like **either** hotel.* *Either one is OK for me.*

We can use **neither** only with a positive verb:
*I want **neither** magazine.* Not *I don't want neither magazine*.

Ⓓ *NEITHER, EITHER* WITH SINGULAR AND PLURAL VERBS

*Neither Bob nor Slim **is** selfish.* (we use a singular verb)
But in informal English, people often use a plural verb: *Neither Bob nor Slim **are** Selfish.*
*Neither the teachers nor the students **agree**.* (we use a plural verb with plural nouns)
A similar use of singular (formal) or plural (informal) verb occurs with **either.**
*Either John or Bob **is/are** available tomorrow.*
*I don't think **either** of them **works/work** on Sunday.*

Ⓔ USING *BOTH, EITHER, NEITHER* WITHOUT A NOUN

We can use **both**, **either**, **neither** without a noun when the meaning is clear:
Would you like tea or orange juice? *I'd like **either**.* (tea or juice)
*I'd like **both**.* (tea and juice)
***Neither**, thank you. I'd prefer coffee.*

1 **Ⓐ** Read the information about Nick and Jill.
Make sentences with *both… and…, either… or…* and *neither… nor… .* Use the verbs in brackets in a suitable form.

> Nick enjoys going on holiday to tropical islands. Jill likes that sort of holiday too. He has two long holidays a year, the same as Jill. Of course, they could have several shorter holidays. That's their choice. Nick has quarrelled with Brigitte the new secretary because she makes lots of mistakes. Jill is always arguing with her. Beth, the other secretary, also makes a lot of mistakes.

0 Both Nick and Jill enjoy going on holiday to tropical islands. (*enjoy*)

1 They can .... (*have*)

2 .... on with Brigitte. (*get*)

3 .... with Brigitte since she started work. (*quarrel*)

4 They can .... her salary. (*dismiss/reduce*)

5 .... a good secretary. (*be*)

6 Brigitte can .... her work .... a new job. (*improve/look*)

2 **Ⓐ - Ⓔ** Write sentences using the word(s) in brackets.

0 Next Saturday afternoon, there is a football match and an art exhibition. (*either*)
   Next Saturday, we'll *either watch a football match or go to an art exhibition.*

1 That road leads to the picnic place. And the other road leads there too.
   .... (*either of*)

2 Teacher X doesn't give a lot of homework. Teacher Y doesn't give a lot of work.
   .... (*neither of*)

3 'Would you like a sandwich or a burger?' 'I'd like the sandwich or the burger.'
   'Would you like a sandwich or a burger?' '...' (*I'd*)

4 'Do you want a present or some money?' 'I want a present and some money!'
   'Do you want a present or some money?' '...' (*want*)

5 Crunchester lost last Saturday. Liverpool lost last Saturday.
   .... (*nor*)

6 Don't answer both Question 1 and Question 2.
   .... (*either*)

7 The socialists don't like the government. The capitalists dislike the government.
   .... (*nor*)

3 **Ⓐ - Ⓔ** Choose the correct answer.

0 Neither of the twins (wants)/want to go to school.

1 You must either stay at home **or/nor** promise not to meet Dan.

2 Ask Tim or Sue – **either of them/both of them** know the answer.

3 'Would you like tea or cola?' '**Either, please/Neither, please.**'

4 **Either driver/Either drivers** might have caused an accident.

5 Neither the police nor the lawyers **likes/like** the new laws.

6 'What did you think of the two films?' 'I didn't like **neither/either.**'

7 Neither Holland nor Belgium **has/have** high mountains.

8 Jim and Gerry **both wanted/wanted both** to marry her.

9 I liked the twins, so I gave **both them/them both** a present.

10 **Both of you/Both you** must keep the secret.

UNIT 43 >> Exclamations with *What...!*, *How...!* etc.

> @ Maggie has passed all her exams with grade A.
> Her parents and teachers say: '**What a great achievement! What marvellous grades!**
> **How fantastic! What brilliant news!** You're **such a clever girl!**'
> Her sister says: '**What a disaster!** I'm **so jealous! How on earth** am I going to match
> those grades?'

A *WHAT* + NOUN

We use **What** + **noun** for exclamations:

What + **a/an** + (adjective) + **singular noun**:   *What a perfect day!*   *What a surprise!*
What + (adjective) + **plural noun**:   *What marvellous grades!* *What results!*
What + (adjective) + **uncountable noun**:   *What great news!*   *What weather!*
What + **a lot of** + **plural/uncountable noun**: *What a lot of people!*   *What a lot of money!*

We can follow these structures with **subject** + **verb**:

*What a perfect day **you've chosen** for the picnic!*   *What great news **this is!***

B *HOW* + ADJECTIVE

We use **How** + **adjective**:

How fantastic! How wonderful!   But not ~~How wonderful news!~~ (not with noun)

We also use this pattern: **How** (+ **adverb**) + **subject** + **verb**:

How you've grown! (to a child)   *How well she plays the piano!*
How London has changed since the 60s!   *How fast it's happened!*

We occasionally use this pattern: **How** + **adjective** + **subject** + **verb**:

How wonderful it is! (**Not** ~~How it is wonderful!~~)
How brave you are!   *How long they took!*

C EXCLAMATIONS WITH *SUCH, SO*

We also use *such/so* to exclaim about something wonderful or surprising:

such + **a/an** + (adjective) + **singular noun**: *It's **such a surprise!** She's **such a good student!***
such + (adjective) + **plural noun**: *They're **such idiots!** They've got **such big noses!***
such + (adjective) + **uncountable noun**: *It's **such good weather**.*
so + **adjective**: *It's **so hot!**   Maggie's **so clever!**   Her sister's **so jealous!***

D *WHAT ON EARTH...!* ETC.

We use **What/How/Why/Where/Who/When on earth...?** * to express surprise, confusion or similar strong emotions:

What on earth is that?   *Why on earth did she hit him!*
How on earth did they escape?   *Where on earth have they gone?*
Who on earth wants to buy a pink and orange dress! *When on earth did that happen?*

* an exclamation mark can also be used: *What on earth is that!*

E NEGATIVE QUESTIONS AS EXCLAMATIONS

We can form exclamations as negative questions (see Unit 55):

Isn't it wonderful!   *Aren't they big!*   *Didn't they do well!*

1 **A B** Rewrite these exclamations by completing the second item in each case.

   0 Bill is very intelligent!   How *intelligent Bill is!*

   1 Susan has very faithful friends!   What .... has!

   2 Her husband is such a handsome man!   What .... is!

   3 We were so lucky to get tickets!   .... we were to get tickets!

   4 They asked such difficult questions!   What .... asked!

   5 Jez-E-bel dances fantastically!   How .... !

2 **A - C** Complete the exclamations. Use *What, What a, How, such, such a, so*. Then listen and check your answers.

The police have arrested Corinne for shoplifting:
(0) *What a* stupid thing to do! She's (1) .... crazy girl to do that! (2) .... terrible news.
(3) .... terrible! She's (4) .... dishonest!

The judge sends her to prison for five years:
That's (5) .... long sentence! (6) .... unfair! She's (7) .... unlucky! (8) ....
bad decision! It's (9) .... unfair punishment.

Her lawyer proves that she's innocent and she leaves prison:
(10) .... miracle! That judge was (11) .... idiot. (12) .... great news! We're
(13) .... glad to see you again! (14) .... clever lawyer!

Corinne invites her friends to a party to celebrate. The sun is shining:
(15) .... good weather! It's (16) .... perfect day for a celebration! Corinne's
(17) .... good person. (18) .... lot of friends have come! The police are (19) ....
incompetent! (20) .... hot it is!

Corinne gives her friends dry bread and stale biscuits:
You're (21) .... terrible friends. I was (22) .... lonely in prison. You were all (23) ....
sure I was guilty! (24) .... horrible food! (25) .... disgusting!

3 **D** Fill the gaps with *What/How/Where/Why/Who/When on earth...*

   0 Hugh is ugly but he's going out with Claudette.
      How on earth did he get such a beautiful girlfriend?

   1 Beth is short of money but she's resigned from her job.
      .... has she resigned from her job?

   2 Gina had on a red blouse; next time you look at her, she's wearing a blue T-shirt.
      .... did she change her top?

   3 Somebody has stolen the rubbish bin from outside your house.
      .... would have stolen the rubbish bin?

   4 You've lost your mobile phone; it must be somewhere in the house.
      .... have I put my mobile?

   5 There is a stranger in your room, taking food from your fridge.
      .... do you think you're doing?

   6 Your room is full of things; but you've bought some new books.
      .... am I going to put them?

   7 Supergirl is in a trap at the bottom of the ocean surrounded by sharks.
      .... will she escape?

4 **E** Rewrite the exclamations in exercise 1 using a negative question.

   0 *Isn't Bill intelligent!*   **2** ....   **4** ....

   1 ....   **3** ....   **5** ....

UNIT 44 >> Nouns and their form

You can often recognise nouns by their endings. But experience of the language is more useful than trying to learn a list of endings. Words often come in 'families'. For example: **friend, friendship, friendliness** (nouns), **befriend** (verb), **friendly** (adjective). But be careful! Many -*ation* nouns are in the same 'family' *as -ate* verbs but, for example, there are no verbs informate or relaxate!

A COMMON NOUN ENDINGS

Many nouns are closely related to adjectives, verbs, adverbs or other nouns. The table in Appendix 9 shows some (but by no means all) common noun endings with examples.

Notice that:

1 **-er/or** usually indicate a **person** or **thing** who/which **carries out work/action**; they are added to verbs and sometimes nouns: *law → lawyer   inspect → inspector*

2 **-ee** usually indicates the **person who 'receives'**: *an employee is employed, a payee is paid*

3 **-ist/-ian/-ant/-ent** often indicate a **person** or **thing** who **carries out work/action**: *a pharmacist, a technician, an attendant, a president*

4 **-ism** often denotes **trends in thought, systems** and **beliefs**: *Communism, Darwinism, Nazism*

5 **-let/-ling/-ette** often indicate **something** which is **small**: *a droplet, a duckling, a couchette*

6 **-dom/-hood/-ship/-t/-th** often denote a (physical or moral) **condition/status**: *freedom, motherhood, friendship, depth*

7 These endings are often related to adjectives:

- **-ance/ence**   *important → importance*   *independent → independence*
- **-ancy/ency**   *constant → constancy*   *dependent → dependency*
- **-y/ity/iety**   *honest → honesty*   *popular → popularity*
  notorious → notoriety
- **-ness**   *sad → sadness*   *happy → happiness*

B SOME COMMON PREFIXES

Here are some common prefixes. A good dictionary will help you with recognising their force:

ab-	*ab*normality	**anti-**	*anti*-perspirant
dis-	*dis*appearance, **dis**appointment	**de-**	*de*contamination, **de**colonisation
il-	*il*literacy, **il**legitimacy, **il**legality	**im-**	*im*maturity, **im**purity
in-	*in*ability, **in**decision	**ir-**	*ir*responsibility, **ir**radiation
mis-	*mis*fortune, **mis**understanding	**un-**	*un*suitability, **un**acceptability
pre-	*pre*diction, **pre**-eminence	**post-**	*post*-modernism, **post**-feminism
super-	*super*market, **super**man	**hyper-**	*hyper*market, **hyper**sensitivity
over-	*over*-enthusiasm, **over**-excitement	**under-**	*under*-employment, **under**-confidence

C NOUN + NOUN

Some nouns are formed from **noun** + **noun**. Here are some examples:
toothbrush/classroom/bedroom/windscreen/football/bodyguard/keyboard

1 **(A)** Using the information in 44A and Appendix 9, form a noun from the word given in each line. Write it in the gap. Then listen and check your answers.

INVENT — Professor Makepeace, the well-known (0) *inventor*, has been creating new
CHILD — machines ever since his (1) .... Even at primary school, he used
ATTEND — to attract the (2) .... of his teachers by his efforts to build strange
EQUIP — pieces of (3) .... from things he found in the rubbish bins. In his
ENTHUSE — teens, he temporarily lost his (4) .... while he devoted his energy
COURT — to the (5) .... of his future wife. Unfortunately for her, he returned
OBSESS — to his (6) .... even during their honeymoon and she soon found it
TIDY — impossible to put up with his (7) .... There were pieces of metal and
NEIGHBOUR — plastic in every room and he annoyed the whole (8) ....with the
EMIGRATE — noise of hammering throughout the night. The (9) .... of his wife
ABSENT — to Australia surprised no one. Did he notice her (10) ....? He continued
FAIL — to work on his inventions, despite the (11) .... of his marriage.

2 **(A)** What are the verbs that are related to these nouns?

0 education *educate*
1 determination ....
2 relaxation ....
3 contamination ....
4 realisation ....
5 inspiration ....
6 generation ....
7 desperation ....
8 colonisation ....
9 purity ....
10 conspiracy ....
11 solution ....

3 **(A)(B)** Form a noun from the word given in each line. Write it in the gap.

GROW — The (0) *growth* of multi-national companies over recent years has
TRANSFORM — caused the (1) .... of many of Britain's high streets. In most towns,
CLOSE — the (2) .... of small traditional shops became inevitable once large
MARKET — supermarkets, and the even larger (3) ...., established themselves
SKIRT — not only in town centres but also on the (4) .... of centres of population.
ABLE — The (5) .... of the small specialist shops such as greengrocer's
COMPETE — and tobacconist's to withstand the (6) .... from the huge chains
CHOOSE — meant that shoppers eventually had less (7) .... There was no
COMPETE — alternative to the supermarkets once their smaller (8) .... had
RIVAL — closed. Instead, there is now great (9) .... between the supermarkets
themselves, leading to price-cutting wars. This may seem like good news for
CONSUME — the (10) .... but in fact it will lead to even bigger companies and
VARY — even less (11) ....

4 **(A)-(C)** Circle the correct alternative.

0 The (lack)/lackness/lacking of clear/(clarity)/clarify in their policies is a sign of their incompetance/incompeteness/(incompetence)

1 There is a severe **short/shortness/shortage** of mathematics teachers in secondary **educate/education/educated**.

2 Astronomers have predicted the imminent **discover/discovery/discoveration** of the **existence/existance/exist** of intelligent life in other galaxies.

3 Many blind people are angry that **architectures/planners/planers** do not take account of their **inabilities/disabilities/unabilities**.

4 I'm hungry! it must be **lunch's time/lunchtime/lunches time**. Why hasn't the school **bell/schools' bell/school's bell** rung yet?

REVISION 4 >> First Certificate Practice

1 For questions 1-12, read the text below and decide which answer, A, B, C or D, best fits each gap. There is an example at the beginning (0).

ARTIFICIAL INTELLIGENCE

Since (0) A Renaissance, there have been (1) ..... stories about intelligent man-made creatures, such as Frankenstein's monster or HAL, (2) ..... in the film *2001*. However, (3) ..... scientists believe that human beings are a long way from producing such creatures in reality. Yes, there are ovens which can search for and download (4) ..... recipes from the Internet, machines which can beat chess champions, cars which can plan the best route from one place to another. However, (5) ..... these constructions possesses true intelligence; they simply have an ability to process (6) ..... much more quickly and more accurately than we can. The makers of *AI*, a film about (7) ..... robotic boy, received (8) ..... from artificial intelligence researchers (9) ..... . The (10) ..... movements and behaviour are based on real-life experience of the difficulties in the field of AI. In fact, there are (11) ..... experts who believe the best approach is to attempt to build an intelligent robot directly; instead, most believe that generations of robots will (12) ..... evolve little by little just as real species have done.

0 (A) the	B –	C a	D an
1 A the many	B little	C many	D a lot
2 A the robot	B robot	C a robots	D an robot
3 A the most	B few	C most the	D most
4 A the	B few	C –	D the many
5 A none	B none of	C none from	D neither
6 A informations	B an information	C information pieces	D information
7 A –	B a	C some	D the
8 A an advice	B advices	C advising	D advice
9 A theirselves	B themselves	C their selves	D themself
10 A actor's	B boys'	C actors'	D boys
11 A lots of	B not a lot	C not many	D not much
12 A itself	B itselves	C himselves	D themselves

2 For these questions, read the text below and think of the word which best fits the gap. Use only *one* word in each gap. There is an example at the beginning (0).

ROBOTS

In (0) many laboratories in Europe and (1) .... USA, researchers are using (2) .... evolutionary approach to develop a robot that thinks for (3) .... In one case, for example, robots play language games with one (4) .... As they play, they build up a shared vocabulary and are able to talk among (5) .... When human beings join in (6) .... games, the robots are able to adapt their language to human languages and, eventually, people and robots will converse with (7) .... other. There is another robot which learns its behaviour from its creators just as babies learn from (8) .... parents. A child learns by interaction with (9) .... world; we cannot learn if we are by ourselves. The same is true for robots. However, (10) .... scientists believe that the first AI robots will look like human beings. They will be more like (11) .... mouse or an insect. (12) .... of these corresponds to our romantic ideas of a humanoid robot.

PAPER 3 PART 4

3 For these questions, complete the second sentence so that it has a similar meaning to the first sentence, using the word given. Do not change the word given. Use from two to five words including the word given. There is an example (0).

0 85% of the pilots had never had an accident.

Most of the pilots had never had an accident.   *MOST*

1 She told me an interesting fact about the life of Elvis Presley.

She gave me an .... about the life of Elvis Presley. *INFORMATION*

2 Robinson Crusoe was all alone on the island until he met Man Friday.

Robinson Crusoe .... on the island until he met Man Friday. *BY*

3 Sam couldn't start the car; and Sheila couldn't start it either.

Neither .... start the car. *COULD*

4 All the people in the neighbourhood know me.

Everybody .... me. *NEIGHBOURHOOD*

5 All of the taxi-drivers have refused to take the drunk man to the station.

Every .... refused to take the drunk man to the station. *HAS*

6 The two libraries lend books to foreign students.

Both.. lend books to foreign students. *OF*

7 There aren't many beaches here, so it's not good for swimmers.

There .... here, so it's not good for swimmers. *FEW*

8 He was away on holiday for three weeks last month.

He had .... last month. *WEEKS'*

OTHER PRACTICE

4 In each set of five, four nouns are normally uncountable. Circle the noun in each list which is not normally uncountable.

0 advice information news (report) knowledge
1 progress research leisure work job
2 luggage computer furniture equipment apparatus
3 imagination courage patience happiness idea
4 milk food vegetable spaghetti meat
5 clothes underwear nylon silk wool

OPEN EXERCISE

5 Write two suitable exclamations for these situations. Use the words in brackets.

situation	exclamation 1	exclamation 2
0 It is very cold and icy.	What cold weather! (*weather*)	How cold it is today! (*cold*)
1 Myra's won an Oscar.	.... (*isn't/wonderful*)	.... (*surprise*)
2 Tim has failed all his exams.	.... (*news*)	.... (*stupid*)
3 Zena's married a billionaire.	.... (*lucky*)	.... (*earth*)
4 It's very hot in mid-winter	.... (*weather*)	.... (*unusual*)
5 Hugh's bought 2 new, modern, luxury sofas.	.... (*furniture*)	.... (*comfortable*)

UNIT 45 >> Relative pronouns

 Someone has tried to rob Gina. 'Yes, Inspector, that's a photo of the man **who** did it. That's the necklace **which** he tried to steal. That's the street **where** it happened. 11.15? Yes, that's the time **when** it happened. And that's the old lady **whose** poodle attacked him.'

Ⓐ USING RELATIVE PRONOUNS

We use relative pronouns to build sentences.

Instead of two simple sentences:	*I met a man. He tried to rob me.*
we can make one sentence:	*I met a man **who** tried to rob me.*
Do not repeat the subject:	**Not** ~~I met a man who he tried to rob me~~.

We use relative pronouns:

1 to **identify the people, animals** or **things** we are talking about (see Unit 46):
  *That's the man **who** did it.*   *I like films **that** have happy endings.*

2 or to **add extra information** about them (**that** is not used in this case: see Unit 47):
  *The man, **who** had a scar on his left cheek, attacked me.*

We use different relative pronouns for different purposes:

	pronoun	example(s)	
people	**who**	*There's the man **who** did it.*	= he
people (object)	**whom***	*I dislike the woman **whom** he married.*	= her
people (possession)	**whose**	*That's the couple **whose** car stopped.*	= their
things/animals	**which**	*Those are the jewels **which** he stole.*	= them
		*I hugged the dog **which** saved me.*	= it
people or things	**that**	*There's the man **that** did it.*	= he
		*I've got the jewels **that** he wanted.*	= them
place	**where**	*This is the street where it happened.*	= here/there
time	**when**	*I remember the day **when** it happened.*	= on that day
reason	**why**	*I don't know the reason **why** he did it.*	= for that reason

* **whom** is nowadays used only in formal English. It may sound rather old-fashioned in normal conversation or writing where we prefer to use **who** or **that**.

Ⓑ *WHICH* FOR THINGS AND *WHO* FOR PEOPLE

We use **that** or **which** (**not who**) for **things** or **animals*** and **that** or **who** (**not which**) for **people**:
*I recognised the thief **that/who** stole my bag.* (person)
*We rewarded the dog **that/which** rescued me.* (animal)
* But we sometimes use **who** for pets or animals that we know well: *I had a cat **who**...*

Ⓒ *WHERE* OR *WHICH*?

We use **where** to **refer to a place** when something happened there:
*That's the school **where** I studied last year.* (or **which** I studied **in**...)
We use **which** when it is the subject of the verb: *That's the car **which** won.*

Ⓓ THE SENTENCE POSITION OF *WHO, THAT* ETC.

We usually place **who**, **that**, **which**, **whose**, **where** directly **after** the **person**, **thing** or **place**:
*She studies with the **teacher who** has a beard.* (Relative clause at the end of the sentence)
*The **teacher who** has a beard is kind.* (Relative clause in the middle of the sentence)

1 **A** **D** Link these pairs of sentences using *who, whose, which, where, when, why.* Put a star (*) against any sentences where it is also possible to use *that.*

0   'Great Expectations' is a novel. Dickens wrote it.
*'Great Expectations' is a novel which Dickens wrote.**

1   Pip is a young boy. His parents have died.

   ....

2   He helped a convict. The prisoner had escaped from a prison ship.

   ....

3   Later, he visits a rich old lady. She lives in a big, decaying house.

   ....

4   A beautiful young girl lives with her. Her name is Estella.

   ....

5   Pip doesn't know the reason. The old lady hates men for a reason.

   ....

6   All the clocks have stopped at a certain time. The lady's fiancé had jilted her at that time.

   ....

7   Pip lives with Joe, a blacksmith. Joe is married to Pip's sister.

   ....

8   A lawyer tells Pip that now he is rich. The lawyer comes from London.

   ....

9   Pip goes to London. He learns to be a gentleman there.

   ....

10   Pip spends the money. It comes from a mysterious benefactor.

   ....

11   The prisoner arrives in London. Pip had helped him.

   ....

12   He tells Pip the truth about the money. He has been receiving it.

   ....

2 **C** Use *where* or *which* to fill the gaps. Then listen and check your answers.

This is the palace (0) *where* the emperor lived. There are underground cells (1) .... he kept his slaves. The slaves looked after the gardens (2) .... the emperor loved. A slave entered the room (3) .... the emperor was sitting. The guards were sleeping in the room (4) .... was above the emperor's. The slave took the emperor to the roof (5) .... he showed him the gardens. He said, 'these are the gardens (6) .... I look after in the hot sun.' The emperor wanted to leave the roof (7) .... was very high. The slave pushed him to the edge (8) .... he stood trembling. The slave pushed him and he fell into the garden (9) .... he broke his neck. They buried him in a piece of land (10) .... the roses grew. The slave sat on the throne (11) .... the emperor had sat on before.

3 **A** Use *who* or *whose* to fill the gaps. Then listen and check your answers.

The slave married the girl (0) *whose* father he had killed. The slave, (1) .... temper was very quick, often punished people. His wife, (2) .... also had a very quick temper, often quarrelled with him. The guards, (3) .... duty was to protect the slave-emperor, would take his wife away. He had ordered them to kill anyone (4) .... quarrelled with him. The wife, (5) .... beauty was famous, persuaded the guards to let her live. She returned to the emperor, (6) .... always forgave her when he was calm. Everyone remembers the slave (7) .... became an emperor.

UNIT 46 >> Defining relative clauses

 The old lady hit him with the umbrella **she was carrying**. Then I took off the shoes **I was wearing** and beat him with them. And of course he was covered in rubbish from a rubbish bin **we'd tipped** over his head. The police said he looked like someone **an army had attacked.**

Ⓐ DEFINING RELATIVE CLAUSES

Some clauses are called **defining relative clauses** because they **define/identify the noun**. In defining relative clauses we can use **who, that, which, whose, where, when** and **why**.

*That's the man **who/that** *tried to rob me.*   (I am identifying the particular man)
*They used the bin **which/that** *was in the street.*   (I am identifying the particular bin)
*This is the street **where** he robbed me.*   (I am identifying the particular street)

* **That** is more informal than **who** or **which** in this kind of clause.

We prefer to use **that**, not **which**, after **all, everything, nothing, superlatives, the day, the year, the time**:
*I've given you **all that** (Not ~~which~~) I have.*
*It's the most beautiful bird **that** (Not ~~which~~) I've ever seen.*

Ⓑ OMITTING THE RELATIVE

We can omit the relative pronoun when it is the **object of the verb** in the relative clause. In informal contexts and in much formal English, we prefer to omit the relative if the meaning remains clear to the reader.

We can say **Either**   *I hit him with the shoes **that/which** I was wearing.* (which = them)
       Or   *I hit him with the shoes I was wearing.*
       Either   *I identified the man **who/that** the police had arrested.* (who = him)
       Or   *I identified the man the police had arrested.*

We sometimes omit other relative pronouns:
*Is that the place (**where**) you're staying?*
*Is that the reason (**why**) you're leaving.*

But when **who, which** or **that** is the **subject of the verb**, we **must** include it:
*We say: That's the man **who/that** robbed me.*   **Not** ~~That's the man robbed me.~~ (who = me)

Ⓒ PREPOSITION + RELATIVE PRONOUN

We can also omit **who** or **which** or **that** when it is the **object of a preposition** in a defining relative clause.

We can say **Either**   *He grabbed the umbrella **which/that** she was hitting him **with**.*
       Or   *He grabbed the umbrella she was hitting him **with**.*
       Either   *The woman **who/that** he was staring **at** got angry.*
       Or   *The woman he was staring **at** got angry.*

Notice: the preposition comes at the end of the relative clause.

However, in formal English, we can use **preposition** + **which** or **whom**:
*He bought the bed **in which** Queen Victoria had slept.* (less formal: ... *the bed she'd slept **in**.*)
*He met the man **with whom** he had argued.* (less formal: ... *the man he'd argued **with**.*)

1 **A** **B** Read the continuing story of *Great Expectations*. Write each pair of sentences as one sentence. Use *who* or *which* ONLY if necessary.

 0 The convict wanted to help the boy. The boy had helped him.
 1 Pip didn't want the money. The convict had given him the money.
 2 He had to forget the dream. He had had the dream since he'd met Estella.
 3 Pip visited the old lady. He had visited her as a child.
 4 Estella told them she wanted to marry a man. She had met him in London.
 5 Pip realised he had lost the woman. He loved her.
 6 Pip and the convict tried to catch a ship. It would take them away from England.
 7 The police wanted to catch the convict. He had returned illegally from Australia.
 8 The convict recognised the man. He hated him most in the world.
 9 They fell under the ship. It was approaching their boats.
10 The man died in the river. The convict had attacked him.

 0 *The convict wanted to help the boy who had helped him.*
 1 ....
 2 ....
 3 ....
 4 ....
 5 ....
 6 ....
 7 ....
 8 ....
 9 ....
10 ....

2 **A** - **C** Put the two ideas into one sentence with a relative clause. Include *who* or *which* or *that* ONLY if they are necessary.

 0 She took off the shoes. She was wearing them. *She took off the shoes she was wearing.*
 1 She thanked the old lady by giving her the necklace. The man had tried to steal it.
   ....
 2 The police arrested the man. She had identified him.
   ....
 3 The robber said he was sorry for the attack. He had made the attack on her.
   ....
 4 The local paper published the story. She had told their reporter the story.
   ....
 5 A TV producer invited her to appear in a programme. He was making the programme.
   ....
 6 In prison, the prisoners watched the programme. She appeared in it.
   ....
 7 The other prisoners laughed at the man. A poodle, a girl and an old woman had caught him.
   ....
 8 He gave up the life of crime. He had started a life of crime.
   ....
 9 He followed a course in prison. It taught him how to shampoo and look after poodles.
   ....
10 The old lady took her poodle to the poodle parlour. The ex-robber had opened it.
   ....

3 **C** Fill the gaps with a preposition from the list + *which* or + *whom*.

about   for   for   for   from   ~~in~~   in   in   on   with   with

0 The magazine in which he was going to publish his story went out of business.

1 The star .... he was telling stories came into the room.

2 She introduced me to the manager of the company .... she was working.

3 This is just the kind of antique furniture .... I've been looking.

4 She introduced me to the people .... she was dining.

5 Do you know the name of the girl .... he is dancing?

6 This is the secret .... so many spies and robbers have died.

7 She has a small salary .... she depends.

8 I went straight to the safe .... he had hidden the diamonds.

9 The police examined the gun .... the bullet had been fired.

10 The train .... we travelled was very hot and uncomfortable.

4 **C** Rewrite sentences 1-6 from exercise 3, without using a relative pronoun.

0 The magazine he was going to publish his story in went out of business.

1 ....

2 ....

3 ....

4 ....

5 ....

6 ....

5 **A** - **C** Make one sentence from these groups of sentences. Omit the relative pronoun if appropriate.

0 The man took away the football. I had kicked it through his window. He lives in the flat above ours.
The man who lives in the flat above ours took away the football I had kicked through his window.

1 The car crashed into the police station. The criminal was driving the car. The criminal had escaped from prison.
The criminal who .... the police station.

2 I showed my aunt the stadium. I had played a professional match there. I scored a goal in that match for the first time.
I showed my aunt ....
the first professional match in ....

3 Her friends didn't like the boy. She had decided to marry him. These friends were very snobbish. But her other friends thought he was nice. These friends were open-minded.
Her friends .... the boy ....
but her other friends ....

4 The computer has a printer. You are using this computer. The printer often breaks down.
The computer .... has a printer
.... down.

5 The man used to be very poor. His girlfriend won the lottery. But now he buys lots of gold and diamonds. He gives them to other girls. Their boyfriends are poor.
The man .... to be very poor but now
.... girls ....

6 Foreign students often complain about English food. They have eaten this food in their school canteens. But they have never tasted English food. This food has been prepared at home.

Foreign students often ....

but they .... at home.

7 I don't want to work for the company. My father owns the company. This is because I want to work in a place. I can be independent there.

I don't want .... owns because

.... I can be independent.

6 **Ⓐ - Ⓒ** **Read the text about coincidences and find all the places where you could A)** *omit* **the relative pronoun or B)** *add* **a relative pronoun or C) where a necessary relative pronoun is used. For type A, put brackets ( ) around the word. For type B, write the possible added pronoun above the place. For type C, underline the pronoun. The first three have been done for you.**

Have you ever met a friend who/that you haven't seen for ten years by chance at a foreign airport? Or have you found in a second-hand shop a ring (that) you lost twenty years before? There are many people <u>who</u> have experienced strange coincidences in their lives. For example, a man whose car had broken down went into the first telephone box he found at the side of the road. As he entered, the phone he'd been about to use started ringing. He picked it up and discovered he was talking to his secretary who had just dialled a wrong number. This kind of incident is not something you can explain logically. Or is it? Mathematicians claim that it is something they'd expect. Of all the things which are happening in the world at one moment, it's logical to expect that there are some which will produce coincidences. This is an explanation which others reject. These people argue that coincidences are signs that we can interpret. They are part of a pattern that Fate has placed in our lives. What's the explanation you would give?

OPEN EXERCISE

7 **Ⓑ** **Complete these sentences by using a relative clause without *who*, *which* or *that*.**

0 I like the ring *she gave you/you bought for your mother etc.*

1 I read the book ....

2 We stayed at the hotel ....

3 She met the man again ....

4 They found the treasure ....

5 He wrote the book ....

6 They hid the photos ....

7 I liked the soup ....

8 She drove the car ....

9 There's only one question ....

10 I agreed with the theory ....

Write ten other sentence-beginnings. Give them to another student to complete.

UNIT 47 >> Non-defining relative clauses

 The old lady, **who had grey hair and a bad leg,** had been very brave. Gina invited her and her poodle, **which had also helped to defend her,** to her house. The dog ate chocolate biscuits and the old lady, **who didn't like tea,** drank tequila. Meanwhile, the robber, **who was only eighteen,** sat in prison, **which was very sad.**

Ⓐ DEFINING RELATIVE CLAUSES

Some relative clauses **define/identify** a **person/people/thing/place**. We have studied this kind of sentence in Unit 46.
Gina says: *'I invited the old lady **who** helped me to my house.'*

                         /   /
                    no comma   no comma

*... **who helped me...*** answers the question: *'Which old lady?'* It identifies her.

Ⓑ NON-DEFINING RELATIVE CLAUSES

Some relative clauses **add extra information**.
Gina says: *The old lady, **who** had nothing else to do, accepted the invitation.*

                    /   \
                comma   comma

*... **who had nothing else to do...*** gives us **extra information** about the old lady.
It doesn't identify her; we already know about her. It is a non-defining relative clause.

Remember: • we **do not** use **that** in non-defining clauses.
               • we **cannot omit who** or **which** in non-defining relative clauses.
               • we **use commas** in non-defining relative clauses.

Here are some more examples:
*The manager, **who** speaks French, talked to the tourists.*
*We went to a new restaurant, **which** serves Italian food.*
*The cook, **whose** food is delicious, is very fat.*

Ⓒ *SOME OF/MANY OF/ALL OF/FEW OF WHICH/WHO/WHOM*

We can use **some of/many of/all of/few of which/who** or **whom** etc.:
*The tourists, **many of who** speak excellent English, understood the guide.*
*The cars, **none of which** had effective brakes, failed the test.*

Ⓓ *WHICH FOR A COMPLETE IDEA*

We can use **which** to refer to a **complete idea**, not just one noun:
*The robber left his fingerprints on the gun, **which** was very stupid.*
(IDEA: which = the fact of leaving his fingerprints)
*The gun, **which** he dropped, had the robber's fingerprints on it.*
(ONE NOUN: which = the gun)
*She is getting married to a singer, **which** makes her parents angry.*
(IDEA: which = the fact that she's getting married to a singer)
*The wedding, **which** will be very small, is next week.*
(ONE NOUN: which = the wedding)

1 **A** **B** **D** Put necessary commas in these sentences OR cross out unnecessary commas. Put a tick (✔) if the sentence is correct.

0 Children roll eggs, all of which are brightly painted, down a hill.   1 The egg, that reaches the bottom of the hill first, is the winner.   2 Fireworks night, which celebrates an event in British history, occurs in November.   3 Often children knock on doors and ask for money which some people don't like.   4 Valentine's Day which is very popular occurs in February.   5 Lovers send cards that have no name which sometimes creates a mystery.   6 Red roses, which are traditional Valentine's gifts, increase in price.   7 This is an example of the kind of commercialism, which spoils these old customs.

2 **B** **C** Add the extra information in brackets ( ) to the sentences by using *who, which, whose* or *where*. Don't forget the commas.

0 Many traditional activities occur at local festivals. (Some of them are very strange.)
   Many traditional activities, some of which are very strange, occur at local festivals.

1 In one place, people compete in gurning. (It is the art of making strange facial (expressions.)
   ....

2 Toe-wrestling is another unusual competition. (Toe-wrestling has a long history.)
   ....

3 On the rivers, people count the swans. (All of the swans belong to the monarch.)
   ....

4 Worm-charming takes place in one village. (It is similar to snake-charming)
   ....

5 The most loving couple win a large piece of bacon. (The bacon is called a 'flitch'.)
   ....

6 A tomato-fight takes place every year. (The fight lasts all day.)
   ....

7 Pancake races take place in the early spring. (In these races women run with frying pans.)
   ....

8 The person who grows the largest leek gets a prize. (A leek is a kind of vegetable.)
   ....

3 **D** In these sentences, *which* refers to a word or a group of words. Underline the word or words.

0 <u>Many local activities have died out</u>, which is rather sad.
1 Old festivals may become commercial, which changes their nature.
2 Tourists love to see traditional activities, which are often very colourful.
3 Often people change the activities to attract tourists, which makes them artificial.
4 Morris dancing, which is traditionally only for men, has a very long history.
5 Now there are many women's groups, which makes the traditionalists angry!
6 But I think this is a good development, which keeps the activity alive.
7 Old activities change with the times, which helps to preserve them.

OPEN EXERCISE

4 **B** - **D** Invent some extra information and add it to these sentences.

1 The painting, ..., is worth two million dollars.   2 My friend, ..., wants to be a fashion model.   3 The weather, ..., changed yesterday.   4 The night club, ..., is going to close.   5 The robber, ..., surrendered to the police.   6 The kidnappers, ..., released their victim.

UNIT 48 >> Reduced relative clauses

 At a party in the Embassy, the old man **seated** next to Mrs Looselips is gossiping about the guests. 'The man **dressed** in black is a famous politician. The woman **drinking** a purple cocktail is a spy. The waiter **serving** caviar is a secret police agent.'

Ⓐ -ING CLAUSES

We can often express the information in a relative clause by using a **present participle** (**verb-ing**):

sentence with *who/which/that*	reduced form with *-ing*
Do you know the woman **who is taking** *photos?* *The servants* **who live** *here are ex-spies.* *There is a tunnel* **that joins** *the house and Big Ben.*	*Do you know the woman* **taking** *photos?* *The servants* **living** *here are ex-spies.* *There is a tunnel* **joining** *the house and Big Ben.*

We use **-ing** clauses to talk about what someone or something is or was doing at a particular time:

The woman **drinking** *a cocktail is a spy.*   *The car* **waiting** *outside was a special limousine.*

We don't use **-ing** clauses to talk about a single completed action:

We say: *I met the man who killed the king.*   **Not** ~~I met the man killing the king~~.

We also use **-ing** clauses to talk about permanent characteristics of things and sometimes people: *The room* **neighbouring** *this one is a prison.*
The men **guarding** *the house are specially trained.*

Ⓑ PAST PARTICIPLE CLAUSES

We can also express the information in a relative clause by using a past participle:

sentence with who/which/that	reduced form with past participle
The disc **that was/had been stolen** *was top secret.*	*The disc* **stolen** *by one of the guests was top secret.*

The past participle form can also be used in the adjective position. For example:

The **stolen** *disc was top secret.*   *The* **recently** *murdered man was a spy.*

For emphasis we can sometimes change the order of the verbs:

They found a bomb in the cellar. It was detonated by the police. = *The bomb* **found** *in the cellar was detonated by the police.* (emphasis on the detonation of the bomb)
The bomb **detonated** *by the police had been found in the cellar.* (emphasis on the finding of the bomb)

Ⓒ CLAUSES WITH *BEING* + PAST PARTICIPLE

We can reduce sentences with **who/which/that** + **a continuous passive construction** like this:

sentence with *who/which/that*	reduced form with *being -ed*
The man **who is being questioned** *is innocent.* *Poison was added to the food* **that was being served.**	*The man* **being questioned** *is innocent.* *Poison was added to the food* **being served.**

Ⓓ *THERE IS/ARE/WAS/WERE* + *-ING* AND PAST PARTICIPLE CLAUSES

We often use **-ing** and **-ed** clauses after **there is/was** etc.:

There wasn't *anyone* **checking** *the food.*   *Is there a guard* **positioned** *on the roof?*

1 **A** - **C** Join the two sentences by using an *-ing* clause or an *-ed* clause.

0 The woman is being photographed. She is kissing the actor.
The woman kissing the actor is being photographed.

1 The man was insulted by the spy. He knows her secrets.

....

2 The woman is smiling at the ambassador. She plans to poison him.

....

3 The musicians have guns. The guns are hidden in their violin cases.

....

4 A man has been arrested in the garden. He was trying to film the party.

....

5 There is a robot at the party. It is disguised as a guest.

....

6 The robot has been programmed to blow up the house. It was invented by the Americans.

....

7 The couple are being given a present by the ambassador. They are expert bomb-makers.

....

8 There is always a lot of blood at the parties. The parties are held in the Embassy.

....

2 **C** Rewrite sentences 0, 2, 4 and 6 from exercise 1 so that there is a change of emphasis.

1 (0) *The woman being photographed is kissing the actor.*

2 (2) ....

3 (4) ....

4 (6) ....

3 **B** Write the 'reduced' form of these sentences.

0 The window which was broken was repaired. *The broken window was repaired.*

1 The train which was delayed arrived at 10.00. ....

2 The bus which was delayed by fog arrived at 12.00. ....

3 The letter which was wrongly addressed got lost. ....

4 My aunt who had been divorced remarried. ....

5 Is that the criminal who was convicted of Tim's murder? ....

6 Is that the criminal who was convicted? ....

4 **D** Write the 'reduced' form of these sentences.

0 There is a man who is waiting at the door. *There is a man waiting at the door.*

1 There is a car which is parked in front of the garage.

....

2 There were several boys who were shouting in the street.

....

3 Are there any students who live in West London here?

....

4 There wasn't any music which was being played during the party.

....

Reduced relative clauses

127

UNIT **49** >> *What* as a relative pronoun

 'Darling! I can't believe **what** you've told me! You've won the lottery and you can buy **what** you want! You can do **whatever** you want. You can travel **wherever** you like. You can meet **whoever** you want. You can have **whichever** jewels you choose.'
'Yes, and I can marry **who** I want. So goodbye, Sam! You're not **what** I want.'

Ⓐ *WHAT*

We can use **what** to mean **the thing which/the things which**:

*I can't believe **what** you've told me.*	*= ... believe the thing which you've...*
*You can do **what** you want.*	*= ... do the thing which you want...*

Ⓑ *WHO, WHERE, WHEN, HOW* FOR UNLIMITED CHOICE

We use **who/whom**, **where**, **when**, **how** in a similar way to talk about an **unlimited choice**:

*I can marry **who** I want/**whom** I want.*	*= ... marry the person that I want...*
*She can go **where** she wants.*	*= ... go to the places where she wants to go...*
*Come **when** you like.*	*= Come at the time that you want...*
*You can do it **how** you want.*	*= ... do it in the way which you want...*

Ⓒ *WHATEVER, WHOEVER* ETC.

We use **whatever, whoever, wherever, however** etc. to emphasise that **a choice is unlimited**.

*I can do **whatever** I like.*	*I can marry **whoever** I like.*
*I can go **wherever** I want.*	*Get the money **however** you can.*

We use **whichever** when there is a free choice from a limited set:
*Look at these CDs. You can listen to **whichever** you like.*

We often use **whichever one**: *You can listen to **whichever one** you like.*

We also use **whatever/wherever + noun**.
*You can drive at **whatever speed** you like on private land.*

Ⓓ *WHAT*-CLAUSE AS SUBJECT

What-clauses (when **what** = the thing(s) which) can be the subject of sentences:

***What** she did was unforgivable.*	***What** I want is a new car.*
***What** matters is not the money.*	***What** we experienced changed our lives.*

Less frequently, we can use other **wh**-clauses in subject position, often if they refer to secrets, mysteries etc.

***Where** they went is a mystery.*	***How** he escaped puzzles me.*
***Why** he did it isn't known.*	

WARNING!!

1 Say ***everything that** is...:*   Not ... ~~everything what is~~....
   *I saw **everything that** was in the museum.*   Not ... ~~saw everything what was~~...
   *You can do **everything that** you want.*   Not ... ~~do everything what you want~~...

2 Do not confuse **what** and **which/that**:
   *I like the flowers **that** you gave her.*   Not ~~the flowers what you gave~~...

1 **Ⓐ Ⓑ** Fill the gaps with *what, who, when, where, how* or *that*.

0 I can live *where* I like.   **1** I can do everything .... I've dreamed of.   **2** I can refuse to do .... the bosses tell me to do.   **3** I can tell the bosses .... I think of them.   **4** I can go out with .... I like.   **5** I can get up and go to bed .... I like.   **6** I can say anything .... I want to say.   **7** On holiday, I can stay .... I like.   **8** I can dress .... I like.   **9** I can do all the mad things .... I've always wanted to do.   **10** I can buy .... they need for all the poor people in the country.   **11** I can invest .... I've won in stocks and shares.   **12** You can't tell me .... I should behave.   **13** I'm free to be .... I've always wanted to be.

2 **Ⓒ** In some cases in exercise 1, we could also use *whatever, whoever, whenever, wherever, however*. Write the word after the number of the sentence. Write *✗* if it's impossible to use an *-ever* word.

0 *wherever*   **7** ....
1 ....   **8** ....
2 ....   **9** ....
3 ....   **10** ....
4 ....   **11** ....
5 ....   **12** ....
6 ....   **13** ....

3 **Ⓓ** Put *what, who, where, why, how, when* in the gaps.

0 *What* he said was wrong.   **1** .... he passed such a difficult exam is a mystery   **2** .... the bus leaves is written on the notice board.   **3** .... the teacher decided to punish him is unclear.   **4** .... we need is this.   **5** .... I'm giving you for your birthday is a surprise.   **6** .... I voted in the election is my business.   **7** .... they choose to be the next president depends on the people.   **8** .... you go on holiday depends on the travel agent.   **9** .... he stole was worthless.

4 **Ⓐ - Ⓓ** Circle all the correct sentences.

0 ~~He gave me the things I had asked for.~~/He gave me what I had asked for. He gave me the things I had asked for them./He gave me which I had asked for./He gave me everything what I had asked for./He gave me everything I had asked for.

1 What caused the accident is a mystery./Which caused the accident is a mystery./We don't know what caused the accident./We don't know the reason what caused the accident.

2 Have you received everything what I sent you?/Have you received what I sent you?/Have you received the things what I sent you?/Have you received the what I sent you?/Have you received the things which I sent you?

3 Here are the computers. You can use whichever you like./You can do anything you want with them./There is nothing what they cannot do./They will solve all the problems which you have./Everything what you want is possible.

4 Martin has left the army. He can wear whatever clothes he likes./He can wear whichever he likes./He can stay out until whatever time he wants./He can do everything that he wants.

5 Why the robber murdered Lady Alice is still not known./The police will be criticised however methods they use./Where the robber hid the jewels hasn't been discovered./Someone will find the jewels wherever he hid them./Wherever the robber goes, he can't escape.

REVISION 5 >> First Certificate Practice

PAPER 3 PART 1

1 For questions 1-12, read the text below and decide which answer, A, B, C or D, best fits each gap. There is an example at the beginning (0).

A LUXURY LIMOUSINE

Would you like the kind of limousine (0) A pop stars and film actors travel around in. This new spacious model (1) ..... occupies three parking spaces of a normal car, can accommodate nine passengers in the back section alone. It has satellite control navigation, (2) ..... means it can speak to you and tell you (3) ..... you want to know. Tell it the name of the place (4) ..... you're heading for and the route that it supplies is the quickest and the most trouble-free according to latest traffic information. The back section provides all the luxuries (5) ..... you could desire, some of which have never been available in a road vehicle before. There is a digital surround sound system (6) ..... provides the highest quality music reproduction with eight speakers. There are refrigerated storage units (7) ..... you can keep your champagne and caviar! There are two flip-down screens (8) ..... you can watch DVDs or videos and a special ceiling panel which displays a star map, a sunny sky or (9) ..... you choose. If privacy is (10) ..... you want, there is a screen to cut you off from the driver. Want one? Well, if you've got £100,000 (11) ..... is the price of the one (12) ..... we're looking at now, you can order it immediately.

0 (A)	which	B that it	C who	D where
1 A	which	B which it	C , that	D , which
2 A	that	B which it	C what	D which
3 A	whatever	B everything what	C , what	D –
4 A	that	B for which	C what	D for where
5 A	–	B for which	C who	D what
6 A	that it	B which it	C what	D which
7 A	which	B in where	C in which	D that
8 A	which	B on which	C on where	D , which
9 A	how	B who	C whichever	D whatever
10 A	that which	B which	C what	D the thing what
11 A	which	B what	C , which	D , what
12 A	–	B what	C , which	D that,

PAPER 3 PART 2

2 For these questions, read the text below and think of the word which best fits the gap. Use only *one* word in each space. There is an example at the beginning (0).

CAR ADVERTISING

In modern society, something (0) which most people consider to be an essential possession is a car. Cars are not just metal boxes which we travel from place to place (1) .... They are also symbols of the position (2) .... we occupy in society. We can easily perceive this if we study what the advertisers choose to emphasise. The technical features (3) .... might attract us to purchase the model are underplayed. Instead of fuel consumption, braking power, basic comfort etc., (4) .... they emphasise is appearance, speed and the status which a particular make of car automatically brings with it. In a current TV advertisement, a group of friends (5) .... are eating together begin to discuss their cars. One couple, (6) .... pride in their newly acquired vehicle is plain, gain social prestige while another, whose embarrassment is equally plain, confess to owning a less expensive vehicle. The link between choice of car and sexual prowess is something (7) .... has long been familiar: the swimsuit-clad young women (8) .... adorn car shows; the advertisements (9) .... which the male driver impresses female admirers; the equation of speed with sexual power (10) .... many advertisements make. However, with changes in the society in (11) .... we live, a change of emphasis has occurred. Now it is the independent woman driver (12) .... choice of car impresses her male colleagues.

PAPER 3 PART 4

3 **For these questions, complete the second sentence so that it has a similar meaning to the first sentence, using the word given. Do not change the word given. Use from two to five words including the word given. There is an example (0).**

0 They rewarded drivers with a good accident record.
   They rewarded drivers *who had avoided* accidents.   *AVOIDED*

1 The car which he had bought from Joe broke down.
   The car Joe .... broke down. *SOLD*

2 This is the office which I worked in for eight years.
   This is the office .... for eight years. *WHERE*

3 The police arrested the man whom I'd identified from his photo.
   The police arrested the man .... identified. *WHOSE*

4 The fact that I took a week's holiday made them angry.
   What .... was the fact that I took a week's holiday. *MADE*

5 I really like the girl with the black sweater and red skirt.
   I really like the girl .... wearing the black sweater and red skirt. *IS*

6 She found him the things which he wanted.
   She found him .... wanted. *WHAT*

7 This is the student with the friends who helped him to cheat in the exam.
   This is the student .... to cheat in the exam. *WHOSE*

8 We went back to the town – he had grown up there.
   We went back to the town .... up. *WHERE*

OTHER PRACTICE

4 **Complete the second items. Omit the relative where possible.**

0 Your friend took some photos at the beach party. You say:
   'Have you got *the photos you took at the beach party*?'

1 Your friend arrives late. The slow train stops at all the stations. You say:
   'Did you come on the train ....?'

2 A girl's brother won the national disco-dancing championship. You say:
   'Do you know the girl ....?'

3 Your friend has been expecting a letter. You ask:
   'Did the postman bring the letter ....?'

4 The youth club is organising a barbecue. You ask:
   'Are you going to the barbecue ....?'

5 There is a car which is blocking the pathway. There is no driver.
   'Can you find the person ....?'

UNIT 50 >> Inversion after negative adverbials

 Nick is angry with Brigitte.
'**Not only** did she lose the company files **but** she forgot to bring me my mid-morning coffee!'

A INVERTING THE VERB

We can move negative adverbials to the front of a sentence (instead of their normal position in mid-sentence). When we do this, we invert the verb, using the same form of the verb as in a question. In other words, the negative adverbial is followed by auxiliary verb and subject:

Never have I known such an incompetent secretary!

We also do this with adverbials such as **little** and **hardly,** which give a negative force to the sentence:

Little did I realise how lazy she was!

B NEGATIVE ADVERBIALS

Here are examples of some of the ones most commonly used:

Never have I seen such a beautiful flower! (Usually: **Never + perfect verb**)
Not only did he win the race but he also broke the record.
Not a penny did he give me.
Not a cloud was there in the sky. (**Not + a + noun**)
Not once did she warn me.
On no account must you press this switch. (Often: **On no account + must...**)
No sooner had we fallen asleep than the storm woke us up. (Often with **perfect verb**)
Hardly had she arrived than she... (**Hardly + perfect verb + than...**)
Little did I think that I'd be homeless one day. (Often: **Little did I think/know/realise...**)

C USE

We generally use this structure in **formal**, often **literary**, **contexts**. We use it to create a **sense of drama** and to place **emphasis** on the negative element of the sentence.

Never have I known such an incompetent secretary,

sounds more formal, old-fashioned than

I've never known such an...

In conversation, the expressions most likely to occur are:

Not only did he...   *No way can...*   *Little did I think...*   *Only...*

Not only did she come first in her class but she also came first in the year.
No way can I get the homework done by tomorrow.
Little did I think that I'd get a job as a pilot.
Only in this butchers can you find such good meat.

Notice: that we do not use inversion when a negative adverbial of time or place is non-emphatic:

Not far from here, you can find wild orchids.

1 **A** - **C** **Rewrite 1-9 by completing the sentences.**

0 I hesitated before employing Brigitte.
Not for nothing *did I hesitate before employing Brigitte.*

1 She makes a lot of mistakes and she also insults our clients.
Not only ....

2 As soon as an important client entered the office, she started whistling.
Hardly ....

3 It's very important that Brigitte doesn't have the key to the safe.
On no account .... (use: *must*)

4 She arrived at the office on time on one occasion only.
Only once ....

5 I forbid her to wear a bikini in the office.
No way .... (use: *can*)

6 She has never typed a letter without spelling mistakes.
Never ....

7 I had no idea that her boyfriend would kiss her in the office.
Little .... (use: *think*)

8 She wears horrible perfume and she leaves lipstick on the coffee cups.
Not only ....

9 You would not often find such easy-going bosses as Nick and Jill.
Rarely ....

2 **A** - **C** **Rewrite 1-6 using expressions from the list in front position.**

little   never   no sooner   not until now   on no account   only   ~~seldom~~

0 My daughters don't often remember my birthday.
Seldom do my daughters remember my birthday.

1 You mustn't tell a Scot that Scotland is part of England.
....

2 You can hear Geordie* nowhere else except in the North East. (* a local dialect)
....

3 As soon as we sat down to have a picnic it began to rain.
....

4 I didn't think it was likely I would become president of the company.
....

5 I didn't understand the reason why she hates me until this moment.
....

6 I have met such a rude person at no time in the past.
....

OPEN EXERCISE

3 **A** - **C** **Write true sentences about yourself or your friends, using structures from this unit.**

1 Never ....
2 Little ....
3 No way ....
4 Only once in my life ....
5 On no account ....
6 Hardly ....
7 Seldom ....
8 Not only ....

Look back at your sentences. Would you use any of them in normal conversation or do they all seem too artificial?

UNIT 51 >> More about inversion

'Hi, Jack. Thanks for phoning. But I can't talk, I've got ten girlfriends with me.'   '**So have I.**'
'They're all fashion models and film stars.'   '**So are mine**.'
'They never look at other boys.'   '**Nor do mine.**'
'OK, I'm lying. I'm all alone tonight.'   '**Yeah, I am too.**'

Ⓐ INVERSION AFTER *SO, NEITHER, NOR*

We use **so** + **auxiliary verb** + **subject** after a **positive** statement, especially in a conversation between two people.

We use **neither/nor** + **auxiliary verb** + **subject** after a **negative** statement. For example:

'*Sue's going to the disco tonight.*'   '*So is Jill.*'
'*I'm not coming home till late.*'   '*Neither am I.*'   or   '*Nor am I.*'
'*My brother passed all his exams.*'   '*So did my sister.*'
'*But I didn't pass any of them.*'   '*Neither did I.*'   or   '*Nor did I.*'

Ⓑ NO INVERSION WITH *TOO* OR *EITHER*

Notice that we can also use **too** after positive statements and **either** after negative statements but in these cases there is **no inversion**:

'*We were at the party last night.*'   '*Gina and Tom were too.*'
'*My brother didn't enjoy the film.*'   '*I didn't either.*'

Ⓒ INVERSION AFTER *AS, THAN, SO*

In a formal style, we may use inversion after **as** and **than**: as/than + **auxiliary verb** + **subject**:
*He went to a private school, **as did** his father and grandfather.* (Not ~~as went...~~)
*I was at the party, **as were** all my friends.*
*The Ancient Egyptians achieved more **than did** the Phoenicians.*

After emphatic **so** + **adjective/adverb** we use an inverted form of the whole verb:
***So difficult did** the teacher **make** the questions that everyone failed.*
***So loudly did** she **scream** that the neighbours called the police!*

Ⓓ INVERSION AFTER ADVERBIAL EXPRESSIONS OF PLACE

In informal spoken English, we often use inversion after **here** or **there** or other short adverbs and adverb particles. Notice that we do this with the simple tenses of intransitive verbs, especially **come** and **go**: *Here comes Susan.* (Not ~~Here is coming Susan.~~)
***There goes** the train. We've missed it!*   *As soon as I got to the stop, **along came** a bus.*

Notice: that we do not use inversion if the subject is a pronoun:
Here she comes. (Not ~~Here comes she.~~)

We also use this kind of inversion with intransitive verbs in formal or descriptive writing:
*At the top of the hill **stands a castle.*   *Outside the front door **was sleeping a huge dog.***

Ⓔ OTHER CASES OF INVERSION

We sometimes use inversion to express a conditional idea (see Unit 110):
***Were she** my daughter, I'd stop her from going out with him.*

Or after direct speech with verbs like **say, ask, exclaim** etc.:
'*Go to the back door,*' **ordered Jack**. (but not with pronouns: ~~... ordered he.~~)

1 **A** Uncle Joe and Aunt Emily are talking. They share the same things. Complete Emily's answers, using *so* or *nor/neither* with the word in brackets.

0 'My legs ache all the time.' *'So do mine.'* (*mine*)

1 'Two of my daughters live in Australia.' '...' (*my son*)

2 'My grandchildren never visit me.' '...' (*mine*)

3 'My family wants to put me in an old people's home.' '...' (*mine*)

4 'I had lots of fun when I was a teenager.' '...' (*I*)

5 'These are my own teeth.' '...' (*these*)

6 'I can't read without my glasses any more.' '...' (*I*)

7 'All my brothers and sisters died a long time ago.' '...' (*mine*)

8 'I don't want a big funeral.' '...' (*I*)

9 'I mustn't forget to write a will.' '...' (*I*)

10 'I'd like to be young again.' '...' (*all our friends*)

2 **B** Rewrite your answers in exercise 1 using *too* or *either*.

0	*'Mine do too.'*	4	....	8	....
1	....	5	....	9	....
2	....	6	....	10	....
3	....	7	....		

3 **C** Complete these sentences using *as, than* or *so* and inversion. A clue to the meaning is in the brackets.

0 Ben went to Cambridge University *as did his brother.* (= *his brother went to Cambridge too*)

1 Lia makes original inventions .... (= *and her father makes them too*)

2 I solved more problems .... (= *the professor solved less*)

3 .... the climate that you can only go out at night. (= *it's a very hot climate*)

4 The Internet contains more information .... (= *a normal library contains less*)

5 I must do my duty .... (= *and you must also do yours*)

6 The tribes were preparing for war .... (= *and the army was also preparing*)

7 On average, girls get better exam results .... (= *boys don't do as well*)

8 .... the forest that no one dared enter it. (= *the forest was very dangerous*)

4 **D** **E** Rewrite each item using inversion. Use *here* or *there* if appropriate. But write ✗ if inversion is not possible.

0 Look! The train is coming. *Look! Here comes the train.*

1 We stopped. Then a policeman walked up. ....

2 The shelf broke. All the books fell down. ....

3 'I love you,' Romeo whispered. ....

4 A river runs through the centre of the town. ....

5 A large lion was lying in the long grass near the jungle. ....

6 'I'll meet you tonight at 10 o'clock,' he promised. ....

7 Look at the harbour. The fishing boats are going. ....

8 As we left, the red sun sank below the western horizon. ....

9 As soon as the cat approached, a thousand birds flew up. ....

10 Look! Here it comes! ....

UNIT 52 >> Verbs with direct and indirect objects

@ Margaret gave **an apron to Frank** for his birthday. For hers, he gave **her a set of golf clubs.** She bought a **cookery book for him** for Christmas. He bought **her an electric drill**. And at New Year she gave **him an iron** while he gave **a World Cup football video to her.**

A SENTENCE STRUCTURES WITH TWO-OBJECT VERBS

Sometimes a verb has two objects.
- We can say: *She gave **Frank a present.***
  Frank is the **indirect object** (often a person); *a present* is the **direct object** (often a thing.)
- or we can say: *She gave **a present to Frank.***

So, there are two possible structures:
either (**1**) *She gave Frank a present.*
or   (**2**) *She gave a present to Frank.* (preposition + indirect object)

B STRUCTURE 1: VERB + INDIRECT OBJECT + DIRECT OBJECT

Here are some examples of Structure 1 with different verbs:

subject	verb	indirect object	direct object
He	*gave*	*me*	*a present.*
I	*lent*	*Tom*	*£100.*
He	*showed*	*them*	*the photos.*
Her friends	*bought*	*her*	*a birthday cake.*
He	*cooked*	*his friends*	*a meal.*
They	*brought*	*their teacher*	*the homework.*
He	*took*	*his girlfriend*	*some roses.*

C STRUCTURE 2: VERB + DIRECT OBJECT + *TO/FOR* + INDIRECT OBJECT

In Structure 2, we use the preposition **to** when there is the idea of **giving** or **passing**:
*He gave a present **to** me.*   *I lent £100 **to** Tom.*   *He showed the photos **to** them.*

We use the preposition **for** when there is the idea of **doing something for somebody** or **helping**: *Her friends bought a birthday cake **for** her.*   *He cooked a meal **for** his friends.*

Sometimes, we can use **either to or for**:   *They brought the homework **to/for** their teacher.*
                                                  *He took some roses **to/for** his girlfriend.*

D CASES WHERE ONLY STRUCTURE 2 IS POSSIBLE

We must use Structure 2 (+ preposition) when the direct object is a pronoun (**it, them** etc.)
He gave it to me.   **Not** ~~He gave me it.~~
They brought it to the teacher.   **Not** ~~They brought the teacher it.~~

Certain two-object verbs can be used **only** with Structure 2. These include:
          admit   describe   dictate   explain   mention   say   suggest

For example, we say:
*I **explained** the problem **to them**.*   **But not** ~~I explained them the problem.~~
*He **suggested** a plan **to his friends**.*   **But not** ~~He suggested them a plan.~~

E QUESTIONS WITH TWO-OBJECT VERBS

We form questions using either structure:
(**1**) *Did you send **him a letter**?*   (**2**) *Did you send **a letter to him**?*

1 Ⓐ - Ⓒ Make sentences from the information, using *while* and the two-object verbs in brackets. Use Structure 1 or 2 as indicated.

0 Bob McGive → wife: diamond ring/Bruce McScrooge → wife: a second-hand hoover.
   Bob gave his wife a diamond ring while Bruce gave a second-hand hoover to his.
   (*gave* (1)/*gave* (2))

1 Myra → Myron: a postcard from the Pyramids/Myron → Myra: a bill (*sent* (1)/*sent* (2))

....

2 Claudette → Jean Grotesque: a silver Mercedes/Jean → Claudette: silk underwear (*bought* (2)/*bought* (1))

....

3 The police → the terrorists: $100,000/the terrorists → the police: the return of Roger Scoop. (*offered* (1)/*promised* (2))

....

4 Slim Skinty → Ellie Tramper: a pair of old boots/Ellie → Slim: some cigarette ends (*gave* (1)/*gave* (2))

....

5 Brigitte → her boyfriend: Nick's secret diary/he → her: his boss's credit card bill (*showed* (2)/*showed* (1))

....

6 Tom Craze → his girlfriend: a million red roses/Slim → his girlfriend: a daisy (*took* (1)/*took* (2))

....

7 Brigitte → boyfriend: snails/Claudette → boyfriend: frogs' legs (*cooked* (1)/*cooked* (2))

....

8 Maggie → her teacher: a 10,000-word essay/Tom → his teacher: a rotten apple (*brought* (1)/*brought* (2))

....

9 Ellie → Slim: her broken umbrella/he → her: 1p (*lent* (1)/*lent* (2))

....

10 Lord Brian → Lady Alice: the sherry/she → him: the whisky (*passed* (2)/*passed* (2))

....

2 Ⓐ - Ⓓ Write 1 or 2 after each sentence below to show if they are Structure 1 or Structure 2. Then rewrite each sentence using the other structure. Remember to use either *to* or *for*. If it is not possible to use the other structure, write *X*.

0 She took her sick aunt some grapes. **1** *She took some grapes to her sick aunt.*

1 They paid the mechanic £100. ....

2 They told a ghost story to me. ....

3 The dog fetched the stick for its owner. ....

4 She gave it to me for Christmas. ....

5 Did you give the message to Tim? ....

6 Have they shown it to the police? ....

7 Please hand it to the receptionist. ....

8 Please pass the salt to her. ....

9 I sold the painting of the forest to her. ....

10 Sorry, I've already lent it to him. ....

11 The magazine paid him £20 for the poem. ....

3 ⓓ Replace the underlined noun(s) with a pronoun (*it, them* etc.). Sometimes you must change the structure.

0 I bought the <u>ice cream</u> for the <u>children</u>. *I bought it for them.*

1 I bought <u>the ice cream</u> for them. ....

2 He lent his best friend <u>some money</u>. ....

3 I gave <u>a computer</u> to <u>my nephew</u>. ....

4 They showed their guests <u>the video</u>. ....

5 We gave each other <u>a calendar</u>. ....

6 They passed <u>the magazine</u> to <u>the man</u>. ....

7 We handed <u>the woman the umbrella</u>. ....

8 She offered the dog <u>a bone</u>. ....

9 Did you send the fax to <u>your boss</u>? ....

4 ⓐ - ⓓ Read the note from Pablo to his friend and find 12 more errors in the use of two-object verbs. Write the corrected sentences below the letter.

Dear Sally,

There's only enough time to write to you a short note. I have had a wonderful Christmas. My parents gave to me a new computer. My grandparents wanted to give me a new car. But I explained them my problem. I don't know how to drive! So, instead, they sent to me a new bicycle. In the middle of the day, my parents cooked for the whole family Christmas lunch. I cannot describe you the food. It was so wonderful! After lunch, my girlfriend brought for me twelve roses. Isn't that strange? Usually the boy brings to the girl flowers. But she explained me her idea. As I never buy her flowers, she thought she would give to me a good example. So, now I feel very guilty.

Well, that's all. Send your news me soon. What did Father Christmas bring you?
love, Pablo.

PS. Did I mention you my birthday party? It is on 8th January. Don't bring for me any presents. I already have enough!

0 There's only enough time to write you a short note. **or** ... to write a short note to you.

1 ....

2 ....

3 ....

4 ....

5 ....

6 ....

7 ....

8 ....

9 ....

10 ....

11 ....

12 ....

5 **A** - **D** Write two sentences for each item 1-10, using both possible structures 1 or 2 UNLESS only structure 2 is possible. In the latter case, write only a single sentence.

0 Bob/give/his wife/a ring. (past negative)
Bob didn't give his wife a ring. Bob didn't give a ring to his wife.

1 Nick/dictate/Brigitte/a letter. (future with *be going to*)

....

2 Carmen/send/an e-mail/Elaine. (Past Simple)

....

3 The generals/explain/the President/the war plans. (Present Perfect)

....

4 Lia/describe/the Professor/her new invention. (Present Perfect negative)

....

5 His parents/bake/a birthday cake/him. (Past Simple)

....

6 I/give/it/my girlfriend/tomorrow. (Future with *be going to*)

....

7 Nerissa/write/a letter/you. (Present Perfect)

....

8 Harry/admit/the crime/the police. (Past Simple)

....

9 She bought some new clothes and/show/them/her friends. (Past Simple)

....

10 I/mention/Peter/the concert. (Past Simple)

....

6 **E** Make questions for these answers. Use Structure 1 where possible. Use ideas from this list:

| Brigitte | a Dior jacket | her family | her father | the French film | a letter |
| her Mercedes | ~~a pearl necklace~~ | Plan A | ~~the robbery~~ | a pullover | vegetables |

0 *Did he give her a pearl necklace?*   No, he gave her <u>a diamond ring</u>.
00 *Did he admit the robbery to the police?*   No, he admitted <u>the murder</u> to the police.
1 ....? No, he explained <u>Plan B</u> to her.
2 ....? No, she sent him <u>an e-mail</u>.
3 ....? No, she's knitting <u>a scarf</u> for him.
4 ....? No, she bought her boyfriend <u>an Armani suit</u>.
5 ....? No, she's cooking <u>her mother</u> dinner.
6 ....? No, he suggested <u>the Russian film</u> to his friends.
7 ....? No, she bought <u>fruit</u> for him.
8 ....? No, he dictated the letters to <u>Beth</u>.
9 ....? No, she bought them for <u>the neighbours</u>.
10 ....? No, she lent him <u>her other car</u>.

OPEN EXERCISE

7 **A** - **E** Write a similar letter to the one in exercise 5 about Christmas/your last birthday/another occasion. Include at least six sentences which contain two-object verbs.

UNIT 53 >> Questions with *who, what, when* etc.

 'What time does the Cardiff train leave? Which platform does it go from? How much does a return ticket cost? How long does it take? When...? Where...? Who...?'
'Sorry, you've missed it. Too many questions.'

Ⓐ TWO TYPES OF *WH*-QUESTION

1 Who did the assassin kill?
(He killed) **the President**.

2 Who killed the President.
The assassin (killed the President).

Question 1 uses the question form of the verb: **did he kill...?** The answer is in **object position** after the verb.

In 2, the question uses the normal form of the verb: **killed...** The answer is in **subject position**.

question word as object	question word as subject
Which train **shall** we **catch**?	Which train **goes** to Cardiff?
Whose ticket **did** you **lose**?	Whose ticket **costs** half price?
How many trains **did** they **cancel**?	How many trains **go** to Cardiff?

Ⓑ QUESTION WORDS

What...? (for things)/**Who...?** (for people)/**When...?** (for time)/**Where...?** (for place)/**Why...?** (for reason, cause)/**How...?** (for method, manner)/**Whose...?** (for possession (see Unit 34)/**Which...? Which of the...?** (for things or people when we are asking about one/some of a limited set)
What did you do yesterday?   *Whose car is this?*   *How did she escape?*
Here are some umbrellas. Which is the one that you lost?
Don't confuse **who's...?** (= who is...? or who has...?) and **whose...?**
Who's there? (is)   *Who's broken it? (has)*   *Whose are these jeans? (possession)*

Ⓒ QUESTION WORDS AND PREPOSITIONS OR PARTICLES

We often use **What... for?** instead of **Why...?** to ask about reason or function:
What did you do that for? (= *Why did you do that?*)   *What are these scissors for?*
Other common question word-preposition/particle combinations include:
What + about: *What's the book about?*
What + up: *What's up* (informal) (= What's happening?)
Sometimes we can ask a question with just a question word and a preposition:
'I mended the chair.' 'What with?' *'I've sold the car.'* *'What for?'*

Ⓓ *WHAT* + NOUN/*HOW* + ADJECTIVE OR ADVERB/*HOW MUCH* AND *HOW MANY*

We often use **What + noun, Which + noun, Whose + noun**:
What time does the train leave?   *Which ticket is yours?*   *Whose bag is that?*
We also often use **How + adjective/adverb**: *How long...?, How often...?* etc.
We use **How long...?** to ask about time or distance:
'How long does the film last?' '2 hours.'   *'How long is the room?' '25 metres.'*
We use **How much...?** and **How many...?** to ask about number or quantity or price:
How much does it cost?   *How much milk is there?*   *How many books have you read?*

Ⓔ QUESTION WORDS + *ELSE*

We can follow **what, who, where, how** etc. with **else**:
What else did you see? (= What other things did you see?)
How else can I help?   (= In what other ways can I help?)

140   54 More about questions   56 Short answers, questions and responses   72 Prepositions
104 Indirect questions

1 Ⓐ **Complete the questions.**

0 Who *fell in love with him*? Betty fell in love with him.

1 Who .... ? He fell in love with Sally.

2 How many .... ? Sixty flights go to Bahrain every week.

3 How many .... ? They cancelled six flights last week.

4 Whose .... ? The police examined Gina's car.

5 Whose .... ? John's car caused the accident.

6 What .... ? A quarrel about sport started the fight.

7 Why .... ? They fought because they supported different teams.

8 Which .... ? The red-haired man started the fight.

9 Which .... ? He supports Crunchester United.

2 Ⓑ **Is it better to use *Which* or *What* in items 1-12?**

0 We've got three kinds of sandwich. *Which* kind do you want?

1 There are three girls in the photo. You ask: '............................... girl is your sister?'

2 You meet someone and want to contact them again. '............................... is your e-mail address?'

3 Hugh has been out with three famous fashion models. '............................... model was the prettiest?'

4 Your friend knows about three cities that you plan to visit. '............................... advice can you give me?'

5 At the same time, you ask the same friend: '............................... city has the best hotels?'

6 You ask your friend: '............................... is your favourite hobby?'

7 Your friend has three hobbies. '............................... hobby is the most satisfying?'

8 He has just taken an exam. '............................... question was the most difficult?'

9 You have seen your friend talking to a detective. '............................... questions did he ask you?'

10 Your friend has got a new girlfriend. '............................... is her name?'

11 'I want to buy you one of these pullovers. .... one do you prefer?'

12 You're going to a disco and you want some general advice. '............................... shall I wear?'

3 Ⓑ **Use *who's* or *whose* in these questions.**

0 *Who's* spilt the wine?

1 .... lost this ring?

2 .... helping us tomorrow?

3 .... got my dairy?

4 .... address is this?

5 .... is that car?

6 .... umbrella can I borrow?

7 .... cooking tonight?

4 Ⓐ Ⓑ Ⓓ **Write questions about the items of information 1-11. The answers are underlined.**

0 Professor Makepeace read <u>a novel about time travel</u>.
What did Professor Makepeace read?

1 Professor Makepeace built <u>a Time Machine</u>.

....

2 <u>His daughter</u> helped him to build it.

....

3 The Time Machine cost <u>£500,000,000</u>.

....

4 <u>His daughter</u> travelled in the Machine on the first voyage.

....

5 She went to <u>Giza in Ancient Egypt</u>.

....

6 <u>Cleopatra's soldiers</u> arrested her.

....

7 Cleopatra shut her <u>in the Great Pyramid</u>.

....

8 <u>A mummy came to life and helped her escape</u>.

.... (use: *to happen*)

9 This happened in <u>AD 32</u>.

....

10 She escaped from Egypt <u>by using the Time Machine</u>.

....

11 <u>The mummy</u> came back to the present with her.

....

5 Ⓓ Put *What* + noun OR *Whose* + noun in the gaps to make suitable questions.

0 '*What colour* is her new blouse?' 'Purple and pink.'
1 '.. of ice cream do you like?' 'Vanilla.'
2 '.. is it?' 'It's June.'
3 '.. of music did they play?' 'Rock and roll.'
4 '.. is this?' 'It's Janine's (photo).'
5 '.. were you married?' '1987.'
6 '.. do you play?' 'Baseball and basketball.'
7 '.. do you play?' 'The guitar and trumpet.'
8 '.. did you borrow?' 'Hester's (dictionary).'
9 '.. do you usually read?' '*The Daily Mail*.'
10 '.. did they give the new baby?' 'Stephen Anthony James.'
11 '.. will she marry?' 'Benny's (brother).'

6 Ⓓ Make questions with *How* + adjective/adverb. The answers are underlined.

0 It takes <u>six hours</u> to get to Cardiff. *How long does it take to get to Cardiff?*
1 Canterbury is <u>70 kms</u> from Guildford. ....
2 The length of the curtain is <u>two metres</u>. ....
3 Myra eats salad <u>three times a da</u>. ....
4 Claudette weighs <u>fifty kilograms</u>. ....
5 The water is <u>75 degrees</u> centigrade. ....
6 The lake is <u>300 metres</u> wide. ....
7 The pool is <u>23 metres</u> deep. ....
8 The statue is <u>10,000 years old</u>. ....
9 My wife is <u>1.5 metres</u> in height. ....
10 <u>Simon</u> has an IQ (= intelligence quotient) of 190. ....
11 A normal football match lasts <u>90 minutes</u>. ....

7 **D** Make questions about items 1-11 with *How much* + noun... or *How many* + noun... .

0 Two thousand cars use this road every day. How many cars use this road every day?

1 A lot of information is irrelevant. ....

2 Myra has won five Oscars. ....

3 Professor Makepeace needs a lot of equipment. ....

4 They stole twenty-three mobile phones. ....

5 A hundred days passed before she forgave him. ....

6 A thousand soldiers attacked the city. ....

7 She used half a kilo of sugar to make the cake. ....

8 You can expect a lot of bad weather this autumn. ....

9 During the war, a lot of soldiers died. ....

10 The Metalheads have recorded five new songs. ....

11 Twenty-five centimetres of rain fell last week. ....

OPEN EXERCISE

8 **E** Write questions with question-words + *else* for these situations.

0 Your sister is changing her flat. You've helped your sister to carry boxes to the car.
You ask: Is there anything more that I can do to help you?
How else can I help you?

1 Kate's come back from the party. She's told you that your ex-girlfriend was there.
You ask: Who were the other people who were there?

....

2 You think that the police have fingerprinted you because they suspect you.
You ask: For what other reason would they fingerprint me?

....

3 Your friend's shown you one of the many things she bought at the shops.
You ask: What are the other things that you bought?

....

4 The travel agent has told you about holidays in Kenya. You ask: What other places in Africa can I visit?

....

5 You've solved a problem but your friends say that you used a stupid method.
You ask: In what other way could I solve it?

....

6 Your friend wants to visit you on Monday but you're busy.
You ask: At what other time can you visit me?

....

Now write the description of three more situations like those in 1-6 and write a question with *else* for each one.

Questions with *who, what, when* etc.

UNIT 54 >> More about questions

Dear Fernando,
How are you? **What** does it **feel like** to be in a new city? **What's** Cambridge **like**? Is it as beautiful as Oxford? **What** do the English girls **look like**? Are they all blonde with blue eyes? And **what's** the food **like**? Are you eating potatoes all the time?
love Claudia.

Ⓐ WHAT + BE + LIKE?/WHAT + LOOK + LIKE?

We use **What** + **be** + **like...?** to ask about somebody's/something's **character**:
'What is your boss like?'   *'He's generous but very strict.'*
'What is Canterbury like?'   *'It's an old city with a beautiful cathedral.'*

We use **What** + **look like...?** to ask about somebody's/something's **appearance**:
'What does your boss look like?'   *'He's tall and fat.'*
'What does the house look like?'   *'It's white with a green front door.'*

But it is also possible to use **What** + **be** + **like?** for appearance:
'What is she like?'   *'She is very beautiful.'* (appearance)
or   *'She is vain.'*   (character)

Ⓑ HOW...?

We use **How...?** to ask about **health/general happiness**:
How are you?   *How is your grandmother? Is she well?*

We can use **How...?** to formally greet someone for the first time: *'How do you do?'*

In informal situations, we use **How** + **be...?** to ask about **experiences**:
'How was the party?'   *'It was great.'*   *'How was the film?'*   *'Terrible!'*
'How is the meal?'   *'It's OK.'*

In formal English, we **do not** use **How** + **be...?** to ask about appearance or character*:
'How is your boss?'   Wrong: *'He's tall and fat.'* or *'He's very kind.'*
          Correct: *'He's very well.'*   or *'He's got a headache.'*

* But this is possible in informal English and American English.

Ⓒ IS HE LIKE...?

We can ask about **resemblance** using **be** + **like**:
Who's he like? (**Is he like** *his mother/his father/his grandfather etc.?*)

Ⓓ WHAT DOES IT FEEL/SMELL/SOUND/TASTE LIKE?

We can use **feel like, smell like, sound like** and **taste like** as well as **look like**.
What does the music sound like?   *What did the soup taste like?*

We can use **What... feel like?** or **How... feel?** to ask about **emotions**:
What did it feel like to see your girlfriend again? or *How did you feel when you saw...?*

We use **feel like** + **verb-ing** or + **noun** to talk about our **wishes/desires**:
'Do you feel like having a meal?'   *'No, but I feel like some chocolate.'*

1 **Ⓐ** Make questions about England with *What + be + like?* OR *What + look like?* Use BOTH patterns if both are possible OR use only one. Use suitable nouns.

0 *What are the police like?/What do the police look like?* Do they wear blue uniforms?

1 ....? Is it raining all the time?

2 ....? Are they very serious and reserved?

3 ....? Is it very green?

4 ....? Is he tall and handsome with wavy hair?

5 ....? Is it too cold to swim in?

6 ....? Are they old-fashioned with red roofs?

7 ....? Has it got central heating?

8 ....? Does it show interesting programmes?

2 **Ⓐ Ⓒ Ⓓ** Use question forms from the theory on the opposite page to rewrite these questions.

0 Was the food delicious, horrible etc.?   *What did the food taste like?*

1 Are you similar in character to your brother?   ....

2 Does the orchestra produce a good sound?   ....

3 Is Benny ill or well?   ....

4 Is Jay ugly, handsome etc.?   ....

5 Do you want to dance?   ....

6 Is the puppy's fur soft or rough?   ....

7 Were you happy or sad when you heard the news?   How ....

8 Were you angry or sad when you lost the race?   What ....

9 Can you describe this perfume?   ....

10 Is the teacher strict, generous, friendly etc.? ....

11 Does the new baby resemble its parents?   ....

12 Is Hull a boring or an interesting place?   ....

3 **Ⓐ Ⓑ Ⓓ** Rewrite the incorrect items. Put a tick (✓) next to the correct items.

0 How is the new boss like? Is she strict or unkind? *What is the new boss like?*

1 How does the singer look like? ....

2 What is her flat like? Is it luxurious? ....

3 How did the food taste like? .... or ....

4 What the college looks like? ....

5 Do you feel like watching a video? ....

6 How are the hotel rooms like? ....

7 I've never seen Myra. What does she look like? ....

8 'How is London?' 'It's got some historic buildings…' ....

9 'How was London?' 'I had a great time!' ....

OPEN EXERCISE

4 **Ⓐ Ⓑ Ⓓ** Your friend has just returned from a trip to South and North America. Ask questions using question forms from this unit about:

the carnival in Rio/New York/Peruvian food/Mexican music/the rainforests/the emotions of your friend when she saw the Amazon/the weather in California/any other people, things or experiences.

UNIT 55 >> Negative questions

> 'Why can't everybody live in peace? Why don't politicians tell the truth? Isn't it ridiculous that the rich nations don't help the poor nations? Why doesn't the government care about people? Why don't you answer my questions?'

Ⓐ FORM OF NEGATIVE QUESTIONS

We form negative questions like this:

Are you a spy? → *Aren't* you a spy?
Do you **speak** German? → *Don't* you **speak** German?
Did he **have** dinner? → *Didn't* he **have** dinner?
Will she **come** to the party? → *Won't* she **come** to the party?

Ⓑ USE

We use negative questions:

1 when we are **surprised**:
Haven't you been to work today?   *Aren't* you at school?

2 when we are **annoyed** or **angry**:
Why aren't you **working**?   *Why didn't* you **help** her?

3 as an **exclamation** (!):
Isn't this meal delicious!   *Wasn't* the weather terrible!

4 when we are **almost sure** about something:
Isn't your name Ted?   *Didn't* you **win** the lottery?

5 when there is a **negative fact** or **happening**:
Why didn't you **finish** the work?   *Which* bird **cannot** fly?

6 when we want to **express an opinion less directly**:
Wouldn't it be better if we went by car?   *Don't* you **think** this colour is better?

Notice that in reply to negative questions 'Yes' means the positive is true while 'No' means the negative is true.

'Don't you speak English?'   'Yes, I do./No, I don't speak English.'

Ⓒ MORE ABOUT USE

We use **Why don't we...?/Why don't you...?** etc. to make **suggestions**:
Why don't we go to the cinema?   *Why doesn't she* change her hairstyle?

We use **Why didn't...?** to **criticise** someone for failing to do something:
Why didn't you remind me to post the letter?

We use **Won't you...** to **persuade** somebody to do something:
Won't you stay for lunch?   *Won't you* help me to write this letter?

We sometimes use **Can't you/he** etc...? to **complain** or be **impolite**:
Can't you shut up?   *Can't they* go somewhere else?

1 **Ⓐ-Ⓒ** Nick is complaining to Brigitte about her lack of efficiency. Make negative questions.

0 *Haven't* you *sent* the faxes yet? (*send*)

1 Why .... you .... the office last night? (*lock*)

2 Look at the mess! Why .... you .... your desk? (*tidy*)

3 Why .... your boyfriend .... you outside working hours? (*can/phone*)

4 .... that top secret file .... in the safe? (*should/be*)

5 .... you .... faster than five words a minute? (*can/type*)

6 .... Jill .... you yesterday to write those letters? (*tell*)

7 .... it .... better to paint your fingernails at home? (*would/be*)

8 .... your last boss .... about you as well? (*complain*)

9 Why .... you polite to Mr Clark when he phoned? He's an important client! (*be*)

10 Why .... you .... for another job? (*look*)

11 'Please, Nick, ... you .... me a pay rise next month?' (*will/give*)

2 **Ⓐ-Ⓒ** Make negative questions for these situations. In some cases there is more than one possible answer.

0 Your friend's sister has a bad stomach-ache. 'Why *doesn't* she *go* to the doctor's? *Hasn't* she got any medicine?'

1 Stella wants to contact her parents but they aren't at home. '.................... they got a mobile number?' '.................... you .... until they return?'

2 Luigi is staying in Luton. He misses Italian food. '.................... there any Italian restaurants in Luton?' '.................... he .... English food?'

3 It's very good weather but Hetty is indoors. '.................... you like to sit outside? .... you got any sun cream? .... you stand the heat?'

4 You want to borrow some money from your parents. '.................... you .... me some money? I'll pay you back soon. .... you believe me? .... I always .... you the truth?'

3 **Ⓐ-Ⓒ** Complete the negative question responses to these items.

0 CRUNCHESTER UNITED BEAT LIVERPOOL. *Aren't Crunchester United* at the bottom of the league? (*be*)

1 *GRAMMAR GOALS* BY CEDRIC POOTER. .... by Derek Sellen? (*be*)

2 NEW FILM: *TITANIC*. .... a few years ago? (*come out*)

3 MYRA DIED LAST WEEK. But .... we .... her at the disco last night? (*see*)

4 HOTTEST DAY OF THE CENTURY. But .... the weather better last month? (*be*)

5 DOLPHIN IS MOST INTELLIGENT FISH. .... dolphins mammals?

6 THE MOON IN ORBIT ROUND THE SUN. .... go round the earth?

7 SHAKESPEARE TO VISIT THE USA. .... dead?

8 BOY NEARLY DROWNED IN POOL. .... he swim? (*could*)

9 NEW HOTEL READY NEXT YEAR. .... they .... building it yet? (*finish*)

OPEN EXERCISE

4 **Ⓐ-Ⓒ** Write suitable negative questions in response to these items.

0 I'm waiting for John to contact me. *Hasn't he phoned you yet?/Can't you phone him?*

1 He's catching a train to London.

2 Geoff's been spending a lot of money recently.

3 She's decided to marry Henry.

4 Sally's sold her car.

UNIT 56 >> Short answers, questions and responses

'Would you like to come to dinner with me?'   **'Thank you, I'd love to.'**
'Would you like to go dancing afterwards?'   **'Yes, I would.'**
'Would you like to come back to my flat for coffee?'   **'No, I'd better not.'**

Ⓐ SHORT ANSWERS

We often give short answers to yes/no questions, using an **auxiliary verb** or **be** or **have**:
'*Do you like chocolate?*'   **'Yes, I do.'**   '*Can you speak Russian?*'   **'No, I can't.'**
'*Are you Spanish?*'   **'Yes, I am.'**   '*Have you got a light?*'   **'Sorry, I haven't.'**
Notice that short answers don't use short forms after **I, you, he** etc.: *Yes, I am.* Not *Yes, I'm*.

The verb in the short answer may be different from the question verb:
***Do** you **want** some chocolate?*   *No, I **mustn't**.* (= I mustn't eat any chocolate.)

Sometimes, we use the same kind of response to a statement, request etc.:
'*Don't forget to write.*'   **'No, I won't.'**   '*You haven't washed.*'   **'Yes, I have!'**

Sometimes a short answer has a tag (see Unit 57): '*It's very hot.*' '*Yes, it is, **isn't it**?*'

Ⓑ SHORT ANSWERS WITH *SO* AND *NOT*

We form some short answers with **so** or **not** after certain verbs:
Positive: *I'm afraid so, I believe so, I expect so, I hope so, I guess so, I imagine so,*
I suppose so, It seems so, I think so
Negative: *I'm afraid not, I don't believe so, I don't expect so, I hope not, I guess not,*
I don't imagine so, It doesn't seem so, I don't suppose so, I don't think so
I believe not, I imagine not, It seems not, I suppose not, I think not are more formal.
'*Will Anne pass the exam?*'   **'I hope so.'**   Not *Yes, I hope*.
'*Is Alaska in Canada?*'   **'I don't think so.'**   Not *No, I don't think*.
'*John looked ill, didn't he?*'   **'Yes, I thought so.'**   Not *Yes, I thought*.
Other short responses with **not** include: *I'd better not, I'd rather not, Of course not*

Ⓒ SHORT RESPONSES WITH VERB + *TO*

With some verbs, we form a short answer with **to**:
Positive: *I'd like to, I'd love to, I have to, He seems to, I want to*
Negative: *I wouldn't like to, I don't have to, He seems not to, I don't want to*
Short answers with the verbs in this list **must** include **to**:
'*Are you coming to the beach?*' '*Yes, I want **to**.*'   Not *Yes, I want*.

Other verbs that are followed by a **to**-infinitive (see Unit 90) can generally be used with
or without **to**.
'*Can you do some extra work on Sunday?*' '*Yes, **I'll try to**.*' or '*Yes, **I'll try**.*'

Ⓓ SHORT QUESTIONS

We sometimes respond to a statement with a short question to express **interest,
disbelief, surprise** etc.:
'*The bridge collapsed yesterday*'.   '*What! **Did it**?*'   (= Did it collapse?)
'*I'm looking for a new job.*'   '*Oh, **are you**?*'   (= Are you looking...?)

Ⓔ SHOWING PRIOR KNOWLEDGE: *SO I'VE HEARD* ETC.

With verbs such as **believe, fear, hear, understand,** we can respond like this, using **So I...:**
'*John's going to study Law.*'   '***So I've heard.***' or '***So I understand.***'

1 **B** Write appropriate responses to the questions, using verbs from 56B – *be afraid, believe, expect, hope* etc. There may be more than one possible answer for some items.

'Is the President going to resign?'

0   You think the President is excellent and that he possibly won't resign: I hope not.

1   You think the President is excellent but that he probably will resign: ....

2   You think the President is bad and that he will possibly resign: ....

3   You believe that he will probably resign: ....

4   There are a lot of signs that he won't resign: ....

5   You don't really know but it seems likely: ....

6   You think the President is bad but that he probably won't resign: ....

2 **A** - **E** Tick (✔) the correct responses. Rewrite the incorrect responses.

0   'Did you like your Christmas presents?' 'Yes, I liked.'   Yes, I did.

1   'Are you coming to the party?' 'Yes, I want.'   ....

2   'The waiter's really handsome.' 'He is, isn't he?'   ....

3   'Is he going to register at the police station?' 'Yes, he has.' ....

4   'There's going to be an election next month.' 'So I am understanding.' ....

5   'John was at the disco.' 'Oh, was he?'   ....

6   'Do you fancy going to see the film at the Odeon?' 'Yes, I'd like.' ....

7   'Are you meeting Tom tonight?' 'Yes, I'm.'   ....

8   'You never help with the housework!' 'Yes, I do!'   ....

9   'Have you done well in your exams?' 'Yes, I hope.'   ....

10 'Come at once to the police station.' 'No, I refuse!'   ....

OPEN EXERCISE

3 **A** - **E** Write any suitable question or statement for these responses.

0   Did you go to school last week?   Yes, I did.

1   ....   So I believe.

2   ....   Of course not.

3   ....   No, she mustn't.

4   ....   Really! Would you?

5   ....   He had to.

6   ....   Thank you, but I'd rather not.

7   ....   So I fear.

8   ....   Yes, there have been.

9   ....   They do, don't they?

10 ....   Has it?

UNIT 57 >> Question tags

> 'Parachuting is great, **isn't it**? You're not afraid, **are you**? You are going to jump, **aren't you**? I'll push you, **shall I**?... WHOOOSH... There, that was great, **wasn't it**? You're not going home, **are you**? You'll come again next weekend, **won't you...?**'

A QUESTION TAGS: FORM AND USE

We most often use question tags in conversation and in informal writing.

verb/tense	positive + negative tag	negative + positive tag
be (present)	I'**m** late, **aren't** I? (Not ~~amn't I~~) She'**s** ill, **isn't** she?	I'**m not** late, **am** I? She **isn't** angry, **is** she?
be (past) Present Simple *Present Cont.* *Present Perfect* *Past Simple* *future* *modals*	She **was** there, **wasn't** she? They often **come** here, **don't** they? He'**s going** to win, **isn't** he? He'**s done** the work, **hasn't** he? He **lost** the match, **didn't** he? You'**ll come** back again, **won't** you? He **can** speak English, **can't** he? They **should** help us, **shouldn't** they.	I **wasn't** wrong, **was** I? We **never win**, **do** we? They **aren't joking**, **are** they? They **haven't finished** yet, **have** they? You **didn't see** Charles, **did** you? He **won't make** trouble, **will** he? She **can't** swim, **can** she? You **shouldn't** steal, **should** you?
There + be	There'**s** a party tonight, **isn't** there?	There **aren't** any problems, **are** there?

Notice:

1 after pronouns like **everyone, everything, no one** we use **they**:
 Everybody enjoyed the party, didn't **they**?   *Nobody* cares, do **they**?
2 we use **it** to refer to **nothing**: *Nothing* bad happened, did **it**?
3 words like **never, hardly, rarely, seldom, scarcely, little** give a negative force to a statement, so that we use a positive tag: It **hardly** matters, **does it**?
 You **rarely** go to the cinema, **do you**?   You **never** lived in France, **did you**?
4 we sometimes use a positive tag after a positive statement (same way tags) to express interest, surprise etc.: So he'**s going** to Oxford University, **is he**?

B ANSWERS TO TAGS

When we reply to tag questions, 'Yes' means the positive is true and 'No' means the negative is true:

'Jo's English, isn't he?' '**Yes, he is.**'   'Jo's Welsh, isn't he?' '**No, he isn't.**'
'Jo isn't English, is he?' '**Yes, he is.**'   'Jo isn't Welsh, is he?' '**No, he isn't.**'

C TAGS AFTER IMPERATIVE VERBS TO MAKE REQUESTS, SUGGESTIONS ETC.

We can follow a positive imperative with **won't you?** to invite someone to do something or to be especially persuasive: *Come in, **won't you**?*   *Kiss me, **won't you**?*

We use imperatives with **will/would/can/can't/could you?** to ask or tell someone to do things: *Help me, **will you**?*   *Shut up, **can't you**?*   *Hold this, **could you**?*

After a negative imperative we use **will you**: *Don't break it, **will you**?*

After **let's...**, we can use **shall we?**:   *Let's go to the cinema, **shall we**?*

Instead of the imperative, we can use **You couldn't/wouldn't..., could/would you?** to be polite: *You couldn't/wouldn't pass me the salt, **could /would you**?*

D INTONATION PATTERNS WITH TAGS

Sometimes, we are asking a real question — we don't know the answer. Then the voice goes up: *This is Smith Street, isn't it?*

But often we expect the other person to agree. It is not a real question. Then the voice goes down: *This is Smith Street, isn't it?*

1 **Ⓐ** We use question tags in many situations. Here are some examples. As you read them, put in the missing question tags.

A *Often, we want to make sure our information is correct:*

  0 This is the Brightsea Hotel, *isn't it*?

  1 You're George Smith, ...?

  2 You paid the money, ...?

  3 There won't be a barbecue, ...?

B *Sometimes, we want to be friendly:*

  4 It's wonderful weather, ...?

  5 That's a new hairstyle, ...?

  6 Sue hasn't changed much, ...?

  7 We haven't been introduced, ...?

  8 Your sister looks like you, ...?

C *Sometimes, we want or expect the other person to agree with us:*

  9 This cake is nice, ...?

  10 Shakespeare was a wonderful writer, ...?

  11 He doesn't dress very well, ...?

D *Sometimes, we expect the other person to do something for us:*

  12 You won't tell him about the accident, ...?

  13 You're going to give me a diamond for my birthday, ..., darling?

  14 You'll lend me the money, ...?

E *Sometimes, we are surprised:*

  15 That's not Tom Craze, ...?

  16 It can't be midnight already, ...?

  17 You haven't won first prize again, ...?

  18 He wasn't rude to the Queen, ...?

  19 You didn't forget your passport, ...?

F *Sometimes, we want to give some unexpected information:*

  20 You didn't know I was a member of the Royal Family, ...?

G *Sometimes we are angry with the other person:*

  21 You didn't tell the truth, ...?

  22 You're not going to tell anyone, ...?

  23 You've stolen my wallet, ...?

  24 It was you who broke the window, ...?

H *Sometimes we want to request something politely*:

  25 You couldn't tell me his phone number, ...?

  26 You wouldn't help me, ...?

2 **Ⓐ** Make statements with question tags to suit these situations. Think carefully about question 3 (see Unit 23 *must* and *don't have to*).

0 I believe that Jenny's in love with Geoff. I say: Jenny's in love with Geoff, isn't she?

1 I don't believe that Ben studied at Oxford: ....?

2 I think that this food is delicious: ....?

3 I don't think that I must wear a school uniform: ....?

4 I don't think that lions live in India: ....?

5 I don't accept that Jill can sack Brigitte: ....?

6 I agree that the government should raise taxes: ....?

7 I don't think it's Tina's birthday today: ....?

8 I am sure that Helen doesn't like sushi: ....?

3 **Ⓐ** Complete these sentences with question tags.

0 Nobody bought any cakes, did they?

1 Somebody must know the answer, ...?

2 Nothing ever goes right, ...?

3 He seldom visits my grandparents, ...?

4 Everyone went to the festival, ...?

5 She hardly ever does anything for other people, ...?

6 You never get nervous before exams, ...?

7 There are no vegetables in the fridge, ...?

8 The police did well last year, ...?

9 No one can see us, ...?

10 It's scarcely worth switching on the heating, ...?

4 **ⒶⒷ** Complete these questions with a tag and write short answers to them. Then listen and check your answers.

0 London's in Germany, isn't it? No, it isn't.

1 Alligators live in Britain, ...? ....

2 It doesn't rain a lot in the Sahara, ...? ....

3 Venus is the nearest planet to the sun, ...? ....

4 The French don't make wine, ...? ....

5 Edinburgh isn't the capital of Norway, ...? ....

6 Jupiter is the biggest planet in the solar system, ...? ....

7 They have a king in the USA, ...? ....

8 They make films in Hollywood, ...? ....

9 Gladiators used to fight in ancient Rome, ...? ....

10 Divorce is illegal in England, ...? ....

5 Ⓐ Ⓓ **Do these questions go up or down? Complete the tags and tick the more likely alternative.**

0 It's a sunny day. You say: It's lovely weather, *isn't it*?　　　　　UP　DOWN ✔

1 You are unsure if Dave's friends live in Wales or not:
   'They live in Wales, ...?'　　　　　UP　DOWN

2 You see a stranger who resembles a person you knew a
   long time ago. Perhaps it's the same person but you're not
   sure: 'You're not Ben Freedman, ...?'　UP　DOWN

3 At a party, a policeman in uniform enters the room. You are
   100% sure that this is someone playing a joke: 'Admit it.
   You're not a real policeman, ...?'　UP　DOWN

4 But he is a real policeman. He handcuffs you and asks:
   'You believe me now, ...?'　　　UP　DOWN

6 Ⓒ **Use an imperative verb + tag to make sentences to suit these situations.**

0 You want Bob to lend you his car: *Lend me your car, will you?* or *Lend me your car, won't you?*

1 You want Tim to turn down his radio. .... ? (use: *can't*)

2 You want to suggest going to the party to your friends. .... ?

3 You want to remind Sam not to forget to write. .... ?

4 You want to persuade Tom to tell you his secret. .... ?

5 You want to invite Joe to sit down. .... ?

6 You want to suggest organising a disco. .... ?

OPEN EXERCISE

7 Ⓐ Ⓒ **Write 2 more questions using tags for these situations.**

1 The police are interrogating a criminal:
   You placed the bomb, didn't you? .... ? .... ?

2 A girl is flirting with a boy:
   You think I'm pretty, don't you? .... ? .... ?

3 A boy wants to invite a girl out:
   Let's go to the disco, shall we? .... ? .... ?

4 You are expressing interest during a conversation by using 'same way' tags.
   So you're from the USA, are you? .... ? .... ?

5 Tom is expecting his friend to agree about the film they are watching.
   The actors aren't very good, are they? .... ? .... ?

6 Bob's parents are telling him to help them.
   Clean your room, won't you? .... ? .... ?

7 You are angry with someone and are asking them to stop doing things.
   Shut up, can't you? .... ? .... ?

8 The teacher is checking her students' general knowledge.
   Paris is in France, isn't it? .... ? .... ?

9 A researcher is asking about someone's past life.
   You grew up in Australia, didn't you? .... ? .... ?

10 An employer is checking the suitability of a candidate for a job.
   You've worked in a factory before, haven't you? ....? .... ?

UNIT 58 >> *To, so that, in case, for* etc.

> We're going to an island **to study** the wildlife. We've learnt the local language **in order to communicate** with the people, and studied their customs **in order not to upset** them. These waterproof tents are **for keeping** our equipment. We'll take medical supplies **in case we get** ill and a radio **so that we can communicate** with the mainland.

Ⓐ *TO/IN ORDER TO* + INFINITIVE (PURPOSE)

We use **to** + **infinitive** to say **why** we do something:
*We're going to an island **to study** the wildlife. 'Why did you go to the embassy?' '**To get** a visa.'*

We can also use **in order (not) to** (more formal) with the same meaning:
*We've learnt the language **in order to communicate**.*
*We've studied their customs **in order not to upset** them.*

We do not use **for** to say **why** we do something:
Not ~~We're going to the island for to study the wildlife.~~

Ⓑ *SO THAT, IN ORDER THAT* (PURPOSE)

We can use **so that** + **subject** + **can/could/would** (**or in order that...**) to say **why** we do/did
something: *We've got a radio **so that we can** communicate with the mainland.*
                *I went to London **in order that I could** meet my friends.*
                *He attended the festival **so that he wouldn't** miss the wedding ceremony.*

Ⓒ *SO AS TO* (PURPOSE)

We can use **so as (not) to** when we are doing something **special** or **avoiding a problem**:
*I sold my car **so as to raise** money for the starving children.* (I had a special purpose)
*I wore thick boots **so as not to damage** my feet.* (I avoided an expected problem)

We don't use **so as to** for simple/obvious tasks:
I went to town to buy some eggs. (**Not** ~~so as to buy~~...)

Ⓓ *IN CASE* (SUGGESTING PRECAUTIONS)

We use **in case** + **subject** + **verb** when we do something because we are worried about a
possible problem: *'Why did you take an umbrella?' '**In case it rained.**'*

Notice that when we are talking about the future, we use a present tense verb after **in case**:
*I will take my driving licence **in case** the police **stop** me.* (**Not** ~~The police will stop me.~~)

When we are talking about the past, we prefer a Past Simple verb, not **would**, after **in case**:
*I took a map **in case I lost** my way.* (**Not** ... ~~I would lose my way.~~)

Notice that **in case** and **if** have different meanings:
*I'll phone her **in case** she's lonely.*   (= I'm going to phone her as a precaution)
*I'll phone her **if** she's lonely.*   (= I'll phone her in a certain situation)

Ⓔ *FOR* + VERB-ING (FUNCTION)

We use **for** + **verb-ing** to talk about the **function** of a **tool/instrument/machine** etc.
*This tent is **for keeping** our equipment.*   *He bought a machine **for making** pasta.*

We can ask the questions **What is/What's it for?** or **What are they for?**
*'**What's** this machine **for**?'*   *'It's **for recording** music.'*

We use **for** + **person** + **to-infinitive** when the purpose of an action involves someone else:
*I've left the door open **for the cat to come** in.*   *I wrote a letter **for Joe to read**.*

Notice the difference between **to do** and **for doing**:
*I bought some scissors **to cut** my nails.*   (Purpose: Why did you buy them?)
*Scissors are **for cutting**.*   (Function: What are they for?)

31 **1** **A** **B** **D** **E** Put *to, so that, in case, for* in the gaps in the text. Then listen and check your answers.

A We're opening a chocolate shop in Bath. We're having a party **(0)** *to* attract customers and giving them free samples **(1)** .... show them how good our chocolate is. We buy cacao direct from Brazil **(2)** .... we can be sure it's good quality and we have special equipment **(3)** .... mixing the ingredients. We haven't given up our jobs yet **(4)** .... the shop isn't a success.

B We're going on holiday in West Africa. We've had injections **(5)** .... we don't catch malaria. We're going to Senegal **(6)** .... listen to the local musicians. We'll buy CDs there **(7)** .... we can't find the same ones in Britain. We've bought an extra ticket **(8)** .... you want to come with us. But you must see the doctor soon **(9)**...................... get your injections.

C Captain Kork is on a new planet. He's brought a laser gun **(10)** .... he can defend himself against aliens, and some scientific equipment **(11)** .... he finds unusual phenomena. What are the diamond rings **(12)** .... ? He's brought them **(13)** .... he meets a beautiful female alien. He would need to contact the Galactic Council **(14)** .... get permission to marry her.

2 **A** - **C** In some cases in exercise 1, you could also use *in order to, in order that* or *so as to*. Write the item numbers in the table below. The first one has been done for you.

in order to	in order that	so as to
0	....	*0* ....
....	....	....
....	....	....

3 **B** - **E** Write a second sentence with the same/similar meaning to the first, using the words in brackets.

0 I didn't drive fast in case I had an accident.
I drove slowly in order not to have an accident. (*slowly/order not*)

1 You can use the Roto-Drill to cut metal and the Z-Saw to cut plastic.
The Roto-Drill .... and the Z-Saw .... (*for/for*)

2 We moved very slowly because we didn't want to frighten the animals.
.... (*so as*)

3 I hid some cash in my pocket because I was afraid somebody would steal my wallet.
.... (*case*)

4 We took plenty of food as we didn't know if there were any restaurants on our route.
.... (*didn't find*)

5 I switched off my mobile phone because I didn't want it to ring in the middle of the concert.
.... (*case*)

6 We've bought a second bed because we want to invite our friends to stay with us.
.... (*so/can*)

7 Tina's dog has to wear a muzzle or else it will bite strangers.
.... (*case*)

8 Phil's best man was afraid of losing the wedding ring so he put it in a safe.
.... (*so as not*)

9 I turned off the music so as to allow the neighbours to sleep.

.... (*so that*)

10 Robin Hood robbed the rich because he wanted to give money to the poor.

.... (*in order that*)

11 What is the function of this pan? Do we use it to make omelettes?

....? ....? (*What/making*)

12 He built a tall fence round the orchard to stop the children from getting in.

.... (*so that*)

4 **Ⓐ - Ⓓ** Put the information in the table in sentence form, using the words at the end.

action	purpose: she/he/they wanted
0 Myra locked her diamonds in the safe	to stop thieves from stealing them
1 Kevin trained every day	to get back his place in the team
2 The professor learnt Russian	to read Russian scientific journals
3 Gina packed her sun lotion	to enjoy the sun if it shone
4 Michelle was waiting in the car	to escape if the alarm rang
5 Nick left home early	to avoid possible traffic jams
6 Captain Kork married the princess	to avoid causing a war
7 The chef visited Naples	to be able to learn new pasta recipes

0 Myra locked her diamonds in the safe so that thieves couldn't steal them.   so that
1 .... order
2 .... so that
3 .... in case
4 .... so that
5 .... in case there
6 .... so as not
7 .... so that

5 **Ⓐ - Ⓔ** Circle all the possible answers.

0 He took his camera to the disco *for taking/to take/so as to take* pictures of Alice dancing.

1 This is a special camera *for taking/so that it takes/so as to take* pictures underwater.

2 They grow bananas here *for exporting/to export/in case they export* them to Europe.

3 She visited Seville *in order to learn/so that she could learn/so as to learn* Spanish.

4 She visited Florence *for learning/for learn/to learn* Italian.

5 He installed security cameras *so that/in case/to avoid* nobody stole his paintings.

6 They held a party *to celebrate/in order to celebrate/in order that they celebrate* her birthday.

7 They held a party *so that they could/so that they can/in case they could* invite all their friends.

8 Maria studied hard *in order to pass/in case she passed/so as to pass* the exam.

9 I'm going to pack my skis *in case it snows/so as to snow/in case it will snow* tomorrow.

6 Ⓐ Ⓔ In each pair of sentences, use *to* in one sentence and *for* in the other. Use verbs from the list (use each verb twice).

examine   improve   lose   make   send   ~~walk~~

0 **a** These are special boots for walking in the mountains.

    b I visit Switzerland every year to walk in the Alps.

1 **a** These exercises are .... your pronunciation in English.

    b Do these exercises every day .... your pronunciation in English.

2 **a** They decided to change their diet .... weight.

    b The company has developed a new diet .... weight.

3 **a** A microscope is an instrument .... very small objects.

    b Professor Makepeace used the microscope .... the meteorite.

4 **a** I borrowed my neighbour's drill .... holes in my wall.

    b A drill is a tool .... holes in materials.

5 **a** I walked ten miles to the postbox .... your birthday card in time.

    b This is lightweight paper .... to people overseas.

OPEN EXERCISE

7 Ⓐ - Ⓔ Finish these sentences in any suitable way. Use language items from this unit.

1 He went to the supermarket ....

2 They bought some olive oil ....

3 Harry bought some dynamite ....

4 They took some warm clothes on holiday with them ....

5 I decided to go to see the doctor ....

6 She burnt her diary ....

7 We added poison to the soup ....

8 She murdered her husband ....

9 I left some money for you ....

10 He built a house for his son ....

11 I'm not going to go out tonight ....

12 She's waiting outside the palace ....

13 They hired a nanny for their baby ....

14 I took all my money out of the bank ....

15 It's a good idea to insure your house ....

UNIT 59 >> Conjunctions and complex sentences

 Last weekend, my aunt had her ninetieth birthday, my sister had a baby **and** my best friend got married. **Although** I was very busy, I enjoyed every minute **because** we had so much to celebrate.

Ⓐ SIMPLE AND COMPLEX SENTENCES

Each part of a sentence with a subject + main verb is a **clause**.
Simple sentences have one clause. **Complex sentences** have two or more clauses:
My aunt was 90, my sister had a baby and my best friend got married. (complex)

Complex sentences need joining words like **and, but, because** etc. You cannot use a comma to join two clauses: ~~I went to London, we bought some clothes.~~

Ⓑ LINKING WORDS: *AND* AND *BUT*

We can use **and** to join subject + verb and subject + verb. If the subject of each verb is the same, we usually do not repeat it:
*I went to London on Saturday **and bought** some clothes.*

We use **but** in the same way but we often include both subjects:
*I bought some new clothes **but (I)** didn't buy any shoes.*

We join three or more clauses with **and** like this:
*I bought some clothes, visited an art gallery **and** met my friend. (same subject)*
*My brother arrived, my sister joined us **and** then we went to the theatre.* (different subjects)

Do not write very long sentences using **and... and... and... but... and...** etc.

Ⓒ MORE LINKING WORDS

Here are some more words which we use to join subject + verb and subject + verb:

1 **for showing contrast:** *Although/Even though it rained, we continued playing football.*
  Never use **although** and **but** in the same sentence:
  ~~Although it rained but he wore his sunglasses.~~

2 **for showing time relationships** (see Unit 20):
  When it rained, we went indoors.   *As soon as it rained, we went indoors.*
  After it rained, the sun began to shine.   *Before it rained, the sun had been shining.*
  While it was raining, we stayed indoors.   *We stayed indoors **until** it stopped raining.*

3 **for showing cause and result relationships:**
  Because it rained, they cancelled the football match.

4 **for expressing conditions** (see Units 106-110): *If it rains, I won't go out.*

We can use these joining words at the beginning of the sentence or in the middle between the two clauses.
Either *Although it rained, we continued playing football.*   (use a comma)
Or   *We continued playing football although it rained.*   (no comma)

Ⓓ *SO/SO THAT*

We also use **so**, especially in informal English, to show **cause** and **result relationships**:
*It rained, **so** we stopped playing football.* (use a comma)

We can use **so that** for **purpose** and **result** (see Unit 58). There is no comma:
*I organised a party **so that** my aunt could celebrate her birthday.* (purpose)

---

1 Ⓐ-Ⓓ Choose the best answer to fill the gaps, A, B, C or D.

0 A collector paid a million for Silvio Copiman's latest painting .... it had Picasso's signature on it.   **A** so   **B** although   Ⓒ because   **D** while

1 But .... Silvio found out that the purchaser was a Mafia member, he was frightened.
A as   **B** when   **C** although   **D** –

2 He decided he had to steal back the painting .... they found out that it was a fake.
A although   **B** when   **C** as soon as   **D** before

3 The guards let Silvio's wife into the house .... she was very beautiful.
A , because   **B** because   **C** although   **D** , although

4 She made a plan of the house .... she was only there for a short time.
A , although   **B** although   **C** because   **D** and

5 Silvio looked at the plan, went to the house at night .... switched off the alarm system.
A and he   **B** and   **C** when he   **D** , he

6 He stole the painting .... no one would discover that he'd cheated the collector.
A because   **B** and so   **C** , so that   **D** so that

7 The gangster knew it was a fake .... had wanted to impress people .... Silvio needn't have stolen it.   **A** but   **B** and   **C** because he   **D** so that he   **E** so   **F** and
G then   **H** but so

2 Ⓐ-Ⓓ Put suitable joining words in the gaps. Use words from the list, each word more than once if necessary. Then listen and check your answers.

although   and   because   before   but   so   when

(0) Although Silvio is an excellent painter, collectors don't pay a lot for his own paintings
(1) .... he isn't famous. (2) .... he was a young man, it didn't matter
(3) .... now that he is married, he needs more money, especially (4) .... his wife likes beautiful things. He has spent a lot of time in art galleries, (5) .... he is familiar with the style of all the famous painters (6) .... is able to copy their work. He doesn't feel guilty (7) .... he says that the collectors should examine the works more carefully
(8) .... they buy them (9) .... if the police find out, Silvio could go to jail. Sam Woodison, his enemy, has never been able to prove that Silvio is a forger (10) .... he has asked many experts to examine them. But (11) .... Silvio makes his first mistake, Sam will be happy.

3 Ⓐ-Ⓒ Put a tick (✓) next to the sentences which are well written. Put a cross (✗) next to the ones which are badly written and rewrite them.

0 Silvio finished the painting and signed it 'Claude Monet' and took it to the museum and sold it. ✗
Silvio finished the painting, signed it 'Claude Monet', took it to the museum and sold it.

1 Although the experts examined the painting carefully, but they didn't realise it was a fake.
....

2 Silvio admires all the great painters but he doesn't feel guilty about copying them.
....

3 Sam has published many articles about Silvio in his magazine but he cannot prove anything.
....

4 He painted a portrait of his wife and he signed it 'Rembrandt' and he gave it to her for her birthday.
....

UNIT 60 >> Linking devices

> Edward Stanton was born in a tiny village in Essex. **However**, he has worked all over the world. **In fact**, he has lived in 37 countries. **Moreover**, he's learnt about many different cultures and had girlfriends of 15 nationalities. **To sum up**, he's had a wonderful life as an EFL teacher.

Ⓐ FORMAL LINKING DEVICES

We often need to show the connection in meaning between sentences. Here are some words/phrases which we often use at or near the beginning of a sentence, especially when we are writing:

for adding information:	*Also, In addition, Besides,*
for adding to an argument emphatically:	*Moreover, Furthermore,* *What's more,* (informal) *To top it all,* (informal)
for introducing an example:	*For example, For instance,*
for showing the result/what happened because of this:	*As a result, Consequently, So,* (informal) *In consequence,* (very formal)
for describing the logical result/conclusion:	*Therefore, Thus,* *Hence,* (especially in mathematics)
for introducing a contrast/something unexpected:	*However, In spite of this, Despite this,* *Nevertheless, On the other hand, On the* *contrary, In fact, Still, All the same,*
for showing the sequence:	*Previously, Before this, Later, Afterwards,* *After this, Firstly/First of all, Secondly,* *Thirdly, Then, Finally/Lastly/Last of all,*
for emphasis before making a supporting point:	*In fact, Indeed,*
for summing up, concluding:	*In conclusion, To sum up,* *As we have seen, As we can see,*
for communicating an emotion:	*Sadly, Fortunately, Unfortunately,* etc.
for generalising:	*On the whole, Generally, In general,*

We generally use a comma after all these linking words if they come first in the sentence:
On the whole, *I agree with the critics.*   **However**, *I think they may be wrong in this case.*

Ⓑ INFORMAL DISCOURSE MARKERS

We also frequently use words and expressions in signposting conversation. These include:
Actually,... After all,... Anyway,... By the way,... I mean,... In other words,... OK,... Now,...
Right,... So,... Talking of...,... You know,... Well,...
We use these in various ways. For example:
Well, I suppose you're right.   (for expressing less than 100% certainty/agreement)
Well, what I think is...   (for introducing a contribution to the discussion)
Well,...   (for pausing, for giving the speaker time to think)

Ⓒ *LAST OF ALL, LASTLY, AT LAST*

Notice the difference between **last of all/lastly** (to show sequence) and **at last** (to show emotion when we have been waiting for something for a long time):
I waited at the bus stop for an hour. **At last**, *the bus arrived!*
Do not use **at last** in a sequence: ~~Firstly,... Secondly,... At last,...~~

1 Ⓐ These ten markers are missing from the text.

1 As a result   2 As we have seen   3 First of all   4 For example   5 However
6 in addition   7 In fact   8 Sadly   9 Secondly   10 Thirdly

Write the numbers in the places where you think the words belong. The first one has been done for you. There may be more than one possible position for some words.

(2) A career in the teaching of English as a Foreign Language has many advantages.   An EFL teacher can experience different cultures.   Salaries are often low and working conditions are sometimes unacceptable.   Many private school owners care only about profit.   They do not pay their staff well.   Many young teachers who answer advertisements for jobs abroad in English magazines are shocked by the conditions they find on arrival.   The accommodation may be substandard.   There may be no free medical care.   The working hours may be excessively long.

2 Ⓐ Ⓑ Fill the gaps with any suitable linking device from the information page.

(0) Previously, school owners have preferred to employ native speakers.
(1) ...., students themselves have lacked confidence in teachers of their own nationality. (2) ...., the standard of English achieved by non-native teachers is now much higher. (3) ...., the situation of English is rapidly changing.
(4) ...., there are now more speakers of English as a second language in the world than native speakers. (5) ...., most conversations in English in the world take place between second-language speakers. (6) ...., authentic English pronunciation and strictly accurate grammar are not so important as communication.
(7) ...., you still need good grammar to pass examinations.
(8) ...., don't burn this grammar book!

3 Ⓐ Ⓑ If the linking device is more likely to occur in formal writing, write FML. If it is more likely to occur in conversation or informal writing, write INFML.

0 Actually, INFML

1 Hence, ...
2 In conclusion, ...
3 By the way, ...

4 Well, ...
5 On the contrary, ...
6 Thus, ...

7 So, ...
8 Indeed, ...
9 Right, ...

4 Ⓒ Put either *last of all* or *at last* in each gap.

0 It snowed for six months. At last, it stopped.
1 She told us several stories, then showed us maps. ...., she showed us photos of her journeys.
2 He asked her to marry him. ...., after six years, she agreed.
3 They built a new village. They constructed the roads, the houses and the shopping centre. ...., they built the church.
4 I was waiting for dinner for ages. ...., they served it.
5 She works all day in the restaurant, serving first breakfast, then lunch and, ..., supper.

UNIT **61** >> Non-finite -*ing* clauses

> **Having built** the Time Machine, Professor Makepeace created an invisibility shampoo. **Showering** herself in the liquid formula, Lia, his daughter, disappeared. For a moment, the Professor was worried, **having lost** his daughter. Then...!!!

Ⓐ SHOWERING,..., HAVING SHOWERED,...

If two things happen at more or less the same time, with **the same subject**, we can use this pattern:

-ing clause	main event (any tense)
Showering *herself in the shampoo,*	*Lia disappeared!*
Producing *instant invisibility,*	*the shampoo is useful to spies and criminals.*

To emphasise that one thing happened **after** the other, we use **having + past participle**:

having clause	main event (any tense)
Having built *the Time Machine,*	*the Professor created an invisibility formula.*
Having sold *the plans for the Time Machine,*	*the Professor is rich.*

Sometimes, we can use either pattern:
Finishing *her work, she went out.*
= **Having finished** *her work, she went out.* (emphasis on time gap)

But often there is a significant difference in meaning:
Phoning *her boyfriend, she felt sad.*   (= she was sad during the phone call)
Having phoned *her boyfriend, she felt sad.*   (= she finished the call and then felt sad)

These patterns are used in writing but not often in speech.

Ⓑ POSITION IN THE SENTENCE

The clause can occupy any suitable position in the sentence:
Front: *Having lost his daughter, he was worried.*   **Back:** *He was worried, **having lost...***
But usually we place the clause **near the performer** of the action.

Ⓒ PERFORMER AS SUBJECT OR OBJECT

The performer of the action in the clause can be the subject or object of the main verb or of a preposition:

performer as subject	performer as object
Standing in the pool, Sue took a photo of her friend. (= Sue was in the pool)	*Sue took a photo of her friend standing in the pool.* (= the friend was in the pool — no comma)

But be careful that the meaning is clear. For example:
✗ *Hanging from the branches and showing his purple bottom, Dick saw a male monkey.* ✗
✓ *Dick saw a male monkey hanging from the branches and...* (no comma) ✓

Ⓓ -ING CLAUSES WITH *AFTER, BEFORE, WHILE, WHEN*

We can use **After/Before/While/When + verb-ing**. For example:
After finishing *her work, she went out.*   **Before going** *out, she finished her work.*
While finishing *her work, she ate an apple.*   **When finishing** *her work, she ate an apple.*
We also use **After + having + past participle**:
After having finished, *she went out.* (emphasis on time gap)
Remember: the subject of both actions must be the same. ~~*While shaving, his dog barked.*~~

1 Ⓐ **Add the appropriate endings from A-J in order to complete the sentences 1-9.**

0 Sleeping on the floor, *she turned restlessly all night.*

1 Having slept on the floor, ...

2 Mixing the eggs and the flour, ...

3 Having mixed the eggs and flour, ...

4 Shouting angrily at his wife, ...

5 Having shouted angrily at his wife, ...

6 Clapping loudly, ...

7 Having clapped loudly, ...

8 Climbing the mountain, ...

9 Having climbed the mountain, ...

A he accused her of ruining his life.

B he returned to his camp in the valley.

C the audience left the theatre feeling happy and excited.

D she turned restlessly all night.

E she suffered from backache all day.

F he breathed the pure Alpine air.

G he begged her to forgive him.

H she poured the mixture into a large bowl.

I the audience also cheered and threw flowers.

J she added salt and pepper at the same time.

2 Ⓐ–Ⓒ **Add one of the clauses A-H to each item by marking the place in the sentence (perhaps more than one possibility) where it could go.**
Then, write the letter from A-H. Also write i or ii or i and ii.

0 ∨ Lia's voice said, 'Father, I'm here.'   H i

1   the Professor took it to the Army, Navy and Air Force chiefs.   ....

2   the three chiefs listened to the Professor.   ....

3   the Professor had brought Lia with him.   ....

4   Lia made the Admiral fall off his chair.   ....

5   she made the General scream.   ....

6   the Air Marshal quickly said that he believed the Professor.   ....

7   the Professor and Lia went back to his laboratory.   ....

A i. *expecting*	ii. *having expected*	this reaction,
B i. *invisibly tickling*	ii. *having invisibly tickled*	him under his chin,
C i. *laughing*	ii. *having laughed*	at his mad idea,
D i. *pulling*	ii. *having pulled*	his moustache,
E i. *seeing*	ii. *having seen*	what had happened,
F i. *selling*	ii. *having sold*	the secret formula,
G i. *testing*	ii. *having tested*	the Invisibility Shampoo,
H i. *whispering*	ii. *having whispered*	in his ear,

3 **Ⓐ** - **Ⓒ** Which of these sentences are badly written? Mark correct sentences with ✓. Mark unclear sentences with ✗.

0 Shining with a bright light, the lovers kissed under the moon.   ✗

1 Threatening to jump from the roof, the policeman tried to calm the man.   ....

2 Dancing with joy, her exam results really pleased her.   ....

3 Having reached the summit, the climbers placed a flag on the mountain.   ....

4 Diving to the bottom of the lake, the swimmers found a secret tunnel.   ....

5 The police chased a man running away from the bank.   ....

6 This plant is suitable for old people requiring little watering or fertilising.   ....

7 Having rescued the boy from the sea, his parents thanked the lifeguard.   ....

8 She danced with the prince wearing a low-cut white gown and glass shoes.   ....

4 **Ⓐ** - **Ⓓ** Rewrite these sentences using *-ing* OR *having -ed* clauses.

0 At the same time as it rotates on its axis, Mars orbits the sun.
Rotating on its axis, Mars orbits the sun.

1 After they had launched several successful test flights, they sent a manned mission to Mars.
....

2 As they looked back at the Earth, the astronauts felt a deep emotion of homesickness.
....

3 As it reached its maximum speed, the capsule separated from the rocket.
....

4 After they had landed on Mars, the crew opened the hatches of the spacecraft.
....

5 When they had explored Mars, the astronauts prepared for the return journey.
....

6 As it re-entered the atmosphere, the spacecraft reached enormous temperatures.
....

7 After they had re-entered the atmosphere, the astronauts parachuted into the ocean.
....

5 **Ⓓ** Combine these sentences, using the words in brackets. Use *-ing* clauses.

0 The General felt a sharp pain. He was laughing at the professor.
While laughing at the professor, the General felt a sharp pain. (*while*)

1 The Professor invented the Time Machine. Before this, he had always failed.
.... (*before*)

2 She had used the Shampoo. Lia was able to enter Buckingham Palace.
.... (*after*)

3 Lia was sitting on the throne. Lia imagined she was Queen of the Universe.
.... (*when*)

4 She stood invisibly in the room. She knocked the crown off the Queen's head.
.... (*while*)

5 She went to the National Theatre. She had left the palace.
.... (*after*)

6 She had wanted to play the Ghost. She had read *Hamlet* as a child.
.... (*while*)

164

7 The actors fainted. They heard a voice coming out of the empty air.

.... (*when*)

8 She left the stage. But first she threw flowers to the audience.

.... (*before*)

9 Lia scared the whole of London. She was moving invisibly through the streets.

.... (*while*)

6 Ⓐ-Ⓓ Read the text and find eight more places, one in each sentence, where you could substitute an *-ing/having -ed* clause. Underline the exact phrase you are replacing and write the clause in the space below. The first one has been done for you. Then listen and check your answers.

They had successfully landed a spacecraft on Mars, so the space centre decided to send a probe to Venus. They knew that the conditions on this planet were extreme, so they designed a specially adapted craft. They sent many unmanned craft to Venus before they attempted the first manned mission. However, Professor Vanessa Dixon, who had left the space centre, criticised the new voyage to Venus. 'We know the dangers, so we shouldn't risk the lives of the astronauts,' she said. After they had listened to her views, the crew refused to board the ship. Because he wanted the mission to succeed, the President himself addressed the crew. 'After we have visited Venus, our country will be the leading nation in space.' However, the crew resigned from the centre and demanded a national investigation into space safety.

0 Having successfully landed a spacecraft on Mars, the space centre...
1 ....
2 ....
3 ....
4 ....
5 ....
6 ....
7 ....
8 ....

OPEN EXERCISE

7 Ⓐ-Ⓓ Complete these sentences in any suitable way, using *-ing* clauses.

0 Having won her fifth Oscar, Myra retired from the film industry.
1 Having ...., the hurricane moved inland.
2 ...., the police arrested Harry.
3 ...., Roger Scoop returned to the UK.
4 ...., Claudette starred in a film.
5 The Metalheads finished their careers, ...
6 ...., Professor Makepeace lay in bed.
7 Lia played lots of tricks on people, ...
8 Brigitte was late for work again, ...
9 Having ...., he decided to resign from his job.
10 While ...., she broke her leg.

Non-finite *-ing* clauses

1 For questions 1-12, read the text below and decide which answer, A, B, C or D, best fits each gap. There is an example at the beginning (0).

SOLAR STUDIES

(0) A do you think about the Sun? (1) ..... as the source of all life by past civilisations, the Sun was once the centre of human culture. (2) ....., for people nowadays, it is just an ordinary, middle-sized star. Not only (3) ..... in cities so that the influence of the Sun on our lives is less obvious, but also other cosmological discoveries, (4) ..... Black Holes, have captured the public imagination. Ask yourself: 'Am I right to be indifferent to the Sun?' Your answer must be: 'No, I'm not.' (5) ..... by internal nuclear fusion, the Sun is a natural laboratory for scientists aiming to make the next big technological advance. (6) ..... one of our prime scientific objectives to generate energy from nuclear fusion? (7) ....., we need to study solar processes in case we can learn from this how to produce radiation-free energy. (8) ....., we need to understand CME's – coronal mass ejections – (9) ..... protect our satellites and spacecraft from these huge, unpredictable bursts of energy from the Sun. No longer (10) ..... wise to neglect our study of solar phenomena. (11) ....., our ancestors recognised the central importance of the sun – and (12) ..... .

0 Ⓐ	How often	B	How	C	What often	D	How many
1 A	Worshipping	B	Worship	C	Revering	D	Worshipped
2 A	Therefore	B	However	C	Moreover	D	Although
3 A	we live	B	we do live	C	do we live	D	live we
4 A	such	B	example	C	such as	D	include
5 A	Driven	B	Driving	C	Drove	D	Drivered
6 A	Is	B	Not is	C	Aren't	D	Isn't
7 A	Thus	B	And	C	Although	D	But
8 A	Consequently	B	However	C	Moreover	D	Therefore
9 A	in order to	B	for to	C	for	D	as to
10 A	it was	B	was it	C	it is	D	is it
11 A	As conclusion	B	Summary	C	At last	D	To sum up
12 A	so we	B	so should we	C	we too	D	so we should

2 For these questions, complete the second sentence so that it has a similar meaning to the first sentence, using the word given. Do not change the word given. Use from two to five words including the word given. There is an example (0).

0 They designed the spacecraft in order to study the Sun.

They designed the spacecraft *so that they could study* the Sun.   *SO THAT*

1 She sent him his birthday present a week late.

She sent .... a week late. *TO*

2 They gave her an explanation of the problem.

They .... her. *EXPLAINED*

3 Tell me about your boss.

Tell me: .... like? *LIKE*

4 The film is very successful – half the population has seen it.

The film .... that half the population has seen it. *SO*

5 She gave him a detailed description of her holiday.
She .... in detail. *DESCRIBED*

6 She apologised sincerely but he was still angry.
Although .... he was still angry. *APOLOGISED*

7 He bought her twelve roses on Valentine's Day.
He .... on Valentine's Day. *FOR*

8 I took an umbrella with me because I was afraid it would rain.
I took an umbrella with me .... rained. *CASE*

OTHER PRACTICE

3 **Rewrite these sentences, following the examples.**

0 I have never seen such a crazy film. *Never have I seen such a crazy film.*

00 I didn't believe you for a minute. *Not for a minute did I believe you.*

1 You seldom get the chance to see wild otters.

....

2 I had hardly sat down – it was time to leave.

....

3 I little thought that I'd become president.

....

4 She was not only intelligent but also very beautiful.

....

5 You must press the red button under no circumstances.

....

6 You can no longer hear the local dialect in this area.

....

7 They'd no sooner started the trip than the car broke down.

....

8 I wouldn't marry him for a million pounds.

....

4 **Complete 1-8 by choosing the best ending.**

0 Please leave the building (when you hear the alarm)/even it is raining outside/because of there is a fire/although it is dangerous to stay.

1 Although the music was very noisy, **but no one complained/I couldn't sleep/nobody would agree to turn the volume down/the music was very quiet.**

2 The shop assistant was very rude to me. **Therefore, I'm never shopping there again/Thus, the manager didn't apologise/However, I was upset/Because I didn't have the right money.**

3 My sister thought that I had lied about her. **On the other hand, she hated me/As a result, she refused to speak to me/So that she complained to our father/However, it was true.**

4 We continued trying to win the match **even we had only ten players/however we lost/although we had several good players/even though we were losing by five goals.**

5 Firstly, add the eggs, then stir the mixture and **at last, put it in the oven/in conclusion, bake it for an hour/to sum up, pour it into the pan/lastly, cook it for thirty minutes.**

6 It is necessary to follow the rules. **In other words, obedience to the regulations is important/For example, everyone must obey the regulations/Such as not walking on the grass/Although there are very harsh punishments for breaking them.**

UNIT 62 >> Adjectives

 A **beautiful, graceful, elegant** lady came into the restaurant. The meal tasted especially **delicious** that evening. 'You are so **handsome** and **intelligent**,' she told him as they drank **smooth, dark-brown, Brazilian** chocolate at the end of the meal. Then he woke up.

Ⓐ ADJECTIVES AND NOUNS

Adjectives describe nouns. We use them:

1 before a noun: *We went to an **expensive** restaurant.*

2 after **be**: *She was **beautiful**.*

3 after the verbs **feel, look, seem, smell, sound, taste** (see Unit 85):
*Tom felt **happy**.*   *She looked **elegant**.*   *The food tasted **delicious**.*

4 after **get, prove, become, make**: *He got/became **angry**.*   *It proved **impossible**.*

Ⓑ ADJECTIVES WITH *AND*

When there are three or more adjectives in front of a noun, we separate them with a comma.

We do not use **and**: *A beautiful graceful, French lady.* (**Not** ~~beautiful, graceful and French~~)

But we use **and** between two colours: *a red **and** white shirt*

But after **be, feel, look** etc., we use adjective **and** adjective:
*He **is** young **and** handsome.*   *She **looks** beautiful, intelligent **and** generous.* (three adjectives)

Ⓒ USUAL ORDER OF ADJECTIVES

value/opinion	size	age	shape	colour	nationality	material	noun/origin
a wonderful,		modern,	round,	Italian,	marble	table	
	a huge,	new,		grey,		concrete	building

We place numbers in first position: *six wonderful, modern, Italian, marble tables.*

Except in expressions like these: *the next two weeks, the last three months, the next two minutes.*

A long value adjective before short is a more common order than short before long:
a wonderful, wise man   **Not** ~~a wise, wonderful man~~

Ⓓ THE RICH, THE POOR ETC.

With a few adjectives, we can use **the + adjective** if we are talking about the general class of people: **the poor, the rich, the young, the old, the sick, the blind, the deaf**:

*He gives money to help **the blind**.*   (general = all blind people)

But *He gave some money to **the blind people**.*   (particular)

We can also use **the + nationality adjectives** to refer to all the people from that country:

*I like **the English**.*   *The French drink a lot of wine.*

Ⓔ FORMING THE OPPOSITES OF ADJECTIVES

With the prefix **un-**: *un comfortable, un happy, un kind, un interesting, un safe, un workable*

But there are other prefixes to form opposites: **ab-, in-, im-** (+ p...), **dis-, il-** (+ l...), **ir-** (+ r...), **non-**: *ab normal, in expensive, im patient, dis similar, il legal, ir regular, non-alcoholic*

We also use the suffix **-less** to form negative adjectives: *hope less, use less, penni less*

1 **Ⓐ** Fill each gap with a verb in its correct form from list 1 and an adjective from list 2.

> **1)** become   feel   feel   smell   sound   sound   ~~taste~~
> **2)** cold   <u>delicious</u>   lovely   rich   Russian   terribile   tired

0 These peaches *taste delicious*. I'll eat some more.
1 The orchestra is no good. The music ....
2 I'm going to put on my coat. I ....
3 Do you ....? You're half asleep.
4 The roses .... but the lilies have no perfume.
5 She .... but really she comes from Wales.
6 Bob McGiven .... by selling second-hand cars.

2 **Ⓐ**-**Ⓒ** Put the adjectives in a suitable order to fill the gaps. Add commas or *and* as necessary.

0 Professor Makepeace invented a/an *enormous, new, silver and black, metal* flying machine.
   (*silver/black/enormous/metal/new*)
1 His laboratory looks .... (*dirty/chaotic*)
2 He's wearing a/an .... lab-suit today.
   (*second-hand/over-sized/nylon/unattractive*)
3 Don't eat there. His food always tastes .... (*strange/artificial*)
4 He didn't know that his wife gave birth to a ....
   baby girl in Australia. (*blue-eyed/healthy/beautiful*)

3 **Ⓓ** Circle all the correct alternatives.

0 Others are often unaware of the problems of the deafs/(the deaf)/the deaf people/(deaf people).
1 **The youngs/The young/The youngers** often don't understand **the olds/the olders/
   the elder/old people.**
2 I've tried **Austrian/Austrians/Austria** food but I've never met any **Austrian/Austrians/Austrian
   people.**
3 There are special classes for **the intelligents/the clevers/the intelligent** children.
4 Florence Nightingale devoted her time to helping **the sicks/the ills/the sick.**
5 I don't think that **the rich/rich people/the rich people** can understand the problems of
   the ordinary/the ordinaries/ordinary people.

4 **Ⓐ**-**Ⓔ** Form adjectives from the words on the left of each line and put them in the gaps. Then
listen and check your answers.

HAPPY	Professor Makepeace was feeling (0) *unhappy*. None of his plans were
EDIBLE	working. The soup made from recycled fish and chips was (1) ....
PRACTICAL	while the banana-powered car was clearly (2) .... since it required
POSSIBLE	several thousand bananas to travel a kilometre. It was (3) .... and also
SAFE	(4) .... to carry so many bananas in the vehicle's fuel tank. He missed
PATIENCE	his wife who had become so (5) .... with his way of life that she had
PENNY	emigrated to Australia 17 years ago. He was alone and (6) ....
SLEEP	and spent (7) .... nights worrying about his inventions. He could
SUCCEED	have been a (8) .... researcher for a big company but he had made the
FOOL	(9) .... decision to devote his life to pursuing his personal fantasies.
PERSIST	Suddenly, there was a (10) .... knocking at his door. He opened it.
LOSE	A sun-tanned young woman stood there. 'I'm Lia, your (11) ....
AUSTRALIA	daughter,' she said with an (12) .... accent. 'I've come to help you.'

UNIT 63 >> Adverbs and adjectives

 Slim Skinty is **fabulously** rich. He gives **generously** to his friends and lives **luxuriously** in each of the castles and palaces he bought **recently**. He drives **expensive** cars **fast** and eats **well**. He has an **absolutely perfect** life. But this is all in his dreams.

Ⓐ ADVERBS

An adverb is a word like **quickly**, **happily**, **well** which describes a verb, e.g. *He writes* **quickly**.
Adverbs often answer the question **How?**: '*How does he behave?*' '**Rudely/Well/Badly**' etc.

Ⓑ RULES FOR ADDING - *LY* TO FORM ADVERBS FROM ADJECTIVES

adjective ending	spelling change	examples
-l	double the l → -lly	*careful → carefully/usual → usually/real → really*
-y	change to -ily	*easy → easily/happy → happily/lucky → luckily*
-e	keep the e → -ely	*immediate → immediately/late → lately* except *truly/wholly/terribly/possibly* etc.
-ic	change to -ically	*dramatic → dramatically/magic → magically* except *publicly*

Ⓒ POSITION OF ADVERBS IN THE SENTENCE

We usually place adverbs after the verb + object:
I parked the car **carefully** *in the street and went into the building.*
But sometimes we put the adverb at the beginning of the clause: **Quickly,** *she took out a gun.*
Do not put the adverb between the verb and the object:
I parked the car **carefully.** (**Not** ~~I parked carefully the car.~~)
For special rules about the position of adverbs of frequency, see Unit 64.

Ⓓ THE -*LY* ENDING

Not all adverbs end in -**ly**. Here are some common examples:
fast, hard, late, often, well (the adverbial form of **good**).
Notice that we can use **fast, hard, late, well** as adverbs or adjectives. For example:
He studied **hard.** (adverb)   *It was a* **hard** *exam.* (adjective)
But some adjectives end in -**ly**: *friendly, lovely, ugly, silly.*
These words have no adverbial form. To form an adverbial phrase with these adjectives,
we use **in a... way/manner:** *My neighbours are friendly.* → *They behave* **in a friendly way.**

Ⓔ ADVERB + ADJECTIVE AND ADVERB + ADVERB

An adverb can make an adjective stronger: *very, extremely, really*, awfully*, terribly**
or make it less strong: *fairly, quite, not very, pretty*, a little* (*informal)
He is **very rich.**   *They are* **extremely poor.**   *We are* **terribly unhappy.**
He is **fairly (not very) rich.**   *It is* **quite (a little) cold.**   *She is* **pretty (fairly) tired.**
We use adverb + adverb in the same way:
He worked **extremely quickly.**   *They danced* **very well.**

Ⓕ ABSOLUTE ADJECTIVES

Some adjectives have strong meanings, e.g. *perfect, impossible, dead, furious, fabulous, unique, disgusting* etc.
Do not use **very** or **extremely** with adjectives like these. But we can use **absolutely** or **really** (informal) to add emphasis: *This music is* **absolutely unique.**   *It sounds* **really perfect.**

1 Ⓐ Ⓑ Ⓓ Ⓔ Ⓕ **Form adverbs from the words on the left of each line and use them to fill the gaps. Then listen and check your answers.**

ADVERSE Case studies show how supermarkets affected communities **(0)** *adversely* in
FAVOUR   the 1970s. At first, people in the village of Mockham reacted **(1)** ....
         when a supermarket opened in the nearest town. They could shop
CHEAP   **(2)** .... by driving to the town instead of relying on the
USUAL   **(3)** .... limited supply of goods in local shops. Customer numbers
DRAMA   declined so **(4)** .... in the village shops that they all had closed
FORTUNE within a year. **(5)** ...., the old suffered since they could not
EASY   **(6)** .... make the long journey to the town. In addition, community
QUICK   social life declined very **(7)** .... since villagers no longer met and
INTIMATE talked **(8)** .... in the local shops. The supermarket was doing so
GOOD   **(9)** .... without any competition that it raised its prices significantly,
REAL   causing poorer customers to be **(10)** .... disadvantaged. This
COMPARE **(11)** .... early study shows the deleterious effect of the advent of
         supermarkets on rural communities.

2 Ⓒ **Put a tick in all the places where you might place the adverb. Put a cross where it is impossible to place it.**

0 CAUTIOUSLY   ✓ he placed ✗ the gun ✓ in his pocket ✓
1 SINCERELY   I told ..... her ..... that I wanted to help her.
2 CARELESSLY   He wrote ..... the homework .....
3 CHEAPLY   They sold ..... the fish ..... in the market .....
4 SADLY   ..... she hugged ..... her husband ..... before he left for the war.
5 CRAZILY   She drove ..... the car ..... down the mountainside ..... as far as the frontier.
6 RAPIDLY   ..... she drove ..... down the mountainside ..... as far as the frontier.

3 Ⓔ Ⓕ **Circle all the correct alternatives.**

0 The food was (very)/(quite)/(pretty) good but the wine was very/(absolutely)/(really) disgusting.
1 This crossword is **very/absolutely/fairly** impossible as the clues are **very/absolutely** hard.
2 The painting is **very/absolutely/fairly** unique; it must be **very/pretty/terribly** expensive.
3 From a formal report: This document is **very/terribly/really** significant.
4 They did the work **extremely/very/really** fast and **absolutely/very** perfectly.

4 Ⓓ **Write ADJ if the underlined word is an adjective. Write ADVB if it is an adverb.**

0 He writes <u>quickly</u>.   ADVB
1 This exercise isn't very <u>hard</u>.   ....
2 He was feeling ill but now he's <u>well</u> again.   ....
3 His car is <u>extremely</u> fast.   ....
4 His car is extremely <u>fast</u>.   ....
5 She decorated the Christmas tree in such a <u>lovely</u> way. ....
6 I have never met such a <u>friendly</u> person.   ....
7 I can't <u>possibly</u> visit you tomorrow.   ....
8 She always arrives <u>early</u>.   ....
9 I watched one of the <u>late</u> films on TV.   ....
10 You're <u>late</u> for class again.   ....

Adverbs and adjectives

UNIT 64 >> Adverbs of frequency

 Showbusiness celebrities **often** come to Stella's hair salon and **sometimes** they tell her gossip about the stars while she styles their hair. But Stella **usually** passes on the stories to her boyfriend, Jake, a tabloid journalist. He **always** publishes them.

Ⓐ ADVERBS OF FREQUENCY

These adverbs answer the question: *How often/How frequently...?*

100%	always	I **always** brush my teeth at night.
90%	usually	I **usually** eat breakfast quickly.
80%	normally/generally	I **normally/generally** get good marks.
70%	often*/frequently	I **often/frequently** visit my friends.
30%	sometimes/occasionally	I **sometimes/occasionally** eat Chinese food.
10%	seldom/rarely	I **seldom/rarely** get angry.
5%	hardly ever	I am **hardly** ever late.
0%	never	I **never** steal.

* Some British people pronounce the **t** in **often** but many people do not pronounce the **t**.

Ⓑ POSITION OF ADVERBS OF FREQUENCY

Adverbs generally go:

1 after the verb **be**: *I **am always** at home on Sundays.*
                           *He **is never** polite to his parents.*
2 before the main verb: *I **often travel** by train.*   *He **rarely goes** out.*
3 between the auxiliary verb (= **has, have, will, must, can, may** etc.) and the main verb:
   *He **has sometimes arrived** early.*   *He **must often work** late.*

Notice the position of adverbs of frequency in questions:
*Do you **usually** watch TV?*   *Does she **ever** play tennis?*

Ⓒ NEVER, EVER, HARDLY EVER

We use **never** and **hardly ever** with a positive verb, **not** with a negative verb:
*I have **never** played baseball.*   *She **hardly ever** goes swimming.*

We use **ever** in questions and in negative sentences:
*Have you **ever** seen that film?*   *They have**n't ever** been to London.*

We sometimes use frequency adverbs in short answers before an auxiliary verb:
*'Do you often go to the cinema?' 'No, I **never** do.'*

Ⓓ EVERY DAY, ONCE A WEEK ETC.

We can also use expressions like **every day, every week, once a month, twice a year, three times a day** to answer the question **How often...?** These expressions usually go at the end of the clause: *I play football **once a week.***
                           *He visits his aunt **every month** when he is in Ireland.*

Ⓔ BEGINNNING SENTENCES WITH ADVERBIALS

It is also possible to place **sometimes, occasionally, normally, usually, often, frequently, every day, once a month** at the beginning of the sentence:
Sometimes, I forget my work.   **Occasionally**, he goes to London.
Every day, I go to school.   **Once a month**, I pay my bills.

but **not ever, hardly ever, rarely, seldom, never, always**.
But see Unit 50 for sentences like: *Rarely does he drink alcohol.*

1 **Ⓐ Ⓑ** Insert a suitable adverb of frequency in the second piece of gossip and write out the whole sentence.

0 Myra and Myron quarrel all the time. = They are quarrelling. *They are always quarrelling.*

1 It's unusual for Tom Craze to tell the truth about his age. = Tom Craze lies about his age.
....

2 A lot of the time, Phoebe Cute has to ask the director to help her remember her lines. = The director helps Phoebe to remember her lines. ....

3 In all her films, Myra hates the other actresses. = Myra is jealous of the other actresses.
....

4 It's usual for the Metalheads to steal ideas from other musicians. = They steal other musicians' ideas. ....

5 It's unusual for Myra to appear in public without her wig. = Myra doesn't appear without her wig. ....

6 It's unusual for Claudette to be on time for her fashion shows. = She is on time for her fashion shows. ....

7 It's unusual to see photos of Claudette's legs because she's ashamed of them. = You see photos of Claudette's legs. ....

8 Many times, she has given money to photographers to prevent them publishing photos of her ugly legs. = She has bribed photographers ....

9 Tom Craze is so vain that he spends all his time in front of the mirror. = Tom is looking in the mirror. ....

10 Have Tom's girlfriends sold his secrets to the media at any time? = Have his girlfriends sold his secrets? ....

2 **Ⓐ Ⓔ** In each piece of text, place the adverbs of frequency in the most suitable position. The first one has been done for you.

1 *always   hardly ever   never   ~~seldom~~*

> *seldom*
> The stars ᵛcomplain. It's good publicity. They realise that the story has come from Stella, so they stop telling her the show business gossip. So Jake's editor is happy.

2 *always   rarely   usually*

> Phoebe Cute falls in love with the male stars in her films. It's a habit! But she continues the love affair after the film is finished. That's because she's choosing her next male leading actor.

3 *occasionally   often   never   seldom*

> Tom Craze is a big star but he's not generous. He pays for the girls' meals when he takes them out to dinner. In fact, the girls pay for him. Although he says thank you, even that happens.

4 *always   never   once a year   twice a year*

> Tom Craze's grandmother watches his films. She's crazy about him. But he only visits her. However, Phoebe Cute treats her 90-year-old uncle even worse. She only phones him and she visits him!

UNIT 65 >> Comparatives

> ***** For a **better** deal, **cheaper** goods, **friendlier** service, *****
> **more advantageous** credit agreements, **more reliable** after-sales care,
> **less inconvenient** opening hours than any of our competitors, come to:
> SLICK VICTOR'S SUPERSTORE!!!!

See Appendix 17 for the comparative form.

Ⓐ COMPARATIVE ADJECTIVES + *THAN*

We use comparative adjectives with **than**. We can compare two people/things/groups etc.:
*My neighbour's car is faster **than** mine.*
*These students are more punctual **than** those.*

We can use **than** + **object pronoun** or **than** + **subject** + **verb**:
*He's taller **than me**.*
or *He's taller **than I am**.*

Comparative adjectives do not always occur with **than**:
I chose the less expensive meal.   She prefers older boyfriends.   Older wines are better.

Ⓑ *LESS* + ADJECTIVE

We can use **less** to make comparisons, with adjectives of one, two, three or more syllables:
*The English are **less friendly** than the Greeks.*
*It's **less hot** in June than July and August.*

Ⓒ INTENSIFYING COMPARATIVES

We can use the words in the table to say **how much** bigger/better/more beautiful etc. someone or something is:

by a large amount: *a lot/far/much/substantially/considerably/a good deal*
*She's **far wittier** than he is.*   *It's **considerably hotter** today.*

by a small amount: *a little/slightly/barely/scarcely/hardly (any)/a bit*
 *It's **a little more expensive**.*   *She's **hardly any taller** than me.*

We also use **any, no, even** with comparatives:
*He's **even taller**.   It isn't **any bigger**.   It's **no better**.*

We can use two comparatives with **and** to suggest a process of increase:
*He drove **faster and faster**.*   *Food is getting **more and more expensive**.*

Ⓓ *AS... AS.../NOT AS/SO... AS...* FOR EQUALITY

When we want to compare two things which are equal in some way we use:
as + **adjective** + **as...** (positive)
*He is **as tall as** I am.*

or **not as/not so** + **adjective** + **as...** (negative)
*She isn't **as tall as** her sister.   It's **not so hot** today **as** yesterday.*

1 **A B** Place comparative forms of the adjectives in the gaps in these advertisements. Use *-er*, *more* or *less*. Then listen and check your answers.

A ~~fashionable~~   intimate   low

Stella's hair salon gives you a **(0)** more fashionable hairstyle for a **(1)** .... price than any other top salon. Other salons are **(2)** .... For top style and top gossip, come to Stella's.

B *exciting*   *good*   *hot*   *sandy*

Do you want to enjoy **(3)** .... weather, **(4)** .... beaches and **(5)** .... night-life? Visit Benny's Spanish Holiday Agency. We provide **(6)** .... holidays than any other agency.

C *cheap*   *a little*   *generous*   *good*   *much*

Enjoy **(7)** .... for **(8)** .... Our meals are **(9)** .... in size and **(10)** .... in price than any other restaurant's. There isn't a **(11)** .... place to eat out in London.

2 **A - C** Use the information to write comparative sentences. Use one of the intensifiers in brackets. Use the adjective in the comparative form.

0 Our restaurant charges £15 for a three-course dinner. Joe's restaurant charges £60.
Our restaurant is a great deal cheaper than Joe's. (*a little/a great deal/cheap*)
Theirs is considerably more expensive than ours. (*scarcely/considerably/expensive*)

1 Ricky has an IQ (= Intelligence Quotient) of 165. Rob has an IQ of 167.
Ricky .... (*slightly/much/intelligent*)
Rob .... (*a great deal/barely/intelligent*)

2 Ted's temperature was 37 degrees yesterday. Today, it's 40 degrees and his headache is terrible.
Ted .... than he was yesterday. (*a little/a lot/ill*)
Ted is in a .... condition today. (*much/slightly/dangerous*)

3 Hong Kong has a very high humidity. North Africa has a low humidity.
Hong Kong .... (*a little/far/humid*)
North Africa .... (*much/scarcely/humid*)

3 Look at the information in the table. Then make sentences with *as... as* or *not so... as...* .

	height	IQ (intelligence)	wealth
June	1.7m	140	£300,000
Kate	1.7m	170	£700,000
Sam	1.8m	140	£300,000

0 June/Kate/tall *June is as tall as Kate.*
1 June/Sam/tall ....
2 June/Kate/intelligent ....
3 June/Sam/intelligent ....
4 Sam/June/rich ....
5 June and Sam/Kate/rich ....

UNIT 66 >> Superlatives

***** COME TO SLICK VIC'S *****

We give **the most reliable** advice, stock only **the highest** quality goods and we sell at **the lowest** prices. We try our **hardest** to satisfy all our customers. Make **the wisest** decision of your life and buy from us!!!!!

See Appendix 17 for the superlative form.

Ⓐ *THE* WITH SUPERLATIVES

We use **the + superlative adjective** to talk about three or more* people, animals or things:
*Harry is **the most famous** bank robber in Britain.*
*Chimpanzees are **the most aggressive** apes.*

* note that informally we sometimes use the superlative about two:
*I like them both but Sue's **the nicest**.*

We often use **the + superlative adjective**:

1 with expressions like **in the world** (Not ~~of the world~~), **in Europe** (Not ~~of Europe~~):
*He is **the most famous** person **in the world**.   It is **the biggest** galaxy **in the universe**.*

We normally use **of** with **time periods** such as year/month:
*Saturday is **the best** day **of the week**.*

2 with **of all/by far/by a long way**:
*She is **the most popular** singer **of all**.   (= of all the singers)*
*She got **the best** mark **of all** in the exam.   (= of all the marks)*

3 with **one of the...-est/most...** + plural noun:
*Oxford is **one of the oldest** universities in the world.*

4 with **ever** + the **Present Perfect** or **Past Perfect**:
*This is **the best** film I've **ever seen** in my life.*
*It was **the longest** story she'd **ever read**.*

We often use the superlative without a noun where the meaning is clear:
*I'm **the best**.   Our last party was **the most successful**.   It's **the worst** that can happen.*

Ⓑ SOME OCCASIONS WHEN WE DO NOT HAVE TO USE *THE*

1 with possessive adjectives: *She tried **her best**.   He's **my closest** friend.*
  or other possessives: *It was Jack's **finest** victory. It was the BBC's **best** programme.*
2 talking about a limited set: *Ben was (the) **fastest**. (= the fastest of a group of runners)*
3 in a defining relative clause: *The prize belongs to the runners who are (the) **quickest**.*
4 giving advice beginning **It's**: *It's **safest** to drive slowly.   It's **best** to be careful.*
5 when we are comparing someone/something with himself/herself/itself etc.:
  *The road's **most dangerous** when it snows.   I'm **happiest** when I'm relaxing.*

Ⓒ *THE* + LEAST + ADJECTIVE

We can use **the + least** with an adjective to talk about three or more people, animals or things:
*This is **the least expensive** restaurant in the city.*
*All the cars are fast but mine is **the least fast**.*

Ⓓ WAYS OF EMPHASISING SUPERLATIVES

We can use words like **simply/easily/quite/by far + the + superlative**:
*It's **simply the best** store!   Jack is **by far the youngest** chess champion.*
Remember:
don't use **most + adjective + -est** : ~~She's the most beautifullest.~~
don't use **more** when you need a superlative: ~~She's the more intelligent person in the class.~~

1 **A** Fill the gaps in these advertisements with the superlative form of the adjectives. Use *the* where necessary. Then listen and check your answers.

A *clear* ___good___ *interesting* *wise*

> *Grammar for Idiots* is simply **(0)** the best grammar book in the world. It has **(1)** ....
> exercises and **(2)** .... explanations. Make **(3)** .... choice, choose
> GFI.

B *large* *experienced* *important*

> Learn Chinese in six weeks. China has **(4)** .... population in the world.
> Soon, Chinese will be **(5)** .... language. Our courses in Mandarin have
> **(6)** .... teachers. Enrol now!

C *cool* *fabulous* *famous* *hot* *late*

> It's **(7)** .... Pop Festival in the world. We're bringing you **(8)** ....
> stars singing their **(9)** .... hits. We can't promise **(10)** .... weather
> of the year but we promise **(11)** .... time!

D *bad* *good* *scary* *strong*

> You need to have **(12)** .... nerves if you're going to watch *Terror House*.
> It's **(13)** .... film you've ever seen. Face your **(14)** .... fears! At
> **(15)** .... cinemas now!

2 **A** **B** Fill the gaps with a possessive adjective, *the* or put ✗ (nothing at all).

0 We all tried our best.   **1** It's .... easiest just to forget it.   **2** They've invited .... best friends
to the party.   **3** He's .... handsomest guy in the world.   **4** You've done .... best, so don't
feel bad.   **5** It's one of .... hottest days of the year.   **6** It's .... safest to wait until sunrise.
7 It's .... safest part of the city.   **8** I've just met .... oldest relative.   **9** It was .... Charles
Dickens's greatest book.   **10** It's .... wisest decision you've ever made.   **11** It's .... wisest
to pay the fine to the police now.   **12** It's .... cheapest to eat at 'The Skware Meel' but the food
is .... worst in town.

3 **C** Rewrite these sentences using *least*.

0 'The Skware Meel' is the cheapest restaurant in the city.
   The 'Skware Meel' is the least expensive restaurant in the city.

1 I don't know anyone who is less successful than Bob.
   Bob .... that I know.

2 I've never slept in such uncomfortable beds as in this hotel.
   This hotel has .... I've ever slept in.

3 She's talented but not as talented as the other musicians in the orchestra.
   She's .... in the orchestra.

4 The river shark is not as dangerous as other sharks.
   .... member of the shark family.

4 **D** Circle all the correct alternatives.

0 We're **simple/perfect/(simply)/easy** the best.

1 That pub is **extremely/a lot/easily/by far** the dullest pub in the town.

2 It's **simply the most/the simply most/the most simply/simplest the most** unexciting.

3 She's **by far the most/by most the far/the farthest** intelligent person I've ever taught.

4 It's **simply easiest/simply the easiest/by far the easiest** exam I've ever taken.

5 He's grown the biggest cucumber **in the world/in my life/by far/of all**.

UNIT 67 >> Comparatives and superlatives – adverbs

 'Nadia, the teenage genius, is the best dancer in the world. She moves **more gracefully**, **more swiftly** and **more sensitively** than anyone else. I'd like to be the same as her. But I move the **most clumsily**, dance **the least rhythmically** and react **the most slowly** of all the students in my class. Nadia dances the best. I dance the worst!'

See Appendix 17 for form.

A We use the comparative adverb + **than** to compare two actions, people, animals, things:

*He finished it **more quickly than** I could.   She answered **more intelligently than** her friend.*
*He drove **faster than** the other drivers.   We arrived **later than** we had expected.*
*She writes **better than** Shakespeare!   She drove **farther than** she had planned.*

We use the superlative of adverbs to talk about three or more actions.

*He finished **the most quickly** of all.   She answered **the most intelligently** of all.*
*He drove **the fastest** and won the race.   He arrived **the latest** out of all the boys.*
*He played **the best**.   Who drove **the farthest**?*

B DEEPER, LONGER, FURTHER

We can use the comparative and superlative of time- and distance-words like **deeper/deepest, longer/longest, further/furthest** to describe verbs:

*It took **longer** than we'd expected.*
*Who dived **deepest**?*
*She drove **further** than before.*

C A LITTLE, A LOT, MUCH

Here are the comparative and superlative forms of **a little** and **a lot/much** (See Unit 38):

	comparative	superlative
(a) little	*less*	*the least*
a lot/much	*more*	*the most*

*Sue drives **a little**.   Sue drives **less** than Tom and Jo.   Sue drives **the least**.*
*Tom drives **a lot**.   Tom drives **more** than Sue and Jo.   Tom drives **the most**.*

We can use **less** + **adverb** to compare two actions:
*She drives **less dangerously** than her brother.*

We can use **least** + **adverb** to talk about three or more actions:
*Juan speaks English **the least fluently** of all the students.*

D MODIFIERS

We can use **a bit/a little/slightly/a lot/far/much** + a comparative adverb:
*Mary drives **a lot more carefully** than her brother.*
*He uses grammar **slightly more accurately** than she does.*

1 **Ⓐ - Ⓑ** Form adverbs from the adjectives in brackets and put them in the comparative or superlative form in the gaps.

0 Nadia sings *better* than the greatest opera singers. (*good*)

1 She drives .... than a Formula 1 driver. (*skilful*)

2 She takes photographs .... than anyone else. (*artistic*)

3 In the ocean with the pearl divers, she dives .... (*deep*)

4 She plays the violin .... than the greatest musicians. (*sensitive*)

5 At the art studio, she paints .... of all. (*good*)

6 She solves mathematical problems .... than a computer. (*rapid*)

7 Out of all the students in her school, she studies .... (*conscientious*)

8 She speaks foreign languages .... than the native speakers. (*fluent*)

9 Who dresses .... in her group of friends? Nadia, of course. (*elegant*)

2 **Ⓒ** Complete the sentences using *less* or *least* + adverb.

0 Nadia behaves more confidently than everyone else.
Everyone else behaves *less confidently than Nadia.*

1 Everyone else moves more noisily than she does.
Out of all the students, she moves ....

2 But her friend, Dania, is the laziest student in the school.
But her friend, Dania, ... hard.

3 Dania is less successful than Nadia in everything.
Dania does everything ....

4 All the other students do the work more carefully than Dania.
Out of all the students, Dania ....

3 **Ⓐ - Ⓓ** Form comparative adverbs from the adjectives in brackets and use them to complete the sentences. Also use *slightly* or *far* with the adverb. The first one has been done for you.

A Nadia took 30 minutes to eat her lunch. Dania took 3 minutes.
Dania ate (0) *far more greedily* than Nadia. (*greedy*)
Nadia's lunch lasted (1) .... than Dania's. (*long*)
Dania eats (2) .... than Nadia. (*graceful*)

B Dania said, 'Thank you very much, sir,' to the teacher. Nadia said, 'I offer you my grateful thanks, sir.' The other students said, 'Thanks.'
Dania thanked the teacher (3) .... than Nadia. (*elegant*)
Nadia and Dania thanked the teacher (4) ....
than the other students. (*polite*)
Nadia always does things (5) .... than most people. (*elegant*)

OPEN EXERCISE

4 **Ⓐ - Ⓓ** Complete these sentences in any suitable way, using comparative or superlative adverbs.

1 He drives ....

2 They swim ....

3 The English ....

4 Teachers work ....

5 She eats ....

UNIT 68 >> More about comparatives and superlatives

> The **harder** you work, **the more** you achieve. **The more** you achieve, **the more confident** you become. **The more confident** you are, **the more successful** you are. But **the less** I work, **the happier** I am.

A *THE MORE..., THE MORE...*

We can use this structure: **the + comparative..., the + comparative...**

TYPE I: ***The harder*** *you work,* ***the more*** *you achieve.*
= **clause** (you work) + **clause** (you achieve)

TYPE II: ***The taller*** *the tree,* ***the longer*** *its shadow.*
= **noun** (the tree) + **noun** (its shadow)

Type II could also be written: *The taller the tree is, the longer its shadow is.*

We want to say that the two things are linked; one leads to the other. We often use this structure to give advice or to form sayings, for example:

'***The bigger*** *they are,* ***the harder*** *they fall.*' (= powerful people suffer more when they fail)

B *LESS* + UNCOUNTABLE NOUN, *FEWER* + PLURAL NOUN

In strict grammar, we use **less + uncountable noun**: *less money, less water, less information* etc.
We should use **fewer + plural noun**: *fewer people, fewer jobs, fewer hospitals* etc.

But in conversation, you will often hear British people use **less + plural noun.** For example:
There were **less people/less dogs** *at the park today.*

This is **wrong**, so don't copy them or use it in examinations!

C *THAN* + CLAUSE

We often follow **comparative + than** with clauses like this:
... I (had) thought   ... he (had) expected   ... she (had) imagined.
He was **shorter than I had expected.**   *It is* **later than I thought**.

It is possible to use **than + when** or **where**:
It is hotter **than when** *I was here last year.*
This flat is nicer **than where** *you lived before.*

D *MOST* + ADJECTIVE

We can use **most + adjective** without **the** if we want to give the meaning **very**:
The race was **most dangerous.** (= very dangerous)
This house is **most damp.** (= very damp)

E 'ABSOLUTE' ADJECTIVES

We **should not** make comparisons using **unique**, **perfect**, **superb** etc. in the comparative or superlative form: ~~*It's the most perfect ring of them all.*~~
~~*This picture is more unique than a Picasso.*~~

However, it is acceptable to use **the most** as an intensifier:
It's **the most perfect** *weather today.*
She's **the most superb** *athlete.*
I had **the most unique** *experience.*

1 **A** Fill the gaps with words from the list. Then listen and check your answers.

*more dishonest   more easily   higher   higher   higher   more   more
more   older   more scandalous   more stupid   more successful*

When Jake was a child, the (0) *more* he discovered about adults, the (1) .... he thought they were. The (2) .... he grew, the (3) .... he believed this. When he got a job as a journalist on a tabloid newspaper, he quickly found that the (4) .... he exaggerated a story, the (5) .... people believed it. The (6) .... the stories, the (7) .... the circulation of the newspaper. And the (8) .... the profits of the paper, the (9) .... Jake's salary. According to Jake, the (10) .... you are, the (11) .... you are. Do you agree?

2 **A** Do you agree with these sayings? Fill the gaps with the comparative form of the words in brackets.
Also classify them as TYPE I (clause + clause) or TYPE II (noun + noun).

0 The *more* you have, the *more* you want. (*much/much*)   TYPE: I
1 The .... it is to get something, the .... we value it. (*easy/little*)   TYPE: ....
2 The .... we smile, the .... the world becomes. (*a lot/happy*)   TYPE: ....
3 The .... the wallet, the .... the head. (*fat/empty*)   TYPE: ....
4 The .... the wrapping, the .... the present inside. (*shiny/cheap*)   TYPE: ....
5 The .... we get, the .... we become. (*old/wise*)   TYPE: ....
6 The .... the hand, the .... the heart. (*cold/warm*)   TYPE: ....
7 The .... we know, the .... we understand. (*much/little*)   TYPE: ....

3 **B D E** Circle ALL the correct alternatives.

0 He ate **fewer/less/littler** food than I did.

1 There were **fewer/less/more** people at the disco than at the lecture.   2 He earns **less/a lot of/fewer** money than his brother.   3 I had **less/fewer/more** friends at school than at university. 4 There is **less/fewer/more** goodness in white bread than in brown bread.   5 He's had far **less/fewer/more** problems since he left London.   6 This painting is **more perfect/more imaginative/more unique** than the *Mona Lisa.*   7 They chose the **most perfect/most superb/most expensive** one of the wedding rings.   8 This has been the **most perfect/most delicious/most enjoyable** meal! Thank you!   9 This diamond is **more/the most/absolutely** perfect! It's the best!   10 Darling, you're looking **most/very/veriest** beautiful tonight.

4 **C** For each situation, write a sentence with a comparative (*more* or *less*) and clause.

0 In his films, Tom Craze looks really tall. When you meet him, he's not as tall as you are.
Tom's shorter than I'd expected. (*short/expect*)
1 On TV, Kelly always looks beautiful. When you meet her she has spots and untidy hair.
She's .... (*attractive/think*)
2 In the advertisement, the hotel looked great. When you arrive, the rooms are small and simple.
The hotel's .... (*luxurious/believe*)
3 You were careful not to choose expensive food at the restaurant. But the bill is huge.
The bill's .... (*big/expect*)
4 You've only spoken to Bob by phone. When you meet, you find he's extremely tall.
Bob's .... (*tall/imagine*)
5 Last week, Tim took you to an expensive disco. This week, the entrance fee is less.
This place .... last week. (*cheap/go*)

UNIT 69 >> *So/such… that, quite/rather a… , too/enough*

Nadia is **so** intelligent **that** she can learn a new language in six hours. She has **such a** quick brain and **such a** sensitive heart **that** all her teachers agree: 'She is **so** lovely. She's **such a** genius. She has **such** elegance. Poor Dania. She's **so** lazy, **so** stupid and wears **such** awful clothes!'

A SO + ADJECTIVE OR ADVERB + *THAT/SUCH (A)* + ADJECTIVE + NOUN + *THAT*

We use **so** + **adjective** + **that** + **result**:
*Nadia is **so intelligent that** she doesn't have to study.*
*Dania is **so lazy that** she never studies.*

We also use **so** + **adverb** + **that** + **result**: *She swims **so well that** she broke the world record.*
*She studied **so little that** she failed every subject.*

We use **such a** + **adjective** + **singular noun** + **that** + **result**:
*She has **such a sensitive heart that** she cries very easily.*

We use **such** + **adjective** + **plural noun/uncountable noun** + **that** + **result**:
*She had **such good marks that** they thought she had cheated.*
*She has **such good taste that** she always looks elegant.*

Sometimes, we omit **that**, especially in informal English:
Dania is so clumsy (that) everyone laughs at her.

B SO MUCH, SO MANY, SUCH A LOT OF

We can use **so** + **much/many/little** and **few**:
*She eats **so much** chocolate that she always has spots.* (**much** + uncountable)
*She's got **so many** diplomas that her room is full.* (**many** + plural noun)
*She has **so little** stress/**so few** problems that…* (**little** + uncountable/**few** = plural)

We can use **such** + **a lot of**: *She ate **such a lot of** chocolate that…*
*She's got **such a lot of** diplomas that…*

C EXCLAMATIONS WITH *SO* AND *SUCH*/MODIFYING WITH *QUITE* AND *RATHER*

We often use **so** and **such** in exclamations (!!!):
*You are **so** beautiful!   He answered the questions **so** quickly!   She has **such a** lovely face!*
*They have **such** expensive clothes!   This is **such** good weather!*

Notice that we must use **such a** with a singular noun: *The film was **such a success**.*

Similarly, we can use **quite a** and **rather a** to modify a singular noun or adjective + singular noun: *The film was **quite a** success.*
*= The film was **rather a** success. = It was **quite/rather a** successful film.*

We can use **quite/rather** + **adjective**: *It was **quite successful**. He is **rather fat**.*

Notice that **so** and **such** are emphatic while **quite** or **rather** lessen the **intensity**.

D *TOO* AND *ENOUGH*

We use **too** before an adjective or an adverb: *He's **too** careless. He drives **too** fast.*
We often use **too**… (for me/you etc.) **to** + **verb**: *It's **too** expensive for me to buy.*
Too always has a **negative** sense:
*It's **too** hot!* (negative) is different from *It's **very** hot.* (emphatic)

We often use **too much** or **too many**: *He's got **too much** furniture / **too many** tables and chairs.*

We use **enough** after an adjective or adverb:
*He's old **enough** to drive. You're driving fast **enough**.*

We use **enough** before a noun: *He's got **enough** money to go on holiday.*

1 **A** Identify eight more pairs of sentences in the text which you can combine with *so… that…* or *such (a)… that…* . Write the sentences under the text.

People call Nadia 'the teenage genius'. She is very intelligent. She can learn a new language in six hours. She is also very sensitive. She can understand other people's problems immediately. But she has physical as well as mental talents. She is a good athlete. She won five golds in the under-18 Olympics. She swims very fast. She has broken two world records. And she is very agile and graceful. She is her country's top gymnast. At home she prepares very delicious food. Her family beg her to cook for them every day. However, her personal life is difficult. She has a very delicate face. Lots of boys fall in love with her. But they are all immature. She finds them boring. She has a very complex personality. It's difficult to find someone who understands her.

0 She is so intelligent that she can learn a new language in six hours.
1 ....
2 ....
3 ....
4 ....
5 ....
6 ....
7 ....
8 ....

2 **B** Rewrite items 1-5, using *so much, so many, so little, so few*.

0 Modern life causes a lot of problems. Some people cannot cope.
   Modern life causes so many problems that some people cannot cope.
1 There is a lot of interest in meditation techniques. Many courses are full.
   ....
2 Many people have very limited chances to relax. They get very stressed.
   ....
3 Many people have very little time to cook. They don't care about their diet.
   ....
4 A lot of advanced technology surrounds us. We feel out of place.
   ....
5 However, we have a great number of advantages. We should be grateful to be living now.
   ....

3 **C** Make exclamations with *so* or *such* or sentences with *quite* or *rather*.

0 The weather is very hot today. It's such hot weather! (*such*) It's so hot! (*so*)
1 This furniture is very stylish. It's ....! (*such*) This furniture ....! (*so*)
2 Your new haircut's really nice. It's ....! (*such*) Your haircut's ....! (*so*)
3 It's about 24 degrees today. It's .... hot. (*rather*) It's .... hot day. (*rather*)
4 He's famous among some people. He's .... famous person. (*quite*)
5 This road is very dangerous. It's ....! (*such*) This road ....! (*so*)

4 **D** Rewrite the sentences using the word in brackets.

0 The bed is too short for him. The bed isn't long enough for him. (*enough*)
1 There are too many suitcases in your room. .... (*luggage*)
2 He is so handsome that he could be a film star. .... to be a film star. (*enough*)
3 The questions were too hard for him to answer. .... (*enough*)
4 He has too little money to buy a car. .... (*enough*)

UNIT 70 >> Adjectives with -ed and -ing

 Uncle Joe tells lots of **boring** stories about the past. I'm so **bored** when I'm with him! But yesterday I overheard Uncle Joe talking to his friend. 'My nephew is so **tiring**,' he was saying, 'I get so **frustrated** listening to his **boring** stories about girls and motorbikes and beach parties.'

Ⓐ THE DIFFERENCE BETWEEN -*ED* AND -*ING* EDJECTIVES

We use adjectives ending in **-ed** to describe the **emotion of a person**:
'*How did you feel?*' '*I was very* **frightened**.'

We use adjectives ending in **-ing** to **describe the thing** or **person that produces the emotion**:
'*What was the film like?*' '*It was very* **frightening**.'

Ⓑ COMMON -*ED*/-*ING* ADJECTIVES

Here are some common **-ed** and **-ing** adjectives:

How did you feel?	What was it like?	examples
amused	amusing	*I wasn't* **amused** *by his joke. The clown was very* **amusing**.
annoyed	annoying	*They were* **annoyed** *by the noise. The drums were* **annoying**.
bored	boring	*I felt* **bored** *in class. The lecturer is* **boring**.
confused	confusing	*I'm* **confused** *by the instructions. This map is* **confusing**.
disappointed	disappointing	*Don't be* **disappointed**. *How* **disappointing** *— we lost!*
disgusted	disgusting	*She was* **disgusted** *by the nude photos.* *The food is* **disgusting**.
embarrassed	embarrassing	*I was* **embarrassed** *by her rudeness.* *It's* **embarrassing** *to sneeze in public.*
excited	exciting	*The dog is very* **excited**. *What an* **exciting** *film!*
fascinated	fascinating	*I'm* **fascinated** *by her beauty. You have* **fascinating** *ideas.*
frightened	frightening	*Are you* **frightened**? *Is the film* **frightening**?
interested	interesting	*Is he* **interested** *in grammar?* *Does he find this book* **interesting**?
pleased	pleasing	*I'm* **pleased** *to be here. The view is very* **pleasing**.
relaxed	relaxing	*Try to be more* **relaxed**. *Listen to some* **relaxing** *music.*
surprised	surprising	*I was* **surprised** *to see you. How* **surprising** *to meet you here!*
terrified	terrifying	*She was* **terrified** *by the monster. The ghost was* **terrifying**.
thrilled	thrilling	*I'm* **thrilled** *to meet such a famous person.* *It's a* **thrilling** *game.*
tired	tiring	*Are you* **tired**? *Mountain climbing is very* **tiring**.

Ⓒ *BE, FEEL* WITH -*ED* ADJECTIVES

We usually use **be** or **feel** with **-ed** adjectives. We often use **get** with **bored/tired**:

I **was fascinated**.   *Don't* **get** *too* **tired**.
She **felt relaxed**.   *I* **got bored** *at the party.*

1 **A**-**C** Fill the gap(s) in each advertisement by using the *-ing* or *-ed* form of the word given.

0 Watch 'SKREME!!!' You'll never be so frightened in your life. (*frighten*)

1 Do you find computers .... ? Buy our 700-page Internet Guide. (*confuse*)

2 Isn't it .... when machines break down? Try our Repair Service. (*annoy*)

3 The most .... thing about our hotel is the low price of a luxury suite. (*surprise*)

4 Are you surrounded by .... people? Use our Dating Agency to make .... friends. (*bore/interest*)

5 Don't be .... by the future. Visit Madam Magistar and hear her .... predictions. (*mystify/astonish*)

6 Problems? Stress? Relax with a .... cup of Old Gaffer Tea. (*comfort*)

7 You'll be .... when you visit our sale. We're reducing prices by 35%. (*amaze*)

8 Bad smells in your home can be .... Use AIRFRESH every day. (*embarrass*)

9 Are you .... by litter in the streets. Join our volunteer KLEEN-UP army. (*disgust*)

2 **A**-**C** Complete the sentences about these situations, using the *-ing* or *-ed* form of the word given. Then listen and check your answers.

A *His trousers fell down in the supermarket.*

0 It was embarrassing when his trousers fell down in the supermarket. (*embarrass*)

1 He felt very .... (*embarrass*)

2 The shoppers were all .... (*amuse*)

3 Has anything as .... as that ever happened to you? (*embarrass*)

B *He parachuted out of the aeroplane and landed in a heap of cow dung in a farm.*

4 Falling through the air was .... but the landing was .... (*thrill/embarrass*)

5 At least he has an .... story to tell people. (*amuse*)

6 The farmer was .... to see him in his farmyard. (*astound*)

7 He was even more .... when the TV news reported it. (*embarrass*)

C *They showed a TV programme about life on a remote island in the Pacific.*

8 The programme was .... (*fascinate*)

9 Many of the islanders felt .... by the film crew. (*irritate*)

10 It must be .... for primitive people to come into contact with technology. (*confuse*)

11 One of the cameramen was so .... that he stayed on the island. (*fascinate*)

D *He buys a lottery ticket every week but he never wins.*

12 When the numbers are announced, he's always .... (*disappoint*)

13 It's very .... not to win. (*disappoint*)

14 His girlfriend gets very .... because he wastes so much money. (*irritate*)

15 If he ever wins, he'll be extremely .... (*excite*)

E *Someone murdered Lady Alice but we don't know the motive.*

16 The police find the crime completely .... (*mystify*)

17 Lady Alice had had a .... day riding her horse. (*tire*)

18 It's really .... that the police can't find any clues. (*surprise*)

19 It's difficult to feel .... when there's an unknown murderer. (*relax*)

Adjectives with *-ed* and *-ing*

185

UNIT 71 >> *Still, yet, already*

 We can't start the circus **yet**. The lions are **still** hungry — they haven't eaten their dinner **yet**! They've **already** eaten three members of the audience this year.

A USE OF *STILL, YET, ALREADY*

We often (but not always) use **still** to express **criticism, surprise** or **impatience**:
*Are you **still** working at the same place?* (surprise)
*He **still** hasn't handed in his work.* (impatience and criticism)

We often use **yet** (in negative sentences and questions) **without** wishing to express criticism.
*He hasn't handed in his work **yet**.* (simple statement: up until this time, he hasn't done it)
*Have you had breakfast **yet**?* (simple question: perhaps with an implied invitation)

We use **already** either simply to **state** that **something has been done** before the time of speaking or to **express surprise** or **praise**:
*He's **already** finished his work!* (surprise)
*I've **already** had breakfast.* (statement)
*She's great! She's written the essay **already**!* (praise)

B *STILL, YET, ALREADY* WITH PERFECT TENSES

We often use these adverbials with perfect tenses (see Unit 7):
Have you finished yet? *When I arrived, he **still hadn't done** it/he'd **already done** it.*

Yet + Future Perfect suggests that we think something hasn't had time to happen by the moment of speaking:
*The letter **won't have arrived yet**.* *Will he **have left yet**?*

We also use **still** and **already** + Future Perfect:
*He **still won't have finished**, even by tomorrow night.*
*They'll **have already finished**.* (we think they've finished by now or by a future time)

C *STILL, YET* AND *ALREADY* WITH PRESENT TENSES

Notice the position in the sentence of **still**, **yet** and **already** in these examples.

Present Continuous

*He arrived ten years ago and he's **still** living here.*	*I'm not leaving **yet**.*	*She's **already** opening her presents.*

Present Simple affirmative

*He **still** lives in London.* *She **still** remembers me.*	we do not use **yet** in positive sentences	*They **already** know how to swim.* *She's **already** here.* *I **already** feel nervous.*

Present Simple negative and questions

*He **still** doesn't eat meat.* *Do you **still** like 60s music?* *Don't they **still** work here?*	*The teacher isn't here **yet**.* *Please don't go **yet**.* *Must you go **yet**?*	*Are they **already** at the party?* *Does he **already** know?*

Notice: yet and **already** occur mainly with **be** or **know**, **feel** etc.: *He doesn't **know yet**.*
Yet also occurs with imperatives and modals: ***Don't** look **yet**.* *I **can't** do it **yet**.*

1 Ⓐ Ⓒ Make sentences with a suitable present tense or imperative and the word(s) in brackets.

0 Myra began acting in films in 1959 and she's in Hollywood now.
Myra is still acting in films. (*still*)

1 Kevin joined Crunchester in 1999 and he hasn't changed team yet.
.... (*still*)

2 Stop! It's too soon to light the fireworks.
.... (*yet*)

3 Mrs Satchelmouth hasn't stopped gossiping since breakfast time.
.... (*still*)

4 Lia got the information yesterday about the party.
.... (*already/know*)

5 Bella used to act in Shakespeare plays. Is it still true?
....? (*still*)

2 Ⓐ Ⓒ Fill the gaps with *still, yet* or *already* + the verb in the Present Simple (negative if necessary).

0 Do you want to take French lessons? No, I *already speak* French. (*speak*)

1 Has Brigitte improved? No, she .... the same mistakes. (*make*)

2 Has Phil passed his exams? No, he .... the results .... (*know*)

3 Have the Collins family arrived? No, they .... here .... (*be*)

4 Shall I tell Bella the news? It's not necessary. She .... (*know*)

5 Would you like to buy a kitten? No thank you, I .... three. (*own*)

6 Is Colin getting used to his new job? Yes, but he .... it difficult. (*find*)

7 Are you planning to go to the film club today?
No, I .... a member .... (*be*)

3 Ⓑ Make sentences using the Future Perfect.

0 I don't think Ben is in London yet. = *Ben won't have arrived in London yet.* (*arrive*)

1 Tim will still be doing the work tomorrow. = ... by tomorrow. (*finish*)

2 I expect Harriet has already left. = ... (*start her journey*)

3 I don't think Minnie's exam results are out yet. = ... (*receive*)

OPEN EXERCISE

4 Ⓐ - Ⓒ Write suitable sentences with *still* for these situations.

0 Myra didn't forgive Myron and she feels the same now.
Myra still hasn't forgiven Myron. / Myra is still angry with Myron.

1 John should have already taken the exam but he hasn't.
....

2 Pete should have been ready when Jill arrived but he wasn't.
....

3 Kate should have arrived 30 minutes ago but she's not here.
....

4 Stella should have stopped going out with Jake but she hasn't.
....

5 Beth should have written the letter by 2 p.m. but she hadn't.
....

6 Tina has refused to talk to me and the situation hasn't changed.
....

REVISION 7 >> First Certificate Practice

1 For questions 1-12, read the text below and decide which answer, A, B, C or D, best fits each gap. There is an example (0).

NEW YEAR'S RESOLUTIONS

The New Year (0) A the traditional time in Britain for making resolutions. The (1) ..... kind of resolution involves giving up something – smoking, chocolate, alcohol, anything which is perceived as (2) ..... . But these promises are seldom kept for more than a few days or weeks. Psychologists suggest that this is because it is (3) ..... to keep a 'negative' vow (4) ..... a 'positive' one. In other words, we can (5) ..... maintain our determination to take a positive action than to make a sacrifice. Keeping fit by taking up a sport seems (6) ..... than depriving ourselves of something we (7) ..... enjoy. However, an (8) ..... important factor in determining whether we keep our resolutions or not is the degree to which the wish to change our lives comes from within ourselves. Nothing is more (9) ..... than trying to conform to other people's idea of what is (10) ..... for you. The more your friends or parents tell you to go to the gym to keep fit, (11) ..... you are to do so regularly. To sum up, a New Year's resolution will not work (12) ..... effectively if it is seen as compulsory or as a sacrifice as if it is seen as your own personal ambition.

0 (A) has always been	B has always	C has been always	D always
1 A most common	B commoner	C commonly	D usuallest
2 A indulgence	B indulgently	C indulgents	D indulgant
3 A difficulter	B the most difficult	C more difficult	D more difficulty
4 A that	B which	C what	D than
5 A more easily	B easier	C more easy	D less easily
6 A most attractive	B attractively	C more attractive	D more attractively
7 A greatly	B much	C very	D more
8 A even most	B extremely more	C extreme	D even more
9 A frustrated	B annoyed	C frustrating	D frustration
10 A worst	B best	C goodest	D worse
11 A the less likely	B the least likely	C the least	D the unlikely
12 A far less	B so	C less	D far more

2 For these questions, read the text below and think of the word which best fits the gap. Use only *one* word in each gap. There is an example (0).

HOGMANAY

New Year is a (0) *more* widely celebrated occasion in Scotland than in the other countries of the UK. In fact, the New Year is celebrated (1) .... exuberantly that people come from all over the world to join in the fun. The (2) .... likely origin of the special name used in Scotland for the festival, 'Hogmanay', is a Gaelic phrase meaning 'new morning'. In ancient times, the pagan practice of sun and fire worship evolved into (3) .... of the most important celebrations of the year, the mid-winter festival. For a time, the Church banned this festival but it had (4) .... great popularity (5) .... it continued underground. Since 1992, Hogmanay has been celebrated on a (6) .... larger scale (7) .... ever before in cities like Edinburgh and Glasgow. During the millennium, some of the (8) .... lasting celebrations took place in Scotland. 'First footing' is one of the (9) .... famous customs associated with Hogmanay. At midnight, if a dark stranger knocks on your door with a lump of coal for your fire, you will have a prosperous year if you let him in. The more hospitable you are, (10) .... luckier you will be. Fireworks and street bonfires are also connected with Hogmanay. They symbolise the bringing of new light to create a (11) .... enlightened world than before. The ancient message of Hogmanay is (12) .... relevant today as it ever has been.

PAPER 3 PART 4

3 For these questions, complete the second sentence so that it has a similar meaning to the first sentence, using the word given. Do not change the word given. Use from two to five words including the word given. There is an example (0).

0 John is not as tall as his brother. John *is shorter than his* brother. **THAN**

1 *Mystery Planet* was one of the most fascinating films I've ever seen.
I have never been .... a film as I was by *Mystery Planet*. **BY**

2 As a result of the festival's success, other cities copied it.
It was .... that other cities copied it. **SUCCESSFUL**

3 The older generation think that Hogmanay used to be more authentic.
The older generation think that nowadays ....
than before. **AUTHENTIC**

4 Everyone was so excited by the match that they didn't want to leave the stadium.
It was .... nobody wanted to leave the stadium. **SUCH**

5 When you drive faster, the risk of accidents increases.
The .... the risk of accidents. **GREATER**

6 The morning post won't come until later.
The morning post ....yet. **ARRIVED**

7 Gina is more intelligent than the rest of her family.
The rest of her family .... **SO**

8 On many occasions the teacher loses our homework.
The teacher .... **OFTEN**

OTHER PRACTICE

4 Form an adjective or adverb from the word given in each line. Write it in the gap.

THE MILLENNIUM BRIDGE

BEAUTY   The Millennium Bridge in London is very **(0)** *beautiful*; it is a slim, modern
GRACE   bridge with a **(1)** .... structure, designed to celebrate the millennium
FORTUNE   in 2000. **(2)** ...., there was a design fault, so that when it was first used
PRONOUNCE by large numbers of people, it was found that it had a **(3)** .... wobble;
DANGER   in other words, it swayed **(4)** .... from side to side. At first the problem
EASY   seemed as if it would be **(5)** .... solved but, in fact, it took two years
THEORY   to find a solution that worked practically as well as **(6)** .... This, of
EMBARRASS course, was highly **(7)** .... for the architect and engineers of the
SUBSTANCE bridge, and added **(8)** .... to the cost, raising it by several million
FINAL   pounds. **(9)** ...., however, the bridge was tested and declared to be
SAFETY   **(10)** .... for the public to use. Now the bridge spans the Thames from
GOOD   St Paul's Cathedral, one of the **(11)** ....-known of all London's
COMPARE   landmarks, to the Tate Modern Gallery, a **(12)** .... recent addition to
          the capital's attractions.

5 Fill the gap(s) by using the *-ing* or -ed form of the word given.

0 It was one of the most *thrilling* experiences of my whole life. (*thrill*)

1 I've never been so .... as when I saw the rats in the kitchen. (*disgust*)

2 It is very .... to know that my old friends still remember me. (*please*)

3 Isn't it ....? I've lost one of my gloves. (*annoy*)

UNIT 72 >> Prepositions

 Madam Magistar predicted a good life **for** Harry and Michelle **with** plenty **of** excitement. 'You can look forward **to** living **in** comfortable conditions **with** lots **of** people to look **after** you. I can see a large building **with** bars **on** the windows... But stop! Don't leave **without** pay**ing** me.'

Ⓐ PREPOSITIONS: THEIR USUAL POSITION IN SENTENCES

Prepositions usually occur:

1 **before nouns and pronouns:**
   *in comfortable **conditions** / **with bars on** the **windows** / **after you***
2 **before verb-ing:** *Don't leave **without paying** me.*   *Thank you **for coming**.*

If a verb follows a preposition, it is **always** in the **-ing** form.

Ⓑ MORE ABOUT PREPOSITION + VERB-ING

The **-ing** verb can be in the **active** form: *He left **without paying** Madam Magistar.*

Or in the **passive** form: *Madam Magistar told Harry's fortune **without being paid**.*

We can use **preposition + noun/pronoun + verb-ing**:

*She went **without anyone paying** her.*
*I congratulated the teacher **on the students passing** the exam.*
*I was grateful **for them helping** me.*
*She did it **without them asking** her.*

Ⓒ TO + VERB-ING

Look at these two different uses of **to** in English:

1 **As part of full infinitive:** *I want **to go**.* (**to** + bare infinitive)
2 **As a preposition:** *I went **to** the bank.* (**to** + noun)

In cases where we use **to** as a preposition before a verb, we **must** use **verb-ing**:

to as a preposition + noun	to as a preposition + verb-ing
*I looked forward **to** my holiday.*	*I looked forward **to going** on holiday.*
*He objected **to** the change of plan.*	*He objected **to changing** the plan.*
*He's used **to** this food.*	*He's used **to eating** this food.* (see Unit 80)

In other words, if you can follow **to** by a **noun** it is a preposition. If you use a verb in the same position as the noun, use the **-ing** form.

Ⓓ PREPOSITIONS IN OTHER POSITIONS IN THE SENTENCE

We may also use prepositions at the end of clauses:

1 in questions with **who/what/which***:
   ***Who** is she going out **with**?*   ***Which** one did you look **at**?*
2 in passive structures: *The meal hasn't been paid **for**.*   *This room isn't lived **in**.*
3 in relative clauses**: *I recognise the person (**who**) she's talking **with**.*
   *That's the team (**which**) he plays **for**.*
4 in infinitive clauses: *I didn't have anyone to play **with**.*

* In very formal, old-fashioned English, someone might use **preposition + wh-word**:
   ***With whom** is she talking?*   ***At what** are you looking?*

** In formal English, we might use **preposition + relative pronoun**:
   *I recognise the person **with whom** she is talking.*   *That is the team **for which** he plays.*

1 Ⓐ Ⓒ Read the text about cricket, the English national summer sport. Fill the gaps with verbs from the list in the correct form.

     bowl   catch   explain   fail   hit   ~~live~~   score   touch   understand   use

Cricket is a mystery to many foreign visitors to England. Even after **(0)** living in the country for several years, they may leave without **(1)** .... the game or its rules. Basically, the game is about **(2)** .... points (called 'runs') with two teams playing against each other over one or several days. The 'batsmen' score runs by **(3)** .... the ball as far as possible while the 'bowlers' try to dismiss them by **(4)** .... the ball and trying to hit their 'wicket'. The 'fielders' can dismiss the batsmen by **(5)** .... the ball without it **(6)** .... the ground. A batsman can also be out through **(7)** .... his legs to stop the ball or through **(8)** .... to complete a 'run'. So, have I made the game easier to understand by **(9)** .... some of the rules?

2 Ⓒ Use the verb given to fill the gap in either the infinitive or the *-ing* form.

0 Some people are opposed to *showing* too much sport on television. (*show*)

1 People who aren't used to .... cricket may find it boring. (*watch*)

2 Women also began to .... in international cricket matches. (*compete*)

3 The matches between Australia and England are exciting to .... (*watch*)

4 Bad light or rain can cause the players to .... the match. (*abandon*)

5 Playing cricket is a little similar to .... baseball. (*play*)

6 It's easier to .... cricket if you understand the rules. (*appreciate*)

3 Ⓐ - Ⓒ Fill the gaps in the sentences with the active or passive *-ing* form of the verbs. Then listen and check your answers.

You can find The Hot Lips Night Club by **(0** *go*) *going* through a network of alleys in the rough part of town. If you're afraid of **(1** *rob*) ...., keep away. But if you want the chance of **(2** *listen*) .... to excellent music, then the small risk of **(3** *meet*) .... a local thief is worth it. The entrance is free but don't count on **(4** *get*) .... cheap drinks here. Drinking at the Hot Lips is a sure way of **(5** *empty*) .... your wallet. If you get tired of **(6** *entertain*) .... by the visiting band, you can go next door to the Hot Lips Casino. The gamblers there are experts in **(7** *take*) .... away your money! Few nights pass without this illegal casino **(8** *raid*) .... by the police but even so, the atmosphere is something you shouldn't leave without **(9** *experience*) ....

4 Ⓓ Complete the sentences so that they end in prepositions. Use the original sentence and the word in brackets to help you.

0 He was looking at something. (question)   What *was he looking at?*

1 Nobody has interfered with the secret papers. (passive)
The secret papers ....

2 I wanted to talk to someone but I was alone. (infinitive clause)
I didn't have ....

3 See that girl. I danced with her. (relative clause)
That's the girl ....

4 He's going to a certain place. (question)
Where ....?

5 It's difficult to do without a TV. (relative clause)
A TV is something I can't ....

UNIT 73 >> Prepositions of time, place and movement

 'On Saturday, she walked **through** the forest **towards** her grandmother's house **next to** the waterfall. But as she got **near** the cottage, she met a wolf, hiding **behind** a tree...!'

A PREPOSITIONS OF TIME

At: We use **at** with **times, names of festivals, meal-times, night** and **weekend**:
at 6 o'clock/at midday/at Easter/at dinner-time/at night/at midnight/at the weekend

In: We use **in** with **centuries, years, months, seasons**:
in the 20th century/in 1999/in January/in May/in August 2007/in (the) summer

Also **in** with **parts of the day**:
in the morning/in the afternoon/in the evening (But **at** night)

On: We use **on** with **days, dates, special days**:
on Wednesday/on Monday the 17th/on the twelfth of July/on Easter Day/on New Year's Eve

Also: *on Monday morning/on Friday evening etc.* (But *in the morning on Monday*)

For more detailed information and for other prepositions of time see Appendix 10.

B PREPOSITIONS OF PLACE OR POSITION

above	around	at	behind	beside	between
far (away) from	in	in front of	inside	near*	
next to	on	opposite*	outside	over	under

* Do **not** use these prepositions with **to**: Not ~~I live opposite to/near to the church.~~

C AT, IN AND ON

Generally, we use **in** when we want to refer simply to place; we mean inside a building/area etc.
*She's **in** the cinema.*   *There's a dog **in** the park.*   *She's **in** the office.*

We use **at** to talk about the activity which happens at the place.
*She's **at** the cinema.* (= she's watching a film)   *She's **at** the office.* (= working)

Prepositions often change the meaning of a phrase. Here are some examples with **at, in** and **on**:

*There's some beer **in** the bottle.* (in = inside)   *He's **on** the bottle.* (= he's drinking heavily)
*Collect your tickets **at** the door.*   *Rita's **on** the door tonight.* (= she's checking entry)
*Her husband's **at** sea.* (= he's in a ship/boat)   *He's **in** the sea.* (= he's swimming or drowning!)
*She's **at** the film.* (= at the cinema)   *She's **in** the film.* (= she has a role in the film)
*He arrived **on** time.* (= punctually)   *He arrived **in** time.* (= at the right moment)

D PREPOSITIONS OF MOVEMENT

We can use various prepositions to talk about movement:

in/into	out of	on/onto	off	to	from	from... to
over	under	through	across	along	past	around/round
between	up	down	towards	away from		

Remember:
We say: *to come/go/arrive/return home* (**Not** ~~to come/go to home~~)
*He **came** home from his holiday yesterday.*

But we say: *I went **to** Jane's home./She came **to** my home.*

1 ⓐ **Put a suitable preposition of time from Appendix 10 in each gap. Then listen and check your answers.**

Aunt Charlotte is talking about her life. 'I was born (0) *on* April 20th 1918. My father was killed
(1) .... the end of the First World War (2) .... a battle in France. (3) .... 1918 to 1930,
I lived with my mother in Brighton. But she died (4) .... April 1930 and I lived with my
grandmother (5) .... the next five years. (6) .... 1935 I fell in love and got married
(7) .... May. But (8) .... the Second World War, my first husband was killed.
(9) .... 1939 to 1945, I worked as a nurse in a military hospital and (10) .... 23rd April 1946,
I married one of the doctors. I gave birth to my first child (11) .... 17th April 1947 but my poor
baby died (12) .... the very cold winter (13) .... New Year's Day (14) .... the early
morning. That was very sad but I had three more children (15) .... the next few years. My
husband caught a serious illness (16) .... 1956 and, although I nursed him (17) .... the
next few months, he died peacefully (18) .... night (19) .... Christmas Day.
Now, it's early (20) .... the 21st century and I'm still alive. I'd like to live (21) .... my hundredth
birthday but that's (22) .... a few years' time from now. I was born, got married and gave birth
(23) .... April, so perhaps I'll die (24) .... the spring too.'

2 ⓑ ⓓ **In each numbered part of the story, mark the places where prepositions are missing and write the preposition from the list that belongs there. The first one has been done for you. Then listen and check your answers.**

1 Andor the Jaguar Boy was born ∨ a village the middle the South American jungle the banks of
   the Amazon River. (*in/in/of/on*)

                                            in

2 The loggers came the rainforest and destroyed his village, killing everyone except the baby.
   He crawled the jungle he reached the foot the great mountains. (*into/of/through/until*)

3 The wild jaguars looked after the human child. He lived a cave a waterfall and learnt to hunt
   with the jaguars the forest. (*in/in/next to*)

4 Once, one of the hottest days of the year, some jaguar hunters came the forest trucks. Andor
   swam the Amazon to find the jaguars and told them to hide an island the river. Then he
   swung the branches the hunters' camp and frightened them. They thought that a forest spirit
   was somewhere the trees so they drove the forest the nearest town and never returned that
   place. (*above/across/in/in/in/in/into/on/on/to/towards/out of*)

3 ⓒ **Put the correct preposition in each gap.**

0 I'm sorry, Captain Sykes isn't here. He's *at* sea. (= *he's away from home, on a ship*)

1 Sarah's worried – her boyfriend's .... the bottle again. (= *he's getting drunk*)

2 The children are probably upstairs .... their bedroom. (= *inside the room*)

3 The children are probably .... the funfair. (= *they're enjoying themselves there*)

4 As you go out, leave your programme .... the door. (= *hand in your programme*)

5 As you go out, give your programme to the man .... the door.
   (= *to the official attendant*)

6 Gina isn't .... the factory because she's on holiday. (= *isn't working*)

7 There's a bird .... the factory – it can't get out. (= *inside the factory*)

UNIT **74** >> More about prepositions

 Have you heard the legend **about** Andor the Jaguar Boy who hunted **like** the jaguars and swam **with** the piranha fish? Was it invented **by** someone? Or do you believe it's true? It's **up to** you.

Ⓐ OTHER USES OF PREPOSITIONS

Here are some prepositions and examples of some of their uses. We use:

1 **about** to talk about the **subject of books, stories, magazines** etc.:
*The programme/book/lesson/film was **about** birds.*

2 **at** with ages, speeds, temperatures:
*He learnt to drive **at** 16.   He drove **at** 100 kph.   Water freezes **at** 0°C.*

3 **by**:
  • to describe the **method of doing something** or **how something was caused**:
  *They made it **by** hand/**by** machine.*
  *He did it **by** mistake/**by** luck/**by** chance/**by** instinct/**by** intuition.*
  But we use **with** when we mention the particular tool/instrument etc.:
  *I cut the plastic **with** some scissors.   He made the hole **with** a drill.*

  • to talk about the **author of a book**, the **writer of a play** etc.
  *I read a book **by** Churchill.   Have you seen any paintings **by** Picasso?*

  • to talk about the **general method of travel**:
  *They arrived **by** bus/**by** train/**by** plane/**by** car/**by** taxi/**by** helicopter.*
  But on *foot/**on** horseback.*

4 **for** to talk about people **receiving a present** etc. *This necklace is **for** my wife.*

5 **in** to **describe the condition of something**:
*Is your grandfather still **in** good health?   Her room's **in** a mess.* (= very untidy)
*The car's **in** good condition.   She's **in** a good mood.*

6 **like** to **compare** someone/something with another person/thing:
*He eats **like** a bird.* (= He eats very little.)   *This house is **like** a concrete box.*
to **give examples:** *I like science-fiction films, **like** Star Wars or Stargate.*

7 **out of order** to mean 'not working' for machines etc.: *The lift is **out of order**.*
  out of sight to mean not visible/hidden: *Harry kept his gun **out of sight**.*

8 **up to me/you/him/her** etc. means *I/you/he/she can choose what to do.*
  *'Shall we go to the cinema?' 'I don't care. It's **up to you**.'*

9 We can use **with** to end a letter, note etc.: *... **with** best wishes, Dave./... **with** love, Ben.*

Ⓑ EXPRESSIONS WITH *ON*

There are several special expressions with **on**:
*I am **on holiday**.*   *I spoke to Dave **on the phone**.*
*I watched a film **on television**.*   *The car is **on loan**.* (= I borrowed it)
*She heard the news **on the radio**.*   *The hotel was **on fire** for hours.*

Ⓒ DESCRIBING PEOPLE/THINGS

Here are some ways to describe people/things using prepositions:

1 ***with** blue eyes/**with** a beard* etc.: *I saw a man **with** red hair and green eyes.*
2 ***in** a jacket/**in** jeans/**in** a suit* etc.: *He came to the beach **in** a suit!*
3 ***with** a red roof/**with** a big garden* etc.: *I want a room **with** a bathroom.*

194   72-3 Prepositions   96 Passive   Appendix 11

1 Ⓐ - Ⓒ **Fill the gaps with prepositions from this unit. Then listen and check your answers.**

Andor learnt a human language for the first time **(0)** *at* the age of 11. They kept him in a room
(1) .... bars on the windows. He was exhibited in a circus **(2)** .... a wild animal. He
hated civilisation: he thought the whole human race was **(3)** .... a mess. He was **(4)** ....
bad health in the town but he was strong enough to bend the bars **(5)** .... his hands. He
knew **(6)** .... instinct how to find the jaguars again, so he travelled through the jungle
(7) .... foot. They searched for him **(8)** .... horseback and **(9)** .... helicopter. The
hunters kept in contact **(10)** .... radio. They left food on the edge of the forest **(11)** ....
him to try to trap him. They hunted him **(12)** .... guns and nets. They even set the jungle
(13) .... fire to try to force him to leave. He covered his face **(14)** .... leaves and ran
through the smoke. He dived into the river and hid **(15)** .... sight **(16)** .... a frog under
the surface. They videoed the search and showed it **(17)** .... television. A film **(18)** ....
him, *Andor the Jaguar Boy,* was made **(19)** .... a famous director. Nobody saw Andor again;
he had escaped from his life with the circus just **(20)** .... time.

2 Ⓐ - Ⓒ **Complete the rewritten sentences by using prepositional expressions from this unit.**

0 They walked to the town centre instead of using their car.
   They went to the town centre *on foot* instead of *by car.*
1 He married a red-haired, blue-eyed girl when he was 19.
   He married a girl .... and .... 19.
2 He wore pyjamas to his brother's wedding which made everyone unhappy.
   He came to his brother's wedding .... which put everyone .... mood.
3 I've read lots of books by Henry James, for example *Daisy Miller* and *The Wings of a Dove.*
   I've read lots of books by Henry James, ... *Daisy Miller* and *The Wings of a Dove.*
4 The television channels showed lots of old films last summer.
   There were lots of old films .... last summer.
5 Shelley is away from work in the Bahamas.
   Shelley is .... in the Bahamas.

3 Ⓐ - Ⓒ **Put a preposition in each gap.**

1 He lives in a house .... a big garden.
2 They have been .... holiday for three weeks.
3 I spoke to her .... the phone yesterday.
4 I can't use the photocopier. It's .... order.
5 The students must arrive .... time for the classes at exactly 9 o'clock.
6 I always arrive .... time for the theatre so that I can choose the best seat.
7 Shakespeare wrote his plays .... a pen made from a bird's feather.
8 Help! The house is .... fire.
9 I bought these flowers .... you, darling.
10 What is this book ....? I want a love story.
11 He began to learn English .... the age of three.
12 The police are looking for a man .... a scar on his cheek.
13 She arrived at the wedding .... a bikini.
14 Sometimes, it is easier to travel .... plane than .... train.
15 He has ears .... an elephant's!

UNIT 75 >> Nouns + prepositions

@ Phoebe Cute denied that there was a **relationship between** herself and Tom Craze. In fact, she said, 'I'd like to announce my **engagement to** my manager, Brett Hargreaves.'

A NOUNS + PREPOSITIONS

In many cases, certain nouns are typically followed by certain prepositions: for example we often use **love + for + noun**:

*She has a great **love for music**.*   *They didn't show much **love for** their **pets**.*

Here is a list of some (but by no means all) common noun + preposition phrases.*

preposition	noun + preposition*	example
about	a story/a novel/a film/ information/news about	I saw a **film about** Pearl Harbour. Can you give me some **information about** Norwich?
between	the difference/contrast/ a relationship between	What's the **difference between** Cheddar and Stilton? There's a strong **relationship between** Sue and Bob.
by	a book/symphony/article by	I listened to a **symphony by** Mozart.
for	a reason/a demand/ a need for	What's the **reason for** the economic crisis? There isn't enough **demand for** British goods.
from	a divorce/a separation from	She got a **divorce from** her husband.
in	an interest/difficulty/ increase/rise/decrease/ fall/pride in	He has a keen **interest in** Arabic culture. I experienced **difficulty in** contacting her. There was a sharp **rise in** the price of coffee. He takes great **pride in** his appearance.
into	an investigation into an intrusion into	The police carried out an **investigation into** the murder. I hate the media's **intrusion into** our private lives.
of	the problem of a picture/photo of the popularity of	She examined the **problem of** unemployment. I saw a **photo of** her as a baby. The **popularity of** the Metalheads declined.
on	an opinion on	What's your **opinion on** capital punishment?
to	an addiction/a reaction/ a solution/ engagement/ marriage of... to	What's your **reaction to** the news about the King? I can't find a **solution to** this puzzle. He announced his **engagement to** Phoebe Cute. He announced the **marriage of** his daughter **to** Tom Craze.
towards	an attitude towards	His **attitude towards** his father is strange.
with	a relationship with a quarrel/argument with an obsession/infatuation with	France has a strong **relationship with** West Africa. Myra had a fierce **quarrel with** Myron. He has an **infatuation with** Phoebe Cute.

* these phrases may vary. For example, we can say:
*Is there any news **about** the war?* or *... any news **of** the war?*

B NOUNS FOLLOWED BY *BETWEEN, OF, WITH*

Many nouns sometimes occur with **between** or **of** or **with** depending on the structure:

*The relationship **of/between** John and Sue.*   *John's relationship **with** Sue.*
*The contrast **of/between** French and Spanish wines.*
*The contrast of French wine **with** Spanish wine.*

1 **A B** Read the text about Henry James. You should find 16 more places where prepositions are missing. Mark the place and write the preposition. The first one has been done for you.

In recent years, there has been an increase ⱽ *in* popular interest the works of Henry James. The demand his novels in bookshops and public libraries has risen sharply. James was an American who had a strong relationship Europe. He lived in Europe and in particular got to know the upper levels English society. This was the reason his obsession the differences American and European manners. The contrast American innocence and European sophistication forms the basis most of his novels. You may find difficulty understanding a late novel James. The problem his complicated style has discouraged many readers. But the reason the current popularity his novels is clear – the number attractive film versions them that have been made.

2 **A B** Fill the gaps in this text with suitable prepositions. Then listen and check your answers.

Phoebe Cute has a difficult relationship (0) *with* the media. They follow her everywhere and publish gossip (1) .... her friendships (2) .... men. Last year they printed photographs (3) .... her sunbathing on a topless beach on the front pages (4) .... all the tabloids. She hates this intrusion (5) .... her private life. The dangers (6) .... this kind of public exposure are obvious. Last year, during an investigation (7) .... the attempted murder (8) .... a famous actress, the police arrested a teenage boy. He had an infatuation (9) .... the actress and had collected over 1,000 articles (10) .... her love-life from magazines and newspapers. He was angered by the announcement (11) .... her engagement (12) .... her manager.

OPEN EXERCISE

3 **A B** Rewrite these sentences using the words in brackets.

1 He announced that his son had promised to marry Phoebe Cute.

   .... (*engagement*)

2 What do you think about the issue of media intrusion?

   .... (*opinion*)

3 People have stopped buying videos of Phoebe Cute films.
   There has been .... (*fall/demand*)

4 She treats the media in a very ambiguous manner.
   She has .... (*attitude*)

5 Phoebe Cute's childhood was very different from her life in Hollywood.
   There is a great .... (*contrast*)

6 Phoebe Cute finds it very difficult to keep her private life out of the press.

   .... (*experiences*)

UNIT 76 >> Adjectives + prepositions

 Paradise Isle is in the Mediterranean. It's **famous for** its night-clubs and its fabulous beaches. If you're **crazy about** music and **fond of** swimming, book your holiday now.

A ADJECTIVES AND PREPOSITIONS

We use some adjectives with a **preposition + noun** or **verb-ing**:

*He's not very **good at maths**.*   *He's **fond of riding**.*

Some examples of common adjective + preposition phrases follow in B and C.

B COMMON ADJECTIVE + PREPOSITION PHRASES

bad at good at	He's **bad at** sport. He's **good at** remembering jokes.	brilliant at lucky at	She's **brilliant at** science. He's **lucky at** card games.
bad for grateful for sorry for	Sugar is **bad for** your teeth. They were **grateful for** our help. I'm **sorry for** disturbing you.	famous for good for	Italy is **famous for** its food. Vitamins are **good for** us.
afraid of frightened of proud of sick of sure of	I'm **afraid of** failing. He's **frightened of** snakes. They're very **proud of** their country. I'm **sick of** these grammar exercises! I'm **sure of** one thing — I love you!	fond of full of scared of short of	Margaret is very **fond of** animals. His pockets were **full of** money. She's **scared of** ghosts. I can't go. I'm **short of** money.
keen on	He's **keen on** becoming a lawyer.		
interested in	They're **interested in** Russian politics.		
angry about crazy about	I'm **angry about** the new taxes. They're **crazy about** rock music. (informal)		
angry with annoyed with busy with fed up with pleased with	Why are you **angry with** me? She's **annoyed with** her boyfriend. I've been **busy with** my work. We're all **fed up with** getting up early. The manager was **pleased with** the result.	bored with careless with	He's **bored with** his girlfriend. He's so **careless with** money!
cruel to good to	You mustn't be **cruel to** animals. She's been so **good to** me.	generous to (un)kind to	He's very **generous to** his friends. Please, don't be **unkind to** her.
different from	English is **different from** Welsh. (Not ~~different than~~)		

Remember: **engaged/married + to somebody**.

*Elizabeth is **married to** Mr Darcy.* (Not ~~married with~~)

C ADJECTIVE + VERB-ING

A few adjectives are followed by **verb-ing** with no preposition:

It's **no good**
It's **pointless**   } **worrying** about the future.
It's **(not) worth**

*The British Museum is **worth visiting**.*   *It's **no good crying**.*

1 **A** **B** Look at these short advertisements and put prepositions in the gaps. Then listen and check your answers.

A Every year, thousands of people are cruel (0) *to* their pets. We're proud (1) .... our record of rescuing these animals. But our animal sanctuaries are short (2) .... money. So please be kind (3) .... an animal today and send your donation to DOGGO ANIMAL SHELTER.

B I'm brilliant (4) .... cooking and fantastic (5) .... cleaning. I'm fond (6) .... looking after children and I'm interested (7) .... learning new skills. But I'm not very lucky (8) .... finding a job. I am grateful (9) .... any offers of employment. Contact me on 01223 657876.

C Are you fed up (10) .... driving to work? Are you sick (11) .... sitting in traffic jams? Do you get angry (12) .... other drivers? Do you want to be different (13) .... the rest? Try our Helicopter Taxi Service.

D Darling Cherie – I'm sorry (14) .... all the mistakes I've made. I didn't mean to be unkind (15) .... you. Don't be afraid (16) .... being hurt by me again. I'm crazy (17) .... you. Please come back! Love Tony.

2 **A** - **B** Complete these sentences by using the correct preposition and the correct form of a verb from this list:

clean   go   know   meet   play   sit   skate   ~~write~~

0 Speaking a language is very different *from writing* it.

1 Please look after your room. I'm fed .... it.

2 When can we go to the beach? I'm bored .... in the hotel.

3 I'd like to go swimming here but I'm afraid .... a shark.

4 Why don't you take Gillian to the ice rink. She's very keen ....

5 Don't read me my horoscope. I'm not interested .... the future.

6 Nigel's a successful man. Is he really scared .... out with girls?

7 Phoebe Cute is famous .... the part of Maisy in *Who Killed Maisy Drake.*

3 **A** - **C** Rewrite these sentences, using the word(s) in brackets with a preposition or verb-ing.

0 Phil and Julie are husband and wife.
Phil and Julie are married to each other. (*each other*)

1 I like giving things to other people.
.... (*generous*)

2 Don't go to the market. You haven't got any money.
.... (*pointless*)

3 I don't think we'll enjoy seeing that film. It's got bad reviews.
.... (*worth*)

4 He doesn't look after his belongings.
.... (*careless*)

5 I'm very worried in case I make a mistake in the exam.
.... (*scared*)

6 I'm absolutely certain that this is the address.
.... (*sure*)

7 Has Tom made you angry again?
.... (*annoyed*)

8 Fiona has promised to marry George.
.... (*engaged*)

Adjectives + prepositions

199

UNIT 77 >> *Like* and *as*

@ ⌐ He walks **like** a duck and smells **like** a pig. But he sings **as** the angels do in heaven! ⌐

Ⓐ USING *LIKE* AND *AS* TO MAKE COMPARISONS

We use **like + noun**:   *Her face shone **like** the **moon**.*   Not ~~Her face shone as the moon.~~
                                *The moon was **like** a silver **disc**.*   Not ~~The moon was as a silver disc.~~

We use **as + subject + verb**:
*I cooked the pasta **as my mother does**.*   *He works hard **as his father does**.*

Notice that in informal English, British people often use **like** as a conjunction:
*I cooked the pasta **like** my mother does.*

But don't do this yourself in formal grammar exercises.

We also use **like** as a less formal alternative to **for example** or **such as**:
*He knows a lot of famous people, **like** Tom Craze and Phoebe Cute.*

Ⓑ USING *AS* + NOUN

But we use **as + noun** to describe the **job** or **function** of somebody or something:
*He works **as a teacher**. The gym was used **as a classroom** when the school was decorated.*

Notice the difference between **as** and **like**:
*She works **like** a slave.* (she is not really a slave)
*The pirates kidnapped her and sold her **as** a slave.* (she is <u>really</u> a slave)
*They live **like** kings.* (they are not really kings)
*They ruled **as** kings from 1300 to 1698.* (they were <u>really</u> kings)

Ⓒ OTHER USES OF *AS* + SUBJECT + VERB

1 We often use **as + subject + verb** in phrases like this: … *as I said…, … as we know…,*
    … as you see…: ***As I mentioned**, my aunt is coming to stay tomorrow.*

2 We use phrases like this, especially in writing: … *as mentioned previously…, … as stated…*:
    ***As stated** in the previous paragraph, we can use 'as' as a preposition.*
    Notice that in the passive we can say: … *as was mentioned…* but
    not ~~… as it was mentioned…~~

3 We use the conjunction **as** to show a **relationship of reason**:
    ***As** we have won £10,000, we can buy a new car.* (= for that reason)

4 We can also use **as** to show a **time relationship**:
    ***As** we were starting to play, it began to rain.* (= at the same moment)

Ⓓ *AS IF*

We use **as if + subject + verb** to make **comparisons**:
*She smiled **as if she knew** a secret.*   *He walked **as if he had** an injury.*

We often (but not always) use the **past** tense when we are using **as if** about the **present**.
This indicates that we are imagining an **unreal** situation (see Units 107-9):
*He dresses **as if he had** a million pounds.*

We use I/he/she/it + **were** (not **was**) to describe **unreal** situations:
*She looks **as if** she **were** a princess.*   *He laughs **as if** he **were** mad.*

We often use **feel/look/seem/smell/sound/taste + as if**:
*The cake **tastes as if** it were stale.*

Ⓔ EXPRESSIONS WITH *AS*

Note these common phrases with **as**.
as advertised   as agreed   as appropriate   as decided   as necessary

1 **A** Put *as* or *like* in the gaps.

Nadia sings (0) *like* an angel but Dania sings (1) .... a dog. Nadia glides (2) .... a swan but Dania moves (3) .... an elephant. Nadia plays the violin (4) .... her music master taught her but Dania plays (5) .... she wants to. Nadia paints (6) .... Picasso but Dania paints (7) .... small children do. Nadia dresses (8) .... a supermodel but Dania chooses her clothes (9) .... a chimpanzee would. Nadia writes (10) .... Shakespeare or Dante did but Dania writes (11) .... Slim Skinty.

2 **A** **B** Use *as* and *like* in each item 1-5.

0   In Spain, Jenny worked *as* a tourist guide. She had to look after the tourists *like* their mother.
1   Sue drives very fast, ... a maniac. She'll never get a job .... a taxi driver.
2   When he was a child, Pete wanted to work .... an animal trainer. Now that he's a vet, it's .... a dream come true.
3   The doctors treat George .... an old friend. But in fact he's in hospital .... a patient.
4   She wrote the story .... a novel. But when I read it, it seemed more .... a film script.
5   I know a little about medicine, so I worked .... the nurse at the summer camp. But I felt .... an impostor.

3 **D** Rewrite these sentences using *as if*. Use the verb in brackets in the correct tense.

0   He behaves like a great professor. *He behaves as if he were a great professor.* (*be*)
1   It sounds like a piece by Mozart. .... (*write*)
2   This perfume smells like roses. .... (*contain*)
3   She dances like a Russian-trained dancer. .... (*study*)
4   He looks like a very poor man without a penny. .... (*not have*)
5   These jewels make you look like a princess. .... (*be*)

4 **A** **B** **E** Rewrite these sentences where necessary so that they are correct. Mark any correct sentences with a tick (✔).

0   When I was younger, I worked as a horse.
    When I was younger, I worked like a horse.
1   As it was agreed, we shall start work tomorrow. ....
2   Repair the furniture like necessary. ....
3   You can buy GLOXO TEA here as advertised on TV. ....
4   She gasped for air as a fish out of water. ....
5   I am too proud to work as a servant. ....

OPEN EXERCISE

5 **A** - **E** Complete these sentences in any suitable way.

1   As you know, ...
2   As I mentioned in the last letter, ...
3   .... as the alarm bell rang.
4   As was agreed, ...
5   As the weather was so bad, ...
6   ...., as advertised in the media.

Like and as

REVISION 8 >> First Certificate Practice

PAPER 3 PART 1

1 For questions 1-12, read the text below and decide which answer, A, B, C or D, best fits each gap. There is an example (0).

SHOPPING

Why is shopping one (0) A the most popular activities? Some psychologists explain the attraction of (1) ..... shopping by suggesting that it is an extension of a primitive urge to go hunting (2) ..... provisions. Stone Age people brought home a mammoth steak or berries; twenty-first century people bring more subtle delicacies (3) ..... Chocko-Mousse or Organic Papaya Sauce. However, are shoppers really (4) ..... primitive hunters? There is the difficulty (5) ..... why women seem generally more enthusiastic (6) ..... shopping than men. Surely, it is men who should look forward to (7) ..... the supermarket if shopping were a disguised form of the predominantly masculine activity of hunting. Also, the modern experience of shopping (8) ..... luxurious malls and boutiques is so far removed (9) ..... the danger and discomfort of the hunt that it is difficult to see any real similarity (10) ..... the two activities. On the other hand, it is perhaps significant that home shopping methods, (11) ..... shopping by mail order or (12) ..... the Internet, have not replaced actual shopping.

	A	B	C	D
0	(A) of	B in	C from	D on
1	A go	B having gone	C to go	D –
2	A with	B for	C on	D after
3	A like	B as	C such like	D such
4	A like	B as	C such as	D as if
5	A for to explain	B of explain	C to explaining	D of explaining
6	A for	B about	C after	D of
7	A raid	B raider	C raiding	D raided
8	A by	B in	C on	D with
9	A from	B of	C with	D out of
10	A to	B in	C between	D among
11	A like to	B as	C such as	D with
12	A in	B by	C on	D among

PAPER 3 PART 2

2 For questions 1-12, read the text below and think of the word which best fits the space. Use only *one* word in each space. There is an example (0).

INTERNET SHOPPING

Various surveys have provided information (0) *about* the internet shopping habits of different nations. (1) .... general, the twenty-four-hour-a-day convenience (2) .... e-commerce ranked above price as the most important factor in choosing this form of shopping. Of course, the majority (3) .... people shop at home but up to 45% of customers make their order while they are (4) .... work. Luckily, few employees have yet been dismissed for (5) .... their shopping from a company computer but employers are increasingly worried (6) .... staff stealing computer time from them. Many purchases over the Internet are made (7) .... night. These night-owl shoppers account for up (8) .... 70% of customers in some countries. Among them are 'shopaholics', people who seem to be addicted to (9) .... on the Net, making more than twenty purchases in a single month. Age is another factor.
(10) .... we could expect, according to these surveys, the elderly make the most use (11) .... internet shopping because for them it saves them the effort of (12) .... on long shopping trips to the supermarket or city centre.

3 For questions 1-8, complete the second sentence so that it has a similar meaning to the first sentence, using the word given. Do not change the word given. Use from two to five words including the word given. There is an example (0).

0 She left the restaurant before she had paid.
She left the restaurant without paying. **WITHOUT**

1 I am really excited about the course that I'm going to attend next month.
I'm looking forward .... next month. *TO*

2 Which programme are you watching?
Which programme .... at? *LOOKING*

3 She was grateful because they paid her quickly for her work.
She was grateful for .... for her work. *PAID*

4 Her dog jumps up and licks her face as soon as she returns from work.
Her dog jumps up and licks her face as soon as ....
home from work. *ARRIVES*

5 Fewer people have been buying mobile phones recently.
The .... has gone down recently. *DEMAND*

6 Can you tell me why this delay has occurred?
Can you tell me .... delay? *REASON*

7 Jack believes that his football team is the best!
Jack is very .... team. *PROUD*

8 They held church services in the town hall after the church roof collapsed.
The town hall was used .... after the church roof collapsed. *CHURCH*

OTHER PRACTICE

4 Fill the gaps with a suitable preposition. Write ✗ if no preposition is necessary.

0 He came to the lecture by helicopter.

1 The baby was born .... 10th December .... night.

2 His new haircut is so ridiculous that I can't look at him .... laughing.

3 Don't phone Joan's home number – she's still .... the office.

4 I learnt to swim .... the age of two .... our neighbours' swimming pool.

5 When he worked .... a ship's doctor, he was often away .... sea.

6 When she worked .... a waitress in a fast food restaurant five hours a day, she felt .... a slave.

7 I detest people who are cruel .... animals. I take pride .... reporting them to the police.

8 Inspector Baxter carried out an investigation .... the murder .... the help of the witnesses.

5 Use the verb given to fill the gap in either the infinitive or the *-ing* form.

0 I'm looking forward to going to the party next week. (*go*)

1 I prefer the cinema to .... a film on video. (*watch*)

2 The teacher encouraged them to .... in English all the time. (*speak*)

3 She's addicted to .... chocolate. (*eat*)

4 He came close to .... his temper when I disagreed with him. (*lose*)

5 It's more difficult to .... a foreign language than to .... it. (*speak/read*)

UNIT 78 >> There + be, it + take

> **There was** a violent storm in the middle of the night. **It took** two days to repair the damage. In fact, **there have been** frequent extreme weather conditions recently. But **it takes** a lot of knowledge to interpret weather patterns.

A THERE + BE

We use **There + be** in all tenses except continuous ones and also with modal verbs. **There + be** usually indicates the presence or absence of something. For example:

There is a jacuzzi in the bathroom.
There has been an accident in the next street.
There weren't many people at the disco.
There's going to be a festival next month.

Are there any tomatoes in the fridge?
There hadn't been any storms before 2003.
There used to be a cinema in the village.
There can't be an alligator in the bath.

B THERE + EXIST

Less commonly, we use **There + exist/stand/occur/seem** and similar verbs. For example:

There exists a serious problem.
There occurred an accident at 3 a.m.

There stands the castle.
There seemed to be a party at Joe's house.

Notice: the verb is singular or plural depending on the noun which follows.
There **appears** to be **a problem**.
There **appear** to be **some problems**.

C IT + TAKE

We use **It + take** to talk about the **length in time** of a journey etc.:
It takes three hours to go to York by train.
It took an hour to reach home.

We also use **It + take** + words like **skill/talent/energy/knowledge/effort/money/fuel**.
It takes a lot of **skill** to solve this puzzle.
It took a lot of **money** to repair the house.

We can reverse the structure like this: **The journey takes** three hours.
We can also use **need** in this way: **It needed** a lot of money to repair the house.

D IT + BE, IT + RAIN ETC.

We can describe the weather like this:
It is rainy/cloudy/misty/foggy/windy/frosty/stormy etc.
It snows/rains/hails a lot in the winter.
There is (a lot of) cloud/rain/sleet/fog etc.
There are (a lot of) clouds/showers/mist patches etc.

E MORE ABOUT STRUCTURES WITH IT

We sometimes use **it** to refer to an **unknown person**, as in these examples:
Who is **it**?   Was **it** a burglar?   Who's there? Is **it** you?

We can use **it + be** or **similar verb** + **relative clause** to add **emphasis**:
It was the teacher **who** murdered them.
It turned out to be the cat **that** had stolen the food.

Notice that we can say:
It's Bob who **will do** it.
It is Sue who **did** it. (especially for a recent action)

or It **will be** Bob who does it.
or It **was** Sue who **did** it.

We can use **it + adjective + to-infinitive**:
It's nice to see you.   **It's good to be** back.   **It was wonderful to see** them again.

1 **A** **Fill the gaps with suitable forms of *there + be*. Use *used to* and various tenses. Then listen and check your answers.**

(0) *There used to be* wet cold winters and dry cool summers in Mockham but recently
(1) .... a change in the climate. During the 90s (2) .... several very wet summers and mild winters but recently (3) .... a further change in the weather pattern. At this moment, (4) .... a very hot summer. Many villagers think
(5) .... a reason for this, such as global warming. Of course, every year,
(6) .... weather problems for the farmers. Last year (7) .... spring frost, this year (8) .... summer drought and perhaps next year
(9) .... autumn flooding.

2 **A** **B** **Write sentences about these situations using *there* + the verb in brackets in the correct form.**

0 A gypsy camp used to be here in Mockham but they've moved away.
  There used to be a gypsy camp in Mockham. (*be*)
1 Mockham Carnival is going to take place next weekend.
  .... (*be*)
2 In the past, they had the custom of sacrificing virgins.
  .... (*exist*)
3 Look! The ancient walls of Mockham Castle are in front of us.
  .... (*stand*)
4 Some clues to the identity of the skeleton in the castle must exist.
  .... (*be*)
5 A violent storm occurred near the castle yesterday.
  .... (*occur*)
6 I thought there was a figure behind the curtain.
  .... (*seem*)
7 Look. That man sitting there is the murderer of my father.
  .... (*sit*)

3 **C** **Write sentences using *it + take* in the correct tense.**

0 We needed five hours to repair the church tower. *It took five hours to repair the church tower.*
1 He needed all his knowledge to solve the problem. ....
2 We'll need a lot of energy to complete the marathon. ....
3 You need a great deal of patience to be a teacher. ....
4 They needed a lot of courage to fight the battle. ....

4 **A** **D** **Put *it* or *there* in the gaps.**

0 *There* was a lot of rain last night.   4 .... is foggy today.
1 .... snowed continuously for three days.   5 .... hailed all night.
2 .... was raining heavily last night.   6 .... was a strong wind. .... kept me awake.
3 .... might be a storm tonight.   7 .... must have rained.

5 **E** **Rewrite these sentences using structures with *it*. Use the words in brackets.**

0 We found out that the dog had stolen the meat. *It was the dog that had stolen the meat.* (*that*)
1 I don't recognise your voice. Am I speaking to Sue? ....? (*is*)
2 I'm very pleased to meet you. .... (*nice*)
3 I discovered that the wind had broken the window. .... (*that*)
4 I really enjoy dancing with the prince. .... (*wonderful*)

UNIT 79 >> *Have* and *have got*

@ 'Harry, are you inside the bank? **Have** you **got** the gold? I'**ve got** the car ready.' 'Yes, but I'**ve got** a problem. Two guards **are having** a chat outside the bank. I'**ve got** to find a way to get past them.'

A *HAVE/HAVE GOT* FOR POSSESSION ETC.

We use both **have** and **have got** to indicate possession of something:
*I **have** a car.* or *I'**ve got** a car.* (= I possess a car/I own a car)

We also use them in wider senses of possession than actual ownership:
*He **doesn't have** a chance of winning.*   *They'**ve got** a serious problem.*   *I'**ve got** no time to do it.*

We use **have** or **have got** to talk about illness: *She'**s got** a cough.*   *I'**ve got** a headache.*

We use **have got** with the meaning of **I've bought** or **I've managed to obtain**:
*I'**ve got** the milk from the shop.*   *She'**s got** the record deal with EMI.*

Notice also that to express obligation, we can use **have got to** in the same way as **have to**:
*I'**ve got to** go. = I **have to** go.*

In American English, it is more usual to use **have** than **have got**: *We **have** a new fridge.*

B FORM AND GRAMMAR INFORMATION

When **have** has the meanings in section A we cannot use a continuous tense:
I have a car.   **Not** ~~I am having a car.~~

We normally use **do**, **does** and **did** to form Present and Past Simple questions and negatives with **have**: *Do you **have** a car?*   *She **didn't have** any money.*
But people also say: *Have you a car?*   *I **haven't** a car.*

Questions and negatives with **have got** are like this:
Has she got a flat?   *Have you got my pen?*   *They **haven't got** a bath in their house.*

We usually only use **have got** in the Present Simple tense. In other tenses we use **have**:
*He **had** a house but it burnt down.*   **Not** ~~He had got a house...~~
*I **will have** a new garage soon.*   **Not** ~~I will have got a...~~

C HAVE AS ACTION VERB

We can also use **have** (without **got**) to describe an action. In this case we can use a continuous tense: *I **am having** a bath.*   *They'**ve been having** a party.*

We always use **do/does/did/didn't** to form Present Simple and Past Simple questions and negatives of **have breakfast/have a walk/have a party** etc.
*Does he **have breakfast** in the morning?*   *He **doesn't have a swim**, except in the summer.*
*We **didn't have a walk** because we were tired.*   *Did you **have a sleep**?*

Compare: *I'**ve got** a shower.*   (= there is a shower in my house)
*I **have** a shower every day.*   (= I wash myself in the shower every day)

D COMMON EXPRESSIONS WITH *HAVE* AS ACTION VERB

Meals and food: *to have breakfast/lunch/dinner/supper/a snack/a picnic/etc.*
Drink: *to have a cup of tea/a coffee/an aperitif etc.*
Activities*: *to have a walk/a swim/a ride etc.*
Games: *to have a game of chess/of cards/of monopoly etc.*
Daily life: *to have a shower/a bath/a wash/a shave/a sleep/a rest etc.*
Special occasions: *to have a party/a meeting/a celebration etc.*
Other uses: *to have a joke/a look/a talk/a love affair/a try/a go/a think etc.*

* With these expressions we can also use **go for**: *go for a walk/a ride etc.* (See also Unit 88).

1 **A**-**D** Use *have got/has got* where possible to fill the gaps. In other cases use *have* in a simple or continuous tense. Use negative forms where necessary. Then listen and check your answers.

Harry (0) has got a problem. The guards (1) .... a long conversation. Harry must (2) .... a go at escaping. He (3) .... a chance of escaping if they recognise him. Harry (4) .... an idea. The bank (5) .... a room with guards' uniforms in it. Harry (6) .... a look for the key to the room. He only (7) .... a few minutes to find the key and disguise himself. Michelle (8) .... a daydream while she is waiting. Harry (9) .... the key. He (10) .... to put on the uniform very quickly. Luckily, Harry (11) .... a lot of courage. He (12) .... to walk past the guards. They (13) .... a drink from a flask of whisky. One of the guards (14) .... a joke and pointing his gun at Harry. Harry and Michelle (15) .... the gold. They're OK.

2 **A**-**D** Use *have* in the Present Simple or the Present Continuous form in sentences 1-12.

  0 Uncle Joe's happy. He's having a game of chess.
00 Uncle Joe has an ancient Indian chess set.
  1 We .... a table tennis competition every Thursday.
  2 'Why is it so noisy?' 'The neighbours .... a party.'
  3 Sue's not at school. She .... a headache.
  4 My sister .... three boyfriends at the moment.
  5 'Is Brian upstairs?' 'Yes, he .... a shower.'
  6 Our neighbours .... a new car.
  7 Tina uses a lot of hot water. She .... a shower five times a day.
  8 .... Phil and Julia .... a love affair?
  9 Poor Charlie. He .... flu.
10 'Is Tom in the office?' 'No, he's out. He .... lunch.'
11 Look at Granny. She .... a dance with the teenagers.
12 Where is Bernie?' 'I don't know, but she usually .... a meeting at this time.'

3 **D** **E** Rewrite these sentences without changing the meaning or the tense. Use an expression with *have*.

  0 They went swimming every morning in Greece. They had a swim every morning in Greece.
  1 Pete and Dave have been playing chess for the last seventy-two hours!
    ....
  2 As soon as I get home, I'm going to go to bed and sleep.
    ....
  3 They were fighting violently when I saw them.
    .... (use: *violent*)
  4 England and France have fought each other many times over the centuries.
    .... (use: *many wars*)
  5 Madame Magistar told me that my boss and I were going to fall in love.
    ....
  6 Elaine always drinks a cup of tea when she feels depressed.
    ....
  7 Are you going to celebrate when you get your exam results?
    ....

UNIT 80 >> Be used to doing, get used to doing

 Kate is a Londoner who is working on a Pacific island. She **isn't used to sleeping** under the stars or **to eating** raw fish. But she'll have to **get used to** it.

Ⓐ BE USED TO + VERB-ING

We use **be used** with the preposition **to** + **verb-ing**.

I'm used to doing something... means that we often do it. We want to **emphasise** that the action is not strange for us. It is a habit:
I won't miss the 6 a.m. train. I'm used to getting up early.
(= getting up early is not a problem for me)
He will pass the exam easily. He's used to studying hard.
(= studying hard is not a problem for him)

We can use **be used to** to talk about past, present or future time:
When I lived in London, I was used to travelling by underground.
She's been used to working hard since she was a child.
It seems strange now but you'll soon be used to working here.

Ⓑ BE USED TO + NOUN

We also use **be used to** + **noun** or **pronoun**:
I'm used to the English **weather**.
She isn't used to life in a big city.
I'm not afraid of flying. I'm used to it.

Remember: we say *I'm used to getting up...* (Not ~~I'm used to get~~) because **to** is a preposition, not part of the infinitive.

Ⓒ GET USED TO

We use **get used to** + **verb-ing** or + **noun** when **something strange becomes familiar**. There is a change:
At first, I didn't like England but I've got used to living here.
(= I've changed. It was a problem but it isn't a problem now.)
When you go to a new school, you have to get used to it.

Ⓔ USED TO AND BE USED TO

Notice that **used to do** (see Unit 14) and **be/get used to doing** are different in meaning:
I used to live in Birmingham.   (something I did in the past but not now)
I was used to living in Birmingham. (we are emphasising: it wasn't strange for me)

We can use **used to do** only about the past.

We can use **be/get used to doing** in all tenses.

1 **A C** Make sentences with *be used to* or *get used to* in a suitable tense. Use negatives where appropriate.

    0 The islanders live without electricity. Kate finds this difficult.
       Kate isn't used to living without electricity.

    1 Kate got up early in London and also gets up early on the island.
       Kate is ....

    2 In London, Kate watched television every evening.
       Kate was ....

    3 The islanders wash their clothes in the river. Now Kate does this.
       Kate has got ....

    4 The islanders haven't seen many Westerners before.
       The islanders ....

    5 Kay still finds it strange sharing her house with animals (a pig, a cow, chickens and a goat).
       Kay hasn't ....

    6 The islanders didn't like having their photographs taken at first. But now it's fun.
       ....

    7 In London, Kate knew all the international news.
       ....

    8 On the island, Kate is very isolated from the world. It's a strange experience.
       ....

    9 On the island, women must obey certain rules of behaviour. Kay still doesn't like this.
       ....

    10 Kate wants the islanders to take modern medicines. But they don't like them.
       ....

    11 Kate and the islanders will start to accept the experience of living together.
       ....

2 **A B D** Complete the sentences 1-8 with a form of either *used to* or *be used to*.

    0 Before going to the island, Kate was used to/had been used to a luxurious life.
    1 When Kate lived in London, she .... drive her own car.   **2** Now, after several months on the island, she .... going everywhere on foot.
    3 In London, Kate .... the noise and the rush.   **4** The islanders, on the other hand, ... peace and silence.   **5** In the old days, the islanders .... fight wars with their neighbours.   **6** The islanders .... living a simple life. Their ancestors .... live in the same way.   **7** Kate .... live a sophisticated life but now she .... the simplicity.   **8** The women .... have arranged marriages but now they .... marrying for love.

OPEN EXERCISE

3 **A C** Make sentences with *be used to, get used to* about these people. Write at least two sentences for each item.

    0 Captain Sykes is an experienced sailor. Billy is a new sailor.
       Captain Sykes is used to living on a ship. Billy hasn't got used to being at sea.
    1 Myra is an experienced Hollywood actress. Verna is a new actress in Hollywood.
    2 Giles has been a farmer for a long time. Hetty is his new farmhand.
    3 Mr Sims is an experienced teacher. Ms Farley has just qualified as a teacher.
    4 Ted is a professional long-distance lorry driver. Bert is driving a lorry for the first time.

UNIT 81 >> Make, do, get, take, pay

'**Make**' and '**Do**' are confusing. When we say '**to make lunch**' we mean 'to cook lunch'. But in informal English, especially in the USA, '**to do lunch**' means 'to meet for lunch together in a restaurant'. It's easy to **make mistakes** — but **do your best** not to.

Ⓐ MAKE

We often use **make** about making something new (**producing**). For example:
- **about cooking or preparing food:**
  make a cake, *make* some tea, *make* a sandwich, *make* dinner/breakfast/lunch/supper
- **about mistakes/noise/mess:** *make* a mistake, *make* noise, *make* a mess, *make* a fuss
- **for certain activities:** *make* a phone call, *make* a TV programme, *make* a film
- **about changes:** *make* a change, *make* a difference, *make* an effort, *make* an improvement, *make* progress
- **about achieving something:** *make* a living, *make* a good teacher/lawyer etc.

We also use **make + someone + adjective** when someone/something causes a feeling in another person:
*The teacher **made me angry**.*   *The ghost story **made them afraid**.*   *The film **made us happy**.*

The expressions **make it/make it big** mean to succeed: *Tom **made it big** in Hollywood.*

Ⓑ DO

We often use **do** about doing a piece of work or doing a job (**process**). For example:
- **about education:** *do* the homework, *do* an exam, *do* research, *do* an exercise
- **about housework and personal activities:** *do* the shopping, *do* the washing up, *do* the ironing, *do* the cooking, *do* your hair
- **about activities:** *do* a crossword, *do* a puzzle
- **about work:** *do* a job, *do* some work, *do* your best

Also: *do* someone a favour (= to do something special to help someone)
       do harm to: *The hooligans **did** a lot of **harm to** the neighbourhood's image.*

Ⓒ GET, TAKE AND PAY

Get, **take** and **pay** are also used in certain expressions. For example:

Get: *He was ill but he **got better** quickly.* (recovered)
*Please help me to **get dinner**.* (prepare)
*It was raining, so they **got wet**.* (became)
*She **got some pasta** from the shop.* (bought)
*She **got some bad news** last night.* (received)
*They **got there** just after nine o' clock.* (arrived)
*They're **getting ready** for the disco.* (preparing)
*She **got ill**.* (became)

Take: *She **took care** of her brother.*   *Drivers mustn't **take risks**.*
*He **took the opportunity** to see the film.*   *I **took a holiday/a break/a trip/a tour**.*
*I'll **take an exam** in June.*   (**Not** *give an exam*)
*She **takes the medicine** every day.*   (**Not** *eat medicine/pills*)
*They **took advantage** of their friend.* (exploited)
*They **took advantage** of the opportunity.* (benefited from)

Pay: *You must **pay attention** to the referee.*
*They **paid the price** for being stupid.* (suffered)

1 **Ⓐ Ⓑ** Put the correct form of *make* or *do* in the gaps in the sentences.

0 Kate is *doing* medical work on the island.

1 The islanders have .... the hospital building themselves.

2 Some island girls will go to New Zealand to .... a nursing course.

3 The island women have .... Kate's hair in a traditional style.

4 The island has .... changes in Kate's life.

5 You never .... any progress if you don't .... mistakes.

6 Kate is proud of what she has .... on the island.

7 Kate's work has .... a big difference to the island.

8 Kate's help is .... the islanders more independent.

9 Kate and the islanders have .... their best to understand each other.

10 Kate wants to .... more research into Pacific societies.

11 Some people want to .... it big in life but Kate just wants to .... what she can for other people.

2 **Ⓐ** Rewrite these sentences using *make* + noun + adjective.

0 I'm sad that you want to leave. It *makes me sad that you want to leave.*

1 He was happy because of his test results.
   His test results ....

2 They were bored in history lessons.
   The history lessons ....

3 She'll be relaxed when she takes the medicine.
   The medicine ....

4 I feel optimistic in the sunshine.
   The sunshine ....

5 My health has got worse in the cold weather.
   The cold weather ....

3 **Ⓒ** Rewrite these sentences using expressions with *get, take* or *pay*.

0 They didn't listen to the President. *They didn't pay attention to the President.*

1 He accepted the opportunity to go to America.
   ....

2 The storm made them very wet.
   .... in the storm.

3 I'll stop work for a short time at 11 o'clock.
   ....

4 He behaved dangerously when he was climbing.
   ....

5 She's preparing for the fashion show.
   ....

6 Her head began to ache while she was using the computer.
   ....

7 She persuaded her rich uncle to give her a lot of money.
   ....

8 He failed because he was lazy.
   .... for being lazy. (use: *price*)

9 Their illness started after they had eaten oysters.
   ....

UNIT 82 >> *Make, let someone do something, get someone to do something*

 The natural beauty of the island **makes** Kate **feel** good. She **got** the wild deer **to feed** from her hand. The dolphins in the bay **let** her **ride** on their backs.

Ⓐ MAKE, GET AND LET

After **make** and **let**, we use the **infinitive without to**.
After **get** we use the **infinitive with to**. Look at the following examples:

The soldiers	**made**	the spy		**tell** them the secret.
The police	**let**	the prisoner		**go.**
His father	**doesn't let**	him		**smoke.**
I	**got**	the manager	**to**	**help** me.
The student	**got**	the teacher	**to**	**correct** his homework.

1 We use **make** when someone **obliges/doesn't oblige** someone to do something or when something or someone **causes/doesn't cause** something to happen:

She didn't **make** him **sell** his car.   (= She didn't oblige him to sell...)
They **made** the spy **tell** them everything.   (= They forced the spy to tell...)
The island's beauty **made** her **feel** happy.   (= It caused her to feel happy)

2 We use **let** when someone **permits/doesn't permit** us to do something:

They **let** him **go.**   (= They gave him permission to go)
That looks difficult. **Let** me **help.**   (= ... Allow me to help)

3 We use **get someone to...** when we want to say that **someone does something for us because we ask them**:

I didn't have an umbrella, so I **got Joe to lend** me his.   (= I asked Joe and he agreed)

In negative sentences, we often use **couldn't get somebody to**:
I **couldn't get her to change** her mind.

Ⓑ ALLOW, CAUSE, FORCE AND PERSUADE + NOUN + TO + VERB

His father	**doesn't allow**	him	**to**	**smoke.**
The bad weather	**caused**	them	**to**	**cancel** the match.
They	**forced**	him	**to**	**tell** them the secret.
I	**persuaded**	Joe	**to**	**lend** me his bicycle.

For more verbs which follow this pattern see Unit 90.

Ⓒ PASSIVE STRUCTURES WITH MAKE AND LET

When we use **make** in the passive, we use **to**:
She was **made to confess.**   I was **made to agree.**

We prefer to use **allow**, not **let**, in the passive:
He was **allowed to enter** the night-club.

1 **A** Make sentences with *make, not make, let, not let* about these situations. Sometimes there is a word in brackets to help you.

0 The dolphins allowed Kate to ride on their backs. The dolphins let Kate ride on their backs.

1 Some of the islanders said to Kate: 'Don't take photographs of us.'
.... (*not let*)

2 Kate kept away from the sacred forest because the islanders told her to.
.... (*make*)

3 Kate said to the islanders: 'You may look at my photographs from England.'
.... (*let*)

4 The islanders could have forced Kate to leave the island but they didn't.
.... (*not make*)
.... (*let*)

5 Some islanders stopped their wives from going to Kate's clinic.
.... (*not let*)

6 The islanders allowed Kate to examine their children.
....

7 Kate's neighbours on the island made it possible for some boys to steal her possessions.
....

8 The island council forced the thieves to return her goods.
....

9 The island girls said to her: 'You may teach us about health care.'
....

10 Some islanders ran away when Kate wanted to give them injections.
....

11 Kate said to them, 'OK. You don't have to come to my clinic.'
....

12 The children wanted to put a tame snake round Kate's neck but she stopped them.
....

2 **A** Write sentences with *get* or *couldn't get* for the situations 1-9.

0 Kate persuaded the islanders to have health checks.
Kate got the islanders to have health checks.

1 The islanders wanted Kate to respect their customs. She agreed.
....

2 Kate wanted the village boys to leave her in peace. But they followed her everywhere.
....

3 Kate planned to build a small hospital. The islanders did it for her.
....

4 The men refused to give their wives more independence despite Kate's wishes.
....

5 Kate asked the women to show her how they tattooed their faces. They showed her.
....

6 The women would have tattooed Kate's body but she refused to let them do it.
....

7 Her boyfriend wanted Kate to come back to Britain. She didn't go.
....

8 Kate contacted the New Zealand government. They began to give more aid to the islanders.

....

9 Kate sent a report about the island to *The Times* but they didn't publish it.

....

3 **A** - **C** **Look at sentences 1-7. There is a mistake in some of these sentences. If the sentence is correct, put a tick (✓) at the end of the sentence. If it is not correct, rewrite it correctly.**

0 He made them to pay back the money. *He made them pay back the money.*

1 The police will get them to confess. ....

2 They were made to show their passports. ....

3 I got the assistant show me the new model. ....

4 Listen to me. Make me give you some advice. ....

5 Please, don't let your dog to come near me. ....

6 I got my uncle to repair my motorbike. ....

7 She was forced to tell them the secret. ....

4 **B** **Study these items and write sentences using *allow, cause, force* or *persuade*.**

0 The gangsters made the bank clerk unlock the safe.
   The gangsters forced the bank clerk to unlock the safe.

1 Myra was nice to the director; he gave her the starring role in his film.

....

2 The fog made all the trains arrive late.

....

3 Please help me to change Bob's mind; he should lend me the money.

....

4 They didn't give permission for the prisoner to phone his girlfriend.

....

5 Nadia doesn't let anyone read her secret diary.

....

6 Nick gave Brigitte no choice; he made her resign from the company.

....

7 The football hooliganism resulted in the authorities cancelling the match.

....

5 **A** **B** **Study the table and then write sentences with the verb in brackets.**

children (11 – 14) must/may/are persuaded to/sometimes…							
0/1 stay out after 11 p.m.	2 help with the housework	3 go to discos alone	4 clean the family car	5 watch over-18 videos	6 take a part-time job	7 run away from home	8 wear clothes that parents choose
38% of parents	78%	65%	59%	17%	85%	5%	6%

0 *38% of parents let their children stay out after 11 p.m.*

1 .... (*not allow*)

2 .... (*get*)

3 .... (*let*)

4 .... (*make*)
5 .... (*allow*)
6 .... (*not let*)
7 .... (*cause*)
8 .... (*force*)

6 **Ⓐ** Read the text. Find and underline 8 more phrases which you can replace with *make* or *let* or *get + somebody* + (to) + verb. Write your complete substitute phrases on the lines below the text. Then listen and check your answers.

Many teachers of English find it difficult <u>to persuade their students to use</u> the language actively. Some teachers simply allow shy students to remain quiet at the back of the class. However, there are ways of encouraging students. There are games that cause the students to use English while enjoying the activity. Group activities and research projects also allow children to communicate in English without suffering from embarrassment.

In the past, many overseas teachers persuaded their students to write to pen-pals in English-speaking countries. Now, the availability of the Internet allows students to contact other children even more easily. E-mailing or chatting online in English causes students to improve in fluency while also enjoying personal contact. Finally, of course, a visit to Britain or another English-speaking country can cause the greatest improvement – but this is expensive which causes some families to think twice.

0 *to get their students to use*
1 ....
2 ....
3 ....
4 ....
5 ....
6 ....
7 ....
8 ....

OPEN EXERCISE

7 **Ⓐ**-**Ⓒ** Finish these sentences in any suitable way, including a second verb.

0 The General made *the soldiers salute him.* **or** *the army march across the desert.* **etc.**
1 My parents don't allow ....
2 When I was a child, I was made ....
3 The advertisement persuaded them ....
4 I was allowed ....
5 The other students got ....
6 I didn't let ....
7 She made the dancers ....
8 The wild music made them ....

UNIT 83 >> Phrasal verbs

 Tania's diary: January 3rd. The alarm clock **went off** at 6 a.m. I **woke up** and **put on** my clothes. I was **looking forward to** another exciting day...

Ⓐ PHRASAL VERBS

A phrasal verb consists of a verb + a word like *up, down, for, with*. The phrasal verb has a different meaning from the verb on its own.
*Maggie **turned up** at eight o'clock.* (**turn** + **up** = appear unexpectedly)
In general, we tend to use phrasal verbs in less formal language situations.

Ⓑ PHRASAL VERBS: VERB + PARTICLE

Many phrasal verbs consist of a combination of a verb and a particle (e.g. *up, off, down, forward*). There are two main types:

- **Type One:** There is **no object**: *He **got up**.*   **Look out!**   Please **shut up!**

to break down	Bill's car **broke down**. (= it stopped working)
get on/get off*	I **got on** at the bus station and **got off** at the park.
to give up**	The problem's too difficult — I **give up**! (= I'll stop trying)
to take off**	The plane **took off** from London Airport.
to wake up	Maggie **woke up** early. (= opened her eyes after sleeping)

 * see also Type Three   ** see also Type Two

- **Type Two:**

*We can say **either** He **turned off** the television.*   **1 verb + particle + noun**
or   *He **turned** the television **off**.*   **2 verb + noun + particle**
Notice: if we use a pronoun (*her, him, it, them* etc.), we **must** use construction 2:
He turned it off.   **Not** ~~He turned off it~~.

to look up	He **looked up** the word in a dictionary.	(= found the meaning)
to put on	She **put on** her new skirt.	(= she got dressed in)
	He **put on** the radio.	(= switched on)
to take off	He **took off** his clothes and had a bath.	
to turn off	He **turned off** the light.	(= switched off)

Ⓒ PHRASAL VERBS: VERB + PREPOSITION

Some phrasal verbs consist of a verb + preposition. With these verbs, the object must come **after** the preposition. There are two main types:

- **Type Three:** (remember: the object must come after the preposition.)
*The nurse **looked after the baby**.* (**verb + preposition + object**)

  If we use a pronoun, it **must** come after the preposition: *The nurse **looked after her**.*

to get on/get off	I **got on** the bus at the airport.	
to look for	She **looked for** her passport.	(= searched, tried to find)
to look after	He **looked after** the baby.	(= took care of)

- **Type Four:** These phrasal verbs consist of a **verb + two items** (a particle and a preposition). The object must come after the preposition, as in Type Three:
*He **puts up with** her bad behaviour.* (tolerates)

to keep up with	She **keeps up with** the news.	(= she knows the latest news)
to look forward to	Sue's **looking forward to** Christmas.	(= she's excited about the future)
to put up with	I can't **put up with** the noise.	(= I can't tolerate it)

See Appendix 6 for a more comprehensive list of all types of phrasal verb.

1 **Ⓐ**-**Ⓒ** Tania has a very boring life! Read her diary and fill the gaps with phrasal verbs from the list. Change the form if necessary. Then listen and check your answers.

> break down   carry on   cheer up   close down   come round   be fed up with
> get back   get on   get on with   get up   look after   look forward to   put off   put up
> put up with   ring up   run down   turn up   wash up   watch out

TANIA'S DIARY

January 3rd. On the way to work, my car **(0)** *broke down*, so I **(1)** .... a bus and **(2)** .... at the office three minutes late. In the evening, I had potatoes and cheese for dinner, then **(3)** .... For the rest of the evening, I **(4)** .... the work of writing my diary.

January 4th. My friend Dorothy **(5)** .... me.................... . She wanted to **(6)** .... for a cup of tea. But instead of that, we went to the town for a meal but our favourite restaurant had **(7)** .... We **(8)** .... walking. Then a car nearly **(9)** .... Dorothy .... but I shouted, '**(10)** .... !' just in time. Then it began to rain. So we **(11)** .... our plans to walk in the park.

January 5th. It's raining again. I **(12)** .... this bad weather. I'm not **(13)** .... next week. I have to stay with my 85-year-old aunt. I can't **(14)** .... her boring conversation about her childhood. My sister will **(15)** .... my goldfish while I'm away. When I **(16)** ...., I'll **(17)** .... some posters of my favourite stars on the walls. That might **(18)** .... me .... It's still raining. It wasn't worth **(19)** .... this morning.

2 **Ⓐ**-**Ⓒ** Rewrite sentences 1-10 by using a phrasal verb instead of the underlined part of the sentence. Choose phrasal verbs from the lists in 83B and C and Appendix 6.

0   The plane <u>left</u> at 9.30.
    The plane took off at 9.30.

1   I like to <u>have up-to-date information about</u> the news.
    ....

2   <u>During my childhood, I lived</u> in the country.
    ....

3   Crunchester were losing 17 – 0 but Kevin didn't <u>lose hope</u>.
    ....

4   The conditions in this hotel are disgusting. I can't <u>accept</u> them any longer.
    ....

5   They <u>found</u> the Mandarin word for 'love' in her Chinese dictionary.
    ....

6   She <u>refused</u> his offer of marriage.
    ....

7   Pete <u>removed</u> his clothes and dived into the ocean.
    ....

8   The driver <u>decelerated</u> when he saw the child in the road.
    ....

9   I <u>am good friends</u> with my bosses.
    ....

10 She <u>put</u> the Metalhead CDs <u>in the rubbish bin</u>.
    ....

3 **Ⓐ - Ⓒ** Rewrite the sentences 1-10 using a pronoun instead of the underlined part of the sentence.

0 He looked up <u>the new words</u>. *He looked them up.*

00 Bill got on well with <u>my sister</u>. *Bill got on well with her.*

1 They put off <u>the festival</u>.

....

2 He's looking forward to <u>the party</u>.

....

3 He cheered up his <u>friends</u>.

....

4 She hasn't got over <u>the surprise</u> yet.

....

5 They put up with <u>the disgusting food</u>.

....

6 Myra showed off <u>her diamonds</u>.

....

7 She put on <u>her pink and yellow scarf</u>.

....

8 They're looking for <u>the hotel</u>.

....

9 I've given up <u>smoking</u>.

....

10 They looked after <u>their grandfather</u> well.

....

4 **Ⓐ - Ⓒ** Use the phrasal verbs 1-10 to replace phrases in the text. The verbs are in the same order as they appear in the passage. Write the complete clause or sentence below the text as in the example. Then listen and check your answers.

> Often, people from one region in a country aren't very friendly with people from another area. For example, the Irish have to tolerate English jokes about their 'stupidity'. Some people from the south consider people from the north as inferior. And be careful in Scotland. The Scottish really don't like being called 'English'. And some Welsh people are always searching for a way to get an advantage over anyone English. Sometimes, relationships between regions or countries go wrong completely because of these stereotypes. But let's all be happy about the future. As people mix more and more, we will stop believing in these prejudices. As a result, the world will start to be a better place.

0 get on with   *Often, people from one region in a country don't get on with people...*

1 put up with ....

2 look down on ....

3 watch out ....

4 be fed up with ....

5 look for ....

6 put down ....

7 break down ....

8 look forward to ....

9 give up ....

10 turn into ....

218

5 Ⓐ - Ⓒ **Underline the phrasal verbs in 1-9 and match them with the more formal alternatives A-J.**

0 It <u>turned out</u> that he was a doctor.   J   A surrendered
1 The fire service put out the fire.   ....   B rejected
2 I really looked up to my father.   ....   C extinguished
3 The army gave up after the bombing.   ....   D tolerated
4 She always showed off in front of boys.   ....   E respected and admired
5 The alarm went off as the fire grew.   ....   F occupied
6 He put up with their rudeness.   ....   G acted ostentatiously
7 They turned down the job offer.   ....   H exhausted
8 His books took up a lot of space.   ....   I sounded
9 She used up her all her money.   ....   J transpired

6 Ⓐ - Ⓒ **Do the same as in exercise 4. But be careful: this time the verbs are not in the same order as in the passage.**

Some people are always trying to follow the latest fashion. They think that others will respect them if they wear the right make-up or the most expensive after-shave. They become depressed unless they have the latest car or fashion accessory. It's easy to show ourselves superior to this kind of fashion victim. But in fact fashion and change occupy a lot of space in all our minds! Maybe, modern life is going to become calmer. But until it does, advertisers will continue to encourage us to get rid of our possessions almost as soon as we buy them.
So don't be shy, my friend! Purchase everything in your local fashion shop.

0 buy up   *Buy up your local fashion shop.*
1 get down   ....
2 go on   ....
3 keep on   ....
4 keep up with   ....
5 look up to   ....
6 put down   ....
7 put on   ....
8 slow down   ....
9 take up   ....
10 throw away   ....

OPEN EXERCISE

7 Ⓐ - Ⓒ **Complete these sentences in any suitable way.**

1 I'm looking forward to ....
2 He crossed out ....
3 Shut up! I'm ....
4 Every weekend, I look after ....
5 If you don't cheer up, ...
6 .... knocked down ....
7 .... to keep up with ....
8 People from my city don't get on with ....
9 Look out! There ....
10 If you carry on ....

UNIT 84 >> Action and state verbs

 Slim Skinty and Ellie Tramper **like** buying second-hand clothes because they **don't cost** much. But they **prefer** looking on rubbish dumps where the clothes **cost** nothing. All the rubbish **belongs** to them.

Ⓐ ACTION AND STATE VERBS

- **Action verbs** describe actions:

  Harry **ran away** from the prison.
  The guards **were firing** their guns.
  Michelle **pulled** Harry into the helicopter.

  Most verbs are verbs of action, for example: *break, cut, dance, read, study, take, write*.
  We can use these verbs in simple tenses (*ran*) or continuous tenses (*were firing*).

- **State verbs** describe states:

  I **have** a car.
  She **likes** pop music.
  They **know** French and Spanish.

  We do not use state verbs in continuous tenses:
  I **have** a car. **Not** ~~I am having a car~~.

Ⓑ STATE VERBS

State verbs include:

1. verbs about **mental activity**: *believe   forget   know   notice   recognise   remember   understand*

He **believes** in God.	**Not** ~~He is believing in God~~.
I **don't recognise** her.	**Not** ~~I am not recognising her~~.
Do you **understand**?	**Not** ~~Are you understanding~~?

2. verbs which describe **emotional states**: *desire   hate   like   love   prefer   want*

She **loves** her parents.	**Not** ~~She is loving her parents~~.
Which one **do** you **prefer**?	**Not** ~~Which one are you preferring~~?
He **wants** a new car.	**Not** ~~He is wanting a new car~~.

3. certain other verbs: *belong   cost   fit   include   mean   need   own   matter*

This book **belongs** to me.	**Not** ~~This book is belonging to me~~.
The ticket **cost** five pounds.	**Not** ~~The ticket was costing five pounds~~.
I **own** three houses.	**Not** ~~I am owning three houses~~.

4. **verbs of perception**: for example *see, hear, smell*. (See Unit 85.)

Ⓒ VERBS WHICH DESCRIBE ACTIONS AND STATES

Some verbs have two or more meanings. They can be used in the continuous tense when they describe an action, but not when they describe a state.

	state	action
Have:	He **has** a headache.	He **is having** a party.
Forget:	I **forget** telephone numbers easily.	She **is forgetting** her old boyfriend.
Think:	I **think** you are right.	I **am thinking** about his new idea.
Come:	He **comes** from the USA.	He**'s coming** from his home by taxi.

See Appendix 5 for a full list of state verbs.

1 **A B** There are 12 verb mistakes in this text. Rewrite the text correctly in the space below. Then listen and check your answers.

> Slim Skinty is wanting to buy a second-hand jacket. He is talking to the shopkeeper. 'How much is it costing? £2? That is seeming expensive. But it is suiting me. If it's fitting Ellie Tramper as well, I'll pay 10p for it. Are you agreeing, Ellie? You are having it at weekends and it's belonging to me during the week. I am also needing a left boot. If it is matching my right one, I'll take it for 2p. We aren't liking wearing old clothes – but we are loving saving money.'

Rewrite correctly here:

Slim Skinty wants to buy a second-hand jacket.

....
....
....
....
....
....

2 **A** - **C** In each sentence 1-17, put the verb in brackets in the Present Simple or the Present Continuous tense.

0 How *do* you *say* 'I love you' in Polish? (*say*)   **1** .... you .... about your dead friend? You seem very sad. (*think*)   **2** Why .... you .... at that boy? .... you .... me any more? (*look/not love*)   **3** .... your friend .... from Austria? (*come*)   **4** .... you .... me? I'm your old teacher. (*recognise*)   **5** Our teacher .... every mistake. (*notice*)   **6** What .... you .... to do next week? (*want*)   **7** I .... that I .... my memory. (*think/lose*)   **8** I .... Shakespeare's plays but I .... his sonnets. (*hate/adore*) **9** Look at Phil and Julie. They .... a good time. (*have*)   **10** 'Pass me a magazine, please.' 'Which one .... you ....?' (*mean*)   **11** Look at Myra! She .... some more jewellery. (*buy*)   **12** She already .... a lot of jewellery. (*own*) **13** .... you .... that Myra will win another Oscar? (*think*)   **14** What size shoes .... you ....? (*take*)   **15** How much money .... he .... to borrow? (*want*)   **16** Which TV channel .... you .... now? (*watch*)   **17** .... you .... the answer to this question? (*know*)

3 **C** Match the questions 1-6 to the situations a-f by writing 1a or 1b etc.

1 How much does it cost?

2 How much is it costing?

3 Where is he coming from?

4 Where does he come from?

5 What are you thinking about?

6 What do you think?

You want to ask about:

a the price of an item in a shop

b the cost of something you are in the process of using at this moment, like a hired boat

c somebody's country of birth

d the starting point of somebody's journey

e somebody's opinion

f what is in somebody's mind at this moment

ANSWER HERE: 1 *a*   **2** .....   **3** .....   **4** .....   **5** .....   **6** .....

UNIT 85 >> Verbs of perception

@ I **saw** Lia **walking** in the garden. Then I **couldn't see** her any more. It **sounds as if** I'm mad but I **saw** her **disappear**!

A VERBS OF PERCEPTION: *SEE, HEAR, TASTE, FEEL, SMELL*

We do not use them in continuous tenses when they are state verbs (see Unit 84).
We often use them with **can** or **could**:

Can you *hear* that music?   Not ~~Are you hearing that music?~~
I couldn't taste the onions in the soup.   Not ~~I wasn't tasting the onions...~~
It's dark. I can feel you but I *can't see* you.   Not ~~I am feeling but I'm not seeing...~~

We often use **taste, feel** and **smell** with an adjective, like this:

The soup tastes good.   Not ~~The soup is tasting good~~.
The silk feels soft.   *The roses smell beautiful.*
Also: *The music sounds good.*   *You look handsome.*

We often use **smell** and **taste + of**: *It smells of honey.*   *It tastes of garlic.*

We usually use **look as if/sound as if** in simple tenses: *He looks as if he is ill.*
The car sounds as if there is something wrong with the engine.

B ACTION VERBS

But we can also use **taste, feel, smell** and **see** as action verbs when they describe an action:

state	deliberate action
The wine tastes good.	*I am tasting the wine.*
I can feel the wind.	*He is feeling the cloth to see if it is soft.*
I can smell cigarette smoke.	*She is smelling the flowers.*
I can see you.	*He is seeing my sister.* (having a romance with)

We can also use the following action verbs: **look/watch/listen/touch** to talk about our senses. e.g.:

He touched her face tenderly.   *We listened to the symphony.*

We also use **feel** to talk about our **emotions** or **physical condition**. In this meaning, we can use it in continuous tenses if necessary: *I am feeling sick.*   *Are you feeling OK?*

We use **I see** to mean **I understand**: '*x + y = 17 if y = 9.*'   '*I see.*'

C *SEE SOMEONE CROSSING/SEE SOMEONE CROSS* ETC.

We often use these structures with **feel, hear, notice, see, witness**:

I: **perception verb + noun/pronoun + verb-ing:**   *I saw him crossing the road.*
II: **perception verb + noun/pronoun + verb:**   *I saw him cross the road.*

We use structure I when we see/hear/feel someone or something **in the middle of carrying out an action**: *I heard her playing the violin.*
                    (= I heard her in the process of playing, perhaps not from start to finish)

We use structure II for a **complete action**: *I heard the orchestra play the 7th Symphony.*
                         (= I heard the whole symphony from start to finish)

We also use structure II for a **short, immediate action**:
I heard the window break.   *I felt the wasp sting me.*

Often there is no important difference between I and II. We might say:
Either *I heard her calling me.*   or *I heard her call me.*

We use **only** structure I (+ **-ing**) with **smell, find** or **discover** or with **can see, can hear**:
I smelt the food burning.   *I found/discovered him stealing the money.*   *I can see them coming.*

1 **Ⓐ Ⓑ** Use the verbs in past or present tenses or with *can/could* to fill the gaps.
Use continuous forms where possible.

A *hear   feel   see   smell   ̶t̶a̶s̶t̶e̶*

The professor's new cola **(0)** *tastes* delicious. It **(1)** .... of wild flowers.
But if you drink too much, you disappear. No one **(2)** .... you.
But they **(3)** .... still **(4)** .... and **(5)** .... you.

B *feel   hear   listen   see   see   sing   smell   touch*

Lia disappeared after she drank it. Nobody **(6)** .... her. But
I **(7)** .... her hand on my shoulder. She **(8)** .... me. Also, we
(9) .... her voice. She **(10)** .... an aria by Puccini. We
(11) .... her perfume. For an hour, we **(12)** .... to her singing.
Then she reappeared. First, we **(13)** .... her legs, then her body, then her face.

C *not see   not see   see   sound   watch   watch*

'I don't believe you. You **(14)** .... the professor, so you **(15)** ....
Lia hide. It **(16)** .... as if the professor is a magician, not a scientist.'
'I **(17)** .... that you don't believe me. But now I'm going to drink the cola.
(18) .... me disappearing! You **(19)** .... me, can you?'

2 **Ⓒ** Write sentences with the pairs of verbs of perception + verbs from the list. Choose the more
appropriate structure from 85C, I or II.

discover/open   feel/crawl   hear/play   hear/sing   ̶n̶o̶t̶i̶c̶e̶/̶b̶o̶r̶r̶o̶w̶
see/rob   smell/burn   watch/beat   watch/act   witness/rob

0 When I was in the bank, I saw Harry with a gun, demanding money.
I witnessed Harry robbing the bank.

1 Ali saw Harry come in the bank, take the money, run out and escape.
....

2 I watched Nadia sit down with the chess computer, move the pieces and win the game.
....

3 While I listened, Nadia took out her violin, played the sonata and left the room.
....

4 When I was in Jill's kitchen, I smelt smoke from Nick's dinner.
....

5 When Nick was in the office, he came in the room as Brigitte was opening the safe.
....

6 Every morning when Kate wakes up on the island, her room is full of the song of birds.
When Kate wakes up, ...

7 Kate woke up in the night; there was a tropical spider tickling her leg.
When Kate woke up, ...

8 When I was in the library, I saw Myra. She had a book about the French Revolution.
....

9 I watched a film from start to finish where Myra acted the role of Marie Antoinette.
....

UNIT 86 >> *Raise, rise, arise/lie, lay, lie* etc.

 Problems often **arise** with verbs which are similar in meaning or appearance but are different grammatically. For example, **lay** is an object verb but **lie** is a no object verb. The past form of **lie** looks like the infinitive form of **lay**. Even British people make mistakes with these verbs!

A RAISE/RAISED/RAISED, RISE/ROSE/RISEN, ARISE/AROSE/ARISEN

Raise is an object verb (transitive verb). In other words it occurs with a direct object.
Rise and **arise** are no-object verbs (intransitive verbs). They occur without a direct object.

basic meaning	subject + verb	object	rest of sentence
raise = to lift = to increase = to look after animals/children = introduce a question	He **raised** The shops **raised** He **raises** She **raised**	his hand their prices pigs and goats the question	to answer the question. last month. on his farm. of tax reform.
rise = to move upwards = to go up	The sun **rises** Prices **rose**		in the east. by 20%.
arise = to occur	A problem **has arisen**		during the meeting.

Compare these examples: *The boss **raised** her salary.*   *Her salary **rose**.*
*We **raised** the problem in Parliament.*   *The problem **arose** in Parliament.*

B LAY/LAID/LAID, LIE/LAY/LAIN, LIE/LIED/LIED

basic meaning	subject + verb	object	rest of sentence
lay = put other meanings e.g.	I **laid** The chickens **laid**	the money twenty eggs	on the table. yesterday.
lie (1) = to be horizontal = to describe position or location	He **lay** (past form) Cairo **lies** The temple **lies**		on the beach yesterday. on the Nile. at the foot of the hill.
lie (2) = not to tell the truth	They **lied**		about everything.

Compare: *She's **laying** the gun on the chair.*   *The gun **is lying** on the chair.*
We also use **lay** in various idiomatic expressions:
*He **laid** the problem to rest.*   (= He settled the problem)
*She **laid** her cards on the table.*   (= She was completely honest about her intentions)

C APPEAR, DISAPPEAR, VANISH

These are no-object verbs: *He often **appears** on television.*
*It **appears** that she has got married.*   *The thief **vanished** in the crowd.*
Wrong: ~~*The magician disappeared the rabbit.*~~   **Correct:** *He made the rabbit disappear.*

D BECOME

Become is a complement verb. It occurs with a noun or an adjective.
*She **became** an actress.* (noun complement)   *She **became** very rich.* (adjective complement)

E PASSIVE FORMS

We can use object verbs in the passive:
*His salary **was raised**.*   *The books **were laid** on the table.*
We **cannot** use no-object verbs or complement verbs in the passive (see Unit 96A):
~~*It was disappeared.*~~   ~~*He was become...*~~

1 **A** Fill the gaps with a form of *raise, rise* or *arise*.

0 Nick and Jill raised the price of their company's goods.
1 Brigitte hoped that her salary would .... too.
2 A problem .... when Nick reduced her salary.
3 The people of Mockham met to .... money for a new hospital.
4 At the meeting, the question of location ....
5 The price of the project has .... by 50% since 2000.
6 Kate usually wakes up when the sun ....
7 Many of the villagers .... goats.
8 A problem .... when the animals ate her clothes from the washing line.

2 **B** Rewrite these items, making sentences with *lay, lie* (1) or *lie* (2).

0 London is located on the River Thames.   London lies on the River Thames.
1 The geese have produced 25 eggs.   ....
2 I'm putting the plates and knives and   ....
forks on the table.   ....
3 She's resting on the sofa.   ....
4 I was in bed all day yesterday.   ....
5 Somebody isn't being honest.   ....
6 The letters are there on the mat.   ....
7 She put her head on the table and cried.   ....

3 **C** Rewrite these items, making sentences with *appear* or *disappear/vanish*.

0 Nobody could find Roger Scoop.   Roger Scoop had disappeared. (*disappear*)
1 The money isn't in the safe now.   .... from the safe. (*vanish*)
2 Don't leave until we've had   ....
time to talk.   ....
3 The magician had a rabbit;   ....
then it wasn't there!   .... (*vanish*)
4 The police are looking for a   ....
man who is missing.   .... (*disappear*)
5 If you use this cream, your   ....
spots will go away.   .... (*vanish*)
6 We've heard that he's very ill.   It ....

4 **D** Rewrite these items, making sentences with *become*.

0 In 1998, Bob earned his first million pounds.   In 1998, Bob became a millionaire.
1 Next year, Sam will join the army.   ....
2 Carla lost her eyesight last month.   ....
3 Julie and Phil will have a baby soon.   ....
4 He lost his job last year.   ....

5 **E** Is it possible to make these sentences passive. Write YES or NO.

0 My grandmother raised me in Texas   YES
1 The balloon rose over the mountain.   ....
2 My father became president of the company.   ....
3 Someone laid the money on the table.   ....

UNIT 87 >> *Speak and talk* etc.

@ If you watch British soap operas, listen to the characters **talking** to each other. In East Enders, they **speak** with a London accent. In Coronation Street, they **speak** with a northern accent.

Ⓐ *SPEAK* AND *TALK*

There is not much difference between **speak** and **talk**:

Structure: *speak/talk to somebody*
             speak/talk about something

We use **speak**: 1 **about languages**: *She **speaks** Spanish and French.*
                   2 **about the way of pronouncing etc.**: *She **spoke** slowly/clearly/quickly.*
                   3 **on the telephone**: *Can I **speak** to Charles, please?*
                   4 **when one person is speaking**: *The professor **spoke** for an hour.*
                   5 **in formal situations**: *May I **speak**?*

We use **talk**:   1 **when two or more people are speaking together**:
                      *They **talked** about the film.*
                   2 **in certain expressions**: *to **talk** business/sense/nonsense/rubbish.*
                      *'I was **talking** business with Anna,' he said.*
                      *'Don't **talk** nonsense,' said his girlfriend, 'you were flirting.'*

Ⓑ *LEND* AND *BORROW*, *HOPE* AND *EXPECT* ETC.

Here are some other pairs of verbs. Make sure you know the difference:

Lend and **borrow**:	*My brother **lent** me five pounds.* (= he gave) *I **borrowed** three books from the library.* (= I took)
Hope and **expect**:	*I **hope** that the sun will shine tomorrow.* (= I wish...) *They **expect** that it will rain next week.* (= They think...)
Meet and **find**:	*I **met** my friends at the restaurant.* (to meet + somebody) *You'll **find**/see the station on the left.* (to find + a place)
Invent and **discover**:	*Bell **invented** the telephone.* (to invent a machine etc.) *Columbus **discovered** America.* (to discover a new planet/a country etc.)
Prevent and **protect**:	*The police **prevented** him from entering the palace.* (= The police stopped him...) *The police **protected** the Queen.* (= The police kept her safe)
Watch and **look at**:	*A lot of people **watched** the football match.* (to watch something moving, e.g. a film) *I **looked at** the statues in the square.* (to look at sth. static, e.g. apainting)
Steal and **rob**:	*He **robbed** the bank/the old lady/the house.* (to rob a bank/a person etc.) *He **stole** the diamonds from the safe.* (to steal money/jewels etc.)
Remind and **remember**:	***Remind** me to do my homework.* (= Help me to remember to do...) *I didn't **remember** to do my homework.* (= I forgot to do...)
Beat and **win**:	*My boyfriend **beat** me at tennis.* (to beat another team/a person etc.) *I didn't **win** the match.* (to win a competition/a cup etc.)
Forget and **leave**:	*Oh no! I've **forgotten** my keys.* (to forget your keys/wallet etc.) *I've **left** my umbrella at home.* (to leave sth. at home/on the train etc.)
Hear and **listen to**:	*I **heard** some people talking but I didn't **listen** to what they were saying.* (to hear = involuntary sense; to listen to = deliberate use of the sense)

1 Ⓐ In each sentence 1-9, put the correct form of *speak* or *talk*. In each case, decide which one is better.

0 Where do they *speak* the best English? That is a difficult question.

1 Every Christmas, the reigning monarch .... to the nation on television.

2 You can often tell the social background of a person from the way that he or she ....

3 British television presenters often .... with a 'mid-Atlantic' accent.

4 British people tend to hide behind their newspapers on trains instead of .... to strangers.

5 People say that women .... more about their emotions than men.

6 In British society, it is impolite to interrupt someone when he is .... even if he's .... nonsense.

7 It is also impolite to .... about money, wealth, salaries etc.

8 Generally, the British don't like .... about themselves, money, sex or politics.

9 So what do they .... about? Well, British people love .... about the weather and their pets. But this is a stereotype. In fact, modern British people .... about everything.

2 Ⓑ Circle the correct word.

0 I forgot/*left*/forgotten my grammar book in the classroom.

1 Our security system **prevents/watches/protects** crime.

2 I **expect/look forward/hope** that you get well soon.

3 Harry and Michelle **robbed/stole/took** five banks in a week.

4 I love **hearing/listening/listening to** classical music and jazz.

5 When you **meet/see/watch** the station, turn left.

6 Galileo **discovered/invented/found** the telescope.

7 Did the Vikings **discover/meet/invent** America before Columbus?

8 They **stole/robbed/stealed** the equipment from Kate's clinic.

9 This lotion **protects/makes/prevents** the sun from causing skin cancer.

10 I didn't **remember/remind/forgot** to buy any fruit at the market.

11 Crunchester **beat/won/beated** the Football Cup.

12 Can you **borrow/lend/take** me some money until Thursday?

3 Ⓑ Use one of the verbs from 87B to replace the underlined phrases.

0 Professor Makepeace underlined created the first Time Machine. *invented*

1 I keep a gun in the house to ensure the safety of my family. ....

2 These injections should stop the development of the illness. ....

3 Harry never takes property from private houses. ....

4 I sincerely wish that everything goes well for you. ....

5 I am certain that Crunchester will get the league title next year. ....

6 Please tell me when it's time to make the phone call. ....

7 Walk straight ahead until you see a church. ....

8 I was aware of some music in the background but I wasn't paying attention. ....

9 Captain Kork has found for the first time several planets. ....

10 Sheila gave me her book to use until I found mine. ....

11 Can I use your pen for ten minutes? – I've lost mine. ....

UNIT 88 >> Verbs + -ing (1)

@

> Bella **loves flirting**. She wouldn't **mind going** out with someone like Tom Craze but she'd **hate being** with someone like Professor Makepeace. She **loves categorising** her boyfriends. She thinks there are only five main types.

A SUBJECT + VERB + VERB-ING

subject + main verb	+ verb-ing
Bella **loves**	**flirting**.
Professor Makepeace	**likes inventing** things.

Here are some verbs which are followed by **verb-ing** (for more verbs see next unit):

adore	appreciate	enjoy	fancy	feel like	like*	love*
miss	detest	dislike	hate*	resent	can't stand	can't bear
can't face	(not) mind**	finish	keep	start*	stop	

I **adore listening** to Mozart.	He **enjoys playing** football.	They **like cooking**.
He **hates eating** potatoes.	They **can't stand living** with her.	He **can't stop talking**.
We **can't bear walking** so far.	She **doesn't mind** waiting.	Did you **finish painting**?

* But see also Unit 91.

** **mind** is usually used in negative statements and questions:

> I **don't mind** working all day.   **Do** you **mind** helping me?

B PASSIVE FORM

subject + main verb	being + past participle	(by + agent)
Phoebe hates	being photographed	by the paparazzi.
	(= Phoebe hates it when the paparazzi photograph her.)	

The passive form often occurs with **by**. Here are some more examples:

I don't **like being examined** by the doctor.	Harry **keeps being arrested** (by the police).
Kate **can't stand being woken** up by goats.	Nadia **detests being given** low marks.

C *TO GO FISHING* ETC.

We use **go** + **verb-ing** (or **come** + **verb-ing**) for many sports and activities:

to go/come:	ballooning	cycling	dancing	diving	fishing	flying
	hang-gliding	hunting	jogging	riding	running	sailing
	shopping	skating	skiing	walking	rock climbing	

Anne **goes jogging** every morning.	We **went skating** on the lake yesterday.
Bill **came shopping** with us.	Would you like to **come fishing**?

D POSITION OF *VERY MUCH/REALLY*

Study the position of **very much** (see also Unit 37) and **really** in these examples:

I like going to museums with my family **very much**.	(at the end of the clause)
They **really** enjoy looking after dogs and cats.	(before the main verb)

1 (A)-(C) Here are examples of Bella's FIVE TYPES OF MAN. Girls, which do you like? Boys, which are you? Use the pairs of verbs to fill the gaps. Use the passive where there is a star (*). Then listen and check your answers.

TYPE A: THE STUDENT PRINCE: Simon (**0** *not mind/be*) *doesn't mind being* poor while he's a student. After he (**1** *finish/study*) .... he plans to (**2** *start/lecture*) .... at Oxford University. He (**3** *love/teach*) .... his girlfriends about ancient history or geology but (**4** *can't stand/talk*) .... about fashion or soap operas with them. He (**5** *love/tell**) .... how intelligent he is.

TYPE B: THE PLAYBOY: James (**6** *enjoy/drive*) .... fast cars. He (**7** *go/ski*) .... in St Moritz every winter. He always (**8** *fancy/go*) .... to night-clubs and he really (**9** *adore/see**) .... with glamorous women. He (**10** *can't bear/talk*) .... about marriage. He (**11** *keep/change*) .... his girlfriend, his car and his image.

TYPE C: THE MUMMY'S BOY: Teddy (**12** *not mind/live*) .... with his mother even though he's 42 years old. He (**13** *adore/eat*) .... her home cooking. He (**14** *like/spoil**) .... and (**15** *love/bring**) .... breakfast in bed by his mum. He sometimes (**16** *go/dance*) .... with a girlfriend but he really (**17** *prefer/listen*) .... to Frank Sinatra CDs with his mother and (**18** *drink*) .... cocoa.

2 (A)-(C) Rewrite the description of Type D using verb + verb-ing. Use the verb in brackets. Follow it with a passive verb-ing where there is a star (*).

TYPE D: THE ROMANTIC: **0**   Byron is always talking about himself. (*never stop*)
Byron never stops talking about himself.

1 He goes to operas by Wagner – They're great! (*adore*)

....

2 He discusses suicide and passion whenever he can. (*love*)

....

3 He doesn't want to stay in one place. (*can't bear*)

....

4 He often travels in the jungle or the desert. (*go*)

....

5 He expects his girlfriends to worship him. (*enjoy**)

....

3 (A)-(D) Add the missing adverb in the brackets and verb-ing in the most suitable positions.

TYPE E: THE HE-MAN: **0** Bruce detests salad. (*really/eat*) *Bruce really detests eating salad.*
1 He can't stand about art or poetry. (*really/talk*)

....

2 He likes. (*very much/box, weight-lift and hang-glide*)

....

3 He likes about guns, cars and football. (*very much/talk*)

....

4 He dislikes by a woman in an argument. (*really/beat**)

....

5 He likes violent computer games with his friends. (*very much/play*)

....

UNIT 89 >> Verbs + -ing (2)

@ Harry **admitted robbing** the bank but he **denied attacking** the guard. 'I wouldn't **risk going** to prison for murder,' he said. 'I've always **avoided killing** anyone.'

A MORE VERBS WHICH CAN BE FOLLOWED BY A SECOND VERB + -ING

admit	excuse	postpone
avoid	forgive	practise
burst out (laughing or crying)	give up	put off (= postpone)
consider	imagine	risk
delay	involve	suggest
deny	mention	
escape	miss	

Harry **admitted robbing** the bank.   Michelle **avoided crashing** into the police barrier.
They **delayed launching** the rocket.   Harry **denied attacking** the guard.
I can't **imagine living** without chocolate. This language course **involves studying** grammar.
I **miss living** in the city.   They **practised shooting** at the target.
He **risked climbing** without ropes.   They **suggested building** a better school.

A negative form exists: *She risked not arriving in time.* (**verb** + **not** + **verb-ing**)
But generally we prefer to use a positive form where possible: *She risked being late.*

B VERB + OBJECT + VERB-ING

Some of the verbs in 88A and 89A can be followed by **object** + **verb-ing**:
*I **hate other people giving** me advice.*   *I **resent you trying** to steal my boyfriend.*
*She couldn't **stop her son smoking**.*   *Do you **mind me listening** to the radio?*

Stop and **prevent** often go with **from**: *She couldn't **stop/prevent** him **from** smoking.*

In a very formal style, we use **verb** + **possessive** + **verb-ing**. For example:
*Do you **mind my listening** to the radio?*   *I **hate their giving** me advice.*

C CAN'T + VERB + VERB-ING

We use **can't help** + **verb-ing** to say that we **can't stop ourselves** from doing something.
For example: *I **couldn't help noticing** that you've been crying.*
                  *She **can't help telling** lies — It's a habit.*

Other verbs which follow the same structure are:
can't resist: *I **couldn't resist** reading her secret diary.*
can't face/stand/bear: *I just **can't face going** back to school.*

D ADMIT AND DENY + HAVING + PAST PARTICIPLE

We use this structure when we want to make it clear that **the action occurred previously**:
*Harry **admitted having robbed** the bank.*
(he admitted that, at a time in the past, he had robbed it)
*He **denies having attacked** the guard.*

Similarly, we can use **confess** with this structure but **confess** is used with the preposition
to: *She **confessed to having** driven the get-away car.*

The only difference between (1) *... **admitted having robbed**...* and (2) *... **admitted robbing**...*
is the emphasis on the time gap in structure (1).

1 **Ⓐ Ⓒ** Read these short advertisements and use the pairs of verbs to fill the gaps. Then listen and check your answers.

A *consider/call* ~~*postpone/repair*~~ *risk/find*

> Don't (0) postpone repairing your house. If you do, you (1) .... that the roof is collapsing and the floors are rotting. Why not (2) .... the NU-HOME REPAIR SERVICE now.

B *give up/search* *imagine/find* *miss/have* *suggest/enrol*

> Do you (3) .... a special person in your life? Have you (4) .... for true love? Or can you still (5) .... your soul-mate? We (6) .... with the TRU-DATE AGENCY now.

C *consider/re-train* *delay/start* *involve/learn* *miss/take* *practise/use*

> Have you (7) .... for a new career in information technology? Our computer courses (8) .... all the basic keyboard skills. You will also (9) .... the Internet to locate information. Don't (10) .... on the road to a prosperous future. Don't (11) .... advantage of our special 25% reduction if you enrol before July.

2 **Ⓑ** Make sentences with the structure verb + object + verb-ing. Use the verb in brackets.

0 She was eating chocolate. I took it away from her. I stopped her eating chocolate. (*stop*)

1 I want to open the window. Is that OK with you? .... (*mind*)

2 I don't believe it. Tom's working on a farm. .... (*can't imagine*)

3 I feel awful when my mother tells me what to do .... (*can't stand*)

4 I'm grateful that Harry collected me in his car. .... (*appreciate*)

5 I'm sad because Tina doesn't visit me any more. .... (*miss*)

6 It's impossible to forgive him for cheating me. .... (*can't excuse*)

7 He didn't complain when we used his car. .... (*mind*)

3 **Ⓒ** Make sentences with *can't help* + verb-ing for these situations.

0 If there's chocolate in the house, I have to eat it.   I can't help eating chocolate.

1 I always whistle at pretty girls in the street.   ....

2 Whenever I'm in a shop, I start shop-lifting.   ....

3 I always break the hearts of the boys I go out with.   ....

4 I've got into the habit of falling asleep in class.   ....

4 **Ⓓ** Make sentences with *admit or deny + having... .*

0 He said that he had never seen her before the murder.
  He denied having seen her before the murder.

1 She confessed that she'd broken the window but said that she hadn't drawn the graffiti.
  ....

2 He said that he had not lost all their money at the casino.
  ....

3 He told the police that somebody else must have broken into the mayor's office.
  ....

4 She told Fred that she'd gone to the party with his best friend but she hadn't kissed him.
  ....

5 They said that they had lied about the robbery.
  ....

UNIT 90 >> Verbs + *to* + infinitive

> **@** Bella **agreed to go** to a Formula One Grand Prix with James. But she forgot that she had **arranged to meet** Bruce at a pub in London.

A VERB + *TO* + INFINITIVE

subject + verb	(not) + to + infinitive
James **decided**	**to go** to the French Grand Prix.
They **tried**	**not to miss** the plane to Paris.

Verbs which are followed by **to + infinitive** of the second verb include:

afford   agree*   appear   arrange   dare****   decide   decline   expect fail   forget   happen**   help****   hope   intend   manage   offer plan   pretend   promise   refuse*   seem   try   want***

Can you **afford to buy** a new jacket?	They **decided not to get** married.
He **failed to catch** the plane.	We **managed to find** the ring.
She **refused to give** him the money.	He **seemed to be** ill.

Notice: * we can say: *He refused/agreed to do it.* **But not** ~~He accepted to do it.~~
   ** we use **happen to...** for something that happens by chance: *I **happened to meet** Paul.*
   *** we do **not** say: ~~I want that...~~   ~~I want that you help me.~~
   **** we can use **help** and **dare** with or without **to:**   *I didn't **dare (to)** move.*
                                                                            *I **helped (to)** do it.*

B PASSIVE FORM

subject + verb	+ (not) to + be + past participle
We **wanted**	**to be informed** about the result.
They **agreed**	**to be paid** by cheque.
They **tried**	**not to be** frightened by the robber's threats.

C VERB + OBJECT + *TO* + INFINITIVE

We use this structure with some verbs:

advise   allow   ask   cause   encourage   forbid   force   get   help invite   order   permit   persuade   remind   teach   tell   want   warn

subject + verb	object	+ (not) + to + infinitive
They **advised**	**him**	**to change** his job.
They **forced**	**the girl**	**to give** them her money.
We **ordered**	**the soldiers**	**not to shoot.**

We can also use **would like** in this way (see Unit 26): *I **would like you to help** me.*

Remember that after **make** and **let** and (optional) **help/dare**, we use the infinitive without **to** (see Unit 82):

They **made** him **help** them.   She **let** us **take** the money.   We **helped** them **pack**.

D VERBS + CONTINUOUS OR PERFECT INFINITIVE

Some of these verbs may be followed by **to be verb-ing** or **to have + past participle:**
*He **seems to be sleeping**.* (at this moment he is in the middle of the action)
*They **happened to be working** when I visited them.*
(at that moment they were in the middle of the action)
*I **seem to have left** my book at home.* (the action took place before the time of the main verb)
*I **hoped to have finished** by now.* (the action should have taken place before the time of speaking)

1 **A** Use the pairs of verbs to fill the gaps, putting the verbs in the correct form. Then listen and check your answers.

afford/upset   arrange/meet   decide/not publish   fail/arrive   manage/calm
plan/return   promise/take   promise/visit   try/find   want/fight   want/give

Bella forgot that the same day she had **(0)** *arranged to meet* Bruce in a pub. Also, she had
(1) .... Teddy to have tea with his mother. Also, Byron
(2) .... from a trip to the Arctic and **(3)** .... her a fur
coat. 'I can't **(4)** .... James,' she thought, 'he has **(5)** ....
me to New York. But how can I **(6)** .... down Bruce? He might
(7) .... James. Also, if I **(8)** .... at Teddy's house for tea
and biscuits, he might ask the police to **(9)** .... me. Byron might
(10) .... his love poems about me.'

2 **B** Write a second sentence with a passive structure.

0 She wasn't frightened by his threats.   *She refused to be frightened by his threats.* (*refuse*)
1 Perhaps he would be promoted.   .... (*hope*)
2 The police might fine him.   .... (*can't afford*)
3 The doctor could examine Harry.   .... (*agree*)
4 He might be released from prison.   .... (*expect*)

3 **C** Write sentences using the verbs in brackets. Use the structure: verb + object + *to* + verb.

0 The police told everyone: 'Don't go near the bomb.'
   The police warned everyone not to go near the bomb. (*warn*)
1 James asked Bella, 'Please come to New York with me.'
   .... (*persuade*)
2 Teddy sent a note to her: 'Don't forget to come and have tea at 4.30.'
   .... (*remind*)
3 Bella told Bruce: 'You mustn't take revenge on James.'
   .... (*forbid*)
4 Bruce said to his mates, 'Help me teach the rich playboy a lesson.'
   .... (*ask*)
5 Byron told Bella: 'You may kiss me if you want to.'
   .... (*allow*)
6 Byron told her: 'You shouldn't fall in love with me.'
   .... (*advise*)

4 **D** Write sentences with the continuous or perfect infinitive, using the verbs in brackets.

0 I arrived at their home. They were trying to phone me at that moment.
   They happened to be phoning me. (*happen*)
00 It seems that he has missed his train. *He seems to have missed his train.* (*seem*)
1 Gina was in the middle of the lake. I thought she was drowning.
   .... (*seem*)
2 Their house is empty. Perhaps they have gone on holiday.
   .... (*appear*)
3 I looked out and by coincidence my old girlfriend was passing my house.
   .... (*happen*)
4 I hope that I'm going to stay in London during the summer.
   .... (*hope*)

Verbs + to + infinitive

Bella **started to explain** about the five different types of men to James. He **started laughing**. 'Would you **like** me **to describe** the five varieties of women to you?' he asked.

Ⓐ *START TO DO = START DOING*

We can use some verbs with **either to + infinitive or verb-ing**. There is little or no difference in meaning:

She **started to explain**. = She **started explaining**.
They **continued to talk**. = They **continued talking**.

These verbs include: *begin   continue   hate   intend   like   love   prefer   start*

Ⓑ *LIKE DANCING* ETC.

In general, we prefer to use **like, hate, love, prefer + verb-ing**:

I **like dancing**.   I **love going** to the cinema.   I **hate studying** maths.

But we tend to use **like, hate, love, prefer + to + infinitive** to talk about **habits** or **choices**.

He **likes to drink** tea in the morning.   She **hates to see** people drop litter.

Ⓒ *WOULD LIKE + TO + INFINITIVE*

We use **would like/would hate/would love/would prefer** with **to + infinitive**:

I'**d like to have** a cup of tea.   She'**d prefer to be** in the beginners' class.

We use **Would you like to...?** to **invite** somebody: **Would you like to watch** TV tonight?

We use **Do you like + verb-ing...?** to ask for **general information**:
Do you like watching TV? (usually/generally)

Ⓓ *REMEMBER TO DO/REMEMBER DOING* ETC.

There are a few verbs which have one meaning with **to + infinitive** and a different meaning with **verb-ing**:

1 **Remember + verb-ing:** refers to **things you did in the past**.
   I **remember posting** the letter. = I posted the letter and now I remember I did it.

   Forget/remember + to: refers to **things you still have or had to do**.
   I **remembered to post** the letter. = I had to post the letter and I did it. I remembered!
   I **forgot to meet** her.   = I had to meet her but I didn't do it. I forgot!

   We also use **forget + verb-ing**, usually in negative sentences.
   I'll never **forget meeting** her. = I met her and I will never forget it.

2 We use **try + verb-ing** when we talk about **making an experiment**:
   I **tried studying** Spanish. = I studied Spanish because I wanted to see if I liked it.
   I **tried collecting** stamps. = I collected stamps for a short time to see if I liked it.

   We use **try + to** when we talk about **making an effort to do something difficult**.
   I **tried to** study Spanish.   = I worked hard at studying Spanish.
   I **tried to** climb the mountain. = I made an effort to climb the mountain.

3 We use **stop + verb-ing** when we **finish an activity**.
   I **stopped smoking**.   = I used to smoke but I stopped.

   We use **stop + to** to **show purpose**.
   I **stopped to smoke**.   = I was walking/driving etc.
                  but I stopped in order to smoke.

1 🅐 🅑 🅓 Here are James's FIVE TYPES OF WOMEN. Fill the gaps with the pairs of verbs, using the second verb in either the *-ing* form or the *to* + infinitive form. If both are possible, write both. Use a passive form where there is a star (*). Then listen and check your answers.

TYPE A: THE DRAMA QUEEN

Melanie (**0** *love/have*) loves having/loves to have quarrels with people. She usually (**1** *start/scream*) .... because she (**2** *like/attract*) .... attention. Recently, she has (**3** *start/attend*) .... film premieres in low-cut dresses but if the photographers (**4** *begin/take*) .... pictures, she (**5** *pretend/insult**) .... and (**6** *try/scratch*) .... their faces. She only (**7** *agrees/go out*) .... with rich, successful men.

TYPE B: THE EARTH MOTHER

Rosie (**8** *love/cook*) .... for her boyfriends. She (**9** *can't help/give*) .... them hot vegetable soups even when it's high summer. She (**10** *intend/have*) .... at least twenty children and (**11** *want/live*) .... in the middle of the forest. She (**12** *plan/die*) .... at 99 years old and (**13** *want/surround**) .... by 100 grandchildren.

TYPE C: THE IRON LADY

Victoria (**14** *plan/be*) .... president of her company before she's 35. She (**15** *encourage/learn*) .... her boyfriend .... how to cook and clean because she has to (**16** *avoid/waste*) .... time on domestic tasks. She will (**17** *stop/kiss*) .... him immediately if her mobile phone (**18** *start/ring*) .... She (**19** *forget/buy*) .... birthday presents for her friends but (**20** *expect/invite**) .... to all their dinner parties because she (**21** *like/meet*) .... important people.

2 🅐 🅑 🅓 Rewrite the descriptions of Type D and E using verb + verb-ing or verb + *to* + infinitive. Use the verb in brackets.

TYPE D: THE TOM-BOY

0 Sally climbed lots of trees as a child.
 Sally loved climbing trees as a child. (*love*)

1 She often arm-wrestles with her boyfriends.
 .... with her. (*invite*)

2 She always wins! .... (*keep on*)

3 She experimented with cooking as a hobby.
 .... as a hobby. (*try*)

4 She never made another soup.
 .... (*give up*)

5 Then she studied motor cycle maintenance.
 .... (*start*)

TYPE E: THE SUGAR-PLUM FAIRY

6 Anita remembers ballet-dancing at 3 years old.
 .... (*never forget*)

7 She always wears pink.
 .... (*love*)

8 She doesn't go anywhere without her pet poodle.

.... (*refuse*)

9 She cries at the end of sad movies.

.... (*can't help*)

10 She says she doesn't want to get married.

.... (*deny*)

11 She looks at wedding dresses in shop windows.

.... (*adore*)

3 **Ⓐ-Ⓓ** In some of these sentences, it is possible to use either verb + verb-ing OR verb + *to*-infinitive without changing the basic meaning. In those cases write the alternative structure. If it is not possible, write *X*.

0 She intends studying to be an artist. *She intends to study to be an artist.*

1 It continued to rain heavily. ....

2 The sun kept on shining. ....

3 I love listening to my grandfather's stories. ....

4 Would you like to visit him too? ....

5 I'd prefer to be in Mrs Firth's class. ....

6 We tried putting more sugar in the cakes. ....

7 I denied leaving the rubbish on the floor. ....

4 **Ⓓ** Use the words in brackets to make one sentence. Use the correct form.

0 I went to New York in 1998. I still remember it.
I remember going to New York. (*remember/go*)

1 I wanted to send him a birthday card but I came home without doing it.

.... (*forget/send*)

2 I loved visiting the island in 2003. I still remember it.

.... (*remember/visit*)

3 I almost forgot to see Joe when I was in London but luckily I remembered in time.

.... (*remember/visit*)

4 He couldn't sleep, so he took the new tablets to see if they helped him.

.... (*try/take*)

5 Have I really met you before? I don't recognise you.

.... (*not remember/meet*)

6 I met my favourite singer when I was in the USA. I'll never forget it.

.... (*never forget/meet*)

7 As I was driving to London, I saw a phone box, so I stopped and phoned her.

.... (*stop/phone*)

8 I used to phone her every night but she made me angry, so I never phone her now.

.... (*stop/phone*)

9 I dyed my hair once, but I didn't like it, so I didn't do it again.

.... (*try/dye*)

10 I lost contact with my first girlfriend years ago. Later, I hired a detective to look for her.

.... (*try/find*)

11 I'd been travelling for hours, so I stopped at a hotel to sleep.

.... (*stop/sleep*)

12 I dived in the Caribbean and swam among the coral. It was unforgettable.

.... (*never forget/dive*)

5 **C** Rewrite these questions by using *would* + *like* or the Present Simple of *like*.

0 Do you want to watch a video? *Would you like to watch a video?*

1 Is painting one of your hobbies? ....?

2 Do you enjoy cycling? ....?

3 Shall we go for a cycle ride? ....?

4 Do you enjoy studying foreign languages? ....?

5 How about visiting me next week? ....?

6 **D** Circle S if the two sentences have the same meaning. Circle D if they have different meanings.

0 He stopped to drink his beer. He stopped drinking his beer. S Ⓓ

1 They started driving. They started to drive. S D

2 I'll never forget climbing Everest. I'll always remember climbing Everest. S D

3 She tried using the laser. She tried to use the laser. S D

4 Do you like this kind of coffee? Would you like this kind of coffee? S D

5 She began learning to play golf. She began to learn to play golf. S D

6 I don't remember sending the e-mail. I didn't remember to send the e-mail. S D

7 The team continued celebrating their victory. The team continued to celebrate their victory. S D

7 **D** For each situation, choose the more suitable alternative.

1 **Choose A. He tried to eat the chicken soup. OR B. He tried eating the chicken soup.**

   i. Ben had never eaten Thai chicken soup before. He ordered it in the restaurant to see if he liked it. .....

   ii. Sam was a vegetarian. Marta offered him chicken soup at the party. He didn't want to be rude, so he did his best to finish it. .....

2 **Choose A. She didn't remember to meet Robert. OR B. She didn't remember meeting Robert.**

   i. Fenella met Robert at a conference last year. She met him again last week but didn't recognise him. She thought she had never met him before. .....

   ii. Fenella arranged to meet Robert again yesterday in the hotel foyer at 8 p.m. She started watching TV at 7.45 and didn't think about Robert until 8.30. .....

3 **Choose A. She stopped singing. OR B. She stopped to sing.**

   Jane was singing in the night club. Suddenly the electricity failed, the lights went out and she couldn't continue. .....

OPEN EXERCISE

8 **A**-**D** Complete these sentences in any suitable way, using either verb-ing or *to* + infinitive.

1 She loves ....

2 They arranged ....

3 We admitted ....

4 Everyone denied ....

5 The police stopped ....

6 The two armies agreed ....

7 The singers started ....

8 I'll never forget ....

UNIT 92 >> Verbs + prepositions

 Ben has **contributed to** his school's athletics successes but, as a result, he's **failed to** **concentrate on** his studies. But getting a place at Oxford or Cambridge doesn't always **depend** only **on** exam results.

Ⓐ VERBS WITH PREPOSITIONS

Some verbs often occur with a preposition in front of a noun or verb-**ing**.

agree with   apologise for   believe in   belong to   concentrate on   congratulate on
contribute to   depend on   disagree with   happen to   insist on   listen to   look at
object to   participate in   prefer X to Y   prevent from   protect from   spend on
succeed in   wait for

Tom **agreed with** his sister.   What **happened to** you?

When we make questions with **Who...?/What...?/How many...?** etc. we usually put the preposition at the end of the question:
What are you looking **at**?   **How many** CD's did you listen **to**?

Ⓑ PARTICULAR MEANINGS OF VERBS WITH DIFFERENT PREPOSITIONS

Some verbs have different prepositions in different cases:

I **arrived in** Italy.   (for a large area, e.g. a town or a country)
They **arrived at** Victoria Station.   (for a smaller place, e.g. a station or an airport)
He **arrived** home.   (no preposition + home, see Unit 73)

Notice: we never use **arrive + to**:   ~~They arrived to London~~.
The train **left from** platform 9.   (from a point, e.g. a platform, a square)
The tourists **left for** the airport.   (for the destination, the place we are going to)
We **left** the hotel early.   (usually no preposition with building, town etc.)

Notice also:

We **agreed with** each other. We **agreed about** almost everything.	We **agreed on** a plan. (decided together) We **agreed to** the new plan. (accepted)
I **apologised for** the mistake./**for** being stupid.	I **apologised to** the teacher/**to** the lady.
He **applied for** a job in a shop/**for** a course.	He **applied to** the university/**to** the company.
She **asked for** some coffee.	She **asked about** the new system.
They **paid for** the car.	They **paid** the bill. (no preposition)
They **paid by** cheque.	They **paid** the money **to** the salesman.
I **talked to**/**with** my friend for an hour.	We **talked about** our holiday.
She **threw** the ball **to** her friend/**to** the dog. (game)	verbs with **at** indicating aggression She **threw** a stone **at** the thief. (attack)
We **laughed with** the teacher. (together)	He **laughed at** the stupid boy. (ridicule)
She **shouted to** me across the square. (communication)	The angry teacher **shouted at** his class. (anger)

Ⓒ NO PREPOSITION

These verbs do not take a preposition: **reach**, **discuss**, **phone**, **ring**, **enter**
We **reached** the hotel in the evening.   They **discussed** their plan.

1 **A**-**C** Rewrite these sentences, using the verb in brackets and a suitable preposition if necessary.

  0 Ben contacted Cambridge University asking to be a student.
    Ben applied to Cambridge University. (*apply*)

  1 His performance in an interview will influence his chances of success.
    .... (*depend*)

  2 The university has requested a confidential reference.
    .... (*ask*)

  3 His girlfriend said that he was stupid to apply.
    .... for applying. (*laugh*)

  4 Ben likes Cambridge more than Oxford.
    .... (*prefer*)

  5 He has given a lot of time to preparing for his interview.
    .... the preparation for his interview. (*spend*)

  6 His parents think he should pay a lot of attention to being polite.
    .... (*concentrate*)

  7 When Ben reached the college gates, the porter showed him where to go.
    .... (*arrive*)

  8 During the interview, Ben and the professors had a discussion about his exam results.
    .... (*discuss*)

  9 After the interview, there was a two-week delay before the result came.
    After the interview, Ben .... the result. (*wait*)

 10 The letter offered him a place. Everyone said 'well done' to Ben.
    .... (*congratulate*)

 11 Next year, Ben will be a participant in the famous Oxford and Cambridge Boat Race.
    .... (*participate*)

2 **A B** Complete the questions with a suitable preposition.

  0 Who is Phoebe Cute going to the party with?
  1 How many films has Myra starred ....?
  2 How many people has Slim borrowed money ....?
  3 How many paintings have you looked .... in the gallery today?
  4 Who are the police and those tracker dogs looking ....?
  5 Which platform does the train for Glasgow leave ....?
  6 Which job did Pauline Collins apply ....?
  7 What did Nick and Jill talk .... during the secret meeting?
  8 How many prisons has Harry escaped ....?
  9 What are those people laughing ....? Is it the clown?
 10 What factors does the President's decision depend ....?
 11 Who did Bella dance .... at the party?
 12 What kind of music does Nadia like listening ....?
 13 What did she spend her money ....?

3 Ⓐ Ⓑ Now make your own questions ending in prepositions. The answers to the questions should be the underlined phrases.

0 Roland and Jenny were laughing at <u>the cartoon</u>.
What were Roland and Jenny laughing at?

1 Sally and Gina have been gossiping about <u>Mrs Peters</u>.
....?

2 Brigitte had to apologise for <u>spilling Nick's coffee</u> on his new suit.
....?

3 The teachers were shouting at <u>the twins</u>.
....?

4 Henry paid for <u>the coffee</u> but not for the cakes.
....?

5 Pauline has applied for <u>three</u> different jobs in London.
....?

6 George gave his old jacket to <u>Ellie Tramper</u>.
....?

7 Ben participated in <u>five</u> races at the under-18 Olympics.
....?

8 The terrorists were shooting at <u>the police</u>, not at the civilians.
....?

9 They unlocked the box with <u>the key they found in the grave</u>.
....?

10 Christine spent her lottery winnings on <u>a yacht</u>.
....?

11 Nadia played the concerto with <u>the Hungarian National</u> Orchestra.
Which ....?

12 George believes in a <u>Far Eastern</u> religion.
Which ....?

13 Her parents objected to <u>Annie's habit of leaving old chewing gum on the carpets</u>.
What ....?

4 Ⓑ Ⓒ Put a suitable preposition in each gap. In some cases write ✗ for no preposition.

0 Can I pay *by* credit card or do you only accept cash?
1 I'd like to pay .... the bill now.
2 They left .... the office as soon as they finished the work.
3 Bill's very ill. I asked his parents .... him but they didn't tell me anything.
4 The train for York will leave .... platform 6 instead of platform 9.
5 If you throw the stick .... the dog, it'll catch it in its teeth.
6 The trip to the seaside starts early. The coach leaves at 6 a.m. .... Brighton.
7 Some hooligans were throwing stones .... the traffic from the bridge.
8 The teachers are always shouting .... Timothy because he's so naughty.
9 I'd like to pay .... the meal now. Can you bring the bill?
10 Go to the hotel reception desk and ask .... the key to Room 101.
11 Everyone's talking .... Petra – She's won the National Cup.
12 Mike is on the other side of the valley. If you shout .... him, he'll hear you.
13 It was such a good joke. We were laughing .... each other for an hour.

5 **Ⓐ-Ⓒ** Put the correct prepositions or ✗ (= no preposition) in these sentences.

0 Maria prefers Swiss cheese _to_ British cheese.

1 The picnic depends .... the weather. 2 Who does this pen belong ....? 3 We reached .... the mountains at sunset. 4 After they'd discussed .... the route, they started driving. 5 It's not my decision. It doesn't depend .... me. 6 When you phone .... Karl, ask him .... Tina's address. 7 Everything in this room belongs .... me. 8 Why do you prefer Nadia .... Dania? 9 Please phone .... me when you arrive .... the airport. 10 As soon as she arrived .... London, she entered .... a night-club. 11 Have you entered .... the poetry competition?

6 **Ⓐ-Ⓒ** Fill the gaps in the sentences so that they suit the situations. Use each verb from the list once only in the correct form; also add the necessary prepositions.

> apply   apologise   ask   not believe   belong   concentrate   depend   forget
>   disagree   leave   pay   prefer   prevent   shout   succeed   talk

0 Melanie always has a different opinion from James.
  Melanie always _disagrees with James_.

1 Phil and Julie forgot Julie's mother's birthday. They said sorry.
  Phil and Julie .... Julie's mother ....

2 Fiona asked Oxford University to give her a place on a course in Politics.
  Fiona ....

3 Harry wanted to rob the Bank of England. Inspector Clark stopped him.
  Inspector Clark .... robbing the Bank of England.

4 The policeman raised his voice angrily. The teenagers had knocked off his helmet.
  The policeman .... who had knocked off his helmet.

5 Tina's parents didn't give her any of the things on her list.
  Tina's parents didn't give her any of the things she had ....

6 Michelle said that the guns were not hers.
  Michelle said that the guns .... her.

7 Bella finds it difficult to pay close attention to Simon's lectures.
  Bella finds it difficult to ....

8 Roxanne wanted to be company president and she achieved her ambition.
  Roxanne .... becoming company president.

9 Sally gets money from her parents to enable her to buy necessary things.
  Sally .... for money to buy necessary things.

10 He likes playing the guitar but his favourite instrument is the saxophone.
  He .... playing the saxophone ....

11 I don't think it's right to criticise other people for my mistakes.
  I .... criticising other people for my mistakes.

12 The departure point of the Glasgow train is Platform 11.
  The train .... Platform 11 .... Glasgow.

13 He used his credit card to buy the new car.
  He .... credit card.

14 I and my friend had a long conversation. We discussed football.
  I .... for a long time .... my friend .... football.

UNIT 93 >> Gerunds and infinitives

@ Many titles of novels, songs, films etc. use a gerund. Here are two examples of 1990s
films: ***Driving*** *Miss Daisy*
Sleeping *with the Enemy*
Finding more examples is not difficult.

Ⓐ THE GERUND: VERB-ING USED LIKE A NOUN

We can use **verb-ing** or **not + verb-ing** as the **subject** of a sentence. For example:
Learning *a foreign language takes time.*
Using *the Internet can be educational as well as entertaining.*
Not drinking *enough liquid is bad for the health.*

We can also use **verb-ing** after **be, find** etc.:
*The best thing about the holiday **was visiting** Super-World.*
*We **found cooking** for ourselves very difficult.*

In other units, we've looked at:

1 **verb-ing** after certain verbs (see Units 88-9):
   *I **like going** to the cinema.*   *He **prefers watching** TV.*

2 **verb-ing** after prepositions (see Unit 72):
   *He did it **without thinking**.*   *I looked forward **to meeting** her.*

Many nouns end in **-ing: skiing, hang-gliding, a human being, a meeting, sight-seeing.**
We sometimes find **a/an/the + verb-ing**:
*There was **a knocking** at the window.*
*I live near a night-club. **The singing** and **shouting** keep us awake.*

Ⓑ TO + INFINITIVE

We can also use **to + infinitive** as the subject of a sentence. We tend to use it for **specific
ambitions, plans, wishes**:
To dance *with the Moscow Ballet was her ambition.*
To play *for Liverpool football team was always his dream.*
To go *to the junction and then join the M25 is the best route.*

We tend to use the gerund for **habits** or **habitual activities, hobbies, processes**:
*'**Playing** for Liverpool is great,' agreed the players.* **Less likely:** *To play for Liverpool is great.*
Collecting *stamps is my brother's favourite hobby!* **Not** ~~*To collect stamps is his hobby*~~.

Overall, it is more usual to use the gerund as subject than the infinitive.

Ⓒ PARALLEL STRUCTURES: *IT* + ADJECTIVE + *TO* + VERB = VERB-ING + VERB

We can say: ***It is*** *difficult/easy/exciting etc.* ***to learn*** *Russian.*
Or   ***Learning*** *Russian is difficult/easy/exciting etc.*

Ⓓ PASSIVE FORMS

Gerund: **being + past participle:**   ***Being robbed*** *at gunpoint is a terrible experience.*
Infinitive: **to + be + past participle:** ***To be robbed*** *at gunpoint is a terrible experience.*

1 **A** **Complete the sentences after reading the text. Use verbs which occur in the text in the gerund form.**

In the 1990s the Metalheads found it easy to make hit singles. They toured all over the world; it was hard work but the fans enjoyed seeing them perform. After they played in New York, they became very successful. But when their tour-bus crashed, they were out of the public eye for nine months. They lost popularity. In 2001, they lost their recording contract. It wasn't easy to adapt to a normal life for the band members. Four of them started solo careers but failed.

Finally, they re-formed the band and called themselves the Old Metalheads. They don't make CDs but, as Slick the lead guitarist says, 'we want to make music not money.'

0 *Making hit singles* in the 1990s was easy for the Metalheads.
1 .... was exhausting but .... in front of their fans was important.
2 Their biggest break was .... in New York.
3 But .... for nine months damaged their popularity.
4 .... was a big shock in 2001.
5 .... wasn't easy.
6 .... wasn't the answer.
7 .... the band made them happy.
8 .... the Old Metalheads was a joke.
9 .... isn't a problem for them.
10 '... is more important than ....'

2 **B** **Choose the better alternative.**

0 **To sing/Singing** has always been one of my hobbies.
1 **To get married/Getting married** to a celebrity with a big wedding is her ambition.
2 **To accelerate/Accelerating** at the wrong moment is one of his faults.
3 **To drive/Driving** a Formula 1 race car in a grand prix in Italy is my dream.

3 **C** **Rewrite these sentences using a verb-ing as subject.**

0 It isn't easy to remain popular in the world of pop music.
  Remaining popular in the world of pop music isn't easy.
1 Sometimes it's difficult to resist temptation.
  ....
2 It's normal to feel anxious before an examination.
  ....
3 It's inconvenient not to have a car in the big city.
  ....
4 It can be embarrassing not to be able to remember someone's name.
  ....

4 **D** **Use passive forms to fill the gaps.**

0 *Being treated* by a good doctor is essential. (*treat*).
1 To .... to represent your country is a great honour. (*choose*)
2 The best part of the day was .... in a stretch limousine. (*drive*)
3 .... by wild dogs was a terrible experience for him. (*attack*)
4 To .... by fans can be a strange experience. (*worship*)

UNIT 94 >> More about infinitives

 Claire is going **to be moving** soon. Everything was **to have been** packed ready **to be transported** to the new flat. But Claire went to York **to say** goodbye to an old boyfriend — so most things are still waiting **to be put** in boxes and labelled for the removal company **to take away.**

Ⓐ INFINITIVE FORMS

The infinitive has various forms. Here are examples using **clean** as an example verb:
(to) clean   (to) have cleaned (perfect)   *(to) be cleaning* (continuous)   *(to) have been cleaning*
(perfect continuous)   *(to) be cleaned* (passive)   *(to) have been cleaned* (perfect passive)

Ⓑ *BE + TO*-INFINITIVE

We use **be + to + verb** to mean **must/mustn't**:
1 for **orders**: *You **are not to open** the door until I say so!*
2 in **notices** and **instructions**: *No one **is to enter** this area without permission.*
*These tablets **are not to be taken** without medical advice.* (passive)

and also in other contexts:
3 for things arranged by '**Fate**': *I didn't know it then but we **were to become** enemies.*
4 for **plans** and **arrangements**: *The festival **is to close** with a firework display.*

Ⓒ *ONLY TO FIND/DISCOVER/BE TOLD* ETC.

We often follow a verb describing a significant action with **to find, to discover, to see** etc.
We use **only** to add emphasis:
*I arrived at their house **to find** that they were just coming to visit me.*
*I located the treasure **only to discover** that someone had stolen it.*
*He reached the school **only to be told** that it was closed.* (passive infinitive)

Ⓓ *FOR* + NOUN/PRONOUN + *TO*-INFINITIVE

We use **for** when we do something so that another person/animal/thing can benefit from
our action. We use **for** + **object pronoun** (*me, him, her, us, them*):
*I scattered some bread **for the birds to eat.** or ... **for them to eat.***
*They gave some money **for us to buy** some new clothes.*

The same structure frequently follows **ask**: *I **asked for the rubbish to be** removed.* (passive)

We also use **for** + **there** + **to be**: *It's important **for there to be** a good community spirit.*

Ⓔ SOME USES OF INFINITIVE WITHOUT *TO*

Here are some situations where we use the infinitive without **to**:
1 after **Why** (**not**) to make questions: ***Why pay** more than you have to?*
                                              ***Why not save** your money?*
2 after expressions with **do** such as **All I do... What he did... :**
   ***All he does is sleep** all day.*   ***What she did was throw** cold water over him.*

Ⓕ SPLIT INFINITIVES

We can '**split**' an infinitive by using an adverb or phrase between **to** and the verb:
*He decided **to slowly drive** along the coast.*   *It is easy **to unconsciously make** a mistake.*

Note that some people consider that it is bad style to do this although it is now generally
accepted.

1 **A** **B** Complete the sentences. Include an infinitive in the appropriate form, with or without *to*.

0 I think that Claire is worrying about her move. *She seems to be worrying about her move.*

1 The removal company promised to contact her last week but they didn't.
The removal company were ....
OR: Claire was .... by the removal company.

2 I think Claire was on holiday last month instead of following her plan and looking for a new flat.
Claire was .... a flat last month. But in fact,
she seems .... on holiday.

3 It is necessary to pack things made of glass very carefully.
Things made of glass need ....

4 By the time they reached the new flat, the journey in the removal van seemed very long.
They seemed .... for a very long time before
they reached the flat. (include *been*)

5 After she'd moved without any big problems, Claire felt very happy.
It was great .... without any big problems.

2 **C** Write four more sentences with *only to...* based on the text in the box. Then listen and check your answers.

> I went to Louise's home to ask her to marry me but she was with another man. I decided to leave the country but all flights were cancelled because of a strike. I returned angrily to Louise's house but I discovered that the man was her long-lost brother. I showed her the ring but she told me that she didn't love me. She had already chosen a wedding dress but had found I would make a jealous husband.

0 *I went to Louise's home to ask her to marry me only to find that she was with another man.*
1 ....   3 ....
2 ....   4 ....

3 **D** Rewrite these sentences using *for* + noun/pronoun + *to* + verb.

0 We raised money so that the council could help the homeless. *We raised money for the council to help the homeless.*   1 We made several bowls of hot soup so that the homeless could eat it.
....   2 He bought a computer so that I could use it. ....   3 Her godmother produced a beautiful dress so that Cinderella could wear it. ....
....   4 The customs official took out a form which we had to complete. ....
....   5 The author wrote a special play so that they could perform it. ....   6 It is essential that they study *Grammar Goals* before the examination. ....

4 **A** **D** **E** Fill the gaps with an infinitive form (with or without *to*) of a suitable verb.

0 All they did was look at the car instead of repairing it.

1 Why .... money on a new car when you can repair the old one?

2 Why not .... your old car to Slick's Garage .... by our expert mechanics.

3 It's essential for there .... trust between friends.

4 I didn't mean .... the vase. All I did was .... it up to look at it.

5 I didn't have any money, so what I did was .... my uncle .... me some.

6 Sometimes he seems .... but really he's thinking with closed eyes.

More about infinitives

UNIT 95 >> *Wish/if only* etc. + past verb forms

@ I **wish** I **could** stay and chat but **it's time I went** to college. **If only I didn't have** to work so hard!

Ⓐ USING PAST VERB FORMS WITH A PRESENT MEANING

We sometimes use **past verb forms** to show we are talking about a **hypothetical/unreal situation in the present**. For example:
*I **wish** I **had** a dinosaur.* (unreal)   *Stop talking! **It's time** we **left**.* (nobody seems to be leaving)

Ⓑ *WISH* + (*THAT*) + PAST OR PAST PERFECT VERB FORMS

We use a past verb form after **I wish** with a present or future meaning:
*I **wish** I **had** a car.* (present meaning: I want a car now)   **Not** ~~I wish I have a car.~~
*I **wish** I **didn't have** to work tomorrow.* (future meaning)   **Not** ~~I wish I don't have to...~~
If we are talking about the past, we use a Past Perfect verb form:
*He **wishes** he **hadn't married** Hester.*   (= but he **did** marry her)

Ⓒ *WOULD RATHER, IF ONLY, SUPPOSING, IT'S TIME*

We can use the same structure after **would rather, if only, supposing** and **it's time**:

present or future meaning	past meaning
I'd rather she *went* now/*went* tomorrow.	*I'd rather* that he *hadn't asked* me to marry him.
If only I *had a* car! (= I want a car now.)	*If only* I *had had* a car when I knew Betty.

We use **supposing** or **suppose**, mostly in informal speech, to consider a hypothetical/unreal possibility:
Supposing we **had** a car, we could collect the goods by car.   (present meaning)
Suppose we **had gone** to London when we had the chance!   (past meaning)
Supposing John **visited** us, we could go to the circus with him.   (future meaning)
But we say ***Supposing*** John **visits** us, we can go... if there is a high probability that he will visit us.
After **It's time...** we can use a past verb form with a present or future meaning:
*It's time we **went**.* (present meaning = we should go now)   **Not** ~~It's time we go.~~
*It **will** soon **be time** we **did** the washing.* (future meaning)   **Not** ~~It'll soon be time we do...~~
We often use **It's time...** + **past verb** to make a strong suggestion to someone:
*Bobby, **it's time** you **went** to school.* (= go to school now)
In formal English, we use **were** instead of **was** (see also Unit 107C) after these structures
and after **wish**:   *I **wish** I **were** President.*   *If only she **were** my girlfriend!*
               *Supposing he **were** dead...!*   *It's time he **were** here.*

Ⓓ *WISH* AND *IF ONLY* + *WOULD*

We often use **wish/if only** + **would** to talk about the present or future:
*I **wish** he **would visit** me more often.*   *If only he **would invite** me out to dinner.*
We can make semi-polite requests using **would**:
*I **wish** you **would** listen. = **If only** you'd listen!* (= Please, listen!)

Ⓔ OTHER POSSIBLE STRUCTURES AFTER *WISH, IT'S TIME, WOULD RATHER*

1 **wish + to-infinitive**: *I **wish to see** the manager.* (formal, serious)
2 **wish + noun + to-infinitive**: *I **wish my children to inherit** my wealth.*
3 **wish + person + noun**: *He **wishes you a** happy New Year/a speedy recovery etc.*
4 **It's time + to-infinitive**: *It's time to get up!*
5 **It's time + for + noun + to-infinitive**: *It's time for the children to go to bed.*
6 **would rather + verb**: *I'd rather go to the cinema than to the disco.* (see Unit 26)
7 **would rather + have + past participle**: *I'd rather have gone home.*

1 Ⓐ Ⓑ Ⓓ **Complete the second sentence in an appropriate way, using the word in brackets.**

0   Slim Skinty doesn't have a warm overcoat. *He wishes he had a warm overcoat.* (*wish*)

1   There are rats in Ellie Tramper's cave.
    She .... (*wish*)

2   The ice cream companies didn't make a big profit last year.
    They .... (*wish*)

3   The weather wasn't warm last summer.
    .... the weather .... (*only*)

4   Dad took me to the zoo but I wanted to go to the circus.
    I .... that Dad .... (*rather*)

5   I can't swim. I .... (*wish*) or .... (*only*)

6   It isn't likely that a comet will hit the earth.
    .... that a comet .... (*supposing*)

7   Bob McGive didn't have a holiday last year.
    He .... (*wish*)

8   It's class time; the children are still playing.
    .... they .... playing. (use a tense of *stop*)

9   I'm not President.
    .... I ...., I'd give free transport to everyone. (*supposing*)

10 The match was planned for 3 but at 3.15 the teams are still practising.
    .... playing. (*time*)

2 Ⓓ **Make sentences with *would* about these situations. Use the words in brackets.**

0   I want John to help me. *I wish John would help me.* (*wish*)

1   I want the teacher to burn the grammar books. .... (*only*)

2   I want the neighbours to stop playing loud music. .... (*wish*)

3   She wants Tom Craze to ask her to marry him. .... (*wish*)

4   I want Phoebe Cute to make a film about my town. .... (*only*)

5   I want the teacher to give me a good report. .... (*wish*)

3 Ⓐ Ⓑ Ⓒ Ⓔ **Match the sentences and the situations by writing letters from A-I in the gaps.**

A I wish I saw you every day	B I wish to see you every day
C It's time to go	D It's time we went
E I'd rather have a car	F I'd rather I had a car
G I wish you a happy birthday	H I wish you'd had a happy birthday
I Supposing Sheila arrives	J Supposing Sheila arrived

0   Some girls are looking at Sheila's secret diary. One says: J

1   Fran is with Sheila's boyfriend in the café. Sheila often comes there. Fran says: .....

2   Teacher to pupil: 'Don't be absent again. ..... here in class.'

3   Phil can only see his sweetheart, Julie, at weekends. He says: .....

4   Sue's parents are too poor to buy her a car, so they bought her a cycle. She says: .....

5   Tim's parents are rich; they offer to buy him a cycle. He wants a car. He says: .....

6   You want to greet Joe on his birthday. You say: .....

7   Everything goes wrong on Joe's birthday. Afterwards, you say: .....

8   The meeting ends at five o'clock. Bill looks at his watch. 'Oh, ...'

9   The meeting ends at 5 but everybody is still talking at 5.15. Bill says: .....

PAPER 3 PART 1

1 For questions 1-12, read the text below and decide which answer, A, B, C or D, best fits each gap. There is an example at the beginning (0).

LIVING ON MARS

There has (0) A a fascination with the planet Mars ever since science fiction began to be written (1) ..... novels about beautiful Martian princesses or three-headed invaders became a successful way to make readers (2) ..... a world of the imagination. Now, there is even a Mars Society whose members have re-created Martian conditions on Earth. Devon Island (3) ..... in the Canadian Arctic, a vast area which (4) ..... mountains, cliffs and canyons like those on Mars. There is even a massive crater. Scientists are (5) ..... advantage of these similar conditions to (6) ..... whether it would be possible for human beings to live on Mars. On Devon Island, the volunteers are getting used (7) ..... space suits all the time. They have to withstand the extreme temperatures that are also found on Mars. In fact, Mars is not so different from our own planet as most people (8) ..... . There are four distinct seasons and the sun rises and (9) ..... to create days and nights similar in length to ours. In the past, there must have been life on Mars; scientists have discovered river beds where water (10) ..... and evidence that living organisms once existed there. Then the systems that supported life (11) ..... . Perhaps a giant asteroid hit the planet and increased its distance from the sun so that temperatures dropped and Mars (12) ..... a dead, frozen planet.

0 (A)	been	B	be	C	to be	D	being
1 A	Produce	B	Having produced	C	To producing	D	Producing
2 A	to enter	B	enter	C	entering	D	to be enter
3 A	lies	B	lays	C	is lying	D	is laying
4 A	is possessing	B	is possessed	C	possesses	D	possessions
5 A	putting	B	getting	C	making	D	taking
6 A	see	B	be seeing	C	finding out	D	be discover
7 A	to wear	B	to be wearing	C	to wearing	D	to be worn
8 A	imagined	B	are imagining	C	imagine	D	imagination
9 A	sets	B	is falling	C	downs	D	falls
10 A	was used to run	B	used to running	C	was used to running	D	used to run
11 A	fell down	B	did wrong	C	broke down	D	broke
12 A	turned from	B	turned into	C	turned down	D	turned up

PAPER 3 PART 2

2 For questions 1-12, read the text below and think of the word which best fits the gap. Use only *one* word in each space. There is an example at the beginning (0).

BRINGING MARS BACK TO LIFE

The aim of the Mars Society is (0) to bring Mars back to life. Its president (1) .... that it is possible to 'terraform' the red planet, in other words to create Earth-like conditions there. This would (2) .... centuries but it would be technologically possible. Sending an unmanned factory ship to Mars would be the first step. (3) .... done this, scientists would send men to Mars to begin the task of (4) .... it habitable. But how could they get used to (5) .... on a planet with such weak gravity? The Mars Society intends to (6) .... money for an experiment, using artificial gravity, to (7) .... out more about the effects of low gravity. If these problems can be overcome, the first men will arrive (8) .... Mars and begin to (9) .... experiments in primitive agriculture. In the next stage, solar mirrors will be used to reflect the sun's rays and (10) .... the temperature of Mars. The Mars Society says that it is time we (11) .... to make this dream come true. In the future, (12) .... will be two planets in the solar system where human civilisations exist.

PAPER 3 PART 4

3 For questions 1-8, complete the second sentence so that it has a similar meaning to the first sentence, using the word given. Do not change the word given. Use from two to five words including the word given. There is an example at the beginning (0).

0 He has a full English breakfast every morning after he leaves his bed.
He has a full English breakfast every morning after *he gets up*. *UP*

1 Doing homework every night is making me really unhappy.
I .... doing homework every night. *FED*

2 It was such bad weather that we had to postpone the football match five times.
It was such bad weather that we had .... the football match five times. *PUT*

3 Ben has been depressed but he's beginning to look happier now.
Ben has been depressed but he's beginning to .... now. *UP*

4 At first I didn't like living in a small village but I soon accepted it.
I soon .... in a small village. *USED*

5 I said to the lady, 'I'm very sorry that I accidentally kicked your dog.'
I .... accidentally kicking her dog. *APOLOGISED*

6 Does it disturb you if I watch TV while you're reading?
Do .... TV while you're reading? *MIND*

7 I always try to help my friends if they ask me nicely.
I always try to .... if they ask me nicely. *FAVOUR*

8 Please say something to stop me forgetting to post these letters.
Please .... these letters. *ME*

OTHER PRACTICE

4 Here are some statements about grammar. If they are correct, write CORRECT and the numbers of the relevant unit(s). If not, rewrite them.

0 After 'make' and 'let', the following verb is without 'to'.   *correct*   *Unit 82*

1 If a verb follows a verb, the second verb always has *-ing*.   ....

2 We cannot normally use 'belong' or 'fit' in continuous tenses.   ....

3 It is incorrect to say 'I am having a shower'.   ....

4 'I used to work' and 'I'm used to working' have the same meaning.   ....

5 We cannot use 'rise', 'disappear' or 'vanish' in the passive.   ....

6 We usually say 'arrive in the city' but 'arrive at the airport'.   ....

OPEN EXERCISE

5 Complete these sentences in any suitable way. Include a second verb in either the *-ing* form or the infinitive form.

0 I didn't intend *to cause an accident* etc.

1 She refused ....

2 Do you mind? ....

3 I've never forgotten ....

4 I detest ....

5 My father can't stand ....

6 Please remind ....

7 The thief admitted .... last year.

8 I can't help ....

UNIT 96 >> Passive (1) – object verbs

 NEWSFLASH: The first perfect humanoid robot **has been created** by Professor Makepeace. The robot **is modelled** on the Professor's daughter, Lia. It **can** easily **be mistaken** for her twin sister.

For information about form, see Appendix 7.

Ⓐ ACTIVE AND PASSIVE

We can use sentences in the active or passive form to create sentences. The object of the active verb becomes the subject of the passive verb:

object	subject

Active: *They make cars in Birmingham.* **Passive:** *Cars are made in Birmingham.*

main verb   **be** in same tense

If a verb is intransitive (= a no-object verb), it **cannot** have a passive form:
He died. (no passive form)   *They arrived at the station.* (no passive form)

Ⓑ BY + AGENT

In the passive verb sentence, we can choose to include the do-er of the action (= the agent) or not:

we can say **either**   A: (with agent) *Harry was arrested **by the police**.*
      or   B: (without agent) *Harry was arrested.*

We normally include the agent **only** if it is important. In the examples above, we'd probably choose B. It is obvious that the police performed the act of arresting Harry, so we don't need to mention them.

The preposition **by** occurs most commonly with the agent:
*It was written **by Shakespeare**.*

We generally use **with** to refer to the instrument used by the agent:
*It was written **with a quill pen**.*

Ⓒ *AND* AND *BUT* IN PASSIVE CLAUSES

If we link passive clauses with **and** or **but**, we do not usually repeat the subject and the form of **be** if they remain the same:
*The robot **was tested** and then **shown** to the public.* (Not ~~and then it was...~~)
*The hospital **will be built** next year but **won't be opened** to the public until 2015.*

Ⓓ PASSIVE WITH MODAL VERBS

We form the passive of object verbs with modal verbs like this:

subject of passive verb	modal + be or + have been	+ past participle
The robot	can be	mistaken...
The professor	should be	congratulated...
The plans	must have been	concealed.

1 **A** - **D** Rewrite the text, using passive forms of all the object verbs. Include only the underlined subjects by using *by* + agent. Then listen and check your answers.

> In 1999, <u>Professor Makepeace</u> invented a Time Machine. <u>His daughter</u> used the machine to travel back in time. She brought back objects from ancient civilisations. In 2000, he made the Invisibility Shampoo which <u>Lia</u> tested. Cameras filmed Lia as she disappeared. Recently, he has created the first humanoid robot in his laboratories. He has amazed the scientific community. Next year, his lab team is going to build a telepathically controlled television system. The TV will show programmes according to the wishes of the viewer. <u>The viewers</u> will transmit these wishes telepathically. But first, doctors must insert a special transmitter in their brains.

Rewrite here:

In 1999, a Time Machine was invented by Professor Makepeace.

....
....
....
....
....
....
....
....

2 **A** - **D** Rewrite these active sentences in the passive form. Include the agents ONLY where you think it is important to do so.

0 In some ancient civilisations, they used to sacrifice young men and women.
  In some ancient civilisations, young men and women used to be sacrificed.

1 People have written many books about the effects of technology on our lives.
  ....

2 Technology has changed our lives.
  ....

3 The government is going to raise taxes next year.
  ....

4 The owners must repair the roof before the winter storms.
  ....

5 Lord Brian can't have murdered Lady Alice.
  ....

6 The publishing company publish this magazine once a month.
  ....

7 The headmaster himself is punishing the boys.
  ....

8 They should have finished the work by the end of the term.
  ....

9 We have been collecting evidence since the beginning of the year.
  ....

10 Driver Number 17 has won the race.
  ....

11 Have they collected the rubbish yet?
  ....

UNIT 97 >> Passive (2) – choosing the passive

 With many verbs, either active or passive forms **can be used**. Why **do** we sometimes **choose** to use the passive instead of the active? In this unit some of the factors which influence our choice **are listed**.

Ⓐ CONTEXTS WHERE PASSIVE VERBS ARE FREQUENTLY USED

We tend to use the passive form frequently:

1 To describe processes

By using the passive, we focus on the products and the steps in the process. We do not have to mention the agents (e.g. the workers or the machines) unless they are important.
*The oranges **are picked** in the citrus groves and then **transported** to the factory. There, they **are graded** and the diseased fruit **is removed**. This **is done** by a specially designed machine which **is imported** from Italy.*

2 In formal academic or scientific discourse (see also Unit 99)

The passive form occurs frequently in academic/scientific texts or lectures.
*This period of history **has not been studied** extensively. The main events **were caused** by economic and political factors although religious factors **have** also **been cited** by some historians.*

3 In new reports, rules, instructions etc.

- *The HYU Bank **was robbed** last night. Thousands of pounds which **were being transported** by a security firm **were stolen...*** (news report)
- *First of all, both surfaces **should be cleaned**.* (instruction)
- *School uniform **must be worn** at all times on the school premises.* (rule)

4 To give impersonal information, such as statistics

*2,000 new cars **were bought** in June.   50 people **were robbed** in London parks during 2006.*
But we **do not** generally use the passive for personal information of the same kind:
My mother bought a new car.   Not ~~A new car was bought by my mother.~~

Ⓑ REASONS FOR CHOOSING TO USE PASSIVE FORMS

1 To avoid mentioning the agent when not necessary

The subject of an active sentence may be unimportant or too obvious to be mentioned. (see also 96B). By using the passive, we can omit the agent if we wish. In these examples, we omit **the police/the government/the farmers:**
*Harry **was arrested**. / Taxes **were raised**. / Wheat **is grown** in the west.*

2 To avoid mentioning the agent for other reasons

Sometimes, we do not know the identity of the agent or we don't want to name them:
*The window **has been broken**.   The money **was stolen**.   The company **is** badly **managed**.*

3 To reduce the distance between subject and verb

Sometimes the sentence subject is followed by a relative clause which distances the subject and verb too much. It is then advisable to use a passive verb. For example:
*Myra **was kissed** by a man who was carrying a huge bunch of roses and lilies.*
This is better than: *The man who was carrying a huge bunch of roses and lilies kissed Myra.*

4 To maintain the same focus in a piece of writing

Sometimes we can use the passive form to avoid changing the subject from that of previous sentences. In this example, by using **was murdered,** we continue to focus on Lady Alice as subject: *Lady Alice was the daughter of Baron Gerbille, the famous zoologist. She married Lord Brian Worsted, a textile magnate. However, in May, she **was murdered** by a hired killer...*

1 **A B** Read these nine short texts. In each case decide if it is better to rewrite the text using some or all verbs in the passive. Rewrite the text in your notebook, using passive verbs where they seem more appropriate. Then listen and check your answers.

> A: They had repaired the roof of Mockham Castle after the storms of the previous winter. However, they had not used high quality materials and the bad summer weather caused more damage. They are going to replace the roof area completely next year if they can raise the necessary funds.

> B: Chris Healey, the Formula One driver, has won several minor races. This year, he has changed racing teams and has achieved greater success. The authorities disqualified him from the Monaco Grand Prix when he was leading the race. However, he has recovered his confidence and has won the Driver of the Month award.

> C: We have surveyed a sample of 1,000 families and have analysed our results. We will publish an article about our findings in the next issue of *Sociology World*.

> D: Someone stole the college football cup last night. In addition, he or she broke several pieces of furniture. He or she also burnt important documents and painted slogans on the headmaster's office wall. The police are investigating the incident.

> E: First of all, they harvest the vegetables using traditional techniques and send them to the canning factory. At the factory, the workers refrigerate the vegetables immediately. Later they inspect, clean and prepare them before they feed them into the canning machine.

> F: The author wrote these poems between 1580 and 1600. An established writer must have written them since someone published them in an expensive edition. We have analysed their style and compared it with that of Shakespeare's sonnets.

> G: Phoebe Cute has made several films in the USA but now she has decided to make a film in Britain. She will play the role of a seventeenth century princess. They will shoot the film in Scotland.

> H: They prepared the wood carefully. Then they painted it and finally protected it with an anti-decay spray. They must repaint the wood within five years.

> I: A man who had never studied at university and who'd hated school all his life won the quiz.

@ Nadia **was given** a Stradivarius violin for her birthday. Dania **was sent** a harmonica.

Ⓐ TWO-OBJECT VERBS IN THE PASSIVE

Some verbs can have two objects (see Unit 52):
ask give hand offer pay promise sell send show teach tell
*Someone sent **Sue** a letter.*   or *Someone sent **a letter** to **Sue**.*

So, we can make the **person** (Sue) or the **thing** (a letter) the subject of a passive verb.
Sue was sent a letter.   or ***A letter** was sent to Sue.*

We usually make the **person** the subject of a passive verb, not the thing:

They gave Barbara a pony.	→ ***Barbara** was given a pony.*
His brother taught Joe Spanish.	→ ***Joe** was taught Spanish by his brother.*
Will they offer us a discount?	→ *Will **we** be offered a discount?*

But sometimes, we make the **thing** the subject if it is more important:

They gave the work to the teacher.	→ ***The work** was given to the teacher.*
They haven't sent us the money.	→ ***The money** hasn't been sent to us.*

Ⓑ VERB + *TO* + INFINITIVE IN THE PASSIVE

Verbs which are followed by **to** + **infinitive** keep the same structure **to** + **infinitive** in the passive:

*We **allowed** them **to stay** out late.*	→	*They **were allowed to stay** out late.*
*They've **encouraged** us **to sing**.*	→	*We've **been encouraged to sing**.*
*We'll **warn** them **not to go out** alone.*	→	*They'll **be warned not to go** out alone.*

Ⓒ NO-OBJECT VERBS

No-object verbs (intransitive verbs) can **not** be used in the passive. These verbs include:
appear   disappear   exist   lie   live   rise   vanish
Do not say: ~~They were disappeared.~~   ~~He is existed.~~

Active sentences without an object do not have a direct passive equivalent. For example:
*He **hunted** for the whole afternoon.* (no direct passive equivalent)

Compare with: *The police **hunted** him all day.* → *He **was hunted** all day.*

Ⓓ COMPLEMENT VERBS IN THE PASSIVE

There is no direct passive equivalent for: *He became rich.* or *He became a millionaire.*
Do not use: ~~he is become~~...

But we can transform **verb** + **object** + **complement** from active to passive:

subject and verb	object	complement	→	subject	passive verb	complement
They appointed	*her*	*president.*		*She*	*was appointed*	*president*
My boss considered	*me*	*a failure.*		*I*	*was considered*	*a failure.*

Ⓔ *MAKE* IN THE PASSIVE

It is necessary to use **to** in front of a second verb after **make** in passive sentences.
*They **made us change** our plan.* (active) → *We **were made to change** our plan.* (passive)

1 **Ⓐ** Read these sentences about Sebastian Ace. Put them in the passive form, using the person as subject.

0 In Moscow, they gave him poisoned wine. *In Moscow, he was given poisoned wine.*

1 From Baghdad, they sent his girlfriend a bomb.

....

2 In Texas, they paid an assassin $4m to kill him.

....

3 In Istanbul, an agent handed him a death threat.

....

4 In Paris, a chef served a pie full of tarantulas to him.

....

5 In Prague, they promised his friend a horrible death.

....

6 In Oslo, they offered his girlfriend €500 to betray him.

....

7 In London, someone gave an anaesthetic to his guard dog.

....

8 In Cairo, they injected snake poison into him.

....

2 **Ⓐ** Rewrite these sentences, using the thing as the subject of the passive verb.

0 In Tokyo, they gave Sebastian the micro-film. *In Tokyo , the micro-film was given to Sebastian.*

1 In Naples, someone sent him a million-dollar bribe. ....

2 In Mombasa, they showed him a photo of Agent 008. ....

3 **Ⓐ - Ⓑ** Rewrite these sentences in the passive form. Use the verb in brackets.

0 'Don't betray us,' they told him. *He was warned not to betray them.* (*warn*).

1 'Be careful,' he advised her. .... (*advise*)

2 'You can't enter the club,' she told them. .... (*allow*)

3 'You should take the test,' she told me. .... (*encourage*)

4 'Don't shoot,' the General told us. .... (*order*)

5 'Please give me the latest gossip,' Jake asked Stella. .... (*ask*)

4 **Ⓐ - Ⓓ** If possible rewrite these sentences using a direct passive equivalent. If not possible, write *X*.

0 Did they give you the letter? *Were you given the letter?*

1 He was lying in bed all day. ....

2 She laid the gun on the bed. ....

3 They appointed her head teacher. ....

4 They drove for five hundred kilometres. ....

5 The chauffeur drove Bob McGive to the island. ....

6 Superman exists. ....

7 The students from Beijing taught us Chinese. ....

8 The mist disappeared at sunrise. ....

9 The aeroplane rose over the city. ....

10 The soldiers headed west. ....

UNIT 99 >> Passive (4) – *It is said that...*

@ | It is rumoured that the Collins family are in trouble. It is believed that Mrs Collins has lost her job. **Pauline is said** to be bored with playing the violin. **Jack is supposed** to be emigrating to Canada but has been forbidden by his doctor to travel...

A *IT IS THOUGHT THAT..., IT HAS BEEN SAID THAT...* ETC.

We often use **It + be + past participle** of verbs like **decide, find, say, state.** For example:
It is said that he is a thief. (= people generally say that he is a thief)
It has been found that this medicine prevents heart disease. (= doctors have found that...)

This structure often occurs in **news reports, academic and scientific discourse**, various kinds of **information**:
It has been reported that the Lomistan army has invaded Jayland. (news report)
It can be argued that unemployment is caused by inflation. (academic argument)
It is rumoured that Shelley is getting another divorce. (gossip)

Verbs which we commonly use with **It + be...** include: *accept   agree   allege*   announce   argue   assert   assume*   believe*   claim*   conclude   decide   demand   discover*   expect   find*   forbid*   imagine   know*   mention   predict   prove*   report*   rumour*   say*   state   suppose*   think*   understand*   write*

We can use some verbs with **There + be...** These include: **allege, believe, suppose, think, understand:**   *There is thought* to be a bomb in the house.
There were alleged to be two criminals hiding there.

B *HE IS FOUND/SAID/REPORTED TO...* ETC.

With many of these verbs above (marked *), there is a parallel personal structure using **to-infinitive: It has been found** that he was ill. or *He has been found to be* ill. (less formal)

We sometimes use **to + be + verb-ing**:
It is said that she is working hard at the moment. or *She is said to be working* hard.

We sometimes use the perfect infinitive (**to have + p.p.**) to show a time gap:
It was thought that the battle had finished. or *The battle was thought* **to have finished.**

C *IT IS FORBIDDEN TO/THAT...* ETC.

We can use some verbs with both of these structures: **that...** or **to + infinitive**:
It was agreed/not allowed/decided/forbidden/not permitted **that we should change** the plan.
Or *It was agreed/not allowed/decided/forbidden/not permitted* **to change** the plan.

D *SUPPOSED TO BE*

Supposed to be has special meanings:

1 Someone has the **duty/permission** to do something:
   He is supposed to look after the money.

2 We may use it to give the **general opinion** about something/someone:
   That hotel is supposed to be very good.

3 In the past tense, it **suggests a failure to do something**:
   She was supposed to bring the water. (but she didn't)

4 In other tenses it may also often have a **negative force**:
   It's supposed to be sunny today. (but it's raining)
   He wasn't supposed to come back today. (but he has)

5 We can use the **negative** to say that something is **forbidden** or not **advisable**.
   You're not supposed to smoke.

1 **Ⓐ** Replace the phrase in brackets using a passive structure with *it*. But there is one item where you cannot use the structure *it is...* . Mark this item *X*.

0 (*You can argue*) It can be argued that high taxes cause people to work less.
1 (*Many experts assert*) .... that violence in films increases criminal activity.
2 (*Some people have claimed*) .... that private cars should be banned.
3 In this essay, (*I will prove*) .... that girls perform better in examinations than boys.
4 (*The public imagine*) .... that all film stars have a luxurious life.
5 (*My brother thinks*) .... that the sun goes round the earth.
6 (*People cannot prove*) .... that alternative medicine is effective.
7 (*Researchers have found*) .... that men are more romantic than women.
8 (*We can conclude*) .... that there are many arguments which will never be settled.

2 **Ⓐ Ⓑ** Here is some gossip. Complete the examples of parallel structures in this table:

passive	passive with *it*	active (*people say…*)
He is said to have three wives.	(0) It is said that he has three wives.	People say that he has three wives.
They are rumoured to be drinking heavily.	(1)	(2) ....
(3)	It is believed that he has never passed an exam.	(4) ....
(5)	(6)	People think that she is mad.
(7)	(8)	People expect that she will murder her husband one day.
(9)	It is known that they are gangsters.	(10) ....
(11)	(12)	People allege that I am spreading gossip.

3 **Ⓒ** Rewrite these sentences using a passive structure with *it* and the verb in brackets with *to*-infinitive.

0 You cannot park here. (*forbid*) It is forbidden to park here.
1 They made a plan to build a new hospital. (*decide*)
....
2 They all said they would change the date of the match. (*agree*)
....

4 **Ⓓ** Write equivalent sentences using *supposed*.

0 He is not allowed to touch the equipment. He is not supposed to touch the equipment.
1 They should have cleaned the car on Sunday. ....
2 Everyone says that it's an excellent film. ....
3 They predicted snow for today. ....
4 It's his duty to cook the dinner. ....
5 Yesterday I forgot that I should help my father. ....
6 I've heard that Paul's restaurant has poor hygiene. ....
7 We aren't permitted on this private beach. ....
8 Where is he? This is his time to guard the camp. ....

UNIT 100 >> Passive (5) – more about passives

 Having been married and divorced four times, I can't stand being cheated by love. I hate being fooled but I love being told that I'm the greatest, most attractive person in the world. After all, to have been loved and to have been left is better than never having been loved at all.

A PASSIVE OF -ING FORM

To express a passive idea, we can use **being + past participle**. For example:

preposition + being + past participle: *He did the work **without being paid.***
*She insisted **on being contacted** as soon as possible.*

verb + being + past participle: *They **liked being driven** by a chauffeur.*
*I **can't stand being scolded.***

as subject of sentence: ***Being arrested** for shoplifting was embarrassing.*

B *HAVING BEEN* + PAST PARTICIPLE

We can use this structure to emphasise the time-gap. For example:

preposition + having been + p.p.: *He went home **without having been paid.***
verb + having been + p.p.: *She **denied having been arrested.***

The most frequent use occurs in this kind of sentence:

***Having been arrested,** he was taken to the police station.* (sequence of events)
***Having been cleaned,** the plums are canned.* (steps in a process)

We can choose between parallel structures:

***Having been identified,** he was fingerprinted.* or ***After he had been identified,** he was...*
***Having been picked,** the plums are loaded.* or ***After they have been picked,** the plums...*

C PASSIVE INFINITIVE

We use both **to be + past participle** and **to have been + past participle.**

*He wants **to be informed** about the plan.* (verb + to-infinitive)
*She was angry not **to have been paid** for the work.* (adjective + to-infinitive)
***To be arrested** by her own son was her worst experience.* (as subject)

D USING *GET* IN PASSIVE STRUCTURES

We can use **get + past participle** of the verb to express a passive idea.

*The window **got broken.***	= *The window **was broken.***
*Did your clothes **get torn**?*	= ***Were** your clothes **torn**?*

We use this structure in informal English, usually when something bad has happened accidentally. We also use it to describe a routine:

*The rooms **get cleaned** once a week.* = *The rooms **are cleaned** once a week.*

Notice: We don't use this structure with state verbs (see Unit 84): **Not** ~~He got liked.~~

E *NEED/REQUIRE/WANT* + VERB-ING

We can use this structure to express a passive idea:

*The room **needs to be cleaned**. = The room **needs cleaning**.* (active verb but passive idea)

1 **Ⓐ Ⓒ Rewrite these sentences using either *being* + past participle or *to be* + past participle. Include the word in brackets.**

0 He insisted that we served him first. He insisted on being served first. *(on)*

1 The car left the garage before it was tested. .... *(without)*

2 She doesn't want them to photograph her. .... *(be)*

3 She enjoys it when people recognise her. .... *(recognised)*

4 I expect that someone will rob me in London at night. .... *(robbed)*

5 They're going to film my sister. .... *(filmed)*

6 It's nice when other people praise you. .... *(to)*

7 My injury was a terrible experience. .... *(being)*

2 **Ⓑ Rewrite these sentences using *having been* + past participle. Then listen and check your answers.**

0 After she was dismissed from her job, Kelly decided to take a holiday to recover.
Having been dismissed from her job, Kelly decided to take a holiday to recover.

1 After someone had robbed her in the street, she couldn't pay her hotel bill.
....

2 They threw her out of the hotel and she slept on the beach.
....

3 Her luggage sank in the middle of the ocean after it was swept away by the tide.
....

4 She was woken by hunger and stole a melon from a market stall.
....

5 She was spotted by the market trader and ran away.
....

6 She was locked in a cell after the police had arrested her.
....

7 After she had been identified by her family, she was able to return home.
....

3 **Ⓒ Complete these sentences using the Passive Perfect infinitive (*to have been* + past participle).**

0 She was grateful to have been rescued. *(rescue)*.

1 He was happy not .... for the mistake. *(punish)*

2 They were sad not .... to the wedding. *(invite)*

4 **Ⓓ Rewrite these sentences using *get* in the appropriate tense.**

0 A wasp stung Peter. Peter got stung by a wasp.

1 The rain soaked us. ....

2 Somebody stole my wallet. ....

3 Nobody cleaned the rooms yesterday. ....

4 They dismissed Kelly from her job. ....

5 Something always injures Tim when he plays football. ....

OPEN EXERCISE

5 **Ⓔ Write ten sentences using *need, require, want* about a dirty, dilapidated neighbourhood.**

For example: The roads need repairing.

UNIT 101 >> *Have something done, get something done*

> I never **have** my meals **served** by a butler. I'**ve** never **had** my appearance **altered** by a top cosmetic surgeon. I'**ve** never **got** my fortune **told** by a top astrologer. But the people who live on Billionaire's Row **have** everything **done** for them.

A FORM: *HAVE* + NOUN + PAST PARTICIPLE

We can use **have** + **noun** + **past participle** of the verb when something is done for us by another person:

	have	noun	past participle	
He	is having	a suit	made.	(= the tailor is making a suit for him)
They	have had	their house	painted.	(= they have paid somebody to paint their house for them)
She	had	her hair	cut.	(= the hairdresser cut her hair for her)
I'm	going to have	a new shower	installed.	(= somebody is going to install a new shower for me)
We	must have	the roof	repaired.	(= we must hire someone to repair the roof for us)

Questions, negatives and short answers are like this:

'**Do** you often **have** your teeth **checked**?'　　　　　　　'Yes, I **do**.'
'**Did** they **have** their car **repaired** after the accident?'　'No, they **didn't**.'
'**Have** they **had** their homework **corrected** yet?'　　　　'Yes, they **have**.'
He **didn't have** his passport **returned** by the police.

Notice: we use **do/does/did** in Present and Past Simple tenses.

B USING *GET* INSTEAD OF *HAVE*

In informal English, we can use **get something done** (instead of **have**) with the same meaning:

I **got** my bike **mended**.　　　　　　　　*Did* you **get** your teeth **checked**?
Will you **get** your hair **cut**?　　　　　　They **didn't get** the computer **fixed**.

C OTHER USES

1 Sometimes, we use this structure with **get** or **have** for something **bad** or **unusual that happens** to us:

He **got** his head **punched** during the fight.
She **had** her work **criticised** by the teacher.

2 We can also use the structure with **have** to make **threats, promises, warnings** etc.

I'll **have** you **arrested**.
We'll soon **have** you **married**.
He'll **have** her **prosecuted** if she shoplifts again.

We use negative structures, especially with **I won't have** and **I'm not having**, to express **angry resistance**:

I **won't have** my son **insulted**.
I'm **not having** my hairstyle **laughed** at.

1 **A** Rewrite the sentences using *have* + *something* + past participle.

0 The oil tycoon goes to the massage parlour for a back massage every morning.
The oil tycoon has his back massaged every morning.

1 Her personal doctor checked the company president's heart last week.

....

2 A Saville Row tailor in London makes the male model's suits.

.... by a Saville Row tailor.

3 The Mafia boss hires assassins to kill his enemies.

....

4 The film director pays a private tutor to educate his daughters at home.

.... by a private tutor.

5 The lottery winner used to pay a maid to iron her underwear.

....

6 A servant polishes the medals of the admiral.

....

7 A Japanese architect is designing a holiday villa for the computer manufacturer.

....

8 Someone shampoos the actress's poodle twice a day.

....

9 Somebody is going to install a new security system for the ambassador.

....

10 A hairdresser dyes the TV presenter's moustache every week.

....

2 **A** Rewrite these questions and negative sentences using *have* + *something* + past participle.

0 Did they repair the roof for you? *Did you have the roof repaired?*
1 Has the teacher checked your homework yet? ....
2 Will the clinic remove the wart on her nose? ....
3 Does someone clean their rooms for them? ....
4 She didn't ask the authorities to change her name. ....
5 Nobody cut his lawn for him last summer. ....
6 Does a secretary type his letters for him? ....
7 Has the dentist taken out her bad tooth yet? ....

3 **B** **C** Rewrite the sentences using *get* + *something* + past participle. Use a negative where necessary.

0 She washes her laundry herself. *She doesn't get her laundry washed.*
1 The baker makes his sandwiches for him. ....
2 Does he employ someone to wash his clothes? ....
3 Did he hire a photographer to take his photo? ....
4 A builder repaired his garage roof for him. ....
5 Sometimes her maid manicures her fingernails. ....
6 Does anyone deliver your newspaper? ....
7 When did anyone test your eyes? ....
8 The cleaner dry-cleaned my wedding suit for me. ....
9 Somebody smashed his car window. ....

REVISION 10 >> First Certificate Practice

1 For questions 1-12, read the text below and decide which answer, A, B, C or D, best fits each gap. There is an example at the beginning (0).

SILK PRODUCTION

Large-scale production of silk (0) A on huge 'farms' of a certain kind of moth. A cocoon of fine threads of silk (1) ..... by the silkworm, which is the grub of this moth. This cocoon is a small tubular structure designed by nature for the grub (2) ..... while it develops.

The cocoons are transferred from the farm to the factory, where, (3) ..... peeled by machines, they (4) ..... in large tanks of warm water in order to (5) ..... the tightly woven silk. In the next step, the threads of silk (6) ..... off by hand-operated machines. This part of the process is known as 'reeling' and can only (7) ..... out by highly experienced staff. Silk production in the factory (8) ..... by the raising of the silkworms themselves on the farm. As soon as the eggs (9) ..... by the female moths, they are stored in incubators. The grubs (10) ..... only on mulberry leaves which are only available at a certain time of the year. Thus, the eggs (11) ..... to promote hatching, so that the silkworms are born at the same time as the leaves become ready (12) ..... picked.

0	Ⓐ	depends	B	is depended	C	has been depended	D	is depend
1	A	is spinning	B	is spinned	C	is spun	D	are spun
2	A	to protect	B	to be protected	C	to be protect	D	to be protecting
3	A	being	B	been	C	having been	D	having
4	A	are floated	B	are float	C	floated	D	have been floated
5	A	be remove	B	be loosened	C	loosen	D	loosening
6	A	are wound	B	are winding	C	have wound	D	has been wound
7	A	carry out	B	be carry out	C	be carrying out	D	be carried out
8	A	is precede	B	is proceeded	C	is preceded	D	had preceded
9	A	are lay	B	are laid	C	has been laid	D	have been layed
10	A	are feed	B	are feeds	C	are fed	D	are being fed
11	A	must be heat	B	must be hot	C	must be heated	D	must to be heated
12	A	to	B	to have been	C	to be	D	to be being

2 For these questions, read the text below and think of the word which best fits the space. Use only *one* word in each space. There is an example at the beginning (0).

THE SILK ROAD

Many of the products which (0) *are* taken for granted in our time (1) .... first discovered or invented by the Chinese. Porcelain, paper, playing cards and fireworks (2) .... all been introduced from China. Silk is a prime example. In 3,000 BC, it is believed, silk had first (3) .... produced in China but it was not until 200 BC that the Silk Road (4) .... established, the 7,000-mile trade route along which silk, spices and other products (5) .... to be brought from Asia to the West. Religion, culture and scientific ideas (6) .... also transmitted along the route as merchants and buyers from East and West communicated. Silk was important not only because fine clothing was (7) .... from it but also for its use in silk painting. Its manufacture remained a secret for centuries; according to legend, silk (8) .... first presented to a Chinese hero by the 'goddess of the silkworm'. However, in about 400 AD, some silkworm eggs (9) .... smuggled out of China by a princess and from that time silkworm farms began to (10) .... established in Central Asia and Europe. Having (11) .... celebrated for centuries as the most important trade route in the world, the Silk Road declined from about 1400 AD onwards. Today, the Internet and the world media can (12) .... regarded as the contemporary equivalents.

PAPER 3 PART 4

3 For questions 1-8, complete the second sentence so that it has a similar meaning to the first sentence, using the word given. Do not change the word given. Use from two to five words including the word given. There is an example (0).

0 Silkworms produce silk.
Silk *is produced by silkworms*. *BY*

1 Silvia is going to employ somebody to repair her house.
Silvia is going .... repaired. *HAVE*

2 After he was expelled from the school, Justin had to find a private teacher.
Having .... the school, Justin had to find a private teacher. *EXPELLED*

3 I don't like other people telling me what to do.
I don't like .... by other people. *TOLD*

4 They were angry because nobody had told them about the change of plan.
They were angry not .... about the change of plan. *HAVE*

5 Sheila taught Justin mathematics while he was away from school.
Justin .... while he was away from school. *BY*

6 Has anyone given you the new password?
Have .... the new password? *BEEN*

7 Most English people consider Shakespeare a great writer.
Shakespeare .... by most English people. *CONSIDERED*

8 Nobody has offered me any food since I arrived at the hotel.
I .... any food since I arrived at the hotel. *HAVEN'T*

OTHER PRACTICE

4 Rewrite these questions and negative sentences using *have* + *something* + past participle.

0 Did they mend your shoes for you? *Did you have your shoes mended?*

1 Are they going to employ someone to clean their swimming pool?
....

2 Nobody has cleaned her windows since last year.
....

3 Is the cosmetic surgeon going to alter the shape of Myra's nose?
....

4 He hadn't employed anyone to cut the lawn until the neighbours complained.
....

5 Does someone check your car for you?
....

6 Once a month, she pays the beautician to remove the hair from her legs.
....

7 The blind girl is going to pay someone to read the daily newspapers to her.
....

UNIT 102 >> Indirect speech: statements – *say* and *tell*

 Stella **tells** Jake all the gossip about the stars. Jake **tells** his editor. 'Stella **said** that Myra Marvellosa was going to have her fifth face-lift. Then she **told** me that Myron Hunkey wears a chest-wig...'

A THE TENSE CHANGE IN INDIRECT SPEECH

When we report what someone said in the past the tense usually goes 'one step' back.

actual words: *She said,*	→ indirect speech: *She said (that)...*
Present Simple *'I often **go** to the cinema.'*	→ Past Simple *she often **went** to the cinema.*
Present Continuous *'I**'m having** a party tomorrow.'*	→ Past Continuous *she **was having** a party the next day.*
Past Simple/Present Perfect *'I **killed** the spy.'* *'I**'ve** never **been** to New York.'*	→ Past Perfect *she **had killed** the spy.* *she **had** never **been** to New York.*
will: *'My friend **will** meet you.'*	→ would: *her friend **would** meet me.*
am/is/are going to: *'He**'s going** to help me.'*	→ was/were going to: *he **was going** to help her.*
can: *'You **can** pass the exam.'*	→ could: *I **could** pass the exam.*
must: *'We **must** be careful.'*	→ had to: *we **had to** be careful.*
may: *'I **may** see you at the party.'*	→ might: *she **might** see me at the party.*

But notice **no tense change** with:
1 Past Perfect
  *'I **had** never **been** to France before.'* → *... had never **been** to France before.*
2 modals — would, could, should, might, ought to
  *'I **might** go to the disco.'* → *... she **might** go to the disco.*
3 used to: *'I **used to** smoke.'* → *... that he **used to** smoke.*

Notice also that it is not necessary to use **that** in indirect speech.

B NO TENSE CHANGE FOR RECENT STATEMENTS

To report something that is generally true or still true now, we keep the present tense:
*'I**'m** seventeen.'* → *She said that she **is** seventeen.* (it is still true now)
*'Paris **is** in France.'* → *He said that Paris **is** in France.* (general fact)

C CHANGE OF PRONOUNS ETC.

Notice that pronouns, possessive adjectives, time expressions and places also sometimes have to change.
*'**You** must **come here tomorrow**.'* → *She said that **I** had to **go there** the **next day**.*
*'**We** went to **your** sister's* → *They said that **they** had gone to **my** sister's*
*party **yesterday**.'* *party the **previous day**.*

Frequently needed changes include: *now* → *then/immediately*   *today* → *on that day*
tomorrow → *the next day/the following day*   *last Tuesday* → *the Tuesday before*
yesterday → *the previous day/the day before*   *this week* → *that week*
here → *there*   *these shops* → *those shops*   *come* → *go*

D SAY AND TELL

Be careful when you use *say* and *tell*:
- **Say never** has a personal direct object (*me, you, him* etc.) but can have a personal indirect object (*to me, to you, to him* etc.): *She **said to** me...*   Not ~~She said me...~~
  We can use *say* with direct speech: *She **said**, 'I'm going to marry Alan.'*
- **Tell always** has a personal direct object: *She **told** me that...*   Not ~~She told to me...~~

1 **A** **C** **D** Jake is talking to his editor. He is reporting these statements by Stella. Use the verb in brackets in the past and change the tenses. Then listen and check your answers.

0 'Phoebe Cute didn't get the starring role in *Teen Beach* as she is too old.' (*say*)
Stella said that Phoebe Cute hadn't got the starring role in 'Teen Beach' as she was too old.

1 'Tom Craze has to wear high-heeled boots in his films so that he can look taller.' (*tell*)
....

2 'Sebastian Ace has invented all the stories about the things he did as a spy.' (*say*)
....

3 'Myron Hunkey was so angry with Myra that he paid me to give her a terrible hairstyle.' (*tell*)
....

4 'Claudette bribes me to reveal what the other fashion models are going to wear.' (*tell*)
....

5 'I looked in Arson Whales' secret diary and saw that he is planning to sack Phoebe Cute.' (*say*)
....

6 'The Metalheads have to hire musicians because they can't play well themselves.' (*say*)
....

7 'Viola Lace, the starlet, wants to know if you (= Jake) will publish her photo in the paper.' (*say*)
....

8 'Sell-U-Lloyd Studios might make a documentary about my hair salon.' (*tell*)
....

9 'The stars are furious that I've told you about their secrets and they want to boycott my salon.' (*say*)
....

2 **A** - **D** Report these statements. Make the tense change only where necessary.

0 'I'm seventeen years old.' She told me this morning that *she is seventeen years old.*

1 'I'm eighty years old.'
He told me many years ago that ....

2 'My brother is a psychiatrist.'
He mentioned today that ....

3 'I often wear a corset.'
Myron whispered to me last month that ....

4 'I hate the director of this film.'
Myron told me ten years ago that ....

5 'Dallas is the main city in my state.'
Hank informed me last month that ....

6 'The police took away my pet leopard.'
Last year, Myra complained that ....

7 'I've always wanted to travel in space.'
He's told me recently that ....

3 **D** Complete these sentences with *say/said* or *tell/told*.

0 She *said* that she wanted to live in Miami.

1 They .... the reporter that they were making a new film.

2 Myra ...., 'I'd like to be cloned.'

3 'No one came to the premiere,' Myron .... us.

4 They .... that the cocktail party would start at 3 a.m.

UNIT 103 >> Indirect speech: orders, requests, advice etc.

@ When I was a child, my parents always **told me to be** brave and strong. They **reminded me to brush** my teeth properly and **to be polite** to visitors. One day they **decided to send me** to a boarding school...

Ⓐ TELL, ASK AND ADVISE

We give **orders** like this:
Teacher to Tom: *'Give me the homework on Monday.'*
General to soldier: *'Don't shoot.'*

We make **requests** like this:
Sally to Ben: *'Please help me carry this bag.'*
Bill to Anna: *'Please don't go to the party without me.'*

We give **advice** to other people like this:
Sally to Ben: *'You should go to the Fitness Centre.'*
Max to Tim: *'You'd better not borrow any more money.'*

We can report orders, requests, and advice by using: **tell, ask, advise + personal object pronoun** (*me, you, him* etc.) or **name + to + infinitive**:

	subject	reporting verb	object pronoun/name	to + infinitive
order	*She*	*told*	*Tom*	*to give her the homework on Monday.*
	Gen.	*Green*	*told*	*the soldier not to shoot.*
request	*Sally*	*asked*	*Ben*	*to help her carry the bag.*
	Bill	*asked*	*Anna*	*not to go to the party without him.*
advice	*Sally*	*advised*	*Ben*	*to go to the Fitness Centre.*
	Max	*advised*	*Tim*	*not to borrow any more money.*

Ⓑ OTHER VERBS

There are also a lot of other verbs which we can use to report orders, requests, and advice etc. using the same structure: **forbid, order, persuade, remind, warn**:

You mustn't smoke. → *They **forbade** her **to smoke**.*
Don't go out. → *He **warned** me **not to go** out.*

Ⓒ OTHER STRUCTURES AND VERBS

We can use other structures to report speech:

1 **Verb + to + infinitive**: reporting verbs include **agree, decide, decline, offer, promise, refuse**.
   'Can I help you?' → *He **offered to help** me.*
   'We won't be late.' → *They **promised not to be** late.*
   'I won't give you the key.' → *She **refused to give** them the key.*

2 **Verb + preposition + verb-ing**:
   'I'm sorry for breaking the rules.' → *He **apologised for breaking** the rules.*

3 **Verb + verb-ing**:
   'Let's go by plane.' → *I **suggested going** by plane.*
   'I didn't steal the money.' → *He **denied stealing** the money.*

4 **Verb + that + subject + verb** (remember the tense change):
   'We'll help you.' → *They **promised (that) they would help** her.*
   'Our room is dirty.' → *They **complained (that) their room was** dirty.*
   But it is possible not to change the tense if the idea is relevant now:
   *They complained that their room **is** dirty.*
   (The room is still dirty at the time of reporting the complaint.)

5 **Verb + preposition + noun**: *'OK, we agree'.* → *They **agreed with the plan**.*

1 Ⓐ Ⓑ Read the story. Then complete 1–18, using indirect speech. Use the verbs in brackets in the appropriate form, as in the example.

REVENGE!

I said, 'Please don't send me to a boarding school,' but they laughed, 'Don't be stupid.'

At the school, the other children told me, 'Be careful. Don't disobey the teachers.'

But when the sports mistress said, 'Run around the school field in the rain for an hour,' I answered, 'No!'

'Well, you must report to the headmaster for punishment,' she said.

He told me, 'You aren't allowed to leave your room for two weeks.'
And he told the cook, 'Give him only dry bread and water.'
He wrote to my parents: 'Don't send him any pocket money.'

I asked them, 'Please take me home immediately.' But they replied, 'No, we won't.' Instead, they said, 'Be brave and strong.' They added, 'You must stay at the school during the holidays.' They asked the headmaster, 'Make him do lots of work.'

Now, I am an adult and my parents are in a home for old people. They hate it. The nurses say: 'You mustn't have alcohol or chocolate.' The matron says: 'You mustn't watch TV after 6 p.m. You have to go to bed at 8 p.m. And don't forget to brush your teeth properly.' The nurses say: 'Be polite to visitors.' When I see them, they say, 'Please let us live with you.' I say, 'Be brave and strong!'

---

0 I asked my parents not to send me to a boarding school. (*ask*)

1 They .... to me. (*refuse/listen*)

2 The other children .... the teachers. (*warn/disobey*)

3 When the sports mistress .... for an hour,
I .... it. (*order/refuse/do*)

4 She .... for punishment. (*order*)

5 He .... for two weeks. (*forbid*)

6 He .... and water. (*order*)

7 He .... any pocket money. (*ask*)

8 I tried to .... immediately. (*persuade*)

9 But they .... to me. (*refuse/listen*)

10 They .... strong. (*advise*)

11 They .... holidays. (*tell*)

12 They .... lots of work. (*encourage*)

13 Now the nurses .... or chocolate. (*forbid*)

14 The matron .... 6 p.m. (*order*)

15 She .... at 8 p.m. (*tell*)

16 She .... properly. (*remind*)

17 They .... with me. (*ask*)

18 I ....! (*advise*)

2 **A** - **C** Report these words. Use the past tense of the verbs in brackets. Make tense changes where necessary.

0 Susan to Dan: 'Could you lend me £10, please.' (*ask*)
Susan asked Dan to lend her £10.

1 Dania: 'I really want to play in the school concert.' (*insist on*)

....

2 Myra to Arson Whales: 'I'm sorry that I forgot my lines.' (*apologise for*)

....

3 Captain Kork to the aliens: 'Don't touch me with your tentacles.' (*order*)

....

4 Brigitte to Nick: 'I won't forget to send the cheque to the tax office.' (*promise that*)

....

5 Jake to Stella: 'You haven't given me much gossip.' (*complain that*)

....

6 Madam Magistar to Phil: 'Yes, you should marry Julie.' (*advise*)

....

7 Dania to Nadia: 'OK, your idea is the best one.' (*agree with*)

....

8 Manager of the Alpville Hotel to the guests: 'I'll give you free skiing lessons.' (*offer*)

....

9 Tom Craze to agent: 'I'm not going to be a monkey in *Galaxy of the Monkeys*.' (*refuse*)

....

10 Myra to Stella: 'You mustn't sell my beauty secrets to the media.' (*forbid*)

....

11 Silvio to his wife: 'Please steal a Vermeer from the museum so I can copy it.' (*persuade*)

....

3 **A** - **C** Look at this phone conversation. Then complete sentences 1-12 in indirect speech. They are not in the same order as the parts in the conversation. Use the tense change where necessary.

Anna: You haven't phoned me for six hours.
Fred: I'm sorry, I've been revising for my exams.
Anna: I see. Well, can I come over and help you?
Fred: No thanks. I want to revise with Wendy. She knows a lot.
Anna: That's why you haven't phoned. It's because you want to be with Wendy!
Fred: Don't be ridiculous. I'm not in love with her.
Anna: Well, I'm going to tell her to leave you alone.
Fred: No, you mustn't say anything to her.
Anna: OK, but please will you ring me more often. Say that you will.
Fred: Yes, OK. I'm sorry that I've neglected you. Please forgive me!
Anna: That's all right. Everything will be different in the future.
Fred: Yes, it will. I'll call you every night before I go to sleep.

0 Fred apologised *for neglecting her.*
1 Anna threatened ....
2 Anna offered ....
3 Fred denied ....
4 Fred promised ....
5 Anna complained ....
6 Fred forbade ....
7 Anna accused ....
8 Fred explained ....
9 Anna persuaded ....
10 Anna expected ....
11 Fred insisted ....
12 Fred begged ....

4 **Ⓐ** - **Ⓒ** Put words from the list in the gaps. Use a suitable form. Add any necessary words.

advise apologise ask complain insist order promise warn
enter insult lead load paint send surrender travel

0 Her teachers *advised* Nadia *to enter* the World Chess Tournament.
1 Nick .... that Brigitte had been .... important clients.
2 Captain Kork .... on .... the expedition to Mercury.
3 Silvio .... not to .... any more fake Picassos.
4 Ben .... Cambridge University .... him his results as soon as possible.
5 The Galactic Admiral .... Captain Kork not .... to the aliens.
6 Madam Magistar .... Julie not .... on flight 409.
7 Michelle .... to Harry for not .... the gun.

OPEN EXERCISE

5 **Ⓐ** - **Ⓒ** Write a report of a conversation between two or more people, using verbs and structures from this unit and the previous one. Base your report around one of these situations.

1 A business meeting where the managers are deciding how to increase profits.
2 A teacher and students discussing exam results.
3 A football team and their manager discussing a defeat.
4 Friends at a disco discussing the other people at the disco.
5 Someone trying to persuade his/her rich aunt to lend money.

Write between 80 and 150 words. Write your report here. Continue on another sheet if necessary.

....
....
....
....
....
....
....
....

UNIT 104 >> Indirect speech: questions

 The police asked Tony **why** he **kept** stealing things. They wanted to know **where** he **hid** the stuff and **whether** anybody else **helped** him. All he wanted to know was **how long** he **would spend** in prison.

A FORM

Notice two important things about indirect questions:

1 The tense changes are the same as in indirect statements.
   But if the question is still relevant to the present time (now), we can choose to use the present tense in the indirect question:

   '**Are** you John Smith?'   →   He asked if my name **is** (or **was**) John Smith.
   'How much **does** it **cost**?'   →   They asked how much it **costs**. (or **cost**).

2 In indirect questions, we do not use the question form of the verb and there is no question mark (?) at the end. In other words, the subject comes before a verb as in a statement.

   We say: *She asked if I was happy.*   **Not** ~~She asked was I happy?~~
            He asked if I liked English.   **Not** ~~He asked did I like English?~~
            She asked what the time was.   **Not** ~~She asked what was the time?~~

   Notice that we use the same structure in polite requests. But we need a question mark (?) because these are real questions:

   Could you tell me where the bank is?   *Have you any idea when the train leaves?*

B REPORTING *WH*-QUESTIONS USING *ASK*

Here are some questions which use question words (*When, Where, Who, Why, How many* etc.) We can report them by using **ask + the question word**:

actual words	indirect question
'**What's** the time?'	She asked (me) **what** the time **was**.
'**Where do** you **live**?'	He asked (us) **where** we **lived**.
'**Why did** you **come** to England?'	They asked (us) **why** we **had come** to England.
'**How many** children **have** you **got**?'	She asked (us) **how many** children we **had**.
'**Who cooked** dinner?'	They asked (him) **who had cooked** dinner.

C REPORTING *YES/NO* QUESTIONS USING *ASK + IF/WHETHER*

We can report **Yes/No** questions by using **ask if** or **ask whether**:

'Are you happy?'   →   She **asked if** I was happy.
'Will you go home at Christmas?'   →   We **asked if** they would go home at Christmas.
'Do you like English?'   →   He **asked whether** I liked English.
'Did you go to the party?'   →   I **asked whether** she had gone to the party.

We can also use an object after **ask**: *ask **someone** if...*: She **asked Jack** if he was married.

Short answers to **yes/no** questions can be reported in various ways. For example:

'Did you steal the money?'   'Yes, I did.' → He **admitted** that he **had stolen** the money.
or *When she asked him **if** he **had stolen** the money, he **admitted** that **he had**.*
'Can you help me?'   'Yes, I can.' → She **asked** him **if** he **could** help her and she **agreed**.

D OTHER REPORTING VERBS

We can use other verbs than **ask** to introduce indirect questions:
*He **wanted to know** what time the train left.   I **wondered** if you were ill.*

1 **Ⓐ-Ⓒ** Change the direct to indirect questions. Use *asked*. Use the tense change. Then listen and check your answers.

> 0 Judge: 'Have you got anything to say?'
> 1 Researcher: 'When did you start stealing?'
> 2 Journalist: 'How many times have you robbed someone in the street?'
> 3 Detective: 'Where do you sell the things which you steal?'
> 4 Psychologist: 'Have you been influenced by films about criminals?'
> 5 Friend: 'Are you afraid of going to prison?'
> 6 Girlfriend: 'Why didn't you steal a diamond ring for me?'
> 7 Priest: 'Do you feel guilty about robbing people?'
> 8 Teacher: 'Why didn't you concentrate on getting good qualifications?'
> 9 Father: 'Do you promise not to steal anything again?'
> 10 Lawyer: 'Can you prove that you're innocent?'
> 11 Prosecutor: 'Do you confess to these crimes?'
> 12 Tony: 'When are you all going to stop asking me questions?'

0 *The judge asked if he had got anything to say.*
1 ....
2 ....
3 ....
4 ....
5 ....
6 ....
7 ....
8 ....
9 ....
10 ....
11 ....
12 ....

2 **Ⓐ-Ⓒ** These are recent questions, so do not use the tense change.

0 'Are you sorry for your crimes?' *They asked Tony if he is sorry for his crimes.*
1 'How long have you been a thief?' He asked Tony ....
2 'Is it easy to shop-lift?' She asked ....
3 'How did the police catch you?' He asked him ....
4 'Where are you staying at the moment?' I asked him ....
5 'Will you continue stealing?' They asked me ....

3 **Ⓐ-Ⓓ** Circle all the correct answers.

0 They asked if I (wanted)/did I want/do you want to see the film.
1 He asked me what was the time./the time was?/the time was.
2 She asked me would I/if I would/whether I would marry her.
3 They asked what I was writing?/I was writing./was I writing?
4 He asked where I had found/did I find/I find the treasure.
5 She asked me who was my friend?/was your friend?/my friend was.
6 He asked how tall I was/tall were you?/tall are you?
7 They asked, 'How are you?'/They asked how I was./They asked how I am?

UNIT 105 >> *Suggest, insist, request* etc. + *that* + subjunctive or *should*

> **@** Tony is a teenage thief. The psychiatrist **recommended that he go** for a course of psycho-analysis. The police **suggested that he stay** in prison. Tony's solicitor **demanded that he be released**.

Ⓐ THE SUBJUNCTIVE: *I/YOU/HE/SHE/IT/WE/YOU/THEY GO*

We rarely use the subjunctive form of verbs except in formal English; Americans use it more than the British. The subjunctive consists of the basic verb with no added ending. For example, **he go** is the subjunctive form in the present and past of **go**.

Remember: the subjunctive form is the same for all tenses — past, present and future.

Ⓑ *DEMAND, INSIST, RECOMMEND, REQUEST, SUGGEST, BE NECESSARY, BE OBLIGATORY* ETC.

In formal English we sometimes (although not always) follow these verbs and similar expressions with **that + subject + (not) + subjunctive verb**. For example:

She **recommended that he see** an analyst.   They **suggest that she not trust** him.

In less formal English, we use the normal verb tenses:

She recommended that he **saw** an analyst.   They suggest that she **doesn't trust** him.

We use the subjunctive when we are recommending/suggesting/insisting on a possible action:

*He is **suggesting that she lie**.* (= he thinks that her best strategy is to lie — possible action)
*She **insisted that I sell** my car.*   *It **is necessary that he see** a doctor.*
*The **best plan is that he meet** her at the office.*   *It's **best that they hide** in the old farm.*

We do not use it for a fact: *She **insisted that he is** mad.* (she regards it as a fact)
*He is **suggesting that she lied**.* (= he is suggesting that in the past she actually lied — fact)

Ⓒ PASSIVE SUBJUNCTIVE: *(NOT) BE + PAST PARTICIPLE*

We can use the passive form: *He demanded that he **not be imprisoned**.*
*They insisted that the evidence **be produced**.*   *It was necessary that the judge **be informed**.*

Ⓓ OTHER STRUCTURES

We often use **demand, insist, recommend** etc.:

1 with **that + subject + should**: *He **suggested that I should** stay at the Alpville Hotel.*
   *The manufacturers **recommend that this glue should** be used with caution.*

2 with the **infinitive** or **verb-ing**:

+ to + verb	+ object + to + verb	+ verb-ing	+ preposition + verb-ing
It was necessary (for him) to go...	*I recommended him to go...*	*I suggested going...* *I recommended going...*	*I insisted on going...* *I insisted on his going...*

Notice: we do not use **suggest + to do**: ~~He suggested (her) to go to the cinema~~.

Ⓔ OTHER EXPRESSIONS WITH *(THAT) + SUBJECT + SHOULD*

We often use this structure after expressions expressing an emotional reaction to a fact:
*It's **a pity she should** be ill.*   *She's **happy that he should** want to stay.*

Ⓕ OTHER USES OF THE SUBJUNCTIVE

We also use the subjunctive in certain idiomatic phrases. These include:
God bless you!   *God save the queen.*   *Be that as it may...*
Come what may...   *Long live...*   *Heaven forbid!*   *Then so be it.*

1 **Ⓐ Ⓑ** Rewrite these sentences using the verb in brackets in the past + *that* + subjunctive form of the verb. Then listen and check your answers.

0 The priest: 'Let Tony have a private interview with me.'
  The priest requested that Tony have a private interview with him. (*request*)

1 Tony's girlfriend: 'He must stop thieving and marry me.'
  .... (*insist*)

2 Tony's mother: 'I want the police to give him another chance.'
  .... (*suggest*)

3 Tony's victims: 'We want him to go to prison for a long time.'
  .... (*demand*)

4 Tony's teacher: 'I think he should learn a skill and become an apprentice.'
  .... (*recommend*)

5 The judgement: 'Tony has to give everything back to the victims.'
  .... (*be obligatory*)

2 **Ⓑ** Make sentences using the word in brackets + *that* + subjunctive.

0 We have to protect the forest. *It's necessary that we protect the forest.* (*necessary*)
1 She has to sign the form. .... (*obligatory*)
2 He ought to sell his car. .... (*best*)
3 He has to report to the police. .... (*necessary*)
4 She has to stay in hospital. .... (*necessary*)

3 **Ⓒ** Use the passive form of the subjunctive to rewrite these sentences.

0 The prosecutor: 'We must punish him.'
  The prosecutor demanded that he be punished. (*demand*)
1 The jury: 'You should fine him.' .... (*recommend*)
2 The defence counsel: 'You mustn't punish him.' .... (*insist*)
3 His father: 'We must pardon him.' .... (*request*)

4 **Ⓓ** Make sentences with *should*. Use verbs in the past from the list.

be   demand   insist   recommend   request   2 x suggest

0 'Let's go on holiday to Cyprus.' He *suggested that* they *should go on holiday to Cyprus.*
1 'Show me your passports. Now!' The officer .... we ....
2 'You must stay for dinner with us.' Her hosts .... she ....
3 'Please show me your passport.' He .... she ....
4 'Why don't we visit the museum?' She .... they ....
5 'This is a good restaurant. Let's eat here.' She .... they ....
6 'We have to show our passports when we leave.' It .... we ....

5 **Ⓐ - Ⓕ** Circle all the correct alternatives.

0 He suggested to go/(going)/(that they go) to see the film.
1 They recommended us to see/to see/that he see the film.
2 I demanded him to show/that he show/him that he show his visa.
3 The crowd shouted, 'Long live/God bless/Long lives the princess!'
4 It is essential that the house be/are/should be kept warm.
5 It is a pity that Charles should lose/loses his job.
6 I feel very sorry that you should still be/would still be angry with me.

REVISION 11 >> First Certificate Practice

1 For questions 1-12, read the text below and decide which answer, A, B, C or D, best fits each gap. There is an example at the beginning (0).

AGEING

At a conference in 1995 on ageing, the audience asked a panel of experts (0) A they thought that it was possible to extend the lifespan of human beings through science. A medical professor replied that he (1) ..... in doubling the lifespan of certain creatures such as mice in his laboratory. A philosopher interrupted him to ask why anyone wanted to live for 150 years. She pointed out that, for most people, life (2) ..... boring enough! The professor requested her not to be frivolous. He revealed that his team (3) ..... they would soon develop an anti-ageing medicine. An alternative health specialist suggested (4) ..... the key to living longer. A member of the audience asked her how (5) ..... plan his food intake to maximise his chances of a healthy life. The specialist (6) ..... eat lots of vegetables and fresh fruit and limit his calorie intake. However, the physiologist (7) ..... . He claimed that regular exercise was the best way to prolong life. Another audience member asked why (8) ..... longer on average in some areas of the world. She asked, '(9) ..... their diet or their unpolluted environment?' The experts agreed that nobody really (10) ..... . Finally, all the experts concluded that at that time (11) ..... difficult to be certain about the causes of ageing. This conference took place a long time ago and the experts now say that there (12) ..... new theories about ageing and how to prevent it.

0	(A) if	B	what	C	however	D	–
1	A succeeded	B	had succeeded	C	was succeeding	D	succeeds
2	A was	B	were	C	had been	D	has been
3	A believes	B	believe	C	were believing	D	believed
4	A was it diet	B	diet be	C	diet being	D	that diet was
5	A should he	B	he should	C	does he	D	he
6	A said him to	B	told him that he	C	told him to	D	told that he should
7	A disagreed	B	unagreed	C	does not agree	D	not agreed
8	A did people live	B	do people live	C	people lived	D	lived people
9	A Was it	B	It is	C	Is it	D	If it was
10	A knows	B	knew	C	is knowing	D	was knowing
11	A it was	B	it is	C	was it	D	is it
12	A were	B	is	C	are	D	be

2 For questions 1-12, read the text below and think of the word which best fits the gap. Use only *one* word in each gap. There is an example at the beginning (0).

BEAUTY

People sometimes ask (0) *how* important beauty is. Current research shows that it (1) .... very important indeed, especially for women. For example, researchers reported that even babies (2) .... longer at people with beautiful faces than at those with less beautiful ones in experiments conducted last year. In another experiment, people were shown two photographs of similar men with different women and asked (3) .... man was most successful. The subjects always replied that the man with the most beautiful woman companion (4) .... probably the most successful. Of course it is important to ask (5) .... we mean by 'beauty'. In fact, all cultures are reported (6) .... have very similar ideas about beauty. People of all countries said that photos of women with round faces, clear skin, youthful looks (7) .... the most beautiful. When they were asked to rank photos in order of beauty, all chose women with large eyes and child-like features. The research also indicated that the proportions of the face (8) .... important. However, researchers also asked (9) .... the beautiful women in the photos were intelligent. The majority answered that they (10) .... not as intelligent as the less beautiful women. The researchers finally asked twelve 'beautiful' women (11) .... happy they felt with their looks. The women, who included successful models and actresses, all replied that they (12) .... change their appearance if they could.

PAPER 3 PART 4

3 For questions 1-8, complete the second sentence so that it has a similar meaning to the first sentence, using the word given. Do not change the word given. Use from two to five words including the word given. There is an example (0).

0 'How are you?' she asked me. She asked *me how I* was.   *ME*

1 'I don't agree with you,' she said when he said that Tom was a liar.
   She .... when he said that Tom was a liar. *HIM*

2 'Where have you been working since September?' Sheila asked Frank.
   Sheila asked Frank .... since September. *HAD*

3 'Are you Aries or Taurus, Helen?' asked the astrologer.
   The astrologer asked Helen .... Taurus. *WAS*

4 'What will you do tomorrow?' they asked me.
   They asked me what .... day. *NEXT*

5 'Don't touch my things!' she told Hugh.
   She told Hugh .... things. *TOUCH*

6 Daniel apologised for drinking too much at the party.
   'I .... too much at the party,' said Daniel. *THAT*

7 'You oughtn't to see Anna again,' Fred advised Max.
   Max was advised by Fred .... again. *TO*

8 Her boss told her, 'You mustn't smoke in the office.'
   Her boss .... in the office. *HER*

OTHER PRACTICE

4 Complete the second sentences using *that* + subjunctive form of the verb.

0 'Please, park your car somewhere else,' Tim asked George.
   Tim requested *George that he park his car somewhere else.*

1 The general said: 'They must return the land.'
   The general demanded .... (use: passive subjunctive)

2 'Sally should try that restaurant,' said Charlotte.
   Charlotte recommended ....

3 'Penny must attend all her classes,' said Mr Frith.
   Mr Frith said that it was essential ....

4 'You really must visit me next Saturday,' Rachel told Rebecca.
   Rachel insisted ....

5 'We must sell the old car,' said Nigel.
   Nigel insisted .... (use: passive subjunctive)

6 Martin said, 'Everyone must bring his or her identity card to the meeting.'
   Martin said it was obligatory ....

7 Martina asked, 'Please, send every student an e-mail about the meeting.'
   Martina requested .... (use: passive subjunctive)

UNIT 106 >> Zero and first conditionals

> **If** it **rains**, there **are** floods. **If** it **snows**, the roads **are** blocked. **If** it **freezes**, we **can't start** the car. But **if** it **rains**, **snows** and **freezes** tomorrow, I'**ll be** happy. I **won't have** to go and visit Aunt Maud.

Ⓐ THE ZERO CONDITIONAL

When we are thinking about **facts** which are **generally true** we use:

If + Present Simple, Present Simple:
*If you **lie** in the sun too long, you **get** sunburnt.* (always true)
*If I **drink** coffee late at night, I **can't sleep.***

We can reverse the order: **Present Simple + if + Present Simple:**
*I **get** a headache if somebody **starts** smoking.* (no comma is now necessary)

Ⓑ THE FIRST CONDITIONAL

When we are thinking about a **possible situation in the future** we use:

If + present verb*, future verb (* or a modal, especially **can**):
We often use it for **possible plans, warnings, promises, threats** or **for persuading someone:**
*If I **go** to London this weekend, I'**ll go** shopping in Oxford Street.* (intention/plan)
*If you **drive** like that, you'**ll have** an accident.* (warning)
*If he **can find** the time, he'**ll help** you.* (promise)
*If you **lend** me some money, I'**ll mend** your car for you.* (persuasion)

We also find **if + present perfect verb:**
*If you **haven't finished** by Saturday, I **won't pay** you.* (threat).

We can reverse the order: **future verb + if + present verb** (no comma is now necessary):
*What **will** you **do** if it **rains** during the picnic?*

Ⓒ OTHER TENSE COMBINATIONS — *IF* + IMPERATIVE/+ FUTURE/+ CONTINUOUS TENSES

1 Sometimes, we use: **If + present verb, imperative:**
   *If you **see** Anna, please **give** her my love.*
   *If you **go** abroad, **don't forget** to take your passport.*

2 In polite requests, we may use **if + will** or **would:**
   *If you'**ll wait** for me, I'**ll go** and fetch my umbrella.* (= Please wait for me while I fetch...)
   *If you **would wait** for me, I'**ll** ...* (very polite form)

3 We sometimes use **if + Present Continuous/Present Perfect Continuous:**
   *If you'**re going** to Brazil in February, you'**ll see** the Carnival.*
   *If you'**ve been watching** the news, you **must know** about the accident.*
   *If he'**s been studying**, he'**ll be able** to answer the questions.*

Ⓓ *UNLESS*

We can use **unless** to mean **except if.**

We can often use **unless + a positive verb** instead of **if + negative verb:**
*You won't pass the exam **if** you **don't study** hard.*
*= You won't pass the exam **unless** (= except if...) you **study** hard.*

Remember: we cannot use a future verb to follow **if** or **unless:**
*If we **see** John, we'll give him the letter.*   **Not** ~~If we will see John, we'll give him the letter~~.

1 Ⓐ Complete the zero conditionals in the text about Aunt Maud.

The weather has a big influence on Aunt Maud's moods. In very hot weather, she always feels sleepy. If (0 *be cold/sit*) it's cold, she sits by the fire. If (1 *be wet/get*) .... rheumatism. If (2 *be foggy/feel*) .... depressed. If (3 *be fine/not expect*) .... it to last. If (4 *be dull/watch*) .... TV all day. If (5 *be stormy/shout*) .... at her servants. But if (6 *be windy/fly*) .... a kite on the hill. It's her favourite hobby. She (7 *get angry/laugh at*) .... if anyone .... her. She says that even ninety-year-olds (8 *deserve/be*) .... to have fun if they .... fit enough. She (9 *not stop/break*) .... unless her kite-string ....

2 Ⓑ Write first conditional sentences for these situations.

0   I'll probably study hard and then I'll pass my exams.
    If I study hard, I'll pass my exams.
1   I hope to get good grades so I can go to university next year.
    ....
2   I hope to do well in my degree, then work in the civil service.
    ....
3   But I might not pass my exams; then I'll go back-packing.
    ....
4   I might travel around the world and then meet lots of people.
    ....
5   I might meet a beautiful foreign girl and get married to her.
    ....
6   But I might not meet anyone, so I'll come home.
    ....
7   I won't have a degree, but I'll work in a shop.
    ....
8   I might not earn a lot, and no one will marry me.
    ....

3 Ⓓ Rewrite these sentences as *unless*-sentences. Do not change the meaning.

0   The flowers will die if you don't give them fresh water.
    The flowers will die unless you give them fresh water.
1   If you haven't got a car, you can't reach the village.
    ....
2   People won't support a team if it is losing.
    ....
3   She'll like you only if you don't forget her birthday.
    ....
4   The police will arrest Tony; but not if he escapes to Brazil.
    ....
5   You can't sell a new product without organising a big advertising campaign.
    ....
6   She needs to start training soon or she'll lose the race.
    ....
7   The crops will die if it doesn't rain until July.
    .... before July.

Zero and first conditionals

UNIT 107 >> Second conditional

> 'If I **looked** like you, I'**d change** my hairstyle, **buy** a new set of clothes and **burn** the old ones. If I **had** your figure, I'**d go** on a diet and **make** an appointment to see a cosmetic surgeon...'
>
> 'If I **were** you, I'**d shut** up.'

Ⓐ THE SECOND CONDITIONAL

When we are thinking about a situation in the present or future which is **hypothetical**, **unlikely** or **unreal**, we use: If + **past verb**, **would** + **verb** (= conditional verb)

*If I **won** the lottery* (unlikely), *I **would buy** a private aeroplane.*
*If your car **broke** down, where **would** you **go** for help?*
*If you **were working** harder, you'd **be** more successful.*

We use a past verb but we are thinking about the present or future.
Sally writes books but not many people buy them. I say:
*If Sally **wrote** a best-selling book, she **would be** famous.* (**unlikely** in the present or future)

Tim and Sue like travelling but they are poor. I say:
*If Tim and Sue **were** rich, they'd **travel** round the world.*
(they are not rich — we are imagining an **unreal** situation in the present)

We can reverse the order: **conditional verb** + **if** + **past verb** (no comma is necessary)
*They **would be** rich **if** they **sold** their house.*

We sometimes use the continuous form of the conditional verb:
*I'd **be dancing** with Bella at the disco if I didn't have flu.*

Ⓑ COULD AND MIGHT

We can use **could/might** in second conditional sentences:
*If I **didn't pass** the exam, I **couldn't go** to university.* (I expect to pass)
*It **might** rain **if** the wind **changed**.* (I expect the wind not to change)

Ⓒ IF I WERE ETC.

If I/he/she/it were... is grammatically correct in second conditional sentences.
*If she **were** rich, she'd stop working.*

But in informal English, people often use **was**:   *If she **was** rich, she'd stop...*

We use **If I were you...** to give advice. We also say   **If she were me, ... If I were him*, ...** etc.:
*If I **were you**, I wouldn't buy that pullover.*   *If I **were you**, I'd study harder.*

* in strictly grammatically correct English, we'd say **If I were he, ...** but this is hardly ever used.

Ⓓ UNLESS

We can also use **unless** in second conditional sentences:
*I **wouldn't do** it **unless** I **wanted** to.*
*He **wouldn't go unless** they **invited** him.*

1 **Ⓐ**-**Ⓒ** Write second conditional sentences with *if* about these situations.

0 Dania wants to be as talented as Nadia. She wants to represent her country in the Olympics.
If Dania were as talented as Nadia, she'd represent her country in the Olympics.

1 Myra doesn't think she'll win another Oscar. So she won't throw another celebration party.
....

2 It's difficult to rob the Bank of England but Harry wants money to buy Michelle a diamond.
....

3 Professor Makepeace wants to win three Nobel Prizes and be the most famous inventor in history. ....

4 Lia wants to make her father happy by finding the formula to make gold from lead.
....

5 Tony needs to solve his psychological problems so that he can give up being a thief.
....

6 Brigitte always phones her boyfriend for hours each day. Nick is not happy.
....

7 Kate is still on the island and doesn't plan to leave it. She doesn't want to miss the people.
....

8 Julie is pregnant. She almost certainly won't have twins. So she won't need to choose two names. ....

9 A witness may contact the police so they can solve Lady Alice's murder. But perhaps no one saw it. ....

10 The Collins family might win the lottery. They need money to move to a larger house.
....

2 **Ⓒ** Write sentences with *If I were you…*, *If she were me…* etc.

0 You ought to change your hairstyle. *If I were you, I'd change your hairstyle.*

1 She thinks I don't wear bright clothes often enough. .... more often.

2 The President ought to change the law in my opinion. ....

3 He thinks I ought to apply for a job as a dancer. ....

4 I think Kevin doesn't train hard enough. .... harder.

5 I think that film stars ought to be more modest. .... a film star, ...

6 I think she ought to wear a different lipstick. ....

7 I think he should criticise other people less. ....

3 **Ⓓ** Complete these sentences about situations in exercise 1.

0 Kate *wouldn't leave* the island unless it *were* absolutely necessary.

1 Julie .... to choose two names unless she .... twins.

2 Myra .... a celebration party unless she .... another Oscar.

OPEN EXERCISE

4 **Ⓐ**-**Ⓒ** Make appropriate second conditional sentences.

0 No exams = happier students *If there were no exams, students would be happier.*

1 Destruction of the rainforests = climate ....

2 Landing of aliens = panic all over the world ....

3 Cheaper public transport = less traffic ....

4 One world language = better communication ....

5 Live for 150 years = more bored ....

UNIT **108** >> First or second conditional?

 Bob McGive: 'If I **have** some spare money, I'**ll buy** a villa on a Mediterranean island.'
Slim Skinty: 'If I **had** some money, I'**d buy** a second-hand coat.'

Ⓐ *LIKELY/UNLIKELY*

We use the **first conditional** when we think something is **possible**:
*Bob McGive is thinking: If I **have** some spare money, I'**ll buy** a villa.* (he thinks it is possible)

We use the **second conditional** when we think something is **unlikely** or **impossible**:
*Slim is dreaming: If I **had** some money, I'**d buy** a coat.* (he is only dreaming)

Ⓑ COMPARING FIRST AND SECOND CONDITIONALS

Look at these examples:
I think my friend may arrive early tomorrow, so I say:
'*If he **comes** early, we'**ll watch** TV.*' (possible — first conditional)
I think my friend will probably be late tomorrow, so I say:
'*If he **came** early, we'**d watch** TV.*' (unlikely — second conditional)

First conditional	*If England **win** the match with Germany, they'**ll be** in the Cup Final.* (I expect England to win.)
Second conditional	*If England **won** the match, they'**d be** in the Cup Final.* (I think it is possible but not likely that England will win.)
First conditional	*I **will go** on holiday with Chris **if** he **asks** me.* (I expect him to ask me. It is probable.)
Second conditional	*I **would go** on holiday with Chris **if** he **asked** me.* (It is possible but not likely. It is like a daydream.)
First conditional	*He'**ll lose** his job **if** he **keeps** on arriving late.* (He is often late.)
Second conditional	*He **would lose** his job **if** he **kept** on arriving late.* (But he is usually punctual.)

1 **A B** Read about Stella, the hair stylist, and Jake, the tabloid reporter. For each item 1-5, complete one second conditional and one first conditional sentence.

0 Stella hasn't got any gossip to give to Jake. She is thinking:
   a If I had some gossip, the paper would pay me for it. *(have/pay)*
   b If I hear anything tomorrow, I will tell Jake. *(hear/tell)*

1 Bernice, the TV chat-show hostess, often comes to Stella's hair salon. She thinks:
   a If I .... a scandal, Stella .... it. *(invent/believe)*
   b If Stella .... Jake, she .... a spy for his paper. *(not love/not be)*

2 Bernice tells Stella that Phoebe Cute is flying to a secret rendezvous with Tom Craze.
   a Bernice says, 'If Phoebe .... that I'd told you, she .... me.' *(know/kill)*
   b Stella says, 'If anyone .... me about the story, I .... a word.' *(ask/not say)*

3 But Stella was lying; she tells Jake the story. He says:
   a 'If my editor .... the story, he .... it on the front page.' *(like/print)*
   b 'Thank you, Stella. If I .... this story, the editor .... with me.' *(not have/be angry)*

4 The paper prints the invented story. This proves that Stella is a spy. Bernice tells the stars:
   a 'If Stella .... Jake, we .... her.' *(not know/can trust)*
   b 'But if you .... to keep your secrets, ... going to Stella's hair salon.' *(want/stop)*

5 Even more stars come to Stella's hair salon. They all want their photos on the front page! They don't care if Stella is Jake's spy.
   a 'Stella, darling, if I .... you about my secret romances, ... Jake .... them?' *(tell/publish)*
   b Stella thinks: 'If I .... a tell-tale, I .... so many clients.' *(not be/not have)*

2 **A B** Three more of these first conditional sentences are more appropriate as second conditional sentences. Rewrite them. Tick (✓) the remaining two sentences.

0 If money grows on trees, we'll all be rich.
   If money grew on trees, we'd all be rich.

1 What will you say if the President visits you?
   ....

2 What will you do if the weather is fine on Saturday?
   ....

3 If your brother murders someone, will you lie to protect him?
   ....

4 If you accidentally find a copy of next week's exam paper, will you look at it?
   ....

5 If the critics like the new film with Phoebe Cute, will you go to see it?
   ....

3 **A B** Six of these sentences deal with unlikely situations. Put the verbs in the appropriate form. Complete the remaining sentences as first conditionals.

0 Look out! If you walk under that ladder, you'll have bad luck. (*walk/have*)

1 What .... you .... if a vampire .... your bedroom? (*do/enter*)

2 If I .... like a bird, I .... over the mountains. (*can fly/fly*)

3 I'm so honest that if I .... a million pounds, I .... it. (*find/return*)

4 If it .... on Sunday, we .... the picnic. (*rain/cancel*)

5 I .... the army even if a foreign army .... my country. (*not join/invade*)

6 My boss is very angry with me. How .... I .... if he .... me? (*survive/dismiss*)

7 If I .... Tom, of course I .... him your message. (*meet/give*)

8 If I .... a super-hero, I .... the world. (*be/save*)

9 Help! Fire! If the house .... down, we .... everything! (*burn/lose*)

10 If there .... an earthquake in London, Big Ben .... (*be/collapse*)

11 If Sue .... at the party, I .... her to dance with me. (*be/ask*)

4 **A B** Write either a first or a second conditional sentence for each situation. Use the verbs in brackets.

0 I'm probably going to Bath. I want to visit the Roman Baths.
   If I go to Bath, I'll visit the Roman Baths. (*go/visit*)

1 I want to go to London because I want to visit the Tate Gallery. But I have no money for the fare.
   .... (*go/visit*)

2 Ben is the best runner in the school. He is going to take part in the school 100 metres race.
   .... a gold medal. (*win/get*)

3 There are many very good runners at the championships where Ben is running in the marathon next month.
   .... another gold medal. (*win/get*)

4 I am going on holiday overseas. The travel company guarantees sunshine. I expect it will be fine.
   But .... for my money back. (*not shine/ask*)

5 Ted is also going on the same holiday. He thinks it might rain a lot. He says:
   '... .' (*not shine/ask*)

6 I rent a flat from a landlord. As far as I know he has no plans to raise the rent.
   But .... it. (*raise/not pay*)

7 The government wants to raise taxes. I don't want to pay more.
   .... them. (*raise/not pay*)

8 Phil and Julie haven't got a television. But they like soap operas.
   .... a lot of soap operas. (*have/watch*)

9 Sam is ill and must stay in bed. He always goes to the Reading Music Festival at this time of year.
   .... (*not be/go*)

10 James has quarrelled with Bella. He doesn't want to see her. He doesn't think she will contact him.

.... me, ... to her. (phone/not speak)

11 James has also quarrelled with Miranda. But he expects her to ring him. He has forgiven her.

.... (phone/speak)

5 Ⓐ Ⓑ Put the second verb in the correct tense.

0 I'll be able to go to Oxford or Cambridge if I *pass* this special exam. (*pass*)

1 If you exceeded the speed limit, the police .... you. (*arrest*)

2 If the teachers find out that you cheated, they .... you. (*expel*)

3 I wouldn't be scared in the mountains unless I .... a wolf. (*see*)

4 What would you wear if Tom Craze .... you to a cocktail party? (*invite*)

5 Would you get rid of your boyfriend if you .... out he was dating another girl? (*find*)

6 We'll play football all day unless it .... to rain. (*begin*)

7 If she'd agree to go out with me, I .... anything for her. (*do*)

8 Do you think Tessa will forgive me if I .... for stealing her boyfriend? (*apologise*)

9 If Frank changed his mind about marrying Harriet, ... you still .... him? (*marry*)

OPEN EXERCISE

6 Ⓐ Ⓑ Complete these conditional sentences in any suitable way.

1 If it rains tomorrow, ...

2 If they found gold in my garden, ...

3 I won't go to the party unless ....

4 If we didn't have to go to school, ...

5 The world would be a better place if ....

6 If I were rich, ...

7 My heart would break if ....

8 If I could make myself invisible, ...

9 If he's late for school again, ...

10 Unless they lower the price, ...

11 I refuse to lend you the money unless ....

12 If there were no police, ...

7 Ⓐ Ⓑ In each pair of sentences, make one sentence first conditional and the other second conditional. Use suitable verbs to complete them. Also write answers to the questions.

0 i. What *would* you *do* if you *won* the lottery? e.g. *I'd buy a private plane.*

00 ii. What *will* you *do* if you finish 'Grammar Goals?' e.g. *I'll take Cambridge First Certificate.*

1 i. What .... you .... if a film star .... you to marry him/her?

ii. What .... you .... if your teacher .... you to do extra homework?

2 i. What .... you .... if it .... next weekend?

ii. What .... you .... if it .... every day for the next year?

UNIT 109 >> Third conditional

 If Mr Sludge **had cleaned** his teeth regularly, they **wouldn't have gone** rotten. And he **wouldn't have lost** his job **if** he**'d** sometimes **had** a shower. But **if** he **had washed** himself and **cleaned** his house, he **wouldn't be** on TV in 'Britain's Dirtiest Man' competition.

Ⓐ THE THIRD CONDITIONAL

When we are talking about **something in the past which cannot be altered now**, we use:
If + Past Perfect, would have + past participle (Conditional Perfect)
*If you **had studied** 'Grammar Goals', you **would have** ('d have) **passed** the exam.*
(= but you did not study so you did not pass)
*If your fiancée **had seen** you with Mary, how **would** you **have explained** it?*
*If she **hadn't lost** her lottery ticket, she **would have won** a million pounds.*
(= in the real past, she lost her ticket, so she didn't win)
*If the pilot **had been** more careful, we **wouldn't have crashed**.*
(= in the real past, the pilot wasn't careful, so we crashed)
*If Billy **hadn't cheated**, he **wouldn't have passed** the exam.*
(= in the real past, Billy cheated, so he passed the exam)

We can reverse the order: **Conditional Perfect verb + if + Past Perfect verb**:
*I **wouldn't have been** late if my car **hadn't broken** down.* (no comma)
*What **would** you **have done** if the police **hadn't arrived**?*

Ⓑ OTHER FORMS

We can use the short forms of **would have** ('d have) and **would not have** (**wouldn't have**).
*I'**d have** called you if I'd known you were at home.*

We can use **could have/might have** in third conditional sentences:
*If I hadn't passed the exam, I **couldn't have gone** to university.* (in fact, I passed)
*It **might have rained** if the wind had changed.* (the wind didn't change)

We can use continuous tenses:
*If he **hadn't been running**, he wouldn't have fallen over.*
*He **wouldn't have been teaching** that class if the usual teacher hadn't been ill.*

Ⓒ MIXING SECOND AND THIRD CONDITIONALS

Sometimes, we talk about something which happened in the past but the result is now:
He invented a new computer programme in 1995. Now, he is very rich.

Then we use a **mixture** of the **third conditional** and the **second conditional** in an *if*-sentence:
*If he **hadn't invented** a new computer programme, he **wouldn't be** rich.*

Here are some more examples:
*If she **had married** the Prince, she **would be** the Queen now.*
*If they **had lost** the war, they **wouldn't live** in an independent country.*

1 **A** Read about four people who have won awards in TV's 'Britain's Most…' competition. In each case make third conditional sentences using the verbs in brackets. Then listen and check your answers.

> Ms Skinny is 'Britain's Slimmest Woman'. She lost weight because she mostly ate yoghurt and fruit. She won the competition because she cheated. The other competitors resigned because they put on weight. They ate the chocolate which Ms Skinny put in their rooms.

0 (lose weight/eat) She wouldn't have lost weight if she hadn't eaten mostly yoghurt and fruit.
1 (win/cheat) ....
2 (resign/put on weight) ....

> Mr Beefy is 'Britain's Strongest Man'. He developed his muscles by going to the gym every day. He won the competition because he gave up smoking and drinking. He didn't go out with girls so that he was able to spend all his time exercising.

3 (develop/go) ....
4 (win/give up) ....
5 (go out/be able) ....

> Ms Openheart is 'Britain's Most Honest Woman'. She won the competition because she didn't fail a lie detector test. Her boyfriend left her because she always told the truth about everything. Her friends said she was silly but they didn't know she would be on television.

6 (win/fail) ....
7 (leave/tell) ....
8 (say/know) ....

> Mr Sweetheart is 'Britain's Most Romantic Man'. His first girlfriend married him because he brought her flowers every day. Then his boss's daughter married him because he wrote such sweet love letters. The police arrested him for bigamy because, when he appeared on TV, his wives found out about each other.

9 (marry/bring) ....
10 (marry/write) ....
11 (arrest/appear) ....
12 (find out/win) ....

2 **C** For each person in exercise 1, complete a conditional sentence, using the verb in brackets.

0 (cheat) If Ms Skinny hadn't cheated, she wouldn't be on TV.
1 (spend/be) ...., ... 'Britain's Strongest Man'.
2 (pass/be) ...., ... on TV.
3 (marry/be) If Mr Sweetheart .... two wives, he ....
in prison now.

3 **A** We can use the third conditional to make excuses. Write excuses, as in the example, for these situations, using verbs from the original sentences.

0 I was late. The taxi broke down. I wouldn't have been late if the taxi hadn't broken down.
1 She felt ill, so she failed the exam.

....

2 I didn't pass my driving test because the examiner made me nervous.

....

Third conditional

285

3 I didn't buy you a birthday present because someone stole my wallet.

....

4 He forgot to send the fax because he was worried about his sick brother.

....

5 They didn't remember to visit their grandmother because they had a phone call from Canada.

....

6 I didn't get up at 8 a.m. because my alarm clock didn't go off.

....

7 The flowers in the garden died because nobody told me how to look after them.

.... (use *somebody*)

8 I borrowed your car because my friend had to go to hospital.

....

9 I didn't phone you last night because the teacher gave me lots of grammar homework.

....

10 She stole her best friend's boyfriend because she didn't know her friend still loved him.

....

4 **A** **B** **We sometimes use the third conditional to express regret for something that we did wrong. Make third conditional sentences for these situations.**

0 I drove too fast. As a result, I had an accident.
   If I hadn't driven too fast, I wouldn't have had an accident.

1 I burnt the dinner because I left the kitchen to watch a soap opera.

....

2 They were playing football in the garden. As a result, they broke the window.

....

3 My brother went to prison because he went shoplifting with his friends.

....

4 I couldn't open the door because I brought the wrong key.

....

5 She became ill because she didn't eat fresh fruit and vegetables.

....

6 He gave his money to his friend to invest. Consequently, he lost everything.

....

5 **B** **Make third conditional sentences using *might have, mightn't have*. Use verbs from the original sentences.**

0 Phil went to the disco. He met Julie there. Later, he married her.
   If Phil hadn't gone to the disco, he mightn't have married Julie.

1 My brother made friends with Geoff. Geoff was a gangster. My brother was arrested.

....

2 My girlfriend went on holiday. She met and fell in love with Rod. I didn't marry her.

....

3 I laughed at my teacher. He gave me bad marks. I didn't pass the exam.

....

4 My mother was mad about dancing. She met my father at a dance. She married my father.

....

5 It rained last weekend. We'd been looking for something to do. We didn't have a picnic.

....

6 I ate burgers at the barbecue. I got food poisoning and missed a job interview. I didn't get the job.

....

6 Ⓐ - Ⓒ Write *if*-sentences about these situations. Use either the third conditional or a mixture of the third and the second conditional.

0 Many industries closed down. Now there is a lot of unemployment.
  If many industries hadn't closed down, there wouldn't be a lot of unemployment.

1 The government reduced salaries for teachers. As a result, there is a shortage of teachers.

....

2 Universities began to charge higher fees. Poor families couldn't send their children to university.

....

3 There were several wet summers; as a result, many British people went on holiday abroad.

....

4 People recycle so many things because schools began to educate children about the environment.

....

5 The USA is so powerful, perhaps because Europe weakened itself through two wars. (use: *might*)

....

6 China introduced a 'one child' policy because their population was growing dramatically.

....

7 Belarus is an independent country as a result of the Soviet Union breaking up.

....

OPEN EXERCISE

7 Ⓐ - Ⓒ Complete these third conditional sentences using any suitable idea.

1 If we hadn't arrived early, ...
2 They would have won the championship if ....
3 The holiday would have been great if ....
4 If the spy hadn't made a mistake, ...
5 He wouldn't have married her if ....
6 They wouldn't have complained if ....
7 The programme wouldn't have been a success if ....
8 Nobody would have remembered him if ....

> Diana has sent me a letter: 'Should you want to contact me, I shall be at my aunt's house. But were you to visit me, I wouldn't be able to see you.'
> I don't think she loves me any more — it's very cold, formal language!

Ⓐ *IF + SHOULD*

In first or second conditional sentences, we sometimes use **if** + **should** to emphasise that something might happen by chance:

If you should meet Jill, give her my best wishes. (= if, by chance, you meet Jill,...)
If it should rain, I'll come home early. (= if, by chance, it rains,...)
If he should win the lottery, he'd waste it all at the casino.
(unlikely situation — second conditional)

We can use **If it so happens/happened that...** with the same meaning:
If it so happens that you find my wallet, let me know.

Ⓑ *SHOULD* IN FRONT POSITION

If we move **should** to the front of the sentence, we do not use **if**. This structure occurs mainly in formal English:
Should you meet Jill, give her my best wishes.
Should the sun shine, we wouldn't have to wear our coats.

Ⓒ *IF I WERE TO...*

We can follow **If I were/If it were** etc. with a **to**-infinitive in a second conditional sentence:
If I were to sell the car, would you be upset?
If it were to rain, we'd have to cancel the game.

Ⓓ *WERE* IN FRONT POSITION

If we move **were** to the front of the sentence, we do not use **if**. This structure occurs in formal English:
Were I in your position, I'd ask the bank manager for advice.
Were you to win the competition, you'd be famous immediately.

Ⓔ *HAD* IN FRONT POSITION

If we move **had** to the front of a third conditional sentence, we do not use **if**. Phrases such as **Had I known...** or **Had he told me...** are fairly common in conversation and are not especially formal.
Had I known that you were ill, I wouldn't have asked you to do the work. (= If I had known...)
Had he warned me about the bad weather, I'd have changed my plan.

Ⓕ ALTERNATIVES TO *IF*

We can use other phrases such as **provided that... so long as... on condition that...** instead of **if** to express conditional ideas:
Provided that/On condition that you pay me in advance, I'll do the work for you.
I'd do anything for her so long as she didn't make fun of me.

1 **Ⓐ** Write sentences with *if… should…* based on these situations. Use 1st or 2nd conditional as indicated.

0 Uncle Joe might get married again → the oldest bridegroom in history. (1st)
If Uncle Joe should get married again, he will be the oldest bridegroom in history.

1 Ellie Tramper might get pneumonia → stop living outdoors. (2nd)

....

2 Madam Magistar might lose her powers → have no way of earning money. (2nd)

....

3 Phil and Julie might have a daughter → name her Kylie. (1st)

....

4 Brigitte might be dismissed by Nick → demand compensation. (1st)

....

2 **Ⓑ** Rewrite these conditional sentences by beginning *Should…* .

0 If you damage this product by careless handling, the guarantee will not be valid.
Should you damage this product by careless handling, the guarantee will not be valid.

1 If you park your car here without a permit, it will be towed away.

....

2 If the local industry causes water pollution, the government will fine them.

....

3 **Ⓒ Ⓓ** Rewrite the conditional sentences in exercise 2 by beginning *Were… to…* and using second conditional tenses. Also indicate how you would begin *If… were to…* .

0 *Were you to damage this product by careless handling, the guarantee would not be valid.
/ If you were to damage…*

1 ....

2 ....

4 **Ⓔ** Write conditional sentences beginning *Had…* for these situations.

0 I didn't know about the party, so I didn't go. *Had I known about the party I would have gone.*

1 You didn't tell me that it was your birthday, so I didn't give you a present.

....

2 She didn't marry me, so she isn't happy.

....

3 Kevin didn't train enough, so he didn't play for England.

.... (use: *harder*)

4 The King didn't lower taxes, so there was a revolution.

....

5 **Ⓕ** Rewrite these sentences, using the word in brackets.

0 I'll cook dinner for you in return for some help from you with my homework.
I'll cook dinner for you provided that you help me with my homework. (*provided*)

1 If you don't tell anyone, I'll tell you all about the secret plan.

.... (*long*)

2 I'll lend you my car if you bring it back before the weekend.

.... (*condition*)

REVISION 12 >> First Certificate Practice

1 For questions 1-12, read the text below and decide which answer, A, B, C or D, best fits each gap. There is an example at the beginning (0).

THINKING ABOUT POSSIBILITIES

We often think about what might (0) A happened if things (1) ..... different in the past. For example, what would have happened if Napoleon (2) ..... the Battle of Waterloo or the native Americans (3) ..... the European settlers? In your personal life, if your mother and father (4) ....., would you exist now? As for the human imagination, if Shakespeare (5) ..... *Romeo and Juliet*, (6) ..... some other author (7) ..... the story of the doomed lovers? And would it have been a better or an inferior version? In the present, we (8) ..... killed if a meteor (9) ..... on our city. And what (10) ..... in the future if the sea levels rise or a nuclear war (11) ..... out? All this speculation is useless; we must live with all these possibilities without worrying about them if we (12) ..... to survive psychologically. There is enough stress in modern life without imagining potential disasters!

0	(A) have	B	be	C	–	D	have been
1	A would have been	B	had been	C	be	D	are
2	A had won	B	wins	C	won	D	would have won
3	A defeated	B	would have defeated	C	had been defeated	D	had defeated
4	A had met	B	hadn't met	C	wouldn't have met	D	didn't meet
5	A wrote	B	didn't write	C	wouldn't have written	D	had not written
6	A would	B	had	C	did	D	didn't
7	A have written	B	written	C	write	D	have been written
8	A would be	B	could have been	C	wouldn't be	D	had been
9	A falls	B	fell	C	had felt	D	will fall
10	A would happen	B	happens	C	will happen	D	does happen
11	A will break	B	would have broken	C	broke	D	breaks
12	A wanted	B	want	C	will want	D	would want

2 For these questions, read the text below and think of the word which best fits the gap. Use only *one* word in each gap. There is an example (0).

AGAINST HOROSCOPES

Do you believe in horoscopes? (0) If you (1) ...., then I think you're a fool. If horoscopes (2) .... accurate, then everybody with the same birthday would have the same things happen to them each day. Every day, some people die. So, if the horoscope really (3) .... the future, it would have to say, 'You will be dead before the end of the day.' But in fact, horoscopes make very vague predictions, such as: 'If you work hard this week, you (4) .... gain a reward.' or 'If you travel by car this week, (5) .... careful.' I once knew a woman who wouldn't leave her house unless her horoscope (6) .... that it was safe to do so. If it (7) .... a lucky day according to her horoscope, she (8) .... worry about anything that happened to her on that day. She didn't consider that different astrologers predict different things. (9) .... she looked in a different paper, she might (10) .... found a completely different prediction. Many people protest that, although they read their horoscope daily for fun, they don't believe in it. They claim that if their horoscope (11) .... good, they wouldn't be upset. But I think that, if they (12) .... taken the trouble to read their 'stars', they will be influenced by whatever the astrologer says in the paper.

PAPER 3 PART 4

3 For questions 1-8, complete the second sentence so that it has a similar meaning to the first sentence, using the word given. Do not change the word given. Use from two to five words including the word given. There is an example (0).

0 If you go to Paris, please buy me a poster of the *Mona Lisa*.
If you go to Paris, will you please buy me a poster of the *Mona Lisa*? *WILL*

1 If there is a storm during the night, please shut all the windows.
Should .... during the night, please shut all the windows. *THERE*

2 Shelley forgot to fasten her safety belt and, as a result, she was badly injured.
If Shelley .... her safety belt, she wouldn't have been badly injured. *TO*

3 Frank didn't insure his house against fire and now he has nowhere to live.
If Frank had insured his house against fire, he .... now. *HOMELESS*

4 She didn't ask me out, so I stayed in last night.
If .... out, I wouldn't have stayed in last night. *HAD*

5 He was driving too fast and as a result he caused an accident.
If he ...., he wouldn't have caused an accident. *DRIVING*

6 She isn't going to accept the job as the company won't offer her a higher salary.
She wouldn't accept the job .... a higher salary. *UNLESS*

7 I think he was wrong to criticise her publicly and that's probably why she was angry.
She .... if he hadn't criticised her publicly. *MIGHT*

8 They will probably win the competition and as a result they'll get lots of money.
If ...., they'll get lots of money. *WIN*

OPEN EXERCISE

4 Complete these conditional sentences in any suitable way.

1 If it were to snow tomorrow, ...
2 He wouldn't have felt hungry if ....
3 Should the door be locked, ...
4 If you haven't already seen the film, ...
5 If she were the boss, ...
6 If there hadn't been a good film on television that night, ...
7 They don't allow the public into the palace unless ....
8 If the temperature drops below zero, ...
9 You wouldn't have been arrested if ....
10 If Superman existed, ...
11 The disaster might have been prevented if ....
12 Should ...., tell him to call back later.

APPENDIX 1 >> Verb tenses: form

VERB TENSES: FORM

The tables give the short forms of the negative: **don't, doesn't, hasn't, haven't** etc. rather than **do not, does not, has not, have not.**

SIMPLE TENSES		
Present and Past Simple use forms of **do** as a helping verb in questions and negatives		

Present Simple

Affirmative:	I **work**	We **work**
	You **work**	You **work**
	He/She/It **works**	They **work**
Question:	**Do** I **work**?	**Do** we **work**?
	Do you **work**?	**Do** you **work**?
	Does he/she/it **work**?	**Do** they **work**?
Negative:	I **don't work**	We **don't work**
	You **don't work**	You **don't work**
	He/She/It **doesn't work**	They **don't work**
Short answers:	Yes, I/you/we/you/they **do**	Yes, he/she/it **does**
	No, I/you/we/you/they **don't**	No he/she/it **doesn't**

Past Simple

Affirmative:	I **worked**	We **worked**
	You **worked**	You **worked**
	He/She/It **worked**	They **worked**
Question:	**Did** I **work**?	**Did** we **work**?
	Did you **work**?	**Did** you **work**?
	Did he/she/it **work**?	**Did** they **work**?
Negative:	I **didn't work**	We **didn't work**
	You **didn't work**	You **didn't work**
	He/She/It **didn't work**	They **didn't work**
Short answers:	Yes, I/you/he/she/it/we/you/they **did**	
	No, I/you/he/she/it/we/you/they **didn't**	

Future Simple

Affirmative:	I'll/**will work**	We'll/**will work**
	You'll/**will work**	You'll/**will work**
	He/She/It'll/**will work**	They'll/**will work**
Question:	**Will** I **work**?	**Will** we **work**?
	Will you **work**?	**Will** you **work**?
	Will he/she/it **work**?	**Will** they **work**?
Negative:	I **won't work**	We **won't work**
	You **won't work**	You **won't work**
	He/She/It **won't work**	They **won't work**
Short answers:	Yes, I/you/he/she/it/we/you/they **will**	
	No, I/you/he/she/it/we/you/they **won't**	

CONTINUOUS TENSES

These follow this pattern: **present/past/future of be + verb-ing**

Present Continuous

Affirmative:	I'm/am working	We're/are working
	You're/are working	You're/are working
	He/She/It's/is working	They're/are working
Question:	Am I working?	Are we working?
	Are you working?	Are you working?
	Is he/she/it working?	Are they working?
Negative:	I'm not working	We aren't/We're not working
	You aren't/You're not working	You aren't/You're not working
	He/She/It's/isn't working	They aren't/They're not working
Short answers:	Yes, I/you/we/you/they are	Yes, he/she/it is
	No, I/you/we/you/they aren't	No, he/she/it isn't

Past Continuous

Affirmative:	I was working	We were working
	You were working	You were working
	He/She/It was working	They were working
Question:	Was I working?	Were we working?
	Were you working?	Were you working?
	Was he/she/it working?	Were they working?
Negative:	I wasn't working	We weren't working
	You weren't working	You weren't working
	He/She/It wasn't working	They weren't working
Short answers:	Yes, I/you/we/you/they were	Yes, he/she/it was
	No, I/you/we/you/they weren't	No, he/she/it wasn't

Future Continuous

Affirmative:	I'll/will be working	We'll/will be working
	You'll/will be working	You'll/will be working
	He/She/It'll/will be working	They'll/will be working
Question:	Will I be working?	Will we be working?
	Will you be working?	Will you be working?
	Will he/she/it be working?	Will they be working?
Negative:	I won't be working	We won't be working
	You won't be working	You won't be working
	He/she/it won't be working	They won't be working
Short answers:	Yes, I/you/he/she/it/we/you/they will/will be	
	No, I/you/he/she/it/we/you/they won't/won't be	

PERFECT SIMPLE TENSES

These follow this pattern: **present/past/future of have + past participle* of verb**

* past participles of some verbs are regular, others are irregular (see Appendix 3)

Present Perfect

Affirmative:	I've/have worked	We've/have worked
	You've/have worked	You've/have worked
	He/She/It's/has worked	They've/have worked
Question:	Have I worked?	Have we worked?
	Have you worked?	Have you worked?
	Has he/she/it worked?	Have they worked?
Negative:	I haven't worked	We haven't worked
	You haven't worked	You haven't worked
	He/She/It hasn't worked	They haven't worked
Short answers:	Yes, I/you/we/you/they have	Yes, he/she/it has
	No, I/you/we/you/they haven't	No, he/she/it hasn't

Past Perfect

Affirmative:	I'd/had worked	We'd/had worked
	You'd/had worked	You'd/had worked
	He/She/It had worked	They'd had worked
Question:	Have I worked?	Have we worked?
	Have you worked?	Have you worked?
	Has he/she/it worked?	Have they worked?
Negative:	I hadn't worked	We hadn't worked
	You hadn't worked	You hadn't worked
	He/She/It hadn't worked	They hadn't worked
Short answers:	Yes, I/you/he/she/it/we/you/they had	
	No, I/you/he/she/it/we/you/they hadn't	

Future Perfect

Affirmative:	I'll/will have worked	We'll/will have worked
	You'll/will have worked	You'll/will have worked
	He/She/It'll/will have worked	They'll/will have worked
Question:	Will I have worked?	Will we have worked?
	Will you have worked?	Will you have worked?
	Will he/she/it have worked?	Will they have worked?
Negative:	I won't have worked	We won't have worked
	You won't have worked	You won't have worked
	He/She/It won't have worked	They won't have worked
Short answers:	Yes, I/you/he/she/it/we/you/they will/will have	
	No, I/you/he/she/it/we/you/they won't/won't have	

PERFECT CONTINUOUS TENSES

These follow this pattern: **present/past/future of have + been + verb-ing**

Present Perfect Continuous

Affirmative:	I've/have been working	We've/have been working
	You've/have been working	You've/have been working
	He/She/It's/has been working	They've/have been working
Question:	Have I been working?	Have we been working?
	Have you been working?	Have you been working?
	Has he/she/it been working?	Have they been working?
Negative:	I haven't been working	We haven't been working
	You haven't been working	You haven't been working
	He/She/It hasn't been working	They haven't been working
Short answers:	Yes, I/you/we/you/they have/have been	
	Yes, he/she/it has/has been	
	No, I/you/we/you/they haven't/haven't been	
	No, he/she/it hasn't/hasn't been	

Past Perfect Continuous

Affirmative:	I'd/had been working	We'd/had been working
	You'd/had been working	You'd/had been working
	He/She/It'd/had been working	They'd/had been working
Question:	Had I been working?	Had we been working?
	Had you been working?	Had you been working?
	Had he/she/it been working?	Had they been working?
Negative:	I hadn't been working	We hadn't been working
	You hadn't been working	You hadn't been working
	He/She/It hadn't been working	They hadn't been working
Short answers:	Yes, I/you/he/she/it/we/you/they had/had been	
	No, I/you/he/she/it/we/you/they hadn't/hadn't been	

Future Perfect Continuous

Affirmative:	I'll/will have been working	We'll/will have been working
	You'll/will have been working	You'll/will have been working
	He/She/It'll/will have been working	They'll/will have been working
Question:	Will I have been working?	Will we have been working?
	Will you have been working?	Will you have been working?
	Will he/she/it have been working?	Will they have been working?
Negative:	I won't have been working	We won't have been working
	You won't have been working	You won't have been working
	He/She/It won't have been working	They won't have been working
Short answers:	Yes, I/you/he/she/it/we/you/they will/will have	
	No, I/you/he/she/it/we/you/they won't/won't have	

APPENDIX 2 >> The form of modal verbs

A Modal verbs include **can/could/must/may** etc. In the second section of *Grammar Goals* (Units 21-8) we study their use. They generally follow the same pattern:

I/you/he/she/it/we/you/they + **modal** + **verb**   without **to**
                                                                                                           without **-s**
                                                                                                           without **-ing**

Most modal verbs also have these forms:
I/you/he/she/it/we/you/they + **modal** + **be** + **verb-ing**: *You **must be joking**.*
I/you/he/she/it/we/you/they + **modal** + **have** + **past participle**: *They **must have arrived**.*

B A few modal or similar verbs are used with **to** + **verb**:
*I **was able to** help.   I **ought to** work.   He **has to**/They **have to** work.   They **need to** work.*
(negative of **need/needs** without **to** is possible)

C Here is a summary of the form of modal verbs. The table gives the short forms of the negative: **mustn't** rather than **must not**. In some cases, a space is blank where a form is either rarely used or does not exist:

MODAL AUXILIARIES

It is impossible to combine these verbs. For example, I *will must* is **wrong**.

modal	affirmative	question	negative
can	*I **can swim**.* — —	***Can** she **swim**?* — —	*They **can't swim**.* *She **can't be swimming**.* *They **can't have swum** the Channel.**
could	*They **could swim**.* *She **could be swimming**.* *They **could have done** it.**	***Could** you **help** me?* ***Could** she **be working**?* ***Could** you **have done** it?**	*We **couldn't do** it.* *He **couldn't be joking**.* *He **couldn't have waited**.**
must	*I **must work**.* *He **must be working**.* *She **must have worked** hard.**	***Must** you **work**?* — —	*I **mustn't work**.* — —
may	*She **may arrive** soon.* *He **may be phoning** at 9.* *We **may have won**.**	***May** I **help**?* — —	*They **may not pay** me.* *They **may not be coming**.* *They **may not have seen** it.**
might	the same as **may** except that all three question forms exist and short form **mightn't** exists.		
would/should	the same as **might**: short negative forms are **wouldn't** and **shouldn't**.		
ought to	*I **ought to help**.* *He **ought to be studying**.* *She **ought to have done** it.**	***Ought** he **to be** here?* ***Ought** he **to be smoking**?* ***Ought** I **to have told** her?**	*She **oughtn't to say** that.* *I **oughtn't to be drinking**.* *I **oughtn't to have done** it.**

* a continuous perfect form is also used, for example: *They **can't have been swimming** hard.*

MODAL VERBS WHICH ALSO FOLLOW A NORMAL PATTERN

We can use **need** and **dare** like modals — *he **needn't** worry* — but also use them like main verbs — *He **doesn't need** to worry./We'll **need** to finish*. This table shows only present, past and future.

modal	affirmative	question	negative
need	*I **need to drink**.*	***Does** he **need to know**?*	*They **don't need to stay**.* *or They **needn't stay**.*
	*I **needed to do** it.*	***Did** you **need to go** there?*	*She **didn't need to hurry**.* *She **needn't have hurried**.*
	*I'll **need to move** next year.*	***Will** she **need to see** me?*	*They **won't need to know**.*
dare	*He **dares (to) refuse**.*	***Does** he **dare (to) climb** it?* *or **Dare** she **do** it?*	*He **doesn't dare (to) fight**.* *or She **daren't fight**.*
	*He **dared (to) enter**.*	***Did** he **dare (to) do** it?*	*They **didn't dare (to) fight**.*
	*They'll **dare to do** it.*	***Will** they **dare (to) help** us?*	*She **won't dare (to) come**.*

BE ABLE TO/HAVE TO

We use these with similar meanings to **can** and **must** (see Units 21-3). They have the full range of tense forms e.g. *I'll **have to** do it./**Have** you **been able to** give up?* This table shows only present, past and future.

be able to	*She **isn't able to do** it.* *They **were able to help**.* *I'll soon **be able to do** it.*	*I'm **able to help**.* *Was he **able to do** it?* *Will she **be able to come**?*	*Are you **able to solve** it?* *I **wasn't able to come**.* *He **won't be able to help**.*
have to	*He **has to study**.* *Yesterday, I **had to work**.* *Tomorrow, I'll **have to work**.*	*Do we **have to do** it?* *Did they **have to go**?* *Will she **have to leave**?*	*I **don't have to help**.* *She **didn't have to salute**.* *They **won't have to stay**.*

APPENDIX 3 >> Regular and irregular verbs

It is useful to study three forms of every verb:
the **infinitive**, the **Past Simple** form and the **past participle**.

We use the **Past Simple** form in sentences about the past:
*I **visited** my aunt yesterday.* (Unit 4)

We use the **past participle**:

• to form perfect tenses:	*I haven't **phoned** Tina yet.* (Units 6-13) *After she had **phoned** her friends, she...*
• after **must have...**, **can't have...** etc.:	*It must have **rained**.* (Unit 27)
• to form passive verbs:	*It is **designed** in China.* (Units 96-100)
• in some other cases:	*She had her house **painted**.* (Unit 101)
• to form some adjectives:	*He was very **disappointed**.* (Unit 70)

See the next page for the spelling of regular and irregular verbs.

Regular verbs add **-ed/-d** to form the Past Simple and past participle.

	infinitive	Past Simple	past participle
Most verbs add **-ed**:	work clean	work**ed** clean**ed**	work**ed** clean**ed**
For verbs ending **-e** add **-d**:	live telephone	live**d** telephone**d**	live**d** telephone**d**
For verbs ending consonant* + **-y** change **-y** to **-ied**:	study marry	stud**ied** marr**ied**	stud**ied** marr**ied**
For verbs ending consonant + vowel* + consonant (a vowel sandwich) double the final consonant: e.g. **-n, -nned**	plan stop	pla**nned** sto**pped**	pla**nned** sto**pped**
But do not double the final consonant: when verb ends in **-w**, **-y**	follow enjoy play	follow**ed** enjoy**ed** play**ed**	follow**ed** enjoy**ed** play**ed**
and when the final syllable is not stressed: e.g. **ha**ppen/**li**sten/**o**pen/**vi**sit	happen listen open visit	happen**ed** listen**ed** open**ed** visit**ed**	happen**ed** listen**ed** open**ed** visit**ed**
But for all verbs ending consonant + vowel + **-l**: double the final **-l**	cancel travel	cance**lled** trave**lled**	cance**lled** trave**lled**

* for an explanation of consonants, vowels and syllables, see Appendix 15

Irregular verbs do not add **-ed**. They have special forms (Unit 4):

infinitive	Past Simple	past participle
arise	arose	arisen
awake	awoke	awoken
be	was/were	been
bet	bet	bet
beat	beat	beaten
become	became	become
begin	began	begun
bend	bent	bent
bind	bound	bound
bite	bit	bitten
bleed	bled	bled
blow	blew	blown
break	broke	broken
do	did	done
draw	drew	drawn
bring	brought	brought
broadcast	broadcast	broadcast
build	built	built
buy	bought	bought
catch	caught	caught

infinitive	Past Simple	past participle
come	came	come
cost	cost	cost
cut	cut	cut
deal	dealt	dealt
dig	dug	dug
drink	drank	drunk***
drive	drove	driven
eat	ate	eaten
fall	fell	fallen
feed	fed	fed
feel	felt	felt
fight	fought	fought
find	found	found
fly	flew	flown
forbid	forbade	forbidden
forget	forgot	forgotten
forgive	forgave	forgiven
freeze	froze	frozen
get	got	got
give	gave	given

infinitive	Past Simple	past participle
choose	chose	chosen
grow	grew	grown
hang	hung*	hung*
have	had	had
hear	heard	heard
hide	hid	hidden
hit	hit	hit
hold	held	held
hurt	hurt	hurt
keep	kept	kept
know	knew	known
lay	laid	laid
lead	led	led
leave	left	left
lend	lent	lent
let	let	let
lie**	lay	lain
light	lit	lit
lose	lost	lost
make	made	made
mean	meant	meant
meet	met	met
pay	paid	paid
put	put	put
read [ri:d]	read [red]	read [red]
ride	rode	ridden
ring	rang	rung
rise	rose	risen
run	ran	run
say	said	said
see	saw	seen
sell	sold	sold
send	sent	sent
set	set	set
shake	shook	shaken

infinitive	Past Simple	past participle
go	went	gone
shine	shone	shone
shoot	shot	shot
show	showed	shown
shut	shut	shut
sing	sang	sung
sink	sank	sunk
sit	sat	sat
sleep	slept	slept
speak	spoke	spoken
spend	spent	spent
split	split	split
spread	spread	spread
stand	stood	stood
steal	stole	stolen
stick	stuck	stuck
sting	stung	stung
strike	struck	struck***
swear	swore	sworn
sweep	swept	swept
swim	swam	swum
swing	swung	swung
take	took	taken
teach	taught	taught
tear	tore	torn
tell	told	told
think	thought	thought
throw	threw	thrown
understand	understood	understood
wake	woke	woken
wear	wore	worn
weep	wept	wept
win	won	won
wind [waɪnd]	wound [waʊnd]	wound [waʊnd]
write	wrote	written

* we use **hang/hung/hung** in most cases: e.g. *I hung a painting on the wall.* But we use
hang/hanged/hanged to talk about the punishment of hanging: *They hanged the murderer in 1873.*
** the verb **to lie** which means 'not to tell the truth' is regular: e.g. *She lied to her mum.* (see Unit 86)
*** the old forms **drunken** and **stricken** are used in some phrases, e.g. **drunken** *driving,* grief-**stricken**.

The following verbs can be regular or irregular:

infinitive	Past Simple	past participle
burn	burned or burnt	burned or burnt
dream	dreamed or dreamt	dreamed or dreamt
lean	leaned or leant	leaned or leant
learn	learned or learnt	learned or learnt
smell	smelled or smelt	smelled or smelt
spell	spelled or spelt	spelled or spelt
spill	spilled or spilt	spilled or spilt
spoil	spoiled or spoilt	spoiled or spoilt

The second form is more usual in British English.

APPENDIX 4 >> Verb + -ing

We use **verb + -ing**:
- to form continuous tenses: *I am **writing**.* (Present Continuous) (Unit 2)
  *They were **reading**.* (Past Continuous) (Unit 5)
  *Have you been **sleeping**?* (Present Perfect Continuous) (Unit 9)
- to form some adjectives: *That's an **interesting** book.* (Unit 70)
- after certain verbs: *I like **swimming**. I don't mind **helping**.* (Units 88-9)
- to act as a noun. For example, as the subject of a sentence: ***Swimming** is fun.* (Unit 93)
  ***Learning** English is hard.*
- or after a preposition (Unit 72): *He did it without **thinking**. I'm fond of **dancing**.*

SPELLING OF -ING FORM

	infinitive	-ing form
Most verbs: add **-ing**:	feel	feel**ing**
	go	go**ing**
	work	work**ing**
	worry	worry**ing**
For verbs ending in silent **-e** remove **-e** and add **-ing**:	live	liv**ing**
	make	mak**ing**
	ride	rid**ing**
	telephone	telephon**ing**
For verbs ending **-ie** remove **-ie** and add **-ying**:	die	d**ying**
	lie	l**ying**
For verbs ending consonant + vowel* + consonant (a vowel sandwich) double the final consonant: e.g. **-n, -nning**	begin	begi**nning**
	hit	hi**tting**
	plan	pla**nning**
	stop	sto**pping**
	swim	swi**mming**
But do not double the final consonant: when the verbs end in **-w** or **-y** and when the final syllable is not stressed: e.g. **ha**ppen/**lis**ten/**o**pen/**vi**sit	follow	follow**ing**
	enjoy	enjoy**ing**
	play	play**ing**
	happen	happen**ing**
	listen	listen**ing**
	open	open**ing**
	visit	visit**ing**
But for all verbs ending consonant + vowel + **-l** double the final **-l:****	control	contro**lling**
	travel	trave**lling**

* for an explanation of consonants, vowels and syllables, see Appendix 15
** see CD-ROM for American English spelling

APPENDIX 5 >> State and action verbs

These are the most common state verbs (see Unit 3 and Units 84-5).
We do not normally use these verbs in continuous tenses.

Verbs expressing **love/hate** etc.: *adore   desire   hate   like   love   mind   prefer*
Verbs expressing **need**: *need   want*
Verbs about **understanding** etc.: *know   realise   believe   suppose   understand*
Verbs about **perception**: *hear   notice   see   look as if   seem   sound*
Verbs about **possessing**: *belong   have* (when the meaning is possess — see Unit 79)   *own*
Also: *cost   depend   fit   include   matter   mean*

Some verbs are **state verbs** in some situations but **action verbs** in other situations:

verb	state	action
have	They **have** a lot of friends. (= possess)	They **are having** a party.
hope	I **hope** you are well. (= I wish)	I'm **hoping** to visit London.
feel	It **feels** smooth.	I'm **feeling** sad.
forget	He **forgets** everything.	He's **forgetting** about her.
look	She **looks** tired.	She's **looking** at the painting.
remember	He **remembers** her.	He has trouble **remembering** her.
smell	The roses **smell** nice.	She's **smelling** the roses.
taste	It **tastes** good.	He's **tasting** the wine.
think	I **think** he's Spanish. (= I believe)	I **am thinking**... (= something is happening in my mind)

We use some verbs in the Present Continuous or Present Simple without an important difference in meaning:

ache	*My tooth **aches**.*	or *My tooth **is aching**.*
expect	*He **expects** to pass the exam.*	or *He's **expecting** to pass the exam.*
hope	*I **hope** to visit London.*	or *I'm **hoping** to visit London.*
hurt	*My knee **hurts**.*	or *My knee **is hurting**.*
look	*He **looks** ill.*	or *He's **looking** ill.*
look forward to	*I **look forward to** seeing you.*	or *'m **looking forward to** seeing you.*

APPENDIX 6 >> Phrasal verbs

In Unit 83, we studied four main types of phrasal verbs:

Type One — with **no object**;
Type Two — **verb** + **participle** + **noun** or **verb** + **noun** + **participle**;
Type Three — **object must go after the preposition**;
Type Four — **verb** + **two items**. Here is a list of the most common phrasal verbs in each type:

Type One	
break down	*Bill's car **broke down**.* (= it stopped working)
carry on	*She **carried on** speaking.* (= she continued)
come round	*He **came round** for lunch.* (= visited informally)
get on/get off*	*I **got on** at the bus station and **got off** at the park.*
get on	*How are you **getting on**?* (= How are you generally?)
get up	*John is ill; he shouldn't **get up**.* (= get out of bed)
give up**	*The problem's too difficult — I **give up**!* (= I can't do it)
go off	*The fire alarm **went off**.* (= sounded, began to work)
go on	*They **went on**.* (= they continued. N.B. **go on** + **verb-ing** is possible)
grow up	*I **grew up** in London.* (= I spent my childhood in London)
hold on	***Hold on** a minute.* (= wait a minute)
keep on	*She **kept on** complaining.* (= she continued complaining)
look out	***Look out**! There's a lion.* (= be careful)
show off**	*He **showed off** to his friends.* (= he tried to impress other people)
shut up (impolite)	***Shut up**! I'm reading.* (= be quiet)
slow down	*The car **slowed down**.* (= went more slowly)
take off**	*The plane **took off** from London Airport.* (left the ground)
turn out	*She **turned out** to be a spy.* (= we found out in the end that she was a spy)
turn up	*He didn't reserve a room in the hotel — he just **turned up**.* (= arrived)
wake up	*Maggie **woke up** early.* (= opened her eyes after sleeping)
wash up**	*We **washed up**.* (= washed the dirty things after a meal)
watch out	***Watch out**!* (same meaning as *Look out!*)

* see also Type Three   ** See also Type Two

Type Two	
buy up	*She **bought up** the whole shop.* (= he bought all the available things)
cheer up	*His friends **cheered** him **up** after he failed.* (= they made him feel happier)
cross out	*She **crossed out** her mistake.* (= put a cross through it)
fill in	*They **filled** the form **in**.* (= completed)
get somebody down	*Her poor health **got** Sheila **down***.* (= depressed her)
put somebody down	*He **put** Gina **down***.* (= he was publicly rude to her)
give up	*She **gave up** smoking.* (= stopped a habit)
knock down/over	*The car **knocked** her **down/over**.* (there was an accident)
look up	*He **looked** the word **up** in a dictionary.* (= found the meaning)
put on	*She **put on** her new skirt.* (= she got dressed in)
	*He **put on** the radio.* (= switched on)
put off	*They **put off** the party.* (= they postponed the party)
put out	*The fire-fighters **put out** the fire.* (= extinguished)

ring up	She **rang up** all her friends. (= telephoned)
show off	He **showed off** his new girlfriend. (= he used her to impress others)
take off	He **took** his clothes **off** and had a bath.
take up	She **took up** chess when she was 18. (= began to play)
	Your luggage **takes up** a lot of space. (= it occupies a lot of space)
throw away	I **threw away** my old clothes. (= put in the rubbish)
turn down	She **turned down** the new job. (= she refused to accept it)
turn off	He **turned** the light **off**. (= switched off)
use up	I've **used up** my money. (= I've spent all my money)
wash up	We **washed up** the dishes. (= cleaned the dishes after a meal)

* ... got down Sheila/... put down Gina are not usual

Type Three	
break into	The thief **broke into** the bank.
get on/get off	I **got on** the bus at the airport.
get over	Minnie has **got over** her illness. (= she has recovered)
look after	He **looked after** the baby. (= took care of)
look for	She **looked for** her passport. (= searched, tried to find)
turn into	The frog **turned into** a prince. (= changed into, became)

Type Four	
be fed up with	I'm **fed up with** living in this town. (= I'm very bored and unhappy here)
get on with	Don **gets on with** Tim. (= they are friends)
keep up with	She **keeps up with** the news. (= she knows the latest news)
look down on	Rich people often **look down on** poor ones. (= despise, see as inferior)
look forward to	Sue's **looking forward to** Christmas. (= she's excited about the future)
look up to	I **look up to** my parents. (= I respect and admire them)
put up with	I can't **put up with** the noise. (= I can't tolerate it)

This table shows some of the cases where we use **put on**, **put off** etc.:

	the radio/TV/cooker	the light	a candle	a tap
put on	✓*	✓	✗	✗
put off	✗	✓	✗	✗
put out	✗	✓	✓	✗
switch on/off	✓*	✓	✗	✗
turn on/off	✓*	✓	✗	✓
turn out	✗	✓	✗	✗

* **turn on** and **switch on** are more usual than **put on** for radio/TV

Be careful with **get on**, **get off**, **get into**, **get out of**:

	a bus/train/ship/aeroplane	a car/taxi	a bicycle/horse
get on/off	✓	✗	✓
get into/out of	✗	✓	✗

APPENDIX 7 >> Active and passive forms of verbs

Here are some examples of active and passive verbs in all the tenses you have studied (see Units 96-100).

tense	active	passive
Present Simple	I **clean** the house every day. He **washes** the windows every week.	The house **is cleaned** every day. The windows **are washed** every week.
Present Continuous	They **are building** a hospital now. He **is cutting** down the trees.	A hospital **is being built**. The trees **are being cut** down.
Present Perfect	I **have completed** the work. She **has sent** the letters.	The work **has been completed**. The letters **have been sent**.
Present Perfect Continuous	She **has been interviewing** him.	He's **been being interviewed**.
Past Simple	They **cancelled** the match. Someone **stole** all the paintings.	The match **was cancelled**. All the paintings **were stolen**.
Past Continuous	I **was repairing** the car. They **were cleaning** the machines.	The car **was being repaired**. The machines **were being cleaned**.
Past Perfect	Someone **had killed** the President.	The President **had been killed**.
Future (**will**)	They **will cut** the grass tomorrow.	The grass **will be cut** tomorrow.
Future (**going to**)	They **are going to repair** the car. She's **going to burn** the letters.	The car **is going to be repaired**. All the letters **are going to be burnt**.

modal verbs	active	passive
can	They **can solve** the problem.	The problem **can be solved**.
could	They **couldn't move** the stone.	The stone **couldn't be moved**.
must	They **must punish** the thief.	The thief **must be punished**.
should	Someone **should change** the music.	The music **should be changed**.
ought to	They **ought to move** the car.	The car **ought to be moved**.
may	They **may change** the phone number.	The phone number **may be changed**.
might	Someone **might steal** the painting.	The painting **might be stolen**.
need	Someone **needs to wash** the clothes.	The clothes **need to be washed**.

APPENDIX 8 >> Uncountable nouns

Here are some of the most common uncountable nouns (see Unit 32):

materials/substances:	cotton glass gold iron oxygen petrol plastic wool
food etc.:	bread butter cheese coffee meat milk salt sugar tea water wine
weather etc.:	hail ice rain snow sleet
abstract ideas:	beauty education grammar heat love noise

Some words are uncountable in English but countable in many other languages. **Be careful!**

advice baggage behaviour business damage equipment furniture hair
homework information knowledge luggage money news permission progress
rubbish scenery spaghetti traffic travel work/homework

With uncountable nouns
• we cannot use **a/an**:   I gave him advice.   (Not ~~an advice~~)
• we cannot use a plural: He offered me some meat.   (Not ~~meats~~)
• we can use **much/a little**, **not many/a few**:   Did it cost much money?   (Not ~~many money~~)

Some uncountable nouns become countable in certain situations:

cheese	I liked all the **cheeses** at the dairy. (= kinds of cheese)
coffee/tea etc.	We'd like two **teas**, please. (= cups of tea)
wine	I like French **wines**. (= kinds of wine)

Some nouns can be both countable and uncountable with different meanings:

chocolate	They bought **some chocolate**. (= a bar of chocolate) They ate all the **chocolates**. (= individual chocolates in a box)
glass	The window is made of Italian **glass**. (= the substance) I drank three **glasses** of milk. (= containers)
rain	The **rain** began. (= it began to rain) The **rains** began. (= a season of tropical rain)
noise	I don't like **noise**. (= noise in general) They heard **a** strange **noise**. (= a particular noise)

APPENDIX 9 >> Common noun suffixes

ending	example	ending	example
-age	usage, wastage, postage	**-hood**	childhood, adulthood
-ment	government, amazement	**-ness**	happiness, sadness, ugliness
-ship	friendship, relationship	**-ure**	closure, pleasure, failure
-acy/-ecy	privacy, candidacy, conspiracy, secrecy	**-ance**	importance, significance
-ence	existence, independence	**-ency/-ancy**	urgency, fluency, constancy
-al	revival, disposal, removal	**-or**	director, inspector, conductor conspirator, regulator
-er	teacher, writer, leader, farmer	**-sion**	delusion, conclusion, confusion decision, collision, provision
-ee	employee, legatee, payee	**-ant/-ent**	attendant, president
-tion	concentration, relaxation solution, pollution, destruction, reduction, deception, conception	**-ian**	musician, mathematician, magician
-ism	communism, capitalism	**-ist**	communist, artist, violinist
-th	length, width, depth, strength	**-ty**	purity, sanity, loyalty, sincerity

APPENDIX 10 >> Prepositions

PREPOSITIONS OF TIME (SEE UNIT 73)

at	in	on
times: *at 7 o'clock, at half-past two, at 15.30*	**centuries:** *in the nineteenth century, in the twenty-first century*	**days:** *on Monday, on Friday etc.*
noon, midnight etc.: *at sunrise, at midday/noon, at sunset, at midnight*	**years:** *in 1745, in 1990, in 2001*	**dates:** *on 22nd March, on 1st August, on the first of May*
night: *at night*	**seasons:** *in (the) spring, in (the) summer, in (the) autumn, in (the) winter*	*or we say: 'on May the first'*
weekend: *at the weekend(s)*		**special days:** *on Christmas Day, on Easter Sunday (But at Christmas, at the New Year etc.), on my birthday*
festivals: *at Christmas, at the New Year, at Easter*	**months:** *in January, in May etc.*	
meal-times: *at breakfast, at lunchtime, at teatime, at dinnertime*	**parts of the day:** *in the morning, in the afternoon, in the evening (But at night)*	**Also** *on Monday morning, on Friday evening (But in the morning on Monday)*
Also *at the beginning/ end of the day*	**Also** *in the middle of the morning*	

FROM... TO/BETWEEN... AND/DURING/FOR/WITHIN/IN/UNTIL

1 **From** + starting time **to** finishing time:
   *It lasted **from** 9 a.m. **to** 5 p.m.*

2 **Between** + beginning of period **and** + end of period:
   *It happened **between** Monday night **and** Tuesday morning.*

3 **For** + length of time:
   *I lived in London **for** a year/**for** six months/**for** a long time.*

4 **During** + war/holiday/trip etc.:
   *I met her **during** my holiday.* (**Not** ~~during I was on holiday~~.)

5 **In/Within** + length of time:
   *He finished **within** five minutes.*
   *I'll do it **in** a week's time/**in** a week from now.*

6 **Until** + a point in time:
   *I'll stay **until** 9 o'clock.*
   *I was there **until** the end of the party.*

NO PREPOSITION

7 No preposition + **every/last/next/this**   *I go there **every** week.   I saw her **last** night.*
   No preposition + **yesterday**   *We saw them **yesterday**.*

PREPOSITIONS OF PLACE (SEE UNIT 73)

Here is some general information about how we use **at**, **in** and **on** to talk about position.

AT	
a point	He is **at** the door/**at** the bus stop. He sat **at** the desk/**at** the table.
special places	He is **at** the cinema. (= to see a film) He is **at** the airport. (= to fly or meet a friend)
work, home, school	(without **the**) I was **at** work/**at** home/**at** school yesterday.
special events	He's **at** a party/a match/a wedding etc.
full addresses	I live **at** 7 Barton Road.
rail platforms (for trains)	The train is **at** Platform 7.
seaside	We are **at** the seaside.
top, bottom, end (point)	It's **at** the top of the page/**at** the bottom of the hill/ **at** the end of the road.

IN	
an area	He is **in** England/**in** the South/**in** the park.
rooms, buildings	He's **in** the kitchen/**in** the cinema. (= inside the building) (Also: He's **in** prison/**in** hospital (without **the**))
containers	It's **in** the cupboard/**in** my pocket.
cars	I am **in** the taxi.
bed	She's **in** bed.
roads, streets, cities	I live **in** Barton Road/**in** London.
water (area)	The island is **in** the Pacific. We swam **in** the river.
middle	It's **in** the middle of the town.

ON	
a surface	It's **on** the table/**on** the wall/**on** the floor.
pages	It's **on** page 25/**on** the front page. (But **in** the book, **in** the newspaper etc.)
transport	I am **on** the train/**on** the plane/**on** the bus. (But **in** is also possible) I am **on** a horse/a bike etc.
floors of buildings	I live **on** the tenth floor.
rail platforms (for people)	I waited **on** Platform 7.
water (surface)	The ship is **on** the lake.
rivers, coasts etc.	London is **on** the Thames. Aberdeen is **on** the coast.
top, bottom, end (surface)	The helicopter's **on** the top of the building.

APPENDIX 11 >> Phrases with prepositions

Here are some further common phrases with prepositions in addition to those listed in Units 74-5.

	phrases	example
above	above it all etc. (= feeling superior to others)	He's **above helping** us. (= he thinks he's too important to help us)
according to	according to the news/ the papers/the experts etc.	**According to Freud**, everyone has subconscious desires.
against	against the law	It's **against the law** to steal.
at	at university/at school/at college/	My brother's **at university**. (= he's a student)
away from	away from it all (= away from the stress of normal life)	I want to get **away from it all** by having a holiday on a Pacific island.
behind	behind closed doors (= in secret) What's behind...? (= what's the real reason for...?)	They discussed the plan **behind closed doors**. **What's behind** the new plan?
beyond	beyond help beyond me, them etc. (= I/they can't understand)	He's so ill that he's almost **beyond help**. These questions are **beyond me**. They're too difficult.
by	by accident/coincidence	She met him **by coincidence** in the park.
for	for... reason for... sake for God's sake! (strong language)	Nick dismissed Brigitte **for two reasons**... He stole some milk **for** his children's **sake**. **For God's sake**, don't shoot!
from	from my/your/her etc. point of view from a distance	**From my point of view**, it's not worth doing. The painting looks better **from a distance**.
in	in my/your/her etc. opinion in the army/the navy/the air force/ the scouts/the team in public/in secret in the end (= after a long time) in another world/in his own world/ on another planet	**In my opinion**, the plan is stupid. She's **in the** Liverpool **police force**. He quarrelled with her **in public**. I waited hours but **in the end** I saw her. He hasn't been listening — he's **in another world**. (= daydreaming)
into	be into something (= be very interested in)	He's really **into Brazilian music** — he spends all his time listening to samba CDs.
like	like a dream	It worked **like a dream**. (= worked perfectly)
on	on a diet/on a course/on strike on course for/on the right path for	She's **on a degree course**. He's **on a diet**. The workers are **on strike**. She's **on course for** exam success. (i.e. she's doing well)
out of	out of my mind (= mad) out of control out of the question (= impossible)	You must be **out of your mind** to marry him! The robot's **out of control** — it's dangerous. It's **out of the question**. You can't use my car.

over	over the moon (= very happy)	He's been **over the moon** since he got his new job.
	over the top (= behaving in an excessively strong way)	He was very angry — it was **over the top**.
under	under... control	The company is **under the control** of Americans.
	under the weather (= slightly ill)	I'm feeling **under the weather**.
	under discussion/consideration	The plan is **under discussion**.
up/down	up/down the street/the road etc.	He lives just **up the road**. (= near here)
with	with special features etc.	She bought a car **with automatic gears**.
without	without (a) doubt	**Without doubt**, he is the thief.

APPENDIX **12** >> Plural nouns

PLURAL FORMS OF NOUNS

Some nouns change their spelling when we add **-s** in the plural form.

-s, -ch, -sh, -x, -o* + es:	kiss**es**/box**es**/tomato**es**/hero**es**
* but words of recent foreign origin ending **-o:**	biro**s**/disco**s**/photo**s**/euro**s**
consonant + **-y → ies:** ladies/families/cities	**But** day**s**/toy**s**/monkey**s**
-f/-fe + ves kni**ves**/wi**ves**/lea**ves**/shel**ves**/hal**ves**	**But** chief**s**/belief**s**

Some nouns have an irregular plural form or use the original Latin or Greek plural form:

child → children	man → men
woman → women	foot → feet
tooth → teeth	one fish → two fish
mouse → mice	an ox → a herd of oxen
one sheep → 100 sheep	criterion → criteria

fungus → fungi	stimulus → stimuli
crisis → crises	thesis → theses
medium → media	nucleus → nuclei
phenomenon → phenomena	species → species

The regular plural of **brother** is **brothers**. We use the irregular plural, **brethren**, in some religious or humorous contexts: *The Plymouth **Brethren** are a sect.*

The plural of **penny** is **pence**: *I owe you five **pence**.*
But we use **pennies** to refer to the coins themselves:
*Here are three Victorian **pennies**.* (= three individual coins)
Many people say *'One pence'* although strictly this is incorrect.

Remember:
1 We usually say **a person** (singular) but **2, 3, many** etc. **people*** (plural)
2 We say **The police are/have/go...** etc. (**police** + plural verb)
3 We use singular **or** plural verbs after **family/government/company/team** etc.
4 Some nouns have a plural form only: **pyjamas/trousers/scissors** etc.

5   Some nouns end in **-s** but are uncountable: **mathematics/physics/economics is...**

6   There are some nouns which have an identical singular and plural form ending in **-s**.
    For example: *A barracks/a crossroads/a headquarters/a means/a series/a species*

7   Some compound nouns add **-s** to the first part: *passers-by   brothers-in-law*

8   Some plural nouns are often used as if singular: *The media is...   The data shows...*
    This usage is wrong according to strict grammar but quite common.

9   We use singular verbs after *a box of chocolates/a can of beans* etc.

* **people** is normally a plural noun. But we sometimes use **a people/peoples** with the meaning
  of nations

APPENDIX 13 >> Spelling

WORDS ENDING IN -Y + -S/-ED/+ -ER/+ -EST/+ -LY

Ⓐ -y + -s → -ies			
• Nouns ending in **consonant + -y:**			
city	→ cities	family	→ families
lady	→ ladies	mystery	→ mysteries
baby	→ babies	country	→ countries
story	→ stories	etc.	
• Verbs ending in **consonant + -y:**			
study	→ studies	fly	→ flies
marry	→ marries	carry	→ carries
worry	→ worries	try	→ tries
copy	→ copies	etc.	
• Nouns and verbs ending in **vowel + -y:**			
toy	→ toys	destroy	→ destroys
key	→ keys	enjoy	→ enjoys
monkey	→ monkeys	play	→ plays
journey	→ journeys	buy	→ buys

Ⓑ -y + -ed → -ied			
Verbs ending in **consonant + -y:**			
study	→ studied	marry	→ married
carry	→ carried	worry	→ worried
try	→ tried	hurry	→ hurried

Ⓒ -y + -er → -ier/-y + -est → -iest			
Adjectives ending in **consonant + -y:**			
easy	→ easier/easiest	happy	→ happier/happiest
lucky	→ luckier/luckiest	heavy	→ heavier/heaviest
funny	→ funnier/funniest	sunny	→ sunnier/sunniest

Ⓓ -y + -ly → -ily			
easy	→ easily	happy	→ happily
lucky	→ luckily	heavy	→ heavily

COMPARATIVE OR SUPERLATIVE FORM OF ADJECTIVES

For adjectives ending in **-e**: add **-r** or **-st**:		
late	*later*	*latest*
white	*whiter*	*whitest*
wide	*wider*	*widest*

For adjectives ending **consonant** + **vowel*** + **consonant** (a vowel sandwich): double the final consonant:		
big (b-i-g)	*bigger*	*biggest*
hot (h-o-t)	*hotter*	*hottest*
thin (th-i-n)	*thinner*	*thinnest*

Adjectives ending in **consonant** + **-y**: → **-ier/-iest**	
easy → *easier/easiest*	*happy* → *happier/happiest*

* for an explanation of consonants, vowels and syllables see Appendix 15

ADVERBS FROM ADJECTIVES

For adjectives ending **-e**: add **-ly**. Do not remove the **-e**.			
polite	→ *politely*	*immediate*	→ *immediately*
fortunate	→ *fortunately*	*rude*	→ *rudely*
extreme	→ *extremely*	*definite*	→ *definitely*

For adjectives ending **-l**: add **-ly**: → (**-lly**)			
usual	→ *usually*	*real*	→ *really*
careful	→ *carefully*	*grateful*	→ *gratefully*

For adjectives ending consonant + **-y**: → **-ily**			
easy	→ *easily*	*happy*	→ *happily*
lucky	→ *luckily*	*heavy*	→ *heavily*

APPENDIX **14** >> Phonetic alphabet

English spelling is not completely phonetic. The same letters may have different sounds in different words: *enough* (gh = f)   *eight* (gh is silent)   *ghost* (gh = g)

Many dictionaries use the phonetic alphabet to help you pronounce English words. The phonetic alphabet consists of different symbols to represent different sounds:

Vowels			Diphthongs			Consonants					
[ɪ]	*as in*	six	[eɪ]	*as in*	made	[b]	*as in*	bed	[ŋ]	*as in*	sing
[i]	"	happy	[aɪ]	"	five	[k]	"	cat	[p]	"	pen
[iː]	"	see	[aʊ]	"	house	[tʃ]	"	church	[r]	"	red
[e]	"	red	[ɔɪ]	"	boy	[d]	"	day	[s]	"	soon
[æ]	"	hat	[əʊ]	"	home	[f]	"	foot	[z]	"	zoo
[ɑː]	"	car	[ɪə]	"	beer	[g]	"	good	[ʃ]	"	show
[ɒ]	"	dog	[eə]	"	hair	[dʒ]	"	page	[ʒ]	"	measure
[ɔː]	"	door	[ʊə]	"	poor	[h]	"	how	[t]	"	tea
[ʊ]	"	put				[j]	"	yes	[θ]	"	thin
[uː]	"	food				[l]	"	leg	[ð]	"	this
[ʌ]	"	cup				[m]	"	mum	[v]	"	voice
[ə]	"	about				[n]	"	nine	[w]	"	wine
[ɜː]	"	girl									

[r] indicates that the final 'r' is only pronounced before a word beginning with a vowel sound (British English). In American English, the 'r' is usually pronounced before both consonants and vowel sounds.

APPENDIX 15 >> Consonants, vowels, syllables, stress

CONSONANTS AND VOWELS

Consonants are: b c d f g h j k l m n p q r s t v w x y z

Vowels are: a e i o u

The letter **y** often represents a vowel sound: *happy   lazy   shy   worrying* etc.
But not *yet* (consonant), *yellow* (consonant) etc.

The letter **h** is sometimes silent at the beginning of a word: *heir   hour   honest* etc.
But not *hair   hospital   happy   horse* etc.

The letter **u** sometimes represents a consonant sound at the beginning of a word:
university   usual etc. **But not** *uncle   us   unusual* etc.

Some words end in a vowel sandwich = **consonant + one vowel + one consonant**:
plan (l-a-n)   *stop* (t-o-p)   *hit* (h-i-t)
travel (v-e-l)   *happen* (p-e-n)   *big* (b-i-g)

The vowel sandwich influences the spelling of **verb + -ed, verb + -ing, adjective + -er**.
(See Appendices 3, 4, 13)

SYLLABLES

Words have one or more syllables (= separate parts when we pronounce them):
- one-syllable words: *sit*   *tea*   *dream*   *sleep*
- two-syllable words: *gram/mar*   *stu/dent*   *de/scribe*   *hap/py*
- three-syllable words: *dis/cov/er*   *re/mem/ber*   *beau/ti/ful*   *sud/den/ly*
- four-syllable words: *in/tel/li/gent*   *con/tin/u/ous*   *ex/cel/lent/ly*

STRESS

In words of more than one syllable, one of the syllables usually carries the main stress:
ENG/land   LON/don   DUB/lin   GRA/mmar   STU/dent
de/SCRIBE   BEAU/ti/ful   dis/COV/er   in/TELL/i/gent   sci/en/TIF/ic

APPENDIX 16 >> Pronunciation

-S ENDING

We add **-s** or **-es** to the verb in the third person form of the Present Simple. We pronounce
the **-s** ending in different ways depending on the final sound of the basic verb.

A The **-s** ending is pronounced [z] after most voiced consonant sounds — [b, m, v, ð, d, n, g,
l, ŋ] — and also after vowel sounds:
She reads [riːdz], *He plays* [pleɪz], *She robs* [rɒbz], *It rings* [rɪŋz], *She tells* [telz]

B The **-s** ending is pronounced [s] after most unvoiced consonant sounds — [p, f, θ, t, k]:
She talks [tɔːks], *He sits* [sɪts], *She stops* [stɒps]

C The **-s** ending is pronounced [iz] after these sibilant sounds — [tʃ, ʃ, s, ks, z]. These include:
1 verbs which end in **-ch, -sh, -ss, -x, -zz**. We add **-es**:
he/she/it watches [wɒtʃiz], *washes* [wɒʃiz], *kisses* [kɪsiz], *boxes* [bɒksiz], *buzzes* [bʌziz]
2 verbs ending **-se** or **-ze** or **-ge** which are pronounced [iz]:
he/she/it loses, recognises, surprises, amazes, judges

D We also add **-s** or **-es** to a noun to form the plural. (Appendix 12)
We add **-'s** to a noun to make the possessive form. (Unit 34)
The pronunciation follows the same rules as in A-C above.

For example:	[z]	*boys*	*dog's*	*knives*
	[s]	*months*	*one week's time*	*steps*
	[iz]	*churches*	*the judge's*	*boxes*

-*ED* ENDING

We pronounce the **-ed** ending in three ways:

A [d] after verbs ending in voiced consonant sounds except [d] and after vowel sounds:
amused   played   showed   surprised

B [t] after verbs ending in unvoiced consonant sounds except [t]:
kicked   passed   stopped   laughed

C [id] after verbs ending in [d] and [t]: *defended   landed   wanted   spotted*

APPENDIX 17 >> Comparatives and superlatives: form

COMPARATIVE AND SUPERLATIVE FORMS OF ADJECTIVES

adjective		examples	comparative	superlative
one syllable	+ -er/-est	*tall/long*	*taller/longer*	*tallest/longest*
ending in consonant vowel-consonant	**double consonant**	*big/thin* *hot*	*bigger/thinner* *hotter*	*biggest/thinnest* *hottest*
two syllables ending -y	**-y → -ier -iest**	*lucky/happy/ silly*	*luckier/happier sillier*	*luckiest/happiest silliest*
three syllables and more two-syllables	**+ more + most**	*intelligent/ expensive careless*	**more** *intelligent* **more** *expensive* **more** *careless*	**most** *intelligent* **most** *expensive* **most** *careless*
good, bad, far, many, much, a little, old, ill, well (= not ill)	**irregular**	*good* *bad* *far* *many & much* *a little* *old* *ill**** *well*	*better* *worse* *farther/further** *more* *less* *older/elder*** *worse* *better*	*best* *worst* *farthest/furthest* *most* *least* *oldest/eldest*** *worst* *best*

* we can use **further** (but not **farther**) to mean **more, additional**: *There were **further** problems.*
** we use **elder/eldest** to describe family members: e.g. *my **elder** brother, the **eldest** child*
*** notice that we say *He's **worse** than yesterday.* Not ~~*He's iller.*~~

COMPARATIVE AND SUPERLATIVE FORMS OF ADVERBS

		example of adverb	comparative	superlative
1 most adverbs	**more +/most +**	*quickly* *intelligently*	*more quickly* *more intelligently*	*most quickly* *most intelligently*
2 exceptions	**+ -er/+ -est**	*fast/hard* *early/late*	*faster/harder* *earlier/later*	*fastest/hardest* *earliest/latest*
3 irregular adverbs		*well/badly/far*	*better/worse* *farther/further*	*best/worst* *farthest/furthest*

INDEX

The numbers refer to units not page numbers.